# A GUIDE TO OGAM

The Arraglen Ogam stone with its west-face cross incorporating the chi-rho monogram (145 QRIMITIR RON[A]NN MAQ COMOGANN).

MAYNOOTH MONOGRAPHS 4

# A GUIDE TO OGAM

*by*
Damian McManus

An Sagart · Maynooth
1991

Maynooth Monographs

1. The Early Irish Verb

2. Sages, Saints and Storytellers

3. Pagan Past and Christian Present in Early Irish Literature

Published by An Sagart, St Patrick's College, Maynooth, Co. Kildare, Ireland.

First Published 1991

ISBN 1 870684 17 6
ISSN 0890 8806

Printed by the Leinster Leader Ltd., Main Street, Naas, Co. Kildare, Ireland.

# TABLE OF CONTENTS

§4.3 The distribution of the inscriptions.
§4.4 The disposition of the inscriptions on the stones.
§4.5 The present condition of the inscriptions.
§4.6 The contents of the inscriptions.
§4.7 Identifying people commemorated in the inscriptions.
§4.8 Crosses accompanying the inscriptions.
§4.9 Christian versus pagan character of the inscriptions.
§4.10 Non-Ogam inscriptions accompanying Ogams.
§4.11 The British Ogam inscriptions.
§4.12 The importance of the British Ogams.
§4.13 Differences between British and Irish Ogams.
§4.14 British Ogams and the Irish language in Britain.

§5.1 Problems of absolute dating.
§5.2 Problems posed by the script.
§5.3 Scholastic characteristics and dating.
§5.4 Formulae and dating.
§5.5 Crosses and dating.
§5.6 Linguistic dating.
§5.7 MacNeill's archaizing hypothesis.
§5.8 Linguistic dating qualified.
§5.9 Periods in the history of the Irish language.
§5.10 General remarks on the applicability of linguistic criteria.
§5.11 Some Early Primitive Irish developments.
§5.12 Lenition.
§5.13 Shortening of long vowels in unstressed syllables.
§5.14 Vowel-affection.
§5.15 Apocope.
§5.16 Vocalization of certain consonant clusters.
§5.17 Syncope.
§5.18 Delabialization.
§5.19 Palatalization.
§5.20 Early Old Irish.
§5.21 Problems of absolute chronology.
§5.22 Relative chronology of inscriptions.
§5.23 The composition vowel O not a dating criterion.
§5.24 Inscriptions pre-dating vowel-affection.
§5.25 The beginnings of vowel-affection in inscriptions.
§5.26 Early post-apocope inscriptions.
§5.27 Inscriptions showing apocope in all names but not in
        formula words.
§5.28 Inscriptions showing complete apocope.
§5.29 Inscriptions showing syncope.
§5.30 The absolute dating of the inscriptions.
§5.31 Dating the British inscriptions.

Plates    Frontispiece: The Arraglen Ogam stone and west-face cross (145)

*In Memory of*
*my parents and my brother Terry*

# INTRODUCTION

Since the publication of Charles Vallancey's report on the Mount Callan stone in 1785 – the appearance of which sparked off modern research into the subject – there has been a steady flow of learned articles on different aspects of the history of Ogam. These have appeared in a variety of languages and journals and many today are inaccessible except to the most determined of researchers. It was the difficulty this state of affairs presented to me as a teacher which prompted me initially to write this book. My intention was to make available to my own Sophister students a general guide to Ogam in which they would have to hand a convenient synthesis of the more important contributions to its history, reappraised in the light of recent research in Early Irish.

After I had already started on the project I recall the late Professor James Carney advising me against spending too much time with Ogam, reminding me of the intractable nature of so many features of the subject. If I did not heed his advice then there were many times while writing the book when I wished I had. The history of Ogam has to be tentative in many respects owing to the nature of the evidence available to us and the reader will, I hope, forgive the numerous *ifs* and *buts* in the following pages. Notwithstanding this it seemed to me that the Ogamists – who when all is said and done were the first to devise both an alphabet and an orthographical system for the Irish language – had been getting a rather bad press in recent scholarship, and some to my mind dubious and unflattering tenets regarding them and their invention had established themselves. The desire to attempt to redress this imbalance was a strong motivation for writing the book and I have tried throughout to treat the Ogamists with the respect due to all medieval Irish *literati*, whose works are currently undergoing such exciting reappraisal.

The book is divided into eight chapters, the first of which is a general introduction, followed by a survey of the problems of establishing the origin of the script and the identity of the alphabetic prototype. In Appendix 1 I have presented the texts and translation of the Old Irish *Bríatharogam*, which I have edited and commented on in detail elsewhere. Chapters four to six deal with the orthodox Ogam inscriptions and in Appendix 2 I have discussed my own readings of some of the inscriptions in Macalister's *Corpus Inscriptionum Insularum Celticarum* and attempted to bring it up to date by publishing inscriptions discovered since 1945. In the last two chapters the later manuscript tradition of Ogam has been investigated and its general importance assessed. Abbreviations have been kept to a minimum and a key to those used in the Bibliography will be found on page 186. For ease of cross-reference the first digit in paragraph (§) and note (n) numbers indicates the number of the chapter to which they belong. It was not thought necessary to repeat this digit in the notes themselves.

It should perhaps be pointed out here that while the works of the two scholars most closely associated with Ogam, Eoin MacNeill and R. A. S. Macalister, are often challenged in the following pages, the present writer would be the first to acknowledge the enormous debt this book owes to their research. In particular, as Macalister's *Corpus* has been criticized so often, I should mention that there were many times when, confronted with an extremely badly worn inscription,

I could only admire his very keen eye and obvious perseverence in establishing a reading. His greatest fault was perhaps his reluctance to be defeated by an inscription, even when it presented insuperable difficulties, and he was justifiably criticized for failing, especially in the introduction to the *Corpus*, to take stock of the works of more linguistically oriented scholars, like Thurneysen. Nonetheless the *Corpus* continues for the present to be an indispensable work for all interested in Ogam inscriptions.

Inevitably in a work of this kind one finds oneself indebted to a large number of people and a general acknowledgement of thanks will have to suffice for all museum, library and university staff in both Ireland and Wales who so kindly assisted me in my research, together with the numerous obliging individuals who permitted me to examine inscriptions in their care or assisted me in locating their whereabouts. It is a pleasure also to thank both my own university, Trinity College, Dublin, for financing some of the field-work with a research grant, and the Alexander von Humboldt-Stiftung for a very generous fellowship to Germany in 1987, where some of the research for this book and earlier related publications was carried out. To Mr Terence Dunne of the Department of Geography, Trinity College, Dublin, I owe special thanks for his technical assistance with the photographs reproduced here. For permission to reproduce photographs I am also grateful to the Burgerbibliothek Bern, the Biblioteca Apostolica Vaticana and the National Museum of Wales, Cardiff. To the staff of the Leinster Leader, in particular Mr Stan Hickey, I also owe thanks for the speed and care with which they have seen the book through the press.

I am particularly indebted to three of the finest scholars in the field of Early Irish, Jürgen Uhlich, Kim McCone and Liam Breatnach, for reading through all or part of the first draft of the book and suggesting numerous improvements; for any remaining errors, of course, I alone am responsible. Very special thanks are due also to Pádraig Ó Fiannachta not only for his kind invitation to me to publish the book in his much-admired Maynooth Monographs series, but also more generally for his great dedication to publication in Irish Studies which has been a source of inspiration to so many of us.

Finally, my greatest debt is to my wife, Claudia, who drew the figures and maps reproduced here and who was indispensable as navigator and photographer on all field-trips. Her constant companionship, patience and continued interest in the work were a source of great encouragement.

DAMIAN McMANUS
Trinity College, Dublin.
January, 1991.

# CHAPTER ONE

# The Ogam Alphabet: Introduction

§**1.1** Where, when and by whom the Ogam alphabet was invented is not known. What can be said with certainty, however, is that Ogam existed already in the fifth century as a monument script. The distribution of inscriptions in the Ogam character (see §§4.2-3) suggests that it was at home in the south of Ireland, and as it can be shown beyond reasonable doubt that the alphabet was designed for the Irish language (see §3.12) it is likely that its framers were Irish and probable that they resided in the south of the country, possibly in the fourth century. That they were familiar with the Latin alphabet and had at least a rudimentary training in Latin grammar is evident (see §3.10ff.), but why they chose the peculiar internal order of the Ogam alphabet and its most unusual signary remains a matter for speculation.

§**1.2** In its earliest form the Ogam script is made up of a total of twenty characters forming a systematic linear code to a unique sequence of sounds. The early and primary values of some of the characters are subject to debate (see §3.13) but the standard transcription in the later manuscript tradition is as follows:

B L F S N     H D T C Q     M G NG Z R     A O U E I

The division into four groups of five indicated here by spacing is of particular importance to the graphical representation of these values in the Ogam script. Each symbol is characterized by a stem- or reference-line, the groups are distinguished by the orientation of one to five rectilinear strokes or scores relative to the stemline and by the use of one to five notches, individual characters within any group by the appropriate number of the relevant markers. Thus on stone, where Ogam is written vertically, the characters of groups one and two appear as horizontal lateral scores to the right and left respectively of the stemline, the latter usually but not invariably the natural edge or arris of the stone itself. The scores of group three transverse the stemline obliquely, while those of the final group appear as notches or short scores on the line itself as follows:[1]

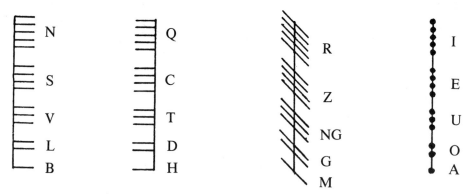

In the manuscripts there is an accommodation to the horizontal left-to-right direction of the standard script and the vowels appear as vertical strokes bisected by the stemline rather than as dots:

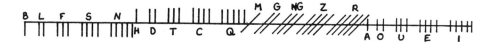

A fifth group of symbols is also commonly included in the manuscript tradition but this did not form part of the original nucleus (see §7.13ff.). Its creators were out of touch with the objectives of the original framers of Ogam, who were concerned to create an alphabet for the Irish language. The *forfeda* 'supplementary characters' were designed with the Latin and Greek alphabets in mind, in particular to accommodate letters of the Latin and Greek alphabets not already matched by Ogam characters. Their framers missed the opportunity of completing the symmetry of the system by having the fifth series mirror the third in the way that the second mirrors the first; the *forfeda* have only the stemline in common with other Ogam characters and tend to mirror their models in shape. This alone would be sufficient to confirm the secondary status of these characters which have been described as being reminiscent more of the inkhorn than the stone-cutter's blade (Hamp, 1954, 312). The first of this group is the exception in that it does occur on the orthodox inscriptions, albeit infrequently and on relatively recent ones (see §5.3), and its existence may have provided the impetus for the creation of this series, which would eventually be straitjacketed into the phonetic scheme of the alphabet by having its characters represent a distinct set of homogeneous sounds (see §7.17). On these symbols in the Ogam inscriptions see §5.3 and on their forms in the manuscript tradition see §7.13.

§1.3 The characters of the alphabet were all assigned names which may have started out as standard examples for teaching purposes but soon assumed greater importance as a fixed series operating on the acrostic principle that the initial sound in the letter name corresponded to the value of the relevant symbol. Unlike their Greek and Latin counterparts these names were meaningful words in the language though some eventually lost currency as such and became semantically redundant, operating solely as letter names. Notwithstanding this the meaning of the majority can be verified and as they represent the mainstay of the tradition these names constitute the most important source of information on the primary values of the symbols (see §3.15). They appear in the manuscript tradition in the following (normalized Old Irish) form:

Beithe, Luis, Fern, Sail, Nin
hÚath, Dair, Tinne, Coll, Cert
Muin, Gort, (n)Gétal, Straif, Ruis
Ailm, Onn, Úr, Edad, Idad
Ébad, Ór, Uilen, Pín/Iphín, Emancholl

§1.4 With the exception of the fifth series, the values of whose symbols are variable, the quinary groups (termed *aicmi*, pl. of *aicme* 'family, class, group') are named after their first components. Thus, *Aicme Beithe, Aicme hÚatha, Aicme Muine, Aicme Ailme*, 'the B group', 'the H group' etc. The symbols of the fifth series are known collectively as *Forfeda* (later *Foirḟeadha*) 'supplementary letters' (also *Aicme na Forfed* 'the group of supplementary letters') demonstrating once again their secondary status within the system. The letters are termed *feda* (pl. of *fid* 'wood, tree'), a term which can also be used specifically of the vowels, in which case the consonants may be called *táebomnai* (*táeb* 'side' *omnae* 'bole of a tree'), a term based apparently on the orientation of consonant symbols relative to the stemline. The latter is known in Irish as the *druim* 'ridge, edge, back' and a single score of a letter is termed *flesc* 'twig' (cp. Modern Irish *fleiscín* 'hyphen'). On the model of the classical term *alphabeta* the Ogam alphabet *in toto* is named *In Beithe-luis* in the Irish Grammatical Tracts but earlier (e.g. in *Auraicept na nÉces*) the name of the fifth character is included in the title, viz. *In Beithe-luis-nin*[2] or *Beithe-luis-nin ind Ogaim*. *Ogam* itself (on which see §8.6) is used as a generic term for the signary, the *Beithe-luis-nin* in this context being referred to as *Cert-ogam* 'correct-Ogam'. In later usage *Ogam* develops the meaning 'written' as opposed to 'spoken' Irish.

§1.5 The following description of the alphabet and how it is read is recorded in the manuscript tradition in the *Auraicept na nÉces* (on which see §8.2):[3] *Is ed a llín: cóic aicmi Oguim ⁊ cóicer cacha aicme ⁊ o óen co a cóic cach aí, conda deligitar a n-airde. It hé a n-airde: desdruim, túathdruim, lesdruim, tredruim, imdruim. Is amlaid im-drengar Ogum amal im-drengar crann .i. saltrad fora frém in chroinn ar tús ⁊ do lám dess remut ⁊ do lám clé fo déoid. Is íar-sin is leis ⁊ is fris ⁊ is trít ⁊ is immi.* 'This is their number: [there are] five groups of Ogam and each group [has] five [letters] and each of them [has] from one to five [scores], and their orientations distinguish them. Their orientations are: right of the stemline, left of the stemline, across the stemline, through the stemline, around the stemline. Ogam is climbed (i.e. read) as a tree is climbed, i.e. treading on the root of the tree first with one's right hand before one and one's left hand last. After that it is across it and against it and through it and around it.'

It is interesting to note that although the alphabet is almost invariably written horizontally (from left to right) in the manuscripts this account would appear to describe a vertically disposed Ogam.

**§1.6** The system outlined above differs in so many ways from the more familiar Latin and Greek alphabets as to belie any connection between them. And yet for all its distinctiveness Ogam shares a principle with its classical counterparts which not only brings it under the same rubric as these but also proves its secondary and derivative status in relation to them. Ogam operates on the alphabetic principle that its characters denote single isolable sounds and it assigns equal status at the graphic level to consonants and vowels alike. This alphabetic principle is the most sophisticated and economic method which has been devised for communicating language in written form, but it is important to note that it is not an invention *per se*. Historically it is the final stage in an evolutionary process characterized by an increasingly minute analysis of speech (word ⟩ syllable ⟩ sound), and a corresponding decrease in the number of symbols required to record it .[4] The sophistication of the alphabetic system is such that it has never appeared in a vacuum. In fact no society in the world has succeeded in avoiding any stage in the evolutionary process of writing except by borrowing (Pulgram, 1976, 16). It follows, therefore, that an alphabetic system must belong to one of two possible categories, the evolved or the borrowed, and most belong to the latter. Some scholars, indeed, maintain that alphabetic writing was perfected once and once only, by the Greeks, all other examples being derivatives of that system (Gelb, 1952, 184).

A cursory glance at the Ogam signary will suffice to show that the alphabetic principle which underlies it must have been borrowed. The system is too regular and too symmetrical to admit of the possibility of evolution from a syllabic or logographic base. The appearance of the vowel symbols as a separate group at the *end* of the alphabetic sequence and their formal distinction from consonantal symbols on stone could scarcely be invoked as an argument in favour of a syllabic base with subsequent alphabetization. There is no evidence for an original syllabic Ogam and even a symmetrical syllabic system such as the first three groups of Ogam would represent would itself have to be a borrowing, and one would be hard pressed to find a suitable model for it in western Europe at the probable time of the creation of the signary.

**§1.7** That Ogam is a derivative of an alphabetic system, then, is scarcely to be doubted, and the model one supposes its framers to have been most familiar with depends ultimately on where one locates the creation of the system, and of course on the identity of its creators. The most likely immediate source is Latin, but Greek and the Germanic runes have also had their adherents. Generally speaking, however, in cases in which borrowing of this kind is suspected it is normally possible to demonstrate the mechanics of the process whereby the prototype influenced the new system by observing correspondences between the forms and sound-values of related symbols. The Latin and Greek alphabets, for example, betray clear affinity with their forerunners (Greek/Etruscan and Phoenician respectively) in their earliest forms, and that affinity could easily be established even on the basis of their evolved classical forms. The forerunner of the Germanic runes is, admittedly, less easily identified but there is a clear connection with North Etruscan alphabets as well as with Latin.[5] In the case of Ogam, on the other hand, the alphabetic principle is clearly present and borrowed, but the mechanics of the borrowing process and the identification of the source pose enormous problems.

The signary, for example, is not an evolved or derived form of any known alphabetic script. It comes into history in a fixed form and with the exception of the elaboration of the fifth series it remains unchanged from the beginning. This uniformity is due primarily to the fact that it is not, strictly speaking, an alphabetic script. The characters of the Ogam signary are not alphabetic graphemes; they are integral parts of a linear code which by its very nature is inflexible, and is clearly unconnected in origin with alphabetic writing. It is, therefore, of little help in establishing the identity of the alphabetic prototype of Ogam. Similarly, the sound-sequence to which the script serves as a code is not that of any of the suspected models nor a mechanically demonstrable variation on them. The separation of vowels from consonants, for example, though a commonplace of grammatical theory, is not a feature of any known contemporary western European alphabet and is therefore likely to be an innovation. This is true also of the *selection* of phonemes which make up the sequence; most of them are sounds for which other scripts employ single symbols but the total inventory is without parallel elsewhere, as indeed are the letter names.

All of this is another way of saying that Ogam is a classic example of 'stimulus diffusion', the process whereby an idea is borrowed from without and given new and independent expression in its adopted form. The principle of alphabetic writing which lies at the base of Ogam is borrowed, but the system represents a new departure, a deliberate once-off creation in which the paraphernalia of the influencing system have been completely overhauled, leaving very little tangible material evidence for identifying that system. Indeed Ogam camouflages its model so effectively that scholars have had considerable difficulty in finding common ground in their attempts to unravel its origins, and the enigma has given rise to some very fanciful and intrinsically improbable solutions. Thankfully, Irish Studies has now matured to the point of recognizing the considerable linguistic ability of the framers of the system, and it is no longer popular or acceptable to dismiss them either as neo-literates casually acquainted with classical script but incapable of reproducing it, or as an ill-defined druidic caste with a consuming distaste for the trappings of the culture of the Roman Empire. Notwithstanding these developments Ogam still poses problems at almost every level and its salient features are best examined in isolation and in their own right. We begin with the outward form of the system, the signary itself.

# CHAPTER TWO

# The Ogam Alphabet:
# The Signary and its Origins

§**2.1** In considering the origin of the Ogam signary it will be best to divorce the characters themselves from the sounds they stand for, and to treat outward form, phonetic value and alphabetic forerunner separately. Admittedly, some theories have been advanced to account economically for both sound and shape (see §2.4 on Arntz), but it may be taken as a general rule of thumb in Ogam studies that the more embracing any theory is the more likely it is to be divorced from reality. The principle underlying the Ogam signary is very different from that underlying, say, the Greek or Latin alphabets, and it calls for a different set of explanations. In the latter conventionalized abstract and, synchronically viewed, arbitrary symbols denote distinctive phonemes, and while both systems have fixed alphabetic sequences the values of the symbols are unrelated to their positions within the sequence. In the Ogam signary on the other hand the sound denoted by the character is directly related to the sequence. Ogam is a position-marking device which indicates the precise position of a sound in a fixed sequence of sounds, and it is by reference to that sequence that the character is decoded into its phonetic value. Typologically speaking Latin and Greek are primary alphabetic systems whereas Ogam is a secondary encoded variety employing a principle which is commonly found in cryptography. This is not to say, of course, that anything written in Ogam characters is necessarily intended to be cryptic in nature. This again is a separate issue.

The only theory on the origin of this script which commands general approval today is that which associates it with the row numerals of the tally stick. These indeed are undoubtedly the most attractive and likely source for it. Before attempting to assess the mode of derivation, however, it will be appropriate at this point to make some comments of a general nature on what has become the accepted view of the efficacy of Ogam as a script. A discussion of two alternative derivations is also called for if only because of the popularity they have enjoyed from time to time.

§**2.2** The formation of the characters of the Ogam signary by the systematic repetition of linear detail has led to the charge that, as a writing system, it is inefficient, monotonous, complicated, awkward, crude, cumbersome, particularly prone to errors and ambiguity, childishly impractical, indeed even barbaric.[1] The potential embarrassment to national pride which the system is seen to represent has been side-stepped by arguing that it was not designed primarily for writing purposes, or by positing as remote a date as possible for its creation, on the grounds that an Irishman of, say, the first or second centuries would be much more likely to have had such bad taste and lack of a sense of propriety than one of, say, the fourth or fifth (see Binchy, 1961, 8-9). It will be as well to dispel this myth immediately.

The obsession with the alleged inferiority of the Ogam script is at best unflattering and at worst dangerously misleading in that it creates the illusion of a retrograde evolution. It is due more to a failure to compare Ogam with its typological equivalents, and to a dubious assessment of the intentions of its creators, than to any lack of judgment or technical virtuosity on their part. Time and again one reads the charge that Ogam is most unsuitable as a vehicle for what is loosely referred to as 'literary expression', and a considerable amount of energy has been wasted by scholars in an attempt to assess its usefulness in such a capacity (see for example Macalister, 1928, 215-6). But there is nothing whatsoever to suggest that the framers of the system had anything quite as ambitious as 'literary expression' in mind for their alphabet, nor is there anything in the tradition of Ogam to suggest that it was ever intended as an alternative to the Latin alphabet in all the domains in which the latter was employed.[2] All we know is that the signary was used and probably designed for inscribing names (possibly also short messages, see §8.10) on hard materials such as wood and stone and it is eminently suited to that purpose. The rectilinear nature of its characters is perfectly designed to cope, for example, with the grain in wood, and we shall see that its employment of the principle of orientation was an added bonus which many of its typological equivalents failed to exploit. It is gratuitous, therefore, to attribute an error of judgment to the framers of the system for creating a script which fails to meet the requirements of an ambitious objective which they are not likely to have entertained and probably would not have endorsed. The Ogam and Latin alphabets were never competitors for adoption as the vehicle for Irish literature in the monastic scriptoria. If it is to be assessed as a script, therefore, this should be done with short dedicatory, votive, commemorative or communicative messages on hard materials in mind. It should not be set alongside insular minuscule.

It has to be admitted, of course, that the character of the script is such that the possibility of human error must be considered when difficulties are encountered in the reading of the inscriptions. The erroneous omission or addition of a single score, faulty spacing or confusion in the orientation can result in a very different reading to the one intended. Now there are several cases in which we can be reasonably sure that an error of this kind has been made. Among examples are (a) the omission of a score (e.g. 108 (numbers refer to inscriptions in Macalister, 1945) LUGUDUC for an expected LUGUDEC, cp. also 97 VORRTIGURN, 297 VORTIGURN, for -GERN and OE for OI in 164 VOENACUNAS, see §6.28, 192 QENILOCGNI for QENILOCAGNI, 300 CUNNETAS for CUNANETAS), (b) the addition of a score (e.g. 3 QUNA- for CUNA, if not due to confusion of /k/ and /kʷ/ §6.29(b), 40 INEQAGLAS for ENEQ- = *Enechglas*, 172 SAGARETTOS for SAGRETTOS ? (cp. 449

SAGRAGNI), possibly iv RITTECC for RETTECC = *Rethech*), (c) too wide
a gap between scores (e.g. 86 CLIUCOANAS for -CUNAS, 242 BRRUANANN
for BRRENANN and 135 AILLUATTAN for -LETTAN see §6.28), (d) too
narrow a gap (e.g. Macalister's -IS in 431 DOVATACIS, the final -IS on which
should be read -EAS, (leg. D[O]V[A]TUCEAS), (e) consonant scores for vowel
scores (e.g. 353 TRENACCATLO for -CATO, witness the accompanying
**TRENACATVS**, the L is clearly an error for O and is corrected by the following
O) and (f) the wrong orientation of scores (e.g. 145 MAN SOMOGAQQ for
MAQ COMOGANN see §5.2 and compare 467 on which the error is corrected
by the lapidary himself, ULCAGNI replacing UDSAGQI). (Others such as the
original omission of a final S in 197 DEGO[S] and the premature insertion of
an S in 198 MAQI-RITE(S)AS are unconnected with the script as such and are
corrected by the lapidary in each case). This danger with position-marking as
a device must always be borne in mind in discussions of chronological features
and morphological irregularities involving minimal distinctions in the representation of sounds in the Ogam script (such as vowel-affection, §5.14, the confusion of /k/ and /k$^w$/, §6.29, and the form of the composition vowel, §6.26).
But to argue that the script is prone to error and ambiguity is to exaggerate the
issue. If the bilingual inscriptions of Britain are a measure of the accuracy with
which the intended letters were correctly engraved, the number of such errors
is not likely to be inordinately high. A comparison of the eleven stones on which
the Ogam and the Latin echo one another (see §4.11) reveals that only one (489)
has errors in respect of more than one character and two (362 and 399) have *possible*, but by no means certain, mistakes in respect of one character only (-ES
in AVITTORIGES for genitive -IAS? on 362, though the construction is
nominative (see §6.25), and a B corresponding to an **M** on 399. The script then
can hardly be fairly described as one which 'might almost have been devised to
ensure the greatest possible chance of making mistakes' (Bergin, 1932a, 142).

§2.3 One derivation of the Ogam signary which has commanded a number of
adherents and which is inspired largely by the alleged unsuitability of Ogam for
writing is the manual gesture theory. According to this the use of Ogam as a
script is to be regarded as secondary and adventitious. The awkwardness of its
characters suggest that it must have been designed for a medium more easily
reconciled with their shape than the written one, and a gesture alphabet is
mooted as one which would fit this requirement. The staunchest supporter of
this view was R. A. S. Macalister, who as doyen of Ogam studies in the present
century was largely responsible for its popularity.[3] Macalister's theory was
presented in a framework which though frequently and forcefully argued is very
much at variance with what the available evidence warrants, and his views on
the matter find very little favour today among Irish scholars. Professor
Macalister believed that Ogam had been created as a manual gesture alphabet
for purposes of secret communication by druids in Cisalpine Gaul in or around
500 B.C. It survived some one thousand years in manual form as part of the
stock-in-trade of druidic freemasonry and finally made the transformation to
a script only at the eleventh hour, in Ireland, with the arrival of Christianity and
the consequent breakdown of the druidic order. As we shall see in the next
chapter (§3.5) the choice of Cisalpine Gaul and 500 B.C. were dictated by an

unduly strict insistence that the alphabetic forerunner of Ogam should conform to certain requirements of detail, and the support for both the role of the druids and the antiquity of the system which Macalister found in the non-Christian character of the inscriptions and their use of an 'archaic' language was quite spurious (see §4.9).

Notwithstanding this unlikely scenario the claim that the finger gesture theory provides a natural explanation for what is considered a most unnatural script must be evaluated in its own right. Macalister points out quite rightly, for example, that the quinary grouping of Ogam can be satisfactorily explained by reference to a medium employing the fingers of the hand, but this is scarcely sufficient to warrant the finger-gesture hypothesis. If the theory is to hold water it must explain more than the arrangement of the characters into groups of five. It should also go some way to accounting for the systematic repetition of the scores and the principle underlying their orientation. In short, if a manual alphabet is to provide the missing link between Ogam and its alphabetic prototype it will be necessary to assume that the finger configurations it employed were such as to generate the Ogam system in the transfer to a written medium, and this is apparently what Macalister had in mind when he described a druid effecting that transformation (1935, 121; 1937, 28).

A glance at what Macalister identifies as the nearest typological equivalents of this hypothetical gesture system, the finger spelling components of modern sign languages,[4] will do little to inspire confidence in the plausibility of reconstructing such a digital code. A comparison of a number of systems used reveals that while there would appear to be no limit to the possible finger configurations and hand orientations employed, most agree in using combinations of arbitrary and iconic shapes and none bear even the remotest resemblance to the symmetrical pattern of configurations which is a prerequisite for the hypothetical Ogam system if it is to account satisfactorily for the Ogam signary. One cannot, indeed, avoid the conclusion that such a system, if it ever existed, would have been as cumbersome and clumsy a means of gesture communication as the advocates of this theory maintain Ogam is as a script. Positing a diversion to a digital gesture medium, therefore, amounts to no more than a displacement of the problem, and brings us no closer to an understanding of the script as we know it.

§2.4 If the finger gesture hypothesis did not take cognizance of the principle underlying the Ogam script, the theory associating Ogam with the cryptic runes did, and thus represented an advance in the investigation of the genesis of the system. In 1876 (462ff.) Graves pointed to the fact that the position-marking principle at the basis of Ogam was identical to that found in some secondary encoded cryptic varieties of the Germanic runes. Some obvious parallels between Ogam and the runes have always been recognized (see §3.6) but formal resemblances between Ogam and the Common Germanic Fuþark or its western and northern offshoots stop at a preference for angular at the expense of rounded shapes and never offered much scope for an explanation of the Ogam signary itself. The secondary cryptic varieties to which Graves drew attention were more promising. These are explained in the so-called *Isruna Tract*,[5] a systematic account of runic cryptography founded on a peculiarity of the old

Common Germanic Fuþark, the division of the twenty-four runes into three groups of eight, known in later Icelandic tradition as *ættir* (pl. of *ætt* 'sex, gender family' but originally probably meaning 'a group of eight', Old Norse *átta*, see further §3.8). As in Ogam this division is exploited for purposes of position-marking and the various methods of indicating position are named so as to reflect the device employed. Thus, *Isruna* (Old English *īs* ⟨ Germanic *\*īsa-*, the name of the *i* rune) are described as being written throughout with the rune *i*, the group to which the relevant rune belongs being indicated first with short (or low-case) *i*-runes, its position within the group next with long (or capital) *I*-runes.[6] The *Hahalruna* are described as follows: *Hahalruna dicuntur istae, quae in sinistra parte quotus versus sit ostendunt, et in dextera quota littera ipsius versus sit.* '*Hahalruna* is the name given to those [secondary runes] which indicate the number of the group on the left-hand side and the number of the letter of that group on the right.' The system may be tabulated as follows:

f u þ a r k g w   h n i j é p R s   t b e m l ng o d

Recognizing the affinity with Ogam, Graves believed that these were the likely source for the latter but he remained of the opinion that Latin rather than the Fuþark was the alphabetic prototype of the system. The latter view was rejected by Arntz who argued that the runes alone provided a satisfactory explanation for many of the features of Ogam and in a very ambitious theory he attempted to account not only for the Ogam script, but also for the values of the characters and their enigmatic sequence by derivation from the *Hahalruna* (1935, 394ff.). According to Arntz the Ogamist, whom he identified as a Pict, adopted the *Hahalruna* and endeavoured to achieve the greatest simplification of the notation possible by limiting the maximum number of scores in any given letter to five, and by deciding to deploy these on one side only of a vertical stemline. His general approach was to subtract the number of strokes on one side of the *Hahalruna* symbol from those on the other, a process which yields the correct number, though not the correct orientation, of scores in the case of Ogam B, L, H M, and NG. Elsewhere, however, as Arntz is forced to admit, a rather more random, if not erratic, approach is required to generate the appropriate Ogam symbol, and here his theory comes to grief. Ogam R for example is produced by ignoring the group marker on the left of the vertical in rune 5, whence the required five scores. Ogam N is created by addition from rune 10, and S by subtraction from rune 16 (whence 6 strokes subsequently reduced to 5). This however yields an Ogam sequence N S, not the attested S N and Arntz is forced to yet another strategy to account for the transposition. Ogam D has to be derived from runic T, G from J, F from P and Q has to be created independently. The structural classification of phonemes in the Ogam sequence finds no explanation in this derivation nor does the separation of vowels from consonants, one of the hallmarks of the Ogam alphabet. What is obviously a carefully organized classification of sounds is portrayed, then, as resulting largely by hit and miss, and the runic cart is put before the Ogamic horse in a similar way in Arntz's explanation of the origin of the term *aicme* (see §3.8).

The antiquity of runic cryptography cannot be established with certainty though it must be conceded that the possibility of creating this type of cipher would have existed from the time the runes were divided into groups, the earliest evidence for which goes back to the sixth century.[7] Arntz does not doubt their existence at a suitably early period for his theory, but while this cannot be disproved there is no reliable evidence for it. But even if it could be demonstrated that the *Hahalruna* did exist at the required time, say in the fourth century (see §3.17), it seems unlikely that a system as symmetrical and systematic as Ogam, with its primary quinary base, could have had such fortuitous beginnings as those outlined in Arntz's derivation. Indeed, the very procedure he envisages is highly unlikely. Arntz became the victim of the complicated and ambitious nature of his own theory. Apart from the graphic, phonetic and chronological difficulties to which it gives rise, there is also the question of the primary status he feels obliged to give the Pictish Ogams, which are undoubtedly later than their Irish counterparts (see §4.2). His derivation was supported by Keller (1936 and 1938) with some modifications, and Ogam is presented as a derivative of the runes in Gelb (1952, tabulation on inside of cover). Most scholars of Irish who have expressed an opinion, however, have rejected it (e.g. Thurneysen, 1937, 201 and Hamp, 1954, 310), and in his discussion of runic cryptography Derolez (1954, 153-4 and 161) acknowledges that the inspiration for the *Hahalruna* may derive ultimately from Ogam rather than vice versa. Runic cryptography in its various forms, therefore, is a valuable source of corroborative evidence for the existence of position-marking as an alphabetic device. As a source for Ogam, however, it is neither formally attractive nor, in the present state of knowledge, chronologically feasible.

§2.5 We may turn then from finger gesture alphabets and secondary varieties of the runes to a more likely source for Ogam. The primary value of the Ogam character, as has been pointed out, is not phonemic, but numerical; it indicates the position of a sound in a fixed immutable sequence. Thus, the orientation and number of scores in the symbol *#* indicates position twelve in the sound-sequence, and it is by reference to that sequence that its value can be decoded. For this reason scholars today are almost unanimous in seeking its origins in the domain of written numbers, particularly in the row numerals of the ubiquitous tally stick. Ogam as we know it, of course, is a monument script and thus at some remove from the primitive tally. But literary references to what are often considered its earliest uses (see §8.10), the practice of inscribing short messages on twigs, rods, staffs and withes, bring it into the cultural ambience of the tally. More importantly, the somewhat bizarre appearance of the signary with its principles of ordering and quinary grouping finds a natural explanation in row numerals, and the theory gives rise to no obvious chronological difficulties since tallies have been employed more or less universally from palaeolithic times.

That tally numerals were the 'idea' behind the Ogam script was suggested by Thurneysen (1937, 196-7) and Vendryes (1941, 110-113), both drawing attention to the outward similarity of the Ogam characters to those of the tally and pointing to the use of tally-based symbols for communicative as distinct from counting purposes on the so-called 'message sticks' (*Botenstäbe, bâtons de messagers*). Menninger (1969, 275) described the Ogam characters as number symbols made 'on the line', strongly reminiscent of tally sticks, and Gerschel (1957 and 1962) set out in detail how he envisaged the adaptation taking place.

§2.6 The main function of the tally was to serve as a written record of a count of items and the principle underlying its notation was relatively straightforward.[8] The items to be counted were translated into a supplementary quantity of row numerals, usually realized as identical notches or scores carved into wood or bone. Thus, in the most primitive form of the tally a count of nineteen would be recorded as nineteen identical notches arranged in a *row* along the tally stick. The necessity of counting out each of the scores of such an unwieldy row when the tally was consulted led in time to the practice of *grouping* the scores at regular intervals by means of a distinctively *marked* notch, and the general choice of quinary and decimal grouping point to the role played by finger counting in the development of these so-called primitive numerals. Stages one and two of the development can be illustrated as follows:

IIIIIIIIIIIIIIIIIII
IIIIVIIIIXIIIIVIIII[9]

The use of specially marked notches or scores led to one of the most important developments in the history of row numerals, namely the facility of *abstraction*. An ordered and grouped sequence such as IIIIVII represents the count *seven*, but since the symbol V presupposes four preceding unit notches, and thus represents *fifth* position in the ordered sequence, it can be abstracted as an abbreviated and unambiguous symbol for the cardinal *five*, and the cardinal *seven* can, accordingly, be abridged as VII. This, clearly, would not have been possible in stage one above. With an abbreviated form of the numeral computation was now greatly facilitated (e.g. VII + VII = VVIIII = XIIII) and the etymology of Latin *computare* (*putare* 'to cut') shows that computing and reckoning began with tallies (Menninger, 1969, 226). The three important principles of the system, therefore, are *ordering*, *grouping* and *abstraction*.

§2.7 In the presentation of the Ogam alphabet above (§1.2) each character is shown in what we may now call its abstracted or abridged form. Thus, just as the Roman numerals I II III IIII V are abstracted from the tally sequence IIIIV, so too Ogam ⊤, ⊤⊤ etc. have been abstracted from an ordered sequence which we may present as follows:

The principles of ordering and grouping[10] are clearly present, and the possibility of abstraction has been demonstrated. The major departure from what we might consider the norm is the absence of rank or group markers, the position of the scores relative to the stemline, formerly the edge of the tally, taking their place. Owing to the absence of rank markers a numeral abstracted from such a sequence will not lend itself easily to computation. Thus, whereas Roman XII and XII can be added to give XXIIII, the addition of Ogam *//* and *//* will yield *///*, which is clearly incorrect. The Ogam numeral, if we may so call it, is more correctly to be regarded as an ordinal than a cardinal. Like its *Hahalruna* counterpart it can be transliterated as a fraction, the numerator indicating the position within a group, the denominator the group itself (e.g. $\frac{1}{1}$ = B, $\frac{1}{2}$ = H, $\frac{5}{3}$ = R etc.), the major difference between Ogam and the *Hahalruna* being that the denominator in Ogam is indicated not by a separate set of notches or scores but by the orientation or shape of the numerator. To recap, therefore, we may say at this point that Ogam shares the principles of ordering and grouping with tally numerals and it also permits of abstraction, though its abridged forms are unattractive for purposes of computation.

The choice of orientation as a means of grouping, with its inherent shortcomings for computation, is one which I believe was made deliberately as part of the adaptation of tally notation to sequential position-marking. Noting some examples of what Menninger (1969, 250-51) calls 'counting on the line' in other tally systems, however, Gerschel (1962, 140-41) envisages orientation of the Ogam kind as a feature of the proto-tally used by the Ogamist. Pointing to the linguistic evidence for quinary and vigesimal gradation in the Celtic languages he reconstructs a vigesimal-base Irish tally with quinary oriented grouping. As he is obliged to recognize that grouping by means of different orientations is not suitable for calculation, he turns to the *forfeda* and assigns them a role as supplementary rank-markers used to turn the grouped ordinals into cardinals. His primitive tally (1962, 153) takes the following shape:

Gerschel's explanation of some of the *forfeda* is certainly very attractive[11] but a tally system combining orientation and rank-marking seems to be an unnecessary complication. Their roles are dissimilar and best regarded as complementary. As we shall see in the next chapter (§3.4), there has always been a tendency in the attempts to identify the alphabetic prototype of Ogam to rely on the 'naturalness' of any argued derivation. Inevitably, however, one is forced to recognize the intervention of a creative individual or school in the formation of the Ogam alphabet, and it does seem appropriate to ascribe at least some of the peculiarities to the *creative* rather than the *natural* input. In the case in hand it is not necessary to assume that the framers of the system actually had as a model a tally featuring the main diagnostic characteristic of the Ogam script, viz. group-marking by orientation. Only two ingredients are necessary to account satisfactorily for the genesis of the script: (1) the principles of ordering, grouping and abstraction available in the standard tally, and (2) the decision to employ position-marking as an alphabetic device. The rest can be safely left to the ingenuity of the creator.

To simplify matters, therefore, we need only assume that the framers of Ogam were in possession of an ordered grouped tally notation of the kind:

IIIIVIIIIXIIIIVIIIIX. The decision to close the system at point *twenty* will have
sufficed to suggest orientation as a more suitable alternative to rank-marking.
It would dispense with the necessity of repeating Vs and Xs (or whatever corresponding markers might have been used), and the shortcomings of this kind
of grouping would not constitute a disadvantage since the symbols were to serve
as position-markers with ordinal values, not as cardinals for computation. For
the limited purposes for which it was devised grouping by orientation actually
constituted a positive advantage affording a much greater facility for abstraction than separate group-markers, especially when one takes into account the
fact that the stemline was to be the side of the tally or stone itself and did not
need to be engraved separately.

   Thus, the most important and significant *creative* element in the system gave
Ogam a conciseness not found in other position-marking devices. One need only
compare the *Hahalruna* above with their separate notation of group and position, or Bede's position-marking Roman numerals with the cumbersome repetition of V or X or XV below (§2.9.) to recognize this. If scholars have tended
to dismiss the Ogamists as framers of a cumbersome script they have done them
a considerable injustice. Subject to all the shortcomings of position-marking as
a device, their script is as sophisticated and efficient an example of it as one
could create.


§**2.8** It emerges then that the outward form of the Ogam alphabet finds a
natural explanation in row numerals. When we address the question as to why
such a system was devised and where its inspiration came from we enter a
domain of speculation where there are no straightforward answers. A common-
sense approach would be to regard the script as an economic compromise, adap-
ting familiar symbols to a new concept, that of writing. Inevitably, however,
with a system so divorced from the norm, ulterior motives will be ascribed to
its framers. MacNeill (1931, 33-4) argued, for example, that the script was
created as a rebuff to Rome, a deliberate expression of anti-Roman sentiment[12]
and Carney (1975, 62-3) suggested that it might have been brought into being
by political or military necessity as a cipher designed not to be understood by
those who had a knowledge of the Latin alphabet.

   Some scholars have opted for the view that Ogam represents a fusion of two
streams, alphabetic writing as we know it, and one of the most important
forerunners of writing, what Gelb (1952, 36ff.) terms the identifying-mnemonic
device (see also Brice, 1976). The latter is a system of conventionalized symbols
not representing a written language but functioning as a memory aid or as a
device for identification, particularly for identifying ownership, status, the parties to a contract or the work of a particular craftsman; the modern counterparts are the heraldic signs of the nobility, military insignia, symbols used by
the professions and crafts, brands on cattle and the like. To bridge the gap
between tally numbers used as a memory aid to a count, and Ogam as a communicative script, Vendryes (1941, 113ff.) highlights the capacity of such conventional symbols for communicating messages of a cryptic kind, and he draws
attention to the use of Ogam in this capacity as described in early Irish literature
(see further §8.10). Gerschel (1962, 522ff. and 543ff.), on the other hand,
emphasizes their capacity as identifying-mnemonic devices, drawing attention

to the use of tally-based symbols for purposes of identification, the pre-literate forerunners of the modern signature, and highlighting the function of the Ogam inscription as a record of the name of a deceased person and, more importantly, as a legal document establishing property rights (on which see §8.13).

According to this school, then, Ogam represents a continuation of an existing and very ancient communicative device overhauled by alphabetization.[13] The theory, of course, cannot be proved conclusively and there is a danger that too much has been read into the manuscript references to the uses of Ogam in this connection (see §8.12). Notwithstanding this the overhaul, if we may so describe it, involved the adaptation of numerals to the principle of position-marking, and it remains to investigate where the inspiration for this device might have come from.

§2.9 Many scholars regard Ogam, not as an alphabet *per se*, but as a cipher to another alphabet (see §3.4), usually the Latin one, and it is frequently suggested that it was designed specifically for purposes of secrecy. Certainly, there is evidence in the manuscript tradition for cryptic varieties of Ogam (see §7.11c) but these amount to no more than variations on the standard type which itself, in these contexts at least, is non-cryptic. In its most dignified role as a monument script, moreover, Ogam can scarcely be described as cryptic since this would defeat the purpose of the inscription and the accompanying Latin on the British stones would make nonsense of any such contention. The idea that an archaic form of the language was used on the inscriptions whether for purposes of secrecy or pedantry is also without foundation (see §4.9).

Notwithstanding these reservations the domain of cryptography (and of telegraphy) certainly offers numerous parallels to the principle underlying the Ogam signary. The fixed sequence of the alphabet gave its characters a numbering quality which we recognize when we use letters in place of numbers, and which the Greeks exploited when they assigned their alphabetic symbols numerical values.[14] Both the established sequence and the numerical character of the letters have been used since classical antiquity for purposes of cryptography. Numerous devices can be employed to this end,[15] such as the substitution for the letter intended of another at a fixed and specified remove from it in the alphabetic sequence, a device which antiquity records as having been employed by Julius Caesar and Caesar Augustus, the former replacing A with D, B with E etc., the latter writing B for A, C for B and so on.[16] Somewhat more transparent is the device whereby the vowels only are encoded by means of substituted dots, their number indicating the position of the intended vowel in the vocalic component of the alphabetic sequence. This is recorded in the tract *De Inventione Linguarum*, a short treatise on the invention of the alphabet usually attributed to Hrabanus Maurus, Archbishop of Mainz from 847-856, where it is styled *Notae Sancti Bonifatii*, though Saint Boniface did not invent it; the earliest record of it can be found in the military handbook of Aeneas the Tactician, dating to the fourth century B.C.[17] The affinity with Ogam, where notches rather than scores are used for the vowels, will be obvious to the reader at this stage, as it was to Graves (1876, 465-6), who suggested that this may have been the starting point for the system.

Another device which is closer to Ogam is to substitute numbers for letters, the value of the number indicating the position of the intended letter in whatever alphabetic sequence is chosen. This is one of the most popular forms of cryptography in the Middle Ages, and Derolez (1954, ch. 2, espc. 156) has shown that the Irish *peregrini* on the continent in the ninth century took a keen interest in it. It normally takes the form of the Roman numerals or of the Greek alphabetic characters with their numerical values, and there are some examples of an attempt to simplify the notation by dividing the letters of the Latin alphabet into groups (Derolez, 1954, 163). The very frequent concordance of Roman and Greek numerals with the letters of the Latin alphabet in manuscripts containing grammatical, alphabetic and computistical materials testifies to the recognition of these forms of cryptography as a subsidiary branch of study in the liberal arts, even if they amount in many cases to no more than a diversion for leisured scholars. It is not surprising, therefore, that the great Anglo-Saxon ecclesiastical historian, the venerable Bede, appends a discussion of it to his discourse on digital computation (*De Computo Digitarum*) which serves as the introductory chapter to his *De Temporum Ratione*. Here he points out that the finger configurations for numbers can be employed as a manual language (*manualis loquela*), and he demonstrates how the warning *caute age* 'go with care' can be communicated to a friend in danger with the appropriate digital symbols for III I XX XIX V and I VII V (CAUTE AGE) respectively.[18] The device can also be employed with written numbers, he says, but it is evident from his remarks (*Potest autem . . . quaedam manualis loquela, tam ingenii exercendi quam ludi agendi gratia figurari*, Jones, 1945, 181) that he considered position-marking, whether in digital or written form, no more than an interesting mental exercise, an intellectual plaything, which he concedes has a certain limited capacity for secretive and telegraphic communication.[19]

These devices have a lot in common with Ogam but the closest approximation by far is offered by the *Hahalruna* and by a telegraphic military signalling system described by Polybius in his history of the rise of the Roman Empire.[20] In the latter the letters of the alphabet were divided into five consecutive groups and the dispatcher signalled his message by means of torches, the number of which held in the left hand indicated the group to which the intended letter belonged, those in the right hand its position within the group. This and the cryptic varieties of the runes have grouping and position-marking in common with Ogam, the only important difference being the superior grouping device in Ogam as outlined above.

In drawing attention to these devices I do not wish to imply that there is a direct connection between any one of them and Ogam, but merely to highlight the fact that the principle which the Ogam signary employs is not an isolated one, though it has been given independent expression unparalleled elsewhere. Most of them, anyway, would be too late to have supplied the model used by the Ogamists. This, as we have seen, is probably the case with the *Hahalruna*, where the roles may in fact have been the reverse. The Irish provenance of much of Bede's *Opera de Temporibus* has now been well established (Ó Cróinín, 1983), and computistics, including finger calculation (see Carey, 1990, 39-41 on *compóid mérda*) were no doubt standard teaching in the monastic schools of seventh-century Ireland, alongside grammar, scriptural exegesis etc. (see further §8.1). Whether the *manualis loquela* had any currency or not is questionable. It would certainly have had its advantages within the monastery itself as a legitimate means of circumventing the rules on the observance of silence, and references to an unspecified system of *signa digitorum* are found in the Saints' Lives (Plummer, 1910, vol. 1, cxvi) though these may have been no more than occasional gestures. But while allusions in the classical authors show that digital computation was known to the Romans (see Bechtel, 1909), computistics in Ireland are largely associated with the stand taken by the Irish Church in the paschal controversy, and are probably far too late for consideration in a discussion of the origins of Ogam. As for the Polybian telegraphic signalling system, the suggestion has been made (Eisler, 1949, n40) that this might have been familiar to Celtic auxiliaries in the Roman army and that it might have provided the model, but one wonders whether we need go as far afield as this for it.

On the face of it, position-marking is too obvious a device not to have arisen independently in different places at different times and it may have suggested itself independently to the Ogamists. If, as seems probable (see §3.10), the framers of the system were familiar with the works of the Latin grammarians – and the inner structure of the alphabet certainly suggests the grammar school rather than the military academy – the inspiration may have been to hand in their study. We have seen that the cryptic devices above were closely associated with the study of the alphabet, and it is not improbable that instruction in the rudiments of Latin grammar might have included a concordance of letters and numbers with its related cryptography.

§2.10 The nature of the Ogam script is such that it is impossible to pinpoint its source of inspiration or to identify its framers in time or space with any degree of accuracy. This may seem like an attempt to bow out of a thorny issue, but it is preferable to positing secret societies of Gaulish or Irish druids, as has all too often been done. With characteristic restraint Thurneysen (1937, 200) suggested that we should seek the framers of Ogam among the Irish learned class of *filid*, and the grammar school would account for many of its features. The script, however, cannot bring us to an identification any more specific than that. What we can say is that if it was originally designed for cryptic purposes it survived long enough to outgrow this mould. It is important to remember this when comparing it with the cryptic devices mentioned above. Ogam differs from these not only in its grouping principle and in shedding its cryptic cloak, if it had one originally, but also in the fact that it does not mark position to an established alphabet. The systems we have referred to are short-lived superficial encoded forms of attested alphabets designed with the limited objective of secret and/or telegraphic communication in mind. Ogam, on the other hand, is a self-contained system marking position to an otherwise unattested sequence of classified sounds. If its written form suggests a similarity with secondary runes, it is in every other respect on a par with the runes themselves. It is not the creation of a dilettante whiling away his leisure time toying with ciphers, but a carefully planned and coordinated writing system designed as a vehicle for a language with a phonemic structure of its own. More than the signary, it was the sequence of sounds memorized as a fixed series of letter names which, as the mainstay of the tradition, guaranteed the esteemed position which Ogam was to retain in the native schools. Long after the script had ceased to exist in any practical capacity and had been reduced to the status of a plaything for leisured scholars with an interest in the abstruse (see §7.12), the alphabet as a series of sounds continued to supply the framework for the study of the grammar of the Irish language and in particular for the study of metrics (see §7.17). It is to its inner structure, therefore, and the problems of its origins, that we must now turn.

CHAPTER THREE

# The Ogam Alphabet: The Internal Structure and its Origins

**§3.1** If the origin of the Ogam script can be outlined in general terms the identification of its alphabetic prototype has proved a much more complicated exercise. Indeed, had the creators set out with the intention of completely covering their tracks and presenting an enigma to modern scholarship they could scarcely have been more successful. A number of plausible solutions to individual problems have been proposed but no one has succeeded in solving all the difficulties associated with this aspect of Ogam and many would probably concede that a lot is irrecoverable on the basis of the evidence available to us. Of the alphabets most frequently mooted as possible prototypes (Latin, the Germanic Fuþark and Greek) the *communis opinio* has by now embraced Latin as the most likely candidate and Ogam today is generally described as a cipher based on the Latin alphabet. In this chapter an attempt will be made to outline the differing views on the matter and to question the conceptual and methodological framework within which they have been formulated.

**§3.2** A large number of origins have been proposed for Ogam and many cannot be discussed in detail in this book. In this connection, however, it is worth noting that the tendency until recently has been to give the system a foreign origin. In the Middle Ages two theories held the field, the one assigning Ogam a divine origin by ascribing its creation to Ogma mac Elathan (see §8.4), the second, the view of the Biblical scholars, bringing it onto the stage of world history as perceived at the time by having it created at the tower of Babel (see §8.3). The supposed Eastern origins of Ogam were popular in the last century at a time when the desire to deny any connections with Latin and Christianity were such that obvious Latin names occurring on the inscriptions such as *Marianus* (16, 188 MARIANI) and *Sagittarius* (56 SAGITTARI) were turned into impossible Irish words, the former explained as 'the field of *Rian*', the latter as 'the sage or priest *Dari* (Brash, 1879, 217 and 118-9).[1] In his 'Lectures on Welsh philology' John Rhys (1879, 312ff.) set out a detailed evolution of Ogam from an ancient Phoenician alphabet and had the system reaching maturity in Britain,[2] whence its introduction to Ireland. Arntz, as we have seen (§2.4), had it created in Pictland on the model of the runes and several scholars, including

19

Macalister, Zimmer (1909, 612-3) and O'Rahilly (1946, 495) considered it an import from Gaul.

Notwithstanding this, no scholar who has argued for the 'introduction' of Ogam to this country from outside has advanced a convincing argument for this contention, nor is there a single piece of reliable evidence to support it. Indeed everything about Ogam suggests its Irish origins. Inscriptions in the Ogam character, for example, are not to be found anywhere outside of Ireland except in areas known to have come under Irish influence through colonization.[3] The language of Ogam inscriptions is invariably Irish as are the names of the characters, and there are compelling reasons for believing that the system was created specifically for the Irish language in its earliest form. The evidence supporting a foreign origin is minimal. It amounts to spurious inferences drawn from a derivation of the word Ogam from the name of Lucian's Gaulish Hercules *Ogmios* (see §8.5), and some highly speculative theorizing on (unattested) Gaulish letter names as the forerunners of the names of Ogam and some runic characters (see nn3.25,26). The fact is that all the evidence suggests that Ogam is the creation of an Irish scholar, or a school of Irish scholars, and Thurneysen may not have been wide of the mark when he suggested that its framers be sought among the *filid*. The exact locus of the creation cannot, of course, be established with certainty, but if the evidence points overwhelmingly to Ireland, or the Irish colonies in Britain, it seems misguided, at least, to seek it elsewhere.

§**3.3** Before embarking on an assessment of the more important or influential contributions to the debate it will be as well at the outset to identify the criteria which may be employed in the search for an alphabetic prototype and to define how they may be used. The distinguishing characteristics of Ogam are its signary, the inventory of phonemes for which it caters, the sequence in which they are arranged alphabetically and the names which they bear. Since the signary itself is likely to be an innovation based on written numerals the inspiration for which cannot be pinned down with accuracy, it is useless as a guide to the identification of the alphabet which underlies the system. Similarly, the Irish (originally Ogam) letter names are innovative in that they are not borrowings of the letter names of any one of the three mooted candidates. Unlike those of the Greek and Latin alphabets they are neither meaningless adaptations of foreign words nor purely perfunctory sound combinations. They share the status of living meaningful words with their runic counterparts and we shall see that their history and importance is analogous to these (see §3.14), but they are not borrowings from Germanic nor can it be demonstrated that they are modelled on runic nomenclature. While they are of the utmost importance as a guide to the earliest form of the alphabet, they offer little assistance in the task of isolating an alphabetic prototype.

We are obliged, therefore, to fall back on two criteria, the inventory of phonemes represented by the signary and their arrangement in an alphabetic sequence, and it is to these that scholars have generally turned in their attempts to identify the prototype of Ogam. It will be appreciated that they do not offer much scope, and what little they do provide would be considerably attenuated were it to be conceded that the choice of phonemes in the system was determined by the requirements of the target language, not dictated by the prototype. This, however, is rarely conceded, though there are convincing, if not compelling, reasons for assuming it.

It is difficult to establish which of these two criteria should be given priority and the approach of scholars has been haphazard and *ad hoc* in this regard. Some, like Marstrander (1928, 183), have emphasized the sequence factor, pointing out that two alphabetic writing systems (Ogam and the runes) which deviate from the classical alphabetic sequence could scarcely be unrelated, but Marstrander could only establish a relationship in the principle of deviation, not in the mechanics of it. Others have employed both criteria without attempting to evaluate the relative importance of either, choosing rather to exploit the cumulative weight of both as evidence in favour of the chosen prototype. This has become the standard approach and it is accompanied by two gratuitous assumptions which have narrowed the perspective of scholars in the field. These are (1) that the key to the values of the Ogam characters as preserved in medieval manuscripts is authentic for the alphabet in its original form, and (2) that Ogam is not an alphabet but a mere cipher.

§**3.4** It is the present writer's view that the assumed authenticity for the early period of the manuscript key to the Ogam alphabet is a fundamental error (McManus, 1986, 13ff. and §3.13 below). Some of the characters of the Ogam script are not reliably attested on the early monuments and the values they are assigned in the considerably later manuscript record bear the marks of interference and artificiality. It would be foolhardy to assume that because *some* of the values of the MS record are confirmed by the inscriptions, *all* necessarily have the same authentic pedigree. Each must be argued on its own merits by evaluating the sources available to the *literati* who handed them down, and until one is satisfied as to the authenticity of any given value its employment as evidence for a preferred alphabetic prototype must be viewed with considerable caution. For the moment it will suffice to say that all scholars who have sought to identify the alphabet used by the Ogamists as a model have assumed that the values they assigned their characters are those recorded in the MS tradition.

It is also generally taken for granted by most scholars that Ogam is no more than a cipher to an otherwise known alphabet. This is stated explicitly, for example, by Graves (1879, 208), for whom the Ogam character represents 'not a sound, but a letter in an alphabet of the ordinary kind' and Diack (1931, 86), who believes it is 'a matter of common agreement that the Ogam alphabet . . . is nothing but a re-writing of letters of the Latin alphabet in a different series of signs.' Binchy (1961, 8) too regarded Ogam as 'an extremely cumbrous way of representing' the Latin alphabet and this assumption, if not always so boldly expressed, represents the framework within which the search for an alphabetic prototype has been conducted. This obsession with the cipher theory has had the unfortunate effect of lowering the level of the debate. For if it is conceded at the outset that Ogam is no more than another alphabet in disguise it at once loses much of its interest and, with the emphasis on the sequence, the attempt to identify the disguised model is in danger of degenerating into an exercise in letter juggling. Regrettably this danger has all too often been realized.

The tyranny of the cipher theory is that it has always tended to highlight the *naturalness* of any proposed derivation of Ogam at the expense of an investigation of the possible *creative* input of the framers of the system. The general approach has been to juxtapose the MS record of the values of the Ogam characters and the letter-sequence of the preferred prototype, to seek one-to-one correspondences, to emphasize their *naturalness*, and to account for any unnatural features by a series of what are often inexplicable, ill-motivated or random reshufflings of the letters of the original. Most attempts to outline the successive stages in the development from the prototype to Ogam amount to no more than exercises in anticipating what one knows became the alphabet in its final form. Inevitably, however, any scholar who adopts the narrow perspective of the cipher theory will eventually find himself in a quandary. It is undeniable that several features of Ogam cannot be explained in terms of a simplistic encoding of the letters of any known alphabet. At some stage the intervention of a creative individual or school must be acknowledged and an attempt to cater for the sounds of Primitive Irish, the target language for the system, must be conceded. If this is so, however, we cannot think in terms of a mere cipher. The difference between regarding a character of the Ogam alphabet as, on the one hand, a mere alternative way of representing a Latin (or Greek or runic) letter, or on the other, a way of representing a sound in the Irish language, is considerable. The distinction is of pivotal importance and should be recognized.

What weight, for example, does the notion that 'Ogam has no character for /p/ because Irish at the time had no /p/' have when placed alongside the argument that Ogam has a character for /h/ because, and only because, the prototype had a *h*? One is surely the antithesis of the other, yet they are commonly found side by side. It is crucial, therefore, to a discussion of the genesis of Ogam to examine whether its framers merely camouflaged a known alphabet or actually created a new one. In the following summary, then, these two qualifications should be borne in mind.

§3.5 The Greek alphabet has never figured largely in discussions of the origin of the Ogam alphabet though it was popularized for a time by Macalister. Once an adherent of the Latin school (1914, 231ff.; 1928, 227-8) Macalister abandoned this allegiance when he found a means of avoiding the difficulty which he felt was presented by the 'unprincipled selection' of Roman letters in Ogam (1935, 119ff.; 1937, 20ff.). In its stead he turned to a Chalcidic variety of the Greek alphabet used in Northern Italy in the sixth-fifth centuries B.C. which, he claimed, was for all intents and purposes identical to Ogam (the twenty-five character form) in its selection of letters and thus removed the awkward problem of the selection process which was baffling the Latin school. The date Macalister gave to the creation of Ogam (circa 500 B.C.) and his identification of the druids of Cisalpine Gaul as its inventors were dictated largely by the age and locus of his perfect-fitting alphabetic prototype. But Macalister's insistence on the forerunner satisfying the requirement of having the same selection of letters as its offspring was misguided, since it allowed for no input whatsoever on the part of the framers, and his inclusion of the supplementary letters in the archetypal Ogam created by Gaulish druids ran counter to Irish tradition itself which clearly acknowledges the secondary and late status of these (see §7.14).

What is more, his Greek prototype is scarcely more attractive than Latin or the runes, even if one were to succumb to the arguments based on the naturalness of the derivation. Like others, Macalister is forced to resort to arbitrary reassignments of values and to letter-shuffling. These shortcomings together with the extended life-span he is obliged to assign the system in gesture form and the tortuous finger configurations made to generate the supplementary letters combine to make a rather incredible theory. In suspecting that his readers might think it 'fantastic, over-elaborate and far-fetched' (1937, 27) he was not wide of the mark and his reviewers did not disagree with this assessment.

§**3.6** Numerous arguments of both a general and a specific kind have been made in favour of the Germanic runes as the likely prototype of Ogam. Among these are: (1) The fact that both the runes and Ogam were designed for hard materials and remained epigraphic to the end, appearing in manuscripts largely as a mere object of antiquarian curiosity. (2) The employment of both scripts for more or less similar purposes and, in particular, their magical associations (Arntz 1935, 369ff.). (3) The fact that some varieties of the runes share the principle employed in the Ogam signary, viz. position-marking (see §2.4 above). (4) The division of the runes into groups (3 x 8) known as *ættir* (Irish *aicmi*) and the naming of the groups after the first character of each *ætt*, viz. *Frøys ætt, Hagals ætt, Týs ætt* (cp. *Aicme Beithe, Aicme hÚatha* etc., see §§1.4, 2.4, Arntz, 1935, 378 and Thurneysen, 1937, 199). (5) The fact that the names of the runes, like the Ogam letter names, were meaningful words in the Germanic languages (Thurneysen, 1937, 199) and the (perceived) partial overlap in meaning (two in the Common Germanic Fuþark and six in the Anglo-Saxon Fuþorc being names of trees, Arntz, 1935, 349ff. espc. 360)). (6) The fact that the Fuþark and Ogam are alone among alphabets in western Europe in deviating from the classical alphabetic sequence together with the argument that the Ogam sequence can be explained by derivation from the Fuþark (Arntz, 1935, 396ff.). (7) That both Ogam and the Fuþark, unlike the classical alphabets, have a special symbol for the sound /ŋ/ (Thurneysen, 1937, 199). (8) That vocalic and consonantal *u* are distinguished in both Ogam and the Fuþark whereas in Latin and classical Greek no such distinction is made at the graphic level (Arntz, 1935, 348). (9) That Ogam H and Z are more readily explained by derivation from the Fuþark than from the Latin alphabet as runic H was not merely graphic and runic Z, unlike Latin Z, was not restricted to foreign words (Arntz, 1935, 348, 395). (10) That the absence of P from Ogam might also be explained by the fact that it was little used in the runic tradition where, at a later period, a dotted *b* was often substituted (Arntz 1935, 395).

§**3.7** As already noted Latin has the greatest number of adherents today as the likely prototype for Ogam. The strongest argument in its favour is probably the fact that it was the most dominant and influential alphabet in western Europe in the period in question and the one an Irishman of, say, the fourth century A.D. is most likely to have come into contact with. Other arguments are (see Thurneysen, 1937, 202-3): (1) That the grouping of sounds in the Ogam alphabet can be explained by reference to the Latin grammarians' classification of the letters of the Latin alphabet into vowels (*vocales*), semivowels (*semi-*

*vocales*), mutes (*mutae*) and Greek letters (*Graecae litterae*). (2) That B and A are the first consonant and vowel respectively of both Ogam and Latin, a remarkable coincidence according to this school if Ogam was not modelled on the Latin alphabet. (3) That both the Ogam and Latin alphabets have five vowels without any graphic distinction of length; Greek has seven, the Fuþark six. (4) That in Ogam as in Latin the sounds /k/ and /kʷ/ are distinguished (symbols 9 and 10, Latin *C/Q*); this is not the case in classical Greek which has dropped *Koppa* (though it did survive in the West Greek alphabet, see Allen, 1968, 15) nor in the Common Germanic Fuþark, the Q rune being a later addition in the Anglo-Saxon and Gothic traditions.

§**3.8** The case for Latin does not appear to be quite as impressive as that for the runes but it is felt that the priority which should be given to Latin is such that the special pleading must be made by the contender. Indeed several of the arguments advanced by the runic school amount to special pleading and carry little conviction. Thus, (3) has already been dealt with above (§2.4). The first part of (1) might be argued equally for Roman capitals and the second part, the similar fates of both systems, is due more to the strength and popularity of the Latin alphabet than to anything else and is scarcely supportive of a derivation of Ogam from the runes. (2) could also be argued for Latin or Greek since both alphabets were used, though not exclusively, in similar domains to the runes and Ogam, and the magical properties of the written word are universal and secondary and do not constitute an argument either way. The magical character of Ogam and the runes, moreover, has been greatly overstated (see §§8.12-13).

The division of the runes into groups (4) is somewhat more to the point but the grouping would appear to be more at home in Ogam than in the Fuþark where there is no internal structure within the *ættir*. In view of the lack of a unifying or characteristic phonemic quality within the Germanic groups some scholars are inclined to believe that the Icelandic term *ætt* 'tribe, family' replaced a word meaning 'eight' or 'group of eight' (Old Norse *átta* 'eight', see Krause 1970, 31, Derolez 1954, xix, Arntz 1935, 378) and this seems reasonable. The term would be perfectly explicable within the runic tradition, where the division was 3 x 8, and a connection with Irish *aicme* would not arise. Arntz's view (1935, 378) that the framer of Ogam could find no use for a word meaning 'eight' or 'group of eight' and therefore understood *ætt* as 'family', whence his *aicme* (see also Krause, 1970, 31), is surely a case of putting the cart before the horse, a classic example of the lengths to which some scholars will go to make the evidence fit the hypothesis. The naming of the groups after their first members is a natural outcome of the division and requires no external influence. The *aicmi* of Ogam therefore do not presuppose familiarity with the Common Germanic Fuþark. Grouping is part and parcel of the position-marking device and requires no external model.

The fact that (5) the Germanic runes and the characters of the Ogam alphabet have meaningful words as letter names together with (6) the deviation of both from the classical alphabetic sequence are interesting correspondences and we shall see that the decision to use meaningful words as letter names had similar consequences in both systems (see §3.14). The similarity however stops there. None of the names of the Ogam characters can be shown to be borrowings from the runic tradition, nor vice versa, nor is there any overall agreement in alphabetic sequence between the two. It seems unlikely, therefore, that these characteristics are the result of borrowing.

Turning to the more specific arguments of the runic and Latin schools, those outlined in (7), (8), (9) and (10) for the former (§3.6) should be balanced against (2), (3) and (4) for the latter (§3.7). The reader will observe that these rest on the assumption that the transition from one alphabet to another should be seen to be as natural as possible, and they will hold water only if this fundamental principle is accepted. One is entitled therefore to question its validity. When it is argued in favour of the runes, for example, that the sixth character of Ogam (H) is more easily reconciled with an origin in an alphabet where it is not purely orthographical, this is tantamount to saying that the framers' choice of letters was dictated, not by the role they intended them to play in their new alphabet, but rather by the status they enjoyed in the prototype. If we accept this as a reasonable line of argument, however, we will have difficulty with the idea that P was abandoned on the grounds that there was no use for it in the projected alphabet, since this is an admission that the framers had their eye on the target language. This is why the runic school emphasizes the weak position of P in the Fuþark as the governing factor on this issue. The same school, however, is then forced into a corner on the question of Ogam C and Q, since this distinction shows a degree of original thinking, there being no model for it in the Fuþark. Similarly, if it is argued that Ogam C/Q favours Latin, the distinction at the graphic level between consonantal and vocalic /u/ (characters 3 and 18 in Ogam) becomes a thorn in this school's side. And if the Latin school is willing to admit that the inventor was ready to abandon what he did not need (e.g. Latin K, F, P etc.), they can scarcely ask us to believe that he incorporated two letters (H, Z) for which he could have no use into his system simply because they were present in his prototype. Finally if they concede that he completely overhauled the order of letters in his prototype, what value attaches to the argument that the positions of A and B in Ogam favour Latin? In short, the idea that natural one-to-one correspondences represent a case for a given prototype is a simplistic one which has been overworked and has permitted scholars to take considerable liberties in their portrayal of the *modus operandi* – not to mention the state of mind – of the framers. When the evidence demands it they are mere dolts toying with a mechanical cipher and straitjacketed by their prototype. If necessary, however, they can be raised to the dignity of grammarians with a keen instinct for phonetics and a refreshing independence of mind.

The latter part of argument (6) for the runes should be balanced against (1) for Latin. Arntz's attempt to account for the Ogam sequence by derivation from the *Hahalruna* has all the shortcomings discussed above in relation to the genesis of the script (§2.4). He failed to substantiate his claim that the runes and the runes alone provide an explanation for this particular enigma. His method does generate some Ogam letters but, for the rest, the juggling and reshuffling he proposes has a very weak motivation and lacks conviction. This admittedly is true also of most of the derivational procedures produced by the Latin school. In fact none of the difficulties associated with Ogam has produced more flights of fancy than that of explaining the sequence. In medieval times when invention was the order of the day the arrangement was explained as being based on a hierarchical classification of trees, or on the names of the twenty-five scholars in the school of Fénius Farsaid arranged in order of merit (see §8.3), and the former of these enjoyed some currency in our own time (Marstrander, 1928 and see n3.25), despite the fact that the letter names will not admit of a homogeneous arboreal classification (see §3.14). Atkinson (1874, 231) has the arrangement in the second *aicme* dictated by the initials of the numbers from one to five in Irish, an explanation which is not only restricted to this group but is also defective in detail,[4] and other more peculiar suggestions have been made from time to time.[5] Meyer (1917), for example, has Ogam as the creation of a Celtic trio whose names happened to contain identical vowel sequences and were chosen to dictate the consonantal arrangement; he identifies them, predictably, as *Balovuseni, Hadotuceqi* and *Magonguzeri*!

§3.9 The 'construct' approach is one adopted by a number of scholars. This is an attempt to account for the Ogam sequence by arranging the letters of the Latin alphabet in rows or columns and then detailing the modifications required to generate the sequence B L V S N etc. The procedure is defective in a number of ways, not least in the predictability of the modifications, all of which are designed to generate what we know became the Ogam sequence. It is in effect a hit and miss approach which cannot miss since it has the benefit of hindsight and its arguments tend to become circular in nature. It is defective too in that it presents the genesis of the Ogam sequence as an arbitrary mechanical adaptation of Latin letters with scant regard for any creative input on the part of the inventors, thus treating Ogam as a mere cipher, and it accepts without question the authenticity of the MS record of the values of the Ogam characters. One example will suffice for illustration.[6]

Of the 'construct' approaches the most recent is that of Carney (1975, 57ff.) who, with characteristic courage, is the only scholar to reject the by now canonical assumption that the Ogamists' immediate prototype was not the Latin alphabet *per se* but the Latin grammarians' classification of it. For Carney the Ogam alphabet, or cipher, as he terms it, is a mechanical adaptation of the *relevant* letters of the Latin alphabet arranged in vertical rows and rearranged partly on the principle of phonetic pairing. The inventor began with a Latin alphabet of twenty-four letters A B C D E F G H I K L M N O P Q R S T U X Y Z NG, the last not existing as such in the Latin alphabet itself but recognized by the grammarians who called it by its Greek name *Agma*. He set out with the intention of arranging these into groups of five and was thus obliged either to add one or discard four. He chose the latter course and abandoned K (for which C could function equally as well), P (because Irish at the time had no /p/), X (because CS could be substituted for it) and Y (which he did not need). He might also have rejected H and Z, according to Carney, but this would have left him two letters short of the desired twenty. The remaining letters were now arranged in vertical rows as follows:

| A | B | C | D |
|---|---|---|---|
| E | F | G | H |
| I | L | M | N |
| O | Q | R | S |
| T | U | Z | NG. |

The inventor now proceeded to rearrange these in a manner which would make good phonetic sense or be convenient as a mnemonic. His vertical groups already have much in common with the Ogam order, and the first or categorizing letter in the eventual 4 x 5 system was to be considered independent of others within its group, not entering into phonetic or mnemonic pairing. A and B at the top of columns one and two were chosen first as categorizing letters and the uppermost letter which was not to be phonetically/mnemonically paired in the remaining columns (M and H) were moved to the top of their columns. The columns already contain four, three, four and two letters respectively of the corresponding Ogam *aicmi*, a very high mathematical probability score according to Carney. Four letters which are to be phonetically paired are now removed temporarily from the construct (T, Q, C, NG), U is moved to the place left vacant by T and G/NG and D/T are now paired. C and Q are also paired and, being stops, are placed after D/T. N and S, which were labelled *semivocales* in Latin, are moved over to column two to accompany F and L. Rearrangements within each group are now made, phonetic pairs being ordered alphabetically, non-phonetic pairs anti-alphabetically (viz. D/T, C/Q, G/NG, O/U, E/I as against L/F, S/N, Z/R).

Carney's approach has the attraction of providing better motivation for some of the reshuffling of letters than have others, but it does have many drawbacks. The *selection* of *relevant* letters it proposes to rearrange, for example, is arrived at by the interaction of a variety of criteria including economy (C taking place of K), observations on the requirements of the target language (the rejection of P) and the desire to achieve a twenty-letter system (retention of H and Z). One wonders which, if any, of these was the guiding principle, or which should be accorded priority. The observation that phonetically paired groups are alphabetically ordered, others anti-alphabetically is interesting but of indeterminate value. In the case of L/F it rests on the assumption that the creators would have used Latin F for Primitive Irish /w/, which is highly unlikely. One wonders, indeed, whether too much is being read into the Ogam sequence. Too close an examination of it runs the risk of leading to observations which, on reflection, might appear inconsequential.[7] In providing statistical probabilities, moreover, Carney concedes, at least implicitly, that his construct is open to a variety of manipulations, and while he himself sought reasonable motivation the idea that the inventors' moves can be traced step by step is always in danger of becoming a licence for the imagination. Graves (1876, 461-2) and Thurneysen (1937, 205) were willing to concede that the precise details of the framers' motivation in establishing the Ogam sequence are irrecoverable, and this is the view too of many runic scholars regarding the Fuþark sequence, which is equally enigmatic.

§3.10 With the notable exception of Carney the consensus of opinion today would appear to be in favour of the view that the framers of Ogam modelled their alphabet on the classification of the letters of the Latin alphabet found in the works of the Latin grammarians. This view was first proposed in some detail by Keller (1936, see also 1938), but the idea that the works of the Latin grammarians were known to the framers of Ogam goes back to de Jubainville (1908, 251-2) who equated Ogam NG with Priscian's *Agma*, whence he considered it a borrowing. Keller's theory is accepted with some modifications by Thurneysen (1937, 203), Vendryes (1941, 101), Van Hamel (1946, 314), Jackson (1953, 156), Kuryłowicz (1961, 1ff.)[8] and Ahlqvist (1982, 8-10).

The Latin grammarians' classification is an adaptation of the analysis of the sounds of the Greek language into vowels and consonants (the latter divided into continuants and stops) which goes back to Plato (Robins, 1979, 23) and was incorporated by Dionysius Thrax (c.100 B.C.) into his *Téchnē Grammatikē*, the first surviving explicit description of the Greek language which remained a standard work for some thirteen centuries and to which Latin grammatical teaching owes a considerable debt (Robins, 1979, 30-31, 48). The Latin grammarians in fact transferred the grammatical system of Thrax's *Téchnē* to their own language producing, in the matter of the classification of sounds, the following system:

| *Vocales* | A | E | I | O | U | | | | |
|-----------|---|---|---|---|---|---|---|---|---|
| *Semivocales* | F | L | M | N | R | S | X | | |
| *Mutae* | B | C | D | G | H | K | P | Q | T |

The influence of Greek on Latin, in particular the borrowing of Greek words and names, led to the extension of the Latin alphabet to include Y and Z, and these were incorporated into the classification above as a fourth group known as *Graecae* or *Graecae litterae* ('Greek letters'). This fourfold classification is found in the works of the Latin grammarians Donatus (4th cent. A.D.) and Priscian (second half of 5th century). Quintilian (1st cent. A.D.) dealt briefly with grammar in his *Institutiones Oratoriae* pointing out (I.iv.6-7, Butler, 1969) that the letters should be classified into vowels and consonants, the latter into *semivocales* and *mutae* (he does not mention Y and Z)[9] but the classification goes back further than this. The relevant portion of Varro's *De lingua Latina* (2nd cent. B.C.) are missing but a fragment indicating his teaching on the matter does survive in an anonymous commentary on Donatus (Gordon, 1973, 14, Ahlqvist, 1982, 9): *Varro dicit consonantes ab* e *debere incipere, quae semivocales sunt, et in* e *debere desinere, quae mutae sunt*: 'Varro says that consonants which are *semivocales* should begin in *e*, those which are *mutae* should end in *e*.'[10] The threefold classification therefore goes back at least to Varro's time and its extension to incorporate the *Graecae* naturally must postdate the adoption of Y and Z into the Latin alphabet. This is first found in a late second or early third century A.D. metrical composition but is probably considerably earlier (Ahlqvist, 1982, 9).

It is important at this point to emphasize that this quasi-phonetic analysis is determined largely by the written rather than by the spoken word. As Robins points out (1979, 23), the Greek alphabet represented the descriptive framework for Greek phonetics. Statements take the form of accounts of the pronunciation of letters and this letter-based approach to phonetics was carried over into Latin grammatical teaching. Letters rather than sounds were considered the smallest parts of speech and were seen to have three qualities, *nomen* 'name', *figura* 'shape' and *potestas* 'power' (Robins, 1979, 24). When Varro speaks, therefore, of the *semivocales* beginning in *e*, he is not referring to sounds as we know them today but rather to the power of the consonant as expressed in its letter name,[11] *semivocales* being *ef, el, em, en* etc., *mutae, be, ce, de, ge* etc. The letter name, therefore, being the expression of the *potestas* of the letter was of the utmost importance, and we shall see that this, together with the letter-based approach, was carried over into Irish grammatical thinking (see §3.14 and §7.17).

**§3.11** Though first to exploit the significance of the Latin grammarians' teachings to the genesis of Ogam, Keller (1936, 34-5) failed to break loose from the runic school as represented by Arntz. Accepting the latter's derivation of the Ogam characters and their sequence from the *Hahalruna* as plausible he advanced the view that while the *order* of the letters within the Ogam *aicmi* was fixed by their runic model, the inventory of each *aicme* was determined by the teachings of Donatus. Thurneysen correctly rejected this compromise as unlikely, arguing that the balance of probability lay in favour of Latin as the model but involved more than a mere casual acquaintance with the Latin alphabet. The inventor of Ogam, according to Thurneysen (1937, 203-4), studied under someone who knew the basics of Latin grammar as taught by Donatus and he modelled his alphabet on the latter's teaching regarding the classification of sounds. Of these he abandoned X and P as unnecessary for Irish and rejected K and Y as superfluous. His second group (H D T C Q) is made up entirely of *mutae*, albeit in a unique sequence, and his first group (B L V S N) contains three *semivocales* (L S N); if one assumes that he identified his V (which Thurneysen believed was a spirant *b* at the time)[12] more closely with Latin F than consonantal V (which is not included among the *semivocales*), and that the position occupied by B was formerly occupied by M (B being later moved forward to harmonize with the position of B in the Latin alphabet sequence), his first group would originally have contained *semivocales* only. The third group was made to accommodate what would not fit into groups one and two and the fourth is self-explanatory. Thurneysen concedes that he has no explanation for the sequences within the *aicmi*.

This outline of the genesis of Ogam has now become the accepted one, allowance being made for minor modifications. These are:

(1) Too close an association of the name of Donatus with the Latin classification of sounds led to a tendency to date the creation of Ogam to the fourth-fifth centuries A.D. Carney (1975, 56), while not accepting the derivation, correctly pointed out that Donatus did not invent the classification, and he argued for greater scope in dating possibilities (first century B.C. – fourth A.D.).

(2) Thurneysen doubted that the Ogamists' teacher would have known anything of the *n adulterinum* (a sound between *n* and *g* conventionally represented by ŋ) recorded in a quotation from Nigidius Figulus in Aulus Gellius' *Noctes Atticae* xix 14.7 (see Allen, 1965, 28, 96)[13], and he left open the question as to where the inspiration for the thirteenth Ogam character came from. In 1941 this 'letter', known to Greek and Latin grammarians as *Agma*, was recovered from obscurity by Richardson, and in 1943 the same scholar argued that *Agma* not only lay behind Ogam NG (as suggested already in 1908 by de Jubainville) but was the origin of the word *Ogam*, the alphabet being named after the peculiarity that it alone had a distinctive symbol for the sound. Notwithstanding this impossible derivation of *Ogam* (see §8.6), it has now become accepted doctrine that the thirteenth letter of Ogam was suggested to the

framers by the teachings of Ion of Chios and Varro as recorded in Priscian to the effect that *Agma* was the twenty-fifth letter of the Greek alphabet and had no distinctive symbol of its own, being written *gg* in Greek and *n(g)* in Latin (*quod ostendit Varro in primo de origine linguae Latinae his verbis: ut Ion scribit, quinta vicesima est litera, quam vocant Agma, cuius forma nulla est et vox communis est Graecis et Latinis, ut his verbis:* aggulus, aggens, agguilla, iggerunt. *In eius-modi Graeci et Accius noster bina g scribunt, alii n et g, quod in hoc veritatem videre facile non est, similiter* agceps, agcora, see Ahlqvist 1982, 10 and Richardson, 1941, 65).[14] In one of the most recent discussions of the matter Ahlqvist (1982, 10) has pointed out that since Priscian is too late as a source for Ogam and *Agma* is not mentioned by the fourth-century gram- marians, the invention of the alphabet must have taken place at a time when Varro's teaching was still reasonably well known in the Roman provinces, and he suggests the end of the second or the beginning of the third century A.D. as a plausible date.

(3) Thurneysen (1937, 205) conceded defeat on the question of the rearrange- ment of the Latin grammarians' classification within Ogam. It is now generally argued that this proceeded along linguistic lines. Carney, as we have seen, emphasized the phonetic pairing within the groups. Hamp (1954, 310-311), who correctly regarded the Ogam letters linguistically as alphabetic symbols roughly covering the segmental phonemes of Primitive Irish and not as a mere cipher, described the arrangement in group four as a compact classification of the allophonic properties possessed by the vowels in juxtaposition with con- sonants,[15] and he regarded the alphabet in general as 'in a limited and muddled way a roster of structurally classified phonemes.' Most scholars, however, do concede that apart from some general principles such as the separation of vowels from consonants and the juxtapositioning of some phonetic pairs the sequence remains in essence as imponderable as its runic counterpart.

§3.12 Several points emerge from this survey of the state of play on the origin of Ogam. The selection of letters in Ogam shows a degree of affinity with pos- sible prototypes but is not explicable *per se* in terms of any one of them. The arrangement of these letters into quinary groups could have been determined by the signary itself, which required grouping, or by the decision to isolate the vowels, of which there were five, and treat them as a separate group. The latter decision suggests that the framers were more than casually acquainted with alphabetic writing. It is consistent with the view that they studied the rudiments, at least, of Latin grammatical teaching, and this course of studies may have introduced them to the principle of position-marking as a cryptic device. The classification of Latin letters, which also would have formed part of such a training, may have influenced them in their arrangement of the letters, but their hands were by no means tied by it.

If we assume that this was the cultural environment in which the Ogamists created their system we must concede that they showed considerable indepen- dence of mind in many respects. They devised a new script as the medium for their writing system. They gave graphic representation to a fundamental distinc- tion made between vowels and consonants by Latin (and Greek) grammarians, a distinction which is irrecoverable, however, from either the Greek or Latin alphabet, though some cryptic devices such as the so-called *notae Sancti Bonifatii* did give it visual expression (see §2.9). In many respects it seems clear that they were thinking on phonetic lines, witness the pairing within the script of phonetically related sounds such as /d/ and /t/, /k/ and /kʷ/, /g/ and /ŋ/ (see however §3.15 under GG *Gétal* on the latter) as well as the peculiarly Irish arrangement of the vowels *a, ou, ei*. Some of their decisions show clearly that they had Primitive Irish in mind as the target language for the alphabet, e.g. the absence of characters for /p/ and /f/, sounds which did not exist in that period of the language. They were not reluctant to part ways with the Latin alphabet in respect of the representation of distinctive sounds. The Latin alphabet provided them with one symbol only for vocalic and consonantal *u*, but their training may have informed them that *vocales sunt. . .numero quinque* a e i o u, *harum duae* i *et* u *transeunt in consonantium potestatem* (Donatus, see Holtz, 1981, 604, 1-2 and Ahlqvist, 1987, 13 and Quintilian, *Institutiones Oratoriae* I.iv.10). They represent these distinctions graphically in the case of *u* (symbols 3 and 18) but not, it would appear (see however §3.15 under H *hÚath*), in the case of *i*. If the NG of Ogam tradition were authentic this too would represent a rejection of the limitations imposed on writing by Latin grammatical teaching which acknowledges the existence of this *littera* but accords it only two of the three properties of letters, viz. *nomen* (*Agma*) and *potestas* (/ŋ/), but not *figura*.

It becomes increasingly obvious, therefore, not only that the creators of Ogam were of an independent frame of mind, but also that they did not intend the alphabet to function as a mere cipher to the Latin alphabet. Ogam is not merely a different way, cumbrous or otherwise, of representing Latin. It follows that the values the framers assigned their characters are not simply those of the corresponding Latin letters in disguise. The evidence suggests that they had a language with a phonemic inventory of its own in mind, that the creation was accompanied by a careful analysis of the sounds of that language, and that the alphabet was designed as a vehicle for them.[16] Put another way the values of the Ogam characters are not to be regarded as those of the Latin alphabet arranged topsy-turvy and camouflaged in a primitive Morse code, but rather as the sounds of Primitive Irish as perceived by the inventors.

§3.13 One of the reasons why the independence of mind which is being emphasized here has not been given due recognition before is the fact that the MS record of the characters of the Ogam alphabet has normally been taken as the starting point for the discussion, and there are clear indications of strong Latin influence in this (see §§7.13-16). Were this an accurate record of the Ogam alphabet in its Primitive Irish form it would have to be conceded that the framers of the system were unduly faithful to their model. This would be the case, for example, with the characters recorded in the MS as having the values H and Z, values which it is difficult to reconcile with an alphabet designed for Primitive Irish in which, to our knowledge, there were no sounds to which these Latin letters would correspond with reasonable accuracy. Similarly, as far as is known, the sound /ŋ/ was no more than a positional allophone of /n/ (i.e. before /g/) in Primitive Irish so that the decision to give it a distinctive character would have to have been dictated from without (either the

Fuþark or the Latin grammarians' *Agma*), since there would have been no obvious need for such a character to write Primitive Irish. As it happens, these three MS values figure largely in the debate on the origins of Ogam and have frequently been employed as evidence by both the runic and Latin schools for their respective contentions. Establishing the authenticity or otherwise, therefore, of the MS record is of paramount importance and should in effect be the preliminary step to an investigation of the origin of the system.

The reader unfamiliar with the nature of the Irish manuscript tradition might consider distrust of the record preserved in it a dangerous liberty. But considerable caution must be taken in evaluating its contents, especially if they presume to record details of a distant past. Our manuscripts are very often much more recent in date than the composition of the texts they record and they seldom preserve a fossilized record of the original compositions. An editor confronted, for example, with an eighth-century text in a manuscript dating from the fifteenth century will seldom, if ever, find the characteristic grammatical, phonological and orthographical features of the period of composition in his copy of it. The texts will usually have been subjected to varying degrees of revision, modernization and corruption and it is one of the editor's tasks to undo the changes brought about during a considerable period of transmission in order to establish the 'original' text. In the case in hand it is even more important to apply this editorial critique as the record of Ogam, which is found in MSS dating in the main from the fourteenth to the seventeenth century, is being used as evidence not for a text of the seventh or eighth centuries, but for the details of an alphabet dating approximately to the fourth. It is a curious fact that whereas no scholar would ever have claimed that the *Auraicept na nÉces* – the major tract in which the Ogam record is found (see §7.9 and §8.2) – was a composition of the Primitive Irish period, most have been content to accept its evidence on the Ogam alphabet as authentic for that period.

The MS tradition, therefore, may be considered a window on the original alphabet, but only in the sense in which this is true of late MS records of early texts; an editorial overhaul is required to remove modernizations and to assess the degree of revision which it might have undergone. It should not be forgotten, moreover, that the MS details on Ogam are found largely in grammatical tracts which in Irish as in Latin and Greek traditions were propaedeutic to a reading of texts and to the study of metrics. Their value, accordingly, is largely as contemporary documents, not as records of a distant past. No one who reads the origin of Ogam and of the Irish language according to the authors of the *Auraicept na nÉces* (see §8.3) would regard it as anything other than a contemporary statement. Why then should the values of the Ogam characters as recorded in this and related material be subject to a different interpretation? Ogam at the time was a living entity on the school curriculum and formed the framework for the analysis of contemporary Irish, not of a long forgotten earlier form of the language (see §7.16). The details, therefore, are essentially synchronic and can only be interpreted at a diachronic level if the necessary precautions are taken.

The key has been considered trustworthy for a number of reasons, not least the fact that many of its details are confirmed by the bilingual inscriptions of Britain (on which see §4.11ff.). In these, however, as in the Irish inscriptions, three characters which figure largely in discussions of the origin of the system (*hÚath*, *Gétal* and *Straif*) are not reliably attested at all (see McManus, 1986, 19ff. on NG). The values they are accorded in the MS key (H, NG and Z), therefore, cannot be tested for authenticity by this yardstick.[17]

Another reason for the assumed authenticity of the MS key was the fact that it records the value of *Cert* as Q, a value confirmed by the most frequently occurring word on the Ogam inscriptions (MAQQI see §4.6). In view of the fact that the sound this symbol represented (/k$^w$/) had merged with /k/ before our MS records came to be written (see §5.18) and that, excepting the case in hand, those records know nothing of it, its appearance in its proper slot in the Ogam alphabet as recorded in the manuscripts lent that record an aura of fidelity to its original which more than anything else was probably responsible for the trust placed in it. But the early Irish grammarians like their Greek and Latin counterparts knew little or nothing about historical phonology and they could not have reconstructed Q (= /k$^w$/) as the original value of symbol 10 (McManus, 1986, 15-16). That the MS record does not preserve Primitive Irish phonemes in cold storage is evident from *Fern*. We know from historical reconstruction and in particular from bilingual inscriptions in Britain that this character had the value /w/ in Primitive Irish and was equated with Latin V. By the Old Irish period the sound had become /f/ in initial position and the symbol is transcribed with Latin F in the MSS. Here, then, we have irrefutable proof of the contemporary nature of that record (McManus, 1986, 16). Since Q cannot be the result either of accurate historical reconstruction or of fossilized preservation, then, there must be an alternative explanation for it.

It is worth noting that when symbol 10 is transcribed with Q we are not told that this represents an ancient value no longer in existence. The manuscript Ogamists treat it as a contemporary value, a fact which itself should have been sufficient to alert suspicion. More importantly, they also use this symbol or the position occupied by it in the alphabet for Latin C and K. This vacillation between Q, K and C suggests that they knew the symbol represented a voiceless velar sound but were not quite sure how to distinguish it from symbol 9. The explanation which I have put forward for this difficulty elsewhere (1986, 15f., 29) is that they had inherited the values of these and all other symbols in the form of the initial sounds of the letter names, and the falling together of /k/ and /k$^w$/ which took place before the manuscript period in all words including the letter names left them with two names (*Coll* and *Cert* see §3.15), two symbols (9 and 10) but only one sound (/k/). They were thus confronted with a dilemma which they resolved quite simply. Looking at the Latin alphabet they saw that K and Q were superfluous (see Isidore, *Etymologiae*, I, iv, 12-13 who describes them as *supervacuae*) and could just as easily have been dispensed with. If this did not constitute a problem for the Latinist there was no reason why it should do so for the Ogamist. The difficulty was resolved, therefore, by equating symbol 10 with the Latin *supervacuae* K and Q, preferring the latter and applying to it the purely Latin rule that it be used before *u*.[18] Thus, far from preserving a fossil from Primitive Irish the transcription with Q is a contemporary solution to an inherited problem, and should arouse suspicion of, rather than copperfasten trust in the authenticity of this record for the Primitive Irish period. In a similar way it can be argued that the manuscript values H (symbol 6), NG (symbol 13) and Z (symbol 14) are also contemporary, cosmetic and Latin-based (see the relevant sections of §3.15 and the discussion of this first revision of the alphabet in §7.16) and were also chosen on the basis of the contemporary forms of their letter names.

§3.14 It emerges from this discussion that the letter names played a pivotal role in the system and can supply vital information regarding the values of the characters. It is all the more curious, therefore, that they have been given scant recognition in this capacity by scholars, the more so indeed when one considers the vital role played by letter names in the traditions of the three alphabetic systems mooted as prototypes for Ogam. In his discussion of Greek letter names, for example, Hammarström (1930, 8ff.) drew attention to their importance in elementary instruction in the alphabet. Quoting van Yzeren's reflection 'Wie hätte die Überlieferung die Namen der Buchstaben, welche den Griechen vollkommen dunkel waren, so treu erhalten können, wenn sie nicht in den ersten Schuljahren dem Gedächtnis gewissenhaft eingeprägt worden wären?',[19] Hammarström went on to show that in the Greek tradition memorizing and mastering the letter names in their fixed order was the first exercise in alphabetic instruction, followed in turn by learning their form and their abstract values, elementary spelling of syllables etc.[20] That this was the method employed by the Romans is also clear from Quintilian's objection *neque enim mihi illud saltem placet, quod fieri in plurimis video, ut litterarum nomina et contextum prius quam formas parvuli discant* 'At any rate I am not satisfied with the course, which I note is usually adopted, of teaching small children the names and order of the letters before their shapes' (*Institutiones Oratoriae*, I, i 25 in Butler, 1969).[21] Letter names were not only useful for what Hammarström calls 'mnemo-technical' purposes; they were an expression of the value of the letter itself and, as already noted (§3.10), in the Latin tradition it is to the position of the supporting vowel *e* in the name of the letter that reference is made in distinguishing between *semivocales* and *mutae* (Hammarström, 1920, 20ff., 1930, 16, Gordon, 1973, 61).

It is generally acknowledged further that the runes were learned and called by their names[22] and the survival of these long after many had become as 'dunkel' to Germanic speaking students as were *Alpha, Beta* etc. to the Greeks also points to a similar memorizing process in instruction. The existence of runic letter names at an early period can be inferred from the use on inscriptions of runes which only make sense if the name is substituted for the value in the same way as *Dcumius, dcimus, cra, bne* etc. can be written for Latin *Decumius, decimus, cera, bene* etc.,[23] and the extremely important role of the runic letter names as bearers of the values of the characters is recognized by Germanic scholars.[24]

Of course we do not have precise information on the nature of instruction received by the framers of the Ogam alphabet or used in the teaching of Ogam in the early period. But if they did undergo elementary instruction in the Latin alphabet, as seems likely, it is probable that they would have recognized the importance of letter names and would have considered them a vital component in their creation. Learning these in their fixed sequence would have constituted an even more important step in instruction in Ogam than in the classical alphabets and Quintilian's objection to the Roman method of his day – which he felt ran the risk of students being slow to recognize letters, paying less attention to their shape than to learning them off in their alphabetic sequence by rote – could scarcely have been raised in the Ogam context. The position-marking nature of the script was such that a memorized fixed sequence of sounds or letter names was an indispensable component and the survival of this fixed sequence in Irish schools of learning right up to the seventeenth century is a measure of its importance to instruction in the alphabet in Ireland. Indeed, if the later manuscript tradition is a yardstick the names must have played a pivotal role as they occupy centre stage in instruction in the later period (see §§7.16-17).

As I have dealt with the Irish letter names in detail elsewhere (McManus 1986, 13ff., 1988 and 1989) a summary of what I consider the important points regarding them will suffice here.

(a) The Irish letter names were coined initially for the Primitive Irish sounds to be represented by the Ogam alphabet. Like the names of the Germanic runes they were the means by which the values of the symbols were learned, memorized and transmitted. They thus represent the mainstay of the tradition and they were the source, in contemporary form, from which the MS values of the Ogam characters were abstracted.

(b) Unlike Greek *Alpha*, *Beta* etc. and Latin *A*, *Be*, *Ce* etc. the Irish and runic letter names were meaningful words which might suffer all the vagaries of nouns in any language, in particular semantic redundancy and phonological change. Whenever the initial sound in the name underwent change *a corresponding change in the value of the symbol took place*. In other words the acrostic principle whereby the initial sound in the name corresponded to the value of the symbol remained in force.

(c) There is no evidence for Gaulish or Continental Celtic precursors of the Irish letter names[25] but the existence and arrangement of the latter into a fixed series to serve the Ogam script can be established with reasonable certainty for, at the latest, the sixth century and it is reasonable to assume that their coining was coeval with the creation of Ogam.

(d) Though there is a small degree of overlap in meaning between Irish and Germanic letter nomenclature there are no compelling reasons for assuming borrowing in either direction.[26]

(e) The letter names, as already noted, have been given scant recognition by scholars and what little attention they have received has been largely misguided by the fiction that they were *all* names of trees. In the Old Irish period the primary meanings of most of the letter names were still known and were the basis for three distinct series of kennings known technically as *Bríatharogam* 'word Ogam' (see Appendix 1). Some of the names, however, were already on the way to semantic redundancy and when their meanings had been obscured a combination of schematism, the fact that the largest single semantic category within the nomenclature was an arboreal one, and the fact that the Irish word for letter(s) *fid/feda* meant 'tree(s)' led to the 'alphabet végétal' fiction, an assertion that *all* the characters of the Ogam alphabet were named after trees.

(f) The letter names survived the decline of the use of the Ogam script and continued to serve as the standard nomenclature for Irish letters until the demise of the Gaelic order in the seventeenth century.

(g) If the meaning of a letter name can be established with reasonable certainty and its etymology ascertained it should be possible to reconstruct its Primitive Irish form. This in turn must be the surest guide to the early value of the character.

§3.15 In the following I give a brief discussion of each letter name and the value it presupposes for the Primitive Irish period. The reader is referred to my 1988 paper on the kennings for fuller details.

B **Beithe**: The name of the first letter of the alphabet is well attested in Irish in its primary meaning 'birch-tree'. It is cognate with Welsh *bedw(en)* 'birch-tree(s)' and Latin *betula* and derives from the Indo-European root *$g^wet$- 'resin, gum'. It establishes /b/ as the value of this letter at all times in the history of Irish.

L **Luis**: The kennings point to an association of this letter name with either *luise/loise* 'flame, blaze' or *lus* 'plant, herb'. The word itself is not reliably attested in a context which would indicate its precise primary meaning but it is clearly related either to the root *leuk-* 'to shine' or *leudh-* 'to grow', either confirming /l/ as the value.

V/F **Fern**: This name is well known in Irish in its primary meaning 'alder-tree' and is cognate with Welsh *gwern(en)* 'alder-tree(s)'. Its Primitive Irish form would have been *wernā*, whence the value /w/ (= V) on the inscriptions. By the Old Irish period /w/ had developed to /f/, whence *Fern* and the manuscript transcription with *f*.

S **Sail**: *Sail* gen. sg. *sailech* is the standard Old Irish word for the willow-tree and is cognate with Welsh *helyg(en)* 'willow(s)', and Latin *salix*. The derivation from the root *sal-* 'dirty' confirms the value for Irish at all times as /s/.

N **Nin**: Nin has the distinction among Irish letter names of having both a specific and general meaning, viz. 'the letter *n*' and 'letters' in general. There appear to have been two words of the form *nin* in early Irish, *nin* 'fork' and *nin* 'loft'. The former is probably to be equated with the letter name though the kennings present some difficulties. The etymology of *nin* is not clear but the initial /n/ is beyond dispute.

H **Úath**: The problem posed by this letter name is self-evident, though it is all too frequently ignored. As it denotes the first letter in a consonantal series it must at one time have begun with a consonant, and there is no evidence for the existence in Primitive Irish, or any other period of Irish for that matter, of a native radical initial /h/, the initial *h* of Old Irish (e.g. *hór* 'hour', *hé* 'he') being purely scribal and based on Latin (unpronounced) *h* (e.g. *hora* 'hour'). It is reasonable, therefore, to suppose that *hÚath* formerly began with a consonant which was lost before the period of the inscriptions, on which the symbol is not attested. In my 1986 paper I suggested an original value /y/, noting the parallel with the Ogam distinction between vocalic and consonantal *u* (symbols 18 and 3 respectively), but I also pointed to difficulties associated with this suggestion (see further §5.11). Not least of these is the problem of an etymology; the nearest one can get to *úath* with an initial /y/ is a Primitive Irish *yōdos* (< *youdos* cognate with Welsh *udd* 'lord' < *youdyos*, from the root *yeudh-* 'to fight')[27] but this would have yielded Old Irish *úad*, not *úath*. A Primitive Irish borrowing *yōtos* from Greek *iota* would solve this difficulty but would make *Úath* exceptional, as a loanword, among the twenty letter names of the original alphabet (only *Ór* and *Pín*, in the *forfeda* category, are borrowings, see §7.15).

The kennings identify *hÚath* with Old Irish *úath* 'fear, horror' and it has been suggested to me by Peter Schrijver of the University of Leiden that if the latter is cognate with Latin *pavere* 'to be terrified', some trace of Indo-European /p/ might have survived into Primitive Irish in pre-vocalic initial position. If so this might explain the appearance of *hÚath* in a consonantal series but the evidence of Continental Celtic, where /p/ in this position is completely lost, does not support the hypothesis.

The letter name, therefore, presents considerable difficulties but one can be reasonably certain that the value *h* which the manuscript tradition accords it is no more than a cosmetic solution to the problem created by the loss of the original initial consonant. Faced with the problem of finding a consonantal value for *Úath* the later Ogamists merely modified the name to *hÚath* on the model of words such as *hór/ór, hé/é* etc. A similar solution to redundancy was adopted in the case of symbols 13 and 14 (see below under GG and Z) as part of the first revision of the alphabet (on which see further §§7.14-16).

D **Dair**: This letter name clearly corresponds to Old Irish *dair/daur*, gen. *daro* 'oak-tree', Welsh *derw(en)* 'oak-tree(s)' from the root *\*deru-*, whence the value /d/.

T **Tinne**: The kennings equate this name with the word *tinne* 'bar, rod of metal, ingot, mass of molten metal'. The word is probably related to Old Irish *tend* 'strong' or *tind* 'brilliant' and the value /t/ is beyond dispute.

C **Coll**: The name of the ninth letter of the alphabet is the word for 'hazel-tree', Old Irish *coll*, cognate with Welsh *collen* pl. *cyll* hazel-tree(s), Latin *corulus* from the root *\*kos(e)lo-*. The etymology confirms /k/ (as opposed to /k$^w$/, see next letter) as the value of this letter in Primitive Irish.

Q **Cert**: This letter name is undoubtedly related to Welsh *perth* 'bush' and cognate with Latin *quercus* ⟨ *\*k$^w$erk$^w$-*, ultimately from the root *\*perk$^w$*. By the Old Irish period, however, it was confused with the word *ceirt* 'rag' (⟨ *\*kert-, \*krāt-* 'turn, plait, interweave') and this confusion is reflected in the kennings. The equation with *perth* confirms /k$^w$/ as the Primitive Irish value of the letter. By the Old Irish period this sound had fallen together with /k/ (whence the confusion of the two words *cert* and *ceirt*) and the manuscript transcription of the value of this letter with Q cannot be original (see the discussion above §3.13).

M **Muin**: The kennings on this letter name point to three distinct Old Irish words, viz. *muin* 'upper part of the back, neck', *muin* 'a wile, ruse, trick' and *muin* 'love, esteem'. It is not clear which of these gave its name to the letter but the probability is that it is the first. 1*muin* is cognate with Welsh *mwn* ⟨*\*mono-* *\*moni-* (Latin *monile*) 'neck, throat', confirming the value of the letter as /m/.

G **Gort**: The name of this letter clearly corresponds to Old Irish *gort* 'field' cognate with Welsh *garth* 'garden', Latin *hortus* from the root *\*gher-, \*ghort-* 'to enclose, enclosure'. The etymology confirms /g/ (as opposed to /g$^w$/, see next letter name) as its value in Irish.

GG **Gétal**: The kennings and commentary on this letter name point clearly to a word meaning 'killing' or 'slaying' and I have suggested in my discussion of it

(1988, 157-9) that it is an old verbal noun of *gonid* 'wounds, slays'. If so it would be cognate with Welsh *gwanu* 'to pierce, stab' from the root *$g^w hen$*- 'to pierce, strike' and it would point to the Primitive Irish value /$g^w$/. Like /$k^w$/ this sound fell together with its non-labialized counterpart (/g/) before the Old Irish period, whence the redundancy of the letter. As the MS value NG is not a radical initial in Irish, no more than is the H of *hÚath*, and is not contained in the letter name itself, it cannot be authentic. It can be explained easily, however, as another example of the recovery of a letter from redundancy, one of the objectives of the first revision of the alphabet (see §7.16). The word *gétal* itself appears to have fallen out of use as such at an early period.

Z *Straif*: All kennings on this letter name point to an identification with *straif, straiph, sraiph* etc. 'sulphur' and as Thurneysen once pointed out (1937, 207), whoever establishes the etymology of this word will have ascertained the earliest value of the letter. As /s/ was catered for by Sail, Straif must originally have stood for some distinctive sound which had become /s/ by the Old Irish period, and the probability is that /st/ was sufficiently distinct from /s/ at the time to warrant being assigned a symbol of its own (on the reflex of *-st-* in the inscriptions see §5.11). The sound /sw/, which must also have existed in Primitive Irish is another, though less likely, candidate. Both /st/ and /sw/ generally fell together with /s/ by the Old Irish period and the manuscript transcription with Z, the only remaining sibilant in Latin with which *Straif* could be equated, is clearly designed to effect an independent status for what was by then a redundant symbol (see the comments on *hÚath* and *Gétal* above). Like many of the *forfeda*, Z was not required to write the Irish language and was inspired by a comparison of Ogam with the Latin and Greek alphabets (see §7.16).

R *Ruis*: The name *Ruis* appears to stand in a similar relationship to the word *ruise* 'red' as Luis does to *luise* (see above). The kennings point to a meaning 'red' or 'redness', in particular the redness in the face brought on by embarrassment. The word therefore derives in all probability from the root *reudh-* 'red', confirming the value /r/.

A *Ailm*: The kennings on this are based on the sound represented by the letter, not on the letter name itself, and as the word is only attested once in anything other than a letter name context (where it appears to mean 'pine-tree') its meaning cannot be established with certainty. There can be no doubt, however, that it always represented /a/. Thurneysen (1937, 204) believed that both it and Beithe had been suggested by Greek Alpha and Beta.

O *Onn*: This letter name is undoubtedly to be equated with Old Irish *onn* 'ash-tree', Welsh *onn(en)* 'ash-tree(s)' from the root *$\bar{o}s$-, *osen-* 'ash'. The word *onn* was replaced already in the Old Irish period by *uinnius/uinnsiu* and some later glossators on the kennings appear to have been unfamiliar with it. The etymology confirms the value /o/.

U *Úr*: All kennings point unambiguously to an equation with *úr/úir* 'earth, clay, soil'. This is the only letter of the vowel series which has an initial long vowel, but of course all can represent either the long or the short form of the vowel. The value /u/ (or /u:/), therefore, is beyond doubt.

E *Edad*: The kennings on this and the last letter of the original twenty (*Idad*) pose considerable problems and the forms of these letter names suggest an artificial pairing (compare Old English *Peorð* and *Cweorð*, Gothic *Pertra* and *Quertra* (see n3.26) and Irish *Beithe/Peithe*, see n7.49). Neither is well attested as a word in its own right. For a discussion of the difficulties see my 1988 paper (163-165).

I *Idad*: See the discussion of Edad above.

On the individual names of the supplementary category of *forfeda* see the discussion below (§7.15).

It will be clear from the above that in any given case in which the initial of the letter name has not undergone any change between the Primitive and Old Irish periods the value of the symbol remains stable. When a change takes place and the new initial remains distinctive it takes over as the new value of the symbol in accordance with the acrostic principle (*\*Wernā* = W ⟩ *Fern* = F). If as a result of the change the initial falls together with another the symbol becomes redundant. In the first revision of the alphabet (see §7.16) the later manuscript Ogamists partially disguised this redundancy by assigning these symbols cosmetic values chosen with discretion from the Latin alphabet. *Úath* required an initial consonantal value and as Latin H was not pronounced it met that requirement perfectly. *Cert* needed an initial voiceless guttural value other than C, whence Q or K. *Gétal* required a sound related in some way to /g/, whence ŋ, and *Straif* needed an initial sibilant value which was met perfectly by Latin Z. This solution also involved a corresponding modification in the spelling of their names, whence *Úath* ⟩ *hÚath*, *Cert* ⟩ *Que(i)rt*, *Gétal* ⟩ *nGétal* and *Straif* ⟩ *Zraif*, and a similar device was employed in the case of the *forfeda* when these underwent revision (see §7.17).

**§3.16** Our editorial critique of the manuscript record reveals, then, that it is a contemporary and cosmetically modified one and should not form the basis for a discussion of the origins of the system. The arguments and counter-arguments of the runic and Latin schools on the issue of Ogam H, NG and Z, which figure prominently in these discussions, bring us nowhere if these are not authentic, and judicious doubt has been cast on their authenticity. Furthermore, our analysis resolves the apparently irreconcilable aspects of the framers' approach to their task, namely the conflict between provision for the target language and fidelity to the prototype. Ogam H, NG and Z are not examples of such fidelity; they are solutions to a problem which arose long after the creation of the alphabet. If the analysis above is correct the target language played the influencing role and the Ogam alphabet can be said to have been created for the purpose of writing Irish, not as a cipher to Latin or any other alphabet. The inevitable conclusion must therefore be that one-to-one correspondences between Ogam and any one of the mooted prototypes loose their significance.

The creative input into Ogam was quite considerable and gives the system an importance it is denied when it is dismissed as a mere cipher. On the other hand it makes the task of identifying the prototype that much more formidable. The surest guide to borrowing among alphabetic systems, viz. similarity in the shape and value of individual characters, can offer no assistance in the case of Ogam, owing to the nature of the script. In its absence it is impossible to identify the model with absolute certainty. Given the Irish character of everything Ogam (see §3.2), however, and the likelihood that it was created in Ireland, Latin must rank as the most probable source of inspiration and, as already noted, the study of Latin grammar could have introduced the framers of the system to most of the concepts to which their alphabet gives individual expression. We have no way of knowing what kind of training in the study of their native language these people had, but their alphabet points to a considerable linguistic awareness. In his review of Gelb's work on the history of writing Hamp (1954, 312) has suggested that the devising of Ogam 'based on a structural phonemic analysis however rudimentary, remains a significant achievement in the history of writing.' It was in fact the earliest manifestation of Irish linguistic thinking, and a very accomplished one at that.

**§3.17** It remains, therefore, to consider the date of the creation of Ogam and for this we have a number of pointers to *termini ante quos*, i.e. times prior to which it must have been created, but nothing concrete. It will be argued in chapter five of this book that the Ogam inscriptions, our earliest surviving documents in Ogam, date in all probability to the fifth and sixth centuries A.D., with the possibility that some may belong to the fourth. In his discussion of the date of the creation of the Common Germanic Fuþark relative to the earliest runic inscriptions Krause (1970, 35) notes that a comparison with other systems, particularly Greek, suggests that the creation of an alphabet precedes its use on inscriptions by approximately one to two centuries. If so, the third or fourth century would be the likely date for the creation of Ogam. Some scholars, on the other hand, maintain that the use of Ogam goes back much further than the inscriptions can take us. Binchy (1961, 8-9), for example, believes that for each occasion it was used on stone it must have been used thousands of times on wood, and many consider saga references to the practice of inscribing messages in Ogam in wood (see §8.10) to point to its earliest use. If so the date of the inscriptions would be irrelevant to the issue and it is certainly true that by the monument period the alphabet and a conventional orthography were well established throughout the country. But details recorded in medieval saga certainly do not constitute reliable evidence for a date prior to the fourth century, and too much has probably been read into the saga references to Ogam in this connection.

The phonology of the alphabet also provides pointers in the matter of dating, particularly if the above analysis of its earliest form is correct. The absence of /p/ is significant as this sound must have been becoming increasingly more common in Latin loanwords by the late fifth century (McManus, 1983, 48). The fact that it never had the honour of being assigned a letter name of its own (McManus,1988, 167 and below n7.49), therefore, is testimony to the date of the coining of the letter names in general, and it is reasonable to suppose that this was contemporaneous with the creation of the alphabet. Similarly, the labio-velars /kʷ/ and /gʷ/ (*Cert* and *Gétal*) are consistent with a date prior to the sixth century, when these were being delabialized to /k/ and /g/ respectively (see §5.18). A period of time must also be allowed for the fact that whatever sounds *Úath* and *Straif* denoted had already disappeared or merged into obscurity with others by the monument period, as they are not attested in the inscriptions.

The evidence, then, appears to suggest the fourth century as a *terminus post quem non*. The fact that Pope Celestine sent Palladius as first bishop to Ireland in the year 431 (*Ad Scottos in Christum credentes ordinatus a papa Caelestino Palladius primus episcopus mittitur*, O'Rahilly, 1942a, 5) suggests the existence, in all probability in the south of the country, of an established Christian community at that time. Given that the Christian religion is a book-based one and required reading skills in Latin, it is possible that this was the locus of the creation of the alphabet. On the other hand, Irish colonies were being established in Wales probably in the fourth century (see n4.10) and these may have provided the link with Latin learning. Jackson (1953, 156), for example, believes the alphabet was created by an Irishman from one of these colonies who attended a Roman grammar school of the late Empire. At any rate archaeological evidence shows that Ireland was by no means cut off materially from the Roman world at the time in question (Bateson, 1973, 37 and Harvey, 1987a, 5-6) and there is no difficulty in assuming cultural contacts of the kind which would have provided the environment and stimulus for the creation of the Ogam alphabet.

## APPENDIX 1

The Old Irish kennings on the letter names, (A) *Bríatharogam Morainn mic Moín*, (B) *Bríatharogam Maic ind Óc*, (C) *Bríatharogam Con Culainn*. For a full discussion of each kenning see my edition (1988). There I described the *Bríatharogam* as circumlocutions which may have been put by a teacher to a student and I compared them with crossword puzzle clues. The connecting alliteration in the B series, however, together with the two-theme structure of each kenning suggests to me now that this comparison does not do them justice. The opposition between *kenning* and *letter name* is that of a semantically marked synonym to an unmarked norm, or of poetic to everyday language. See Watkin's excellent discussion of the 'language of Gods and language of men' (1970).

### TEXTS

|     | A                | B               | C                |
|-----|------------------|-----------------|------------------|
| B   | Féochos foltchaín | Glaisem cnis    | Maise malach     |
| L   | Lí súla          | Carae cethrae   | Lúth cethrae     |
| F   | Airenach fían    | Comét lachta    | Dín cridi        |
| S   | Lí ambí          | Lúth bech       | Tosach mela      |
| N   | Costud síde      | Bág ban         | Bág maise        |
| H   | Condál cúan      | Bánad gnúise    | Ansam aidche     |
| D   | Ardam dosae      | Grés soír       | Slechtam soíre   |
| T   | Trian roith      | Smiur gúaile    | Trian n-airm     |
| C   | Caíniu fedaib    | Carae blóesc    | Milsem fedo      |
| Q   | Clithar baiscill | Bríg anduini    | Dígu fethail     |
| M   | Tresssam fedmae  | Árusc n-airlig  | Conar gotha      |
| G   | Milsiu féraib    | Ined erc        | Sásad ile        |
| GG  | Lúth lego        | Étiud midach    | Tosach n-échto   |
| Z   | Tressam rúamnai  | Mórad rún       | Saigid nél       |
| R   | Tindem rucci     | Rúamnae drech   | Bruth fergae     |
| A   | Ardam íachta     | Tosach frecrai  | Tosach garmae    |
| O   | Congnaid ech     | Féthem soíre    | Lúth fían        |
| U   | Úaraib adbaib    | Sílad cland     | Forbbaid ambí    |
| E   | Érgnaid fid      | Commaín carat   | Bráthair bethi?  |
| I   | Sinem fedo       | Caínem sen      | Lúth lobair?     |
|     |                  |                 |                  |
| EA  | Snámchaín feda   | Cosc lobair     | Caínem éco       |
| OI  | Sruithem aicde   | Lí crotha       |                  |
| UI  | Túthmar fid      | Cubat oll       |                  |
| IO  | Milsem fedo      | Amram mlais     |                  |
| AE  | Lúad sáethaig    | Mol galraig     |                  |

## TRANSLATION

|   | A | B | C |
|---|---|---|---|
| B | Withered foot with fine hair | Greyest of skin | Beauty of the eyebrow |
| L | Lustre of the eye | Friend of cattle | Sustenance of cattle |
| F | Vanguard of hunting/ warrior bands | Milk container | Protection of the heart |
| S | Pallor of a lifeless one | Sustenance of bees | Beginning of honey |
| N | Establishing of peace | Boast of women | Boast of beauty |
| H | Assembly of packs of hounds | Blanching of faces | Most difficult at night |
| D | Most exalted tree | Handicraft of an artificer | Most carved of craftsmanship |
| T | One of three parts of a wheel | Marrow of (char)coal | One of three parts of a weapon |
| C | Fairest tree | Friend of nutshells | Sweetest tree |
| Q | Shelter of a lunatic | Substance of an insignificant person | Dregs of clothing |
| M | Strongest in exertion | Proverb of slaughter | Path of the voice |
| G | Sweetest grass | Suitable place for cows | Sating of multitudes |
| GG | Sustenance of a leech | Raiment of physicians | Beginning of slaying |
| Z | Strongest reddening dye | Increase of secrets | Seeking of clouds |
| R | Most intense blushing | Reddening of faces | Glow of anger |
| A | Loudest groan | Beginning of an answer | Beginning of calling |
| O | Wounder of horses | Smoothest of craftsmanship | Sustaining equipment of warrior/hunting bands |
| U | In cold dwellings | Propagation of plants | Shroud of a lifeless one |
| E | Discerning tree | Exchange of friends | Brother of birch? |
| I | Oldest tree | Fairest of the ancients | Energy of an infirm person? |
| EA | Fair-swimming letter | Admonishing? of an infirm person | Fairest fish |
| OI | Most venerable substance | Splendour of form | |
| UI | Fragrant tree | Great elbow/cubit | |
| IO | Sweetest tree | Most wonderful taste | |
| AE | Groan of a sick person | Groan of a sick person | |

# CHAPTER FOUR

# The Ogam Inscriptions: Introduction

**§4.1** This and the following two chapters deal with what may be called the orthodox Ogam inscriptions, that is inscriptions on stone recording the name of an individual with or without an indication of parentage and/or sept or tribal affiliation and serving either as memorials, whether on tombstone (see §8.8) or cenotaph, or as charters of land ownership (see §8.13), or both. The so-called scholastic Ogams are not in a direct line of descent from the orthodox tradition and will be discussed in chapter seven (see §7.4ff.). Their inspiration is different and the orthographical conventions they observe are recent, dating from a period when the earlier cult was only a memory and its orthography and 'grammar' had lapsed into obscurity.

**§4.2** Orthodox Ogam inscriptions have been found in most counties of Ireland, in Wales, Devon, Cornwall and the Isle of Man, and there are doubtful examples from Scotland and England. Though scattered over a relatively large geographical area there is a marked southern bias in their distribution as will be clear from the maps on pp. 46, 48 and the following details:[1]
  (a) Kerry 121, Cork 81, Waterford 47, Kilkenny 11, Kildare and Mayo 8 (each), Wicklow 5, Carlow 4, Wexford, Limerick and Roscommon 3 (each, possibly 5 in the case of Wexford), Antrim, Cavan, Meath and Tipperary 2 (each), Armagh, Dublin, Fermanagh, Leitrim, Derry, Louth and Tyrone 1 (each).
  (b) Kerry 9 (one gone missing, see under ii/iii), Cork 3, Kilkenny 3, Meath 3, Waterford, Mayo and Louth 1 (each).
  (c) Wales: Pembrokeshire 16, Breconshire and Carmarthenshire 7 (each), Glamorgan 4, Cardiganshire 3, Denbighshire 2, Carnarvonshire 1; Cornwall 5, Devon 2, Isle of Man 5,[2] ?Scotland 2, ?England 1.[3]
  The questionable authenticity of the Silchester stone, the only Ogam inscription recorded for England, is discussed by Fulford and Sellwood (1980) who argue, mainly on archaeological grounds, that it should be considered false until further evidence is found to support it. Similarly, the orthodoxy of the two inscriptions from Scotland has been called into question by Jackson (1983) who points out that the reading given by Macalister for the Gigha stone (506)

contains much that is imaginary.[4] Apart from these there are also some 27 stones from Pictish Scotland bearing inscriptions in the Ogam character, often accompanied by peculiarly Pictish pictorial symbols as well as by ornamented crosses.[5] Unlike inscriptions in the Roman alphabet from the same area which are in Latin (see Okasha, 1985), and the orthodox Ogam inscriptions which are in Irish, these, though they bear Pictish names and some words of Irish origin, are written in an unknown language.[6] They can be dated to a relatively late period (seventh to ninth centuries) and their employment of the Ogam character is generally presumed to reflect the penetration of Pictland at this time by Irish or 'Gaelic' influence deriving both from the missionary zeal of the Columban Church established originally in Iona and the expanding political power of the Dalriadic Gaelic kings. Their Ogams bear all the features of the scholastic type, including for example the use of an incised stemline on the face of the stone as compared with the more common employment of the arris in the orthodox type, the use of long straight scores for the vowels, and of ornamental varieties of the characters such as those which link the ends of the scores (see the Burrian stone in Macalister, 1940, 210), all with parallels in the manuscript record (see §7.11). They are undoubtedly of great significance as the only examples of the Ogam alphabet in anything but an Irish-language milieu. As they fall outside the scope of this book, however, they will not be discussed further.[7]

The inscriptions from Biere in Saxony mentioned by MacNeill (1909, 330), who described them as 'possibly the work of some wandering Gael who knew just a little of the craft' and discussed in detail by Macalister (1902, 138-164) have been shown by Verworn (1917) to be forgeries. Supposed Ogam inscriptions from America recorded in Fell (1978), on the other hand, do not appear to the present writer to belong to the genre.

§4.3 Of the total number of inscriptions recorded approximately 5/7 (or 5/6 of the Irish total) were discovered in the three southern counties of Kerry, Cork and Waterford, with the largest concentration in Kerry, amounting approximately to 1/3 of the full total. The significance of this distribution for pinpointing the *locus* of the creation of the Ogam script is indeterminate. We do not know what span of time intervened between the framing of the alphabet, the establishment of an orthographical system and the actual cult of the inscriptions (see §3.17), and it should be borne in mind that whereas there is general consensus among runologists that the runic writing system was probably framed in or around northern Italy, the majority of runic inscriptions, including the earliest, are to be found in Scandinavia.[8] What can be said is that the cult of erecting monuments with inscriptions in the Ogam character probably originated and was certainly most predominant in southern and particularly south-western Ireland, and this area remained the focal point for it to the end (see §5.3). The distribution suggests that it spread thence in a predominantly eastward direction crossing the Irish sea to south Wales and south-west England, but never succeeded in gaining a secure foothold in the area north of a line drawn from Galway through Dublin across to the north coast of Wales. The distribution in Britain corresponds more or less in relative frequency to that of the respective areas in Ireland from which the colonists who brought it across the Irish Sea probably set forth, being minimal (if not non-existent) in Scotland

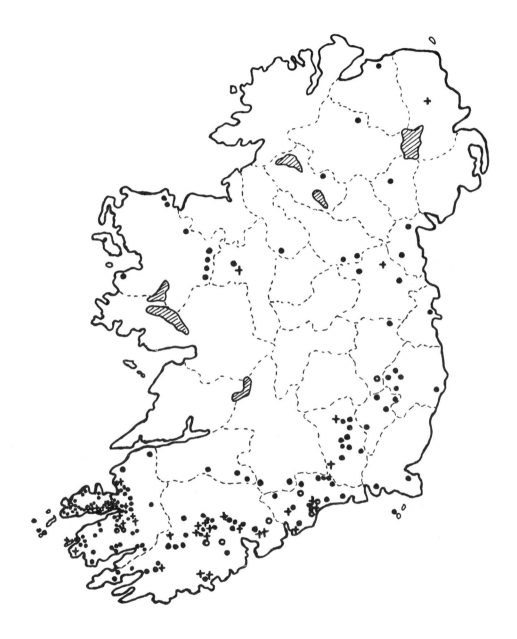

Distribution of Ogam inscriptions in Ireland.
● Single stone.
+ Group of 2–4 stones.
○ Group of 5 or more stones.

as it is in the adjacent area of north-eastern Ireland whence Argyll was settled in or around the fifth century,[9] and maximal in south-west Wales colonized by Irish settlers from the south-east around the fifth century, according to the most recent dating.[10]

§4.4 The inscriptions are normally disposed along the natural arris of the stone beginning in general on the left-hand side and reading upwards, across the top and down the right-hand angle in boustrophedon fashion. This would appear to have been the standard practice though variations on it such as upward or downward readings on each or either angle do occur. Occasionally the inscription might be incised on the face of the stone as in the scholastic Ogams but this is very exceptional and may have been dictated by the condition of the arris or the presence of an earlier inscription on it (e.g. 227; 40, 241). In such cases and on rounded boulders with no natural arris the inscription is normally without a stemline though this can easily be 'imagined' by observing the positioning of the vowel notches. In the case of the British monuments, on which the Ogam inscription is generally accompanied by one in the Latin alphabet, there is some-times an attempt to align the corresponding names in each script, usually resulting in a deviation from the standard disposition of Ogam with a conces-sion on the Latin side in the choice of a perpendicular rather than a horizontal arrangement of the inscription (e.g. 362, 378 and see §4.13). There are occa-sional indications (e.g. v) of the surface of the stone being rubbed smooth in preparation for the inscription.

§4.5 The condition of the inscriptions ranges along a scale from perfect preser-vation to virtual complete illegibility and a high percentage of them is defective in one way or another, a fact which makes the Ogam record a notoriously dif-ficult one to work with. The blame for the high proportion of uncertain readings is often laid squarely at the door of the script itself, but the fact that several inscriptions are perfectly preserved suggests rather that other factors must bear the responsibility. The choice of the natural angle of the stone, for example, though economical for the lapidary, had particularly unfortunate con-sequences in that it left the inscription more exposed to weathering than would have been the case had it been inscribed on the face. This is often highlighted on the bilingual stones of Britain where the inscription in the Latin alphabet is usually in a better state of preservation than the one in Ogam. Of course the script may be indirectly responsible in that it is not always immediately recognizable as such, a fact which may have contributed to the lamentable abuse of much of the record. For Ogam monuments have seldom had the good fortune to function only in the capacity for which they were engraved. Most have been appropriated to other tasks scarcely conducive to the preservation of the inscrip-tion. Many stones, for example, have been employed as building material in souterrains, ringforts, churches, oratories, stone huts, cottages, outhouses and the like, whether as lintels or roofing slabs, or in foundations and surface walls. Such an appropriation could occasionally prove fortunate in that it might pro-tect the inscription from the effects of weathering and the rubbing of cattle (see for example the Coolmagort stones, 197-203 and O'Kelly's comments on the Gearha South stone in O'Kelly-Kavanagh, 1954a, 51). More often than not,

Distribution of Ogam inscriptions in Wales.
● Stone with Latin and Ogam inscriptions.
+ Stone with Ogam inscription.

however, the inscriptions were liable to suffer damage either by trimming in the adaptation, or in the levelling of the structure itself. The charge of sacrilege, if it was ever made, was clearly an ineffective sanction when a good return was to be had from a stone and the list of casualties suffered by Ogam monuments is as varied as it is long. All manners of appropriation are recorded, such as employment as a hearth-stone (218a), a foot-bridge (122), lintels over a drain (82-96), a kneeling stone at a well (5), a seat for weary travellers (47), even an agricultural roller (308). One was built into a chimney-breast (173), another into a wall, despite offers being made for it by interested parties (33), and a third into the gable of a house (245). Many served as gate-posts or as rubbing-posts for cattle (particularly damaging in view of the position of the inscription). The inscriptions on one group of pulvinar boulders were worn down by youths rolling them as a trial of strength (155-63). A hollow sounding stone was broken on suspicion of it housing a treasure (172), another for convenience of carriage (97). If the suspicion of interference with inscriptions by Christian activists in the early period is probably groundless (see §4.9), vandalism has taken its toll in more recent times (e.g. 6, 57, 247 and p. 83). And of course many inscriptions have been lost forever. Among recorded instances are several of stones being smashed to pieces for building purposes (e.g. 20, 143, 144, 169); one fell from a cliff into the sea (174), another disappeared from a museum (56) while a third served first in a souterrain, then as a door-lintel, was subsequently seen lying on a manure heap and eventually disappeared without trace (214).

Appropriations of the kind mentioned above mean, of course, that the original site of erection of the monument may be unknown, though in the case of the larger stones it is unlikely to be far from the site of discovery. Some stones have been found in the most unlikely of places, such as in the bed of a stream (179), on a strand below the tide mark (180, 220) or buried in a bog (128). Many were discovered marking modern graves in cemeteries (e.g. 2, 194, 269) or lying prostrate in open fields and ditches (40, 81). A number were found upright as standing stones, usually of megalithic proportions (7, 66, 76, 164), and several on sites of early structures such as stone circles, old burial mounds and cairns (19-25, 107, 131-3, 148-54, 225). No certain example of a stone associated with a pagan burial has yet been found however (see Mac White, 1960/61, 295).

The Ogams in Britain, despite being accompanied in most cases by an inscription in the Latin alphabet, scarcely fared better than their counterparts at home, a fact which suggests that the peculiar form of the Ogam script cannot be made the scapegoat for the maltreatment of many of these monuments. In Wales one stone was built in on the external face of a church tower, the Ogam being almost completely trimmed away by the masons (328). 341 was rescued just in time from being converted into a gate-post, 368 served as a sill for a door, 409 as a bridge over a ditch, 433 as a gate-post, 446 as a lintel in a church where it has now been built into the window sill, and stone 362, the only Ogam monument commemorating a woman and bearing the Irish word for 'daughter' (on which see §§6.25 and 6.27), was found acting as a step in the path to a church porch, though it can now be claimed to be one of the best protected of all Ogam inscriptions, lying as it does in a large locked chest inside the same church, Eglwys Cymmin in Carmarthenshire.

Plate 1
The Eglwys Cymmin Latin/Ogam stone (362)
**AVITORIA FILIA CVNIGNI** AVITTORIGES INIGENA CUNIGNI
(courtesy of the National Museum of Wales, Cardiff)

§**4.6** The contents of the Ogam inscriptions are regrettably limited. They confine themselves, as do the majority of the Christian inscriptions of Britain, to a mere record of the name of the person commemorated with or without that of his father or some indication of sept or tribal affinity. They never tell us anything about the circumstances of the person's death and only very exceptionally give an indication of his station in life (e.g. 145, the QRIMITIR stone, see §4.9), and unlike the runic inscriptions, the engraver of the Ogams never identifies himself on the stone. As the earliest examples of recorded Irish, however, the onomastic character of their contents is significant, given the pivotal role of the need to record personal names in the history of writing in general (see Gelb, 1952, 66ff.). The challenge to devise an orthographical system for the Irish language was probably first encountered in this way, and Ogam met it with reasonable success. The association of the system with the writing of personal names survived, indeed, long after the general adoption of conventional script (see n7.27 and §8.8 on the term *ainm n-oguim*).

The names and formula words on the inscriptions appear almost without exception (see §6.25) in the genitive case. A governing word (probably meaning 'stone', cf. the **LIE** on the Inchagoill Roman-alphabet inscription 1 **LIE LUGUAEDON MACCI MENUEH**, or 'memorial' or the like) is to be understood though it is never expressed except in the case of the ANM formula (see below). Unlike Gaulish inscriptions on which parentage is indicated by a patronymic suffix attached to the father's name (e.g. **KOISIS TRUTIKNOS** 'Coisis son of Drutos' rendered in Latin on the Todi bilingual as **[C]OISIS DRUTI F.**), or by a possessive genitive of the latter (e.g. **DOIROS SEGOMARI**, 'Doiros (son) of Segomaros')[11] the standard practice on the Ogam inscriptions as in the insular Celtic languages is to use the word for 'son ' (Primitive Irish ( = PI) *maqqas*, gen. sg. *maqqī*, Ogam MAQ(Q)I etc. see §6.27, Old Irish ( = OI) *macc*, gen. sg. *maicc*). Some examples of the **DOIROS SEGOMARI** type are attested (e.g. 47 NETA-CARI NETA-CAGI (see §6.15), 262 ERCAGNI ?MAQI-ERCIAS, 169 MAQI-LIAG MAQI-ERCA, 154 CUNAMAQQI CORBBI MAQQ[I]. . .) but these are exceptional.[12] A different relationship is expressed by AVI (gen. of *\*awias* 'grandson, remote descendant', OI *aue*, gen. sg. *aui*) and MUCOI (E(arly)OI *mocu*, *maccu*); these express kindred and tribal affiliation and are followed by the name of the eponymous ancestor of the sept and tribe to which the person commemorated belonged. CELI (gen. sg. of PI *\*kēlias*, OI *céile*, gen. sg. *céili* 'client, vassal, fellow') appears in later Christian nomenclature in the sense 'devotee' but is probably best translated 'retainer' or 'follower' of the person whose name follows. ANM (⟨ PI *\*anmen* 'name', OI *ainm*) possibly in the sense 'inscription' (cf. the later usage *ainm n-oguim* 'an Ogam inscription consisting of a name' see §8.8) is an exception to the rule that nouns are in the genitive case (PI gen. sg. *\*anmēs*, OI *anm(a)e* should appear as ANMES or ANME on an Ogam inscription) while KOI (or XOI), so transliterated because it is invariably written with the first supplementary letter (see §5.3), appears to be an adverbial locative from the pronominal stem *\*ke*, *\*ko* with the meaning 'here', corresponding to the **HIC IACIT** (seldom **IACET**) of the Christian inscriptions of Britain.[13] These words (which are discussed in greater detail below §6.27), together with the personal names here represented by X, Y and Z, appear in the following customary formulae arranged in order of relative frequency:[14]

(1) X MAQQI Y
(2) MUCOI:
(a) X MAQQI MUCOI Y
(b) X MAQQI Y MUCOI Z
(c) X KOI MAQQI MUCOI Y
(d) X MUCOI Y
(e) X MAQQI Y MAQQI MUCOI Z[15]
(3) Single name inscriptions with no accompanying word.
(4) ANM:
(a) ANM X MAQQI Y
(b) ANM X[16]
(5) AVI:
(a) X AVI Y
(b) X MAQQI Y AVI Z[17]
(6) KOI:
(a) see (2)(c) above[18]
(7) CELI:[19]
(a) X CELI Y[20]

A personal name may also occasionally be prefaced by a noun indicating office such as 145 QRIMITIR RON[A]NN MAQ COMOGANN and 251 VELITAS LUGUTTI, the former containing the gen. sg. of the word for 'priest', Old Irish *cruimther* (nom.), the latter possibly the gen. sg. corresponding to Old Irish *filed*, nom. *fili* 'poet'.[21]

Examples of the more common formulae following the numeration above are:

(1)     85 GRILAGNI MAQI SCILAGNI
(2) (a) 197 DEGOS MAQI MOCOI TOICAKI
    (b) 250 CATTUVVIRR MAQI RITTAVECAS MUCOI ALLATO
    (c) 156 MAQQI-IARI KOI MAQQI MUCCOI DOVVINIAS
    (d) 118 VEQREQ MOQOI GLUNLEGGET
    (e) 244 COILLABBOTAS MAQI CORBI MAQI MOCOI QERAI
(3)     190 GOSSUCTTIAS 191 GAMICUNAS
(4) (a) 187 ANM MAILE-INBIR MACI BROCANN
    (b) 95 ANM MEDDO/UGENI
(5) (a) 66 MAQI-DECCEDDAS AVI TURANIAS
    (b) 288 ?DEBRANI MAQI ELTI AVI OGATOS
(6) (a) See (2)(c)
(7) (a) 215 ALATTO CELI BATTIGNI

§4.7 With the arguable exception of the British inscription 358 **MEMORIA VOTEPORIGIS PROTICTORIS**, VOTECORIGAS, generally assumed to be the memorial of *Guo(r)tepir*,[22] king of Dyfed, who died in the middle of the sixth century – his hair was whitening (*canescente iam capite*) in or around 540 when Gildas is believed to have written his diatribe on the Britons, *De Excidio Britanniae*, in which he addressed him as 'tyrant of Dyfed' (*Demetarum tyranne Vortipori*) – none of the individuals (as opposed to the septs and tribes, on which see §§6.17-18) recorded on the Ogam inscriptions has been identified with certainty in the historical record, a fact which makes absolute dating impossible.

Some attempts in this direction have been made, but most are tentative and doubtful.[23] MacNeill (1909, 332) identified the last person named on the Breastagh stone (10) as *Amlongaid/Amolngaid*, king of Connacht, who died between 440 and 450, and he suggested tentatively that 193 might commemorate *Colmán Oilither*, grandson of Díarmait mac Fergosa Cerrbéoil (†565 or 572). The condition of 10, however, is such as to leave some doubt as to its reading (see McManus, 1986, 22-3) and its language would appear to be more than two generations removed from the mid-fifth century (see below §5.29),[24] while 193, which Macalister describes as a '"scholastic" essay', is even less certain, particularly with regard to the AILITHIR on which the identification is based, *Colmán* otherwise being a commonly occurring name (and the reading COLMAN itself is questionable). MacNeill's identification (1931, 51) of the ADDILONA of 241 with a mid-sixth-century *Saidliu*, son of Ferb, greatgrandfather of Mo Chutu, is also problematic[25] as is that of vi SILLANN MAQ VATTILLOGG with the late eighth or early ninth century *Sílán m. Áedloga* of the Uí Angáin (Fanning/Ó Corráin, 1977, 17) in view of the linguistic and chronological difficulties it raises.[26] The commemorand on 40 MAQI-CAIRATINI AVI INE-QAGLAS has been identified with the *Mac-Caírthinn* of the Leinster poem *Ní dú dír do dermait* who ruled as king of Leinster in the fifth century and may be the same person as the *Mac-Cárthinn* mac Cóelbath who is recorded in the Annals of Innisfallen as having fallen in the battle of Mag Femin in the year 446.[27] The location of the stone (Barony of Duleek Lower, Co. Meath) does not correspond to that of the *Uí Enechglais* at a later time, when they are found on the Wicklow coast (Byrne, 1973, 137-8, and see below §6.18), but they may have held sway in this area of Brega at an earlier period when they were one of the leading Leinster dynastic groups to which the kings mentioned in the said poem belonged (Ó Corráin, 1985, 59). On the other hand the commemorand is known to us only as a member of the *Uí Enechglais* – his father's name is not recorded – while the *Mac-Cárthinn/Caírthinn* of the Leinster poem and the annals is recorded only as such or with his father's name Cóelub. No absolute certainty, therefore, can attach to the equation and the apocope of the final syllable of INEQAGLAS on a mid-fifth century inscription would present a problem for chronology (see §5.30).

Individuals commemorated on the stones can occasionally be identified in relation to one another as members of the same family or tribe. This is sometimes the case, for example, when groups of stones are discovered together. Thus stones 112 and 113, ?MICANAVVI MAQ LUGUN[I] (the unusual spacing suggests that this is not to be read MICAN AVVI MAQ-LUGUN[I]) and VEQIKAMI MAQI LUGUNI, belong to a group found acting as lintels in a souterrain in Knockshanwee, County Cork, and would seem to commemorate brothers, while three of the seven stones from the souterrain at Coolmagort, County Kerry, viz. 197, 198 and 200 (DEGOS MAQI MOCOI TOICAKI, MAQI-RITEAS MAQI MAQI-DDUMILEAS MUCOI TOICACI and MAQI-TTAL MAQI VORGOS MUCOI TOICAC) appear to commemorate members of the *túath* of *Toicacas* and also provide conclusive proof of the consonantal value of the first of the supplementary category of letters (see §5.3). In Wales the two related inscriptions from Llandeilo Llwydiarth (433 **ANDAGELLI IACIT FILI CAVETI/[A]NDAGELLI MACV CAV[ETI]** and 434

**COIMAGNI FILI CAVETI)** also appear to commemorate brothers but Macalister's suggestion that a third generation of the same family appears on the Maenclochog stone (441 **CVRCAGNI FILI ANDAGELLI**), a view supported by Richards (1960, 147), is disputed by Jackson in his review of the *Corpus* (1946, 523) where he points out that inscription 441 is, palaeographically at least, approximately fifty years older than 433. But the most interesting example of this type of relationship is surely provided by inscriptions 243 and 244 from a souterrain in Rockfield, Co. Kerry (MAQI-RITTE MAQI COLABOT [MAQI MOCO QERAI] and COILLABBOTAS MAQI CORBI MAQI MOCOI QERAI) the former of which, even if the restoration is in large part inferential, may record the son (i.e. assuming COILLABBOTAS and COLABOT to be the same person) of the person commemorated in the latter and would thus confirm O and OI as interchangeable spellings of the diphthong, not dialectal variants (see §6.28 and n6.71), as well as showing an interesting linguistic development within a single generation, viz the apocope (see §5.15) of the final syllable -AS.

§**4.8** Several inscriptions in Ireland are accompanied by a cross,[28] some by more than one (104, 145, 170, 185, 291, 301) and some also by another form of ornament (141, 183, 186). The crosses range in size and shape and include the more common plain (occasionally with slightly expanding terminals) linear and outline types (e.g. 34, 146, 163; 147, 217, 231, 235), crosses of arcs (8 and iv), cross pattées (76, 135) sometimes in a circle (141, 145), larger cross potents with square or rectangular terminals (32, 233) and some less easily defined unusual shapes (160, 188). 145 is one of the most interesting monuments with its chi-rho monogram and its Greek cross in a circle complementing an obviously Christian Ogam inscription, but the finest example of design and execution is surely the Maltese cross on the Church Island stone (iv).[29] On most stones the position of the cross is such as not to interfere with the inscription, or vice versa, with the result that it is impossible to establish with certainty whether they are coeval or not. In cases in which the cross is inverted with respect to the inscription (163, 171) or is at the butt of the stone (146, 235),[30] or when its execution contrasts in technique with that of the inscription (184, 186) it may be a subsequent addition which could easily be explained as the result of a later appropriation to serve as a tombstone, analogous to other appropriations already mentioned (see §4.5). Macalister would have it that many crosses postdate the inscriptions and were designed to Christianize what was regarded as a pagan memorial (see, for example, 8, 45, 141, 145, 170, 185), but this raises a number of issues which must be discussed separately (see §4.9). In the case of three stones, on the other hand, the disposition of cross and inscription would seem to confirm the order of priority beyond doubt. In one of these (135) the cross must be subsequent in date to the inscription as it interferes with it, but on 180 it seems that an Ogam score (the second in the L of CALIACI) was cut short to avoid running into the left arm of an existing cross, and on the Church Island stone (iv) several of the Ogam scores actually overlie the cross, thus providing irrefutable proof of the later date of the inscription in this case.

It is worth mentioning that crosses sometimes coincide with late linguistic forms (145, 233, 204), the use of supplementary letters (231, 235, 301, see §5.3), the ANM formula (76, 104, 204, see §5.4), Latin names (188, 265) or a Latin loanword (145). 104 is interesting in combining a cross, ANM, a late-looking spelling (CORRE) and a very Latin-looking spelling (MAQVI, see §6.31) ) but the significance of all of this is indeterminate in view, for example, of 156 which combines a cross with an inscription betraying none of these features.

§4.9 The presence of crosses on the Ogam stones and their relationship to the inscriptions raises the obvious and extremely important question of the religious character of these monuments and the intellectual environment to which they belonged. Notwithstanding the generally acknowledged origin of the Ogam alphabet in the Latin alphabet itself and the fact that, as we shall see, the cult of these monuments falls within the Christian period, the view that they were essentially pagan in character and were the work of a learned class divorced from if not totally unfamiliar with Latin has often been asserted. This is the position championed by MacNeill (1909, 301 ff. and 1931, 34) and Macalister (1945, *passim* and 1937, Chapter 1), and though already challenged by Graves in 1876 (446-7) and 1888 (242ff., see n3.1 above) and again by Thurneysen in 1937 (199) the exposure which the works of its proponents has enjoyed would appear to have copperfastened it in the minds of many. For MacNeill and Macalister the Ogamists, by which is meant those trained in the use of the alphabet and its conventional orthography, are to be sought among the druids, a somewhat nebulous class in early Ireland the very mention of which is always immediately suggestive of paganism and antipathy to Christianity and Christian Latin learning. Though willing to concede a Christian element on some of the stones, supporters of the pagan theory would consider this the exception rather than the rule. MacNeill emphasizes the essentially non-Christian character of the monuments and depicts the culture which produced them as isolated and retrospective, characterizing Ogam as 'pagan to the last' and contrasting it with manuscript Irish which he considered 'Christian from the first', and it is commonplace in general works on early Ireland for Ogam to be described as a pagan or pre-Christian writing system which 'survived' into the Christian period.

   In truth it must be said that the views of the pagan school have been expressed with much greater confidence in their veracity than the available evidence will permit, and while the contrary cannot be demonstrated beyond doubt assertions such as those of MacNeill and Macalister cannot be allowed to go unchallenged. On the linguistic side the view that the language of the inscriptions was of an 'archaic' nature even at the time of the erection of the monuments and might be explained as the speech of a remote period preserved by the druids in their schools of learning (Macalister, 1928, 220-21; 1935, 122) or as the language of an isolated pedantic backward-looking learned tradition (MacNeill, 1931, 34) is quite unfounded.[31] Parts of the formulae on the inscriptions betray a measure of conservatism such as one often finds in the written as opposed to the spoken word, but the language of the inscriptions in general is remarkably fluid and keeps pace with developments which we know were taking place between the Primitive and Early Old Irish periods (see chapter 5). Though undoubtedly the product of a learned tradition, since literacy is unlikely to have been a widespread attainment at the time in question, there is nothing of a linguistic nature on the monuments which necessitates the view that that tradition was isolated in any way or retrospective in its orientation. Indeed, neither of these characteristics could be easily reconciled with the fact that the very erection of inscribed monuments of this kind was itself an innovation probably of the late fourth or early fifth century.

The absence of Christian sentiment from the Ogam formulae is another characteristic advanced by the pagan school in support of its claims but this is equally indeterminate as a criterion. Many of the later semi-uncial inscriptions confine themselves, as do those in the Ogam character, to a mere record of the name and filiation of the person commemorated, yet no scholar would be likely to argue on this basis that they are the product of a pagan milieu. Formulae tend to become stereotyped and those of the Ogam tradition share much with the contemporary inscriptions of Britain, the palaeography of which shows that they derive their inspiration from the *inscriptiones Christianae* of Gaul. The only element which might have raised an eyebrow in Christian circles is the indication of earthly parentage which tended to be avoided on the Christian inscriptions of Gaul in deference to the Gospel injunction 'call no *man* your father upon the earth: for one is your Father, which is in heaven' (Matthew, xxiii, ix, see Nash-Williams, 1950, 6), but no one familiar with Irish nomenclature even in the most Christian of environments would consider the filiation in the formula *X mac Y* anything other than the norm. As Jackson puts it (1953, 167) 'To define a man's name by adding his father's is a formation absolutely typical of all the Celtic languages at all periods.' It is only when contrasted with the later formula of the type $\overline{\text{OR}}$ **DO X**, 'a prayer for X' that the mere record of a name might arouse suspicion, but there is nothing in an Irish name which makes it pagan *per se* and no inference can be drawn from the absence of such sentiment if it was not the convention at the time to express it.

A third category of evidence is that of *assumed* interference with the monuments in the form of the addition of crosses to 'Christianize' them (8, 45, 141, 145, 170, 185), the destruction of 'pagan Ogams' to make way for a Christian inscription (1, 127, 145) and the deliberate mutilation of MUCOI formulae.[32] These are gratuitous assumptions drawn with some imagination from the present condition of the stones and they presuppose rather than prove Christian hostility to the cult. The last is the one most frequently cited as evidence of such hostility, the argument being that the name following MUCOI was often that of a deity of pagan mythology, the tutelary god/goddess of the race, and would have been considered offensive to Christian sensitivities. Against this, however, is the fact recognized by MacNeill, who himself retracted the idol-breaking hypothesis which he was first to put forward,[33] that Ogam MUCOI continues in manuscript usage in the form *mocu, maccu*.[34] This is difficult to reconcile with any notion of ecclesiastical censorship and it will not suffice to argue that *mocu* was merely 'copied' into manuscripts after Christianity had been established, that is at a time when it could no longer represent a threat.[35] The MS sources of the *mocu* formula are largely ecclesiastical in nature and works such as Adamnán's Life of Columba show clearly that MUCCOI/*mocu*-type names were in vogue among ecclesiastics at a time when the Ogam inscriptions were being inscribed. If Brénaind mocu Altai of the Altraige († 577 or 583, better known as St. Brendan), Comgall mocu Aridi of the Dál nAraide († 601 or

602) and Lugaid moccu Ochae of the Corcu Ochae († 609), founders respectively of the monasteries of Clúain-ferta Brénaind (Clonfert), Bennchor
(Bangor) and Clúain-ferta Molúa (Clonfertmulloe), had no difficulty with their
names can we really take seriously the view that MUCOI names on an Ogam
inscription would have been regarded with suspicion and considered justifiable
targets for Christian vandalism? Surely not, and the fact that most MUCOI formula inscriptions survive intact confirms this and suggests that such hostility,
if it existed, could only have been localized. Damaged inscriptions are the rule
rather than the exception in the Ogam corpus and those bearing MUCOI formulae do not form a distinctive category. Such defects as they bear are not
improbably the results in most cases of secondary appropriations, weathering
or accidental damage.[36] When we know that a stone was used for building purposes it is surely reasonable to assume that any damage it might have suffered
is more likely to be the result of that appropriation than of some earlier
hypothetical censorship.

The isolation from Latin learning of those who erected the monuments is seen
as a prerequisite of the pagan school's argument, no doubt owing to the
assumption that the presence of such learning would itself imply a Christian
environment. In support of this MacNeill cites the transcription of the third
character of the Ogam alphabet with *f* in the manuscript tradition, arguing that
the *filid* could not have been in touch with Latin prior to the seventh century
(when /w/ became /f/) since otherwise they would have preserved the earlier
equation of the symbol with Latin *v*.[37] The MS record, however, as has already
been argued (see §3.13), is that of the contemporary alphabet, not of an outdated one, and it is based on the contemporary pronunciation of the letter
names. As evidential value for the intellectual environment of the earlier
Ogamists, therefore, it is quite useless. Its very existence, however, and its
preservation of the salient features of the system is very significant as it will not
allow for the breach between the Ogam and MS traditions which MacNeill
envisaged and which he explained in terms of a pagan/Christian dichotomy.[38]
If the erection of monuments in the Ogam character went out of fashion at some
time in the seventh century (see §5.30) the study of the alphabet itself did not,
and it continued to occupy an important position on the curriculum of the *filid*,
among whose ranks there were many ecclesiastics. There can have been no distrust or boycott of Ogam of the kind which MacNeill proposes when he interprets the questions 'Why is Irish said to be a worldly language?' and 'Why is
he who reads Irish said to be unruly in the sight of God?' as jibes directed at
Ogam.[39] He failed to demonstrate that Ogam as distinct from the Irish language
itself was the target of the implied criticism, and it is improbable that these dicta
reflect anything other than an understandable perception of Latin, the language
par excellence of the church and one of the *tres linguae sacrae quae toto orbe
maxime excellunt* (Calder, 1917, xxxiv, quoting Isidore) as more spiritual and
thus less worldly than the vernacular. Indeed it is this very perception of Latin
which explains the defensive position of the Irish grammarians of the *Auraicept
na nÉces* tradition in their evaluation of the merits of both languages (see §8.2).

The isolationist view is reinforced to some extent by the conventional assessment of the Ogam character as an intrinsically inefficient transcription or cipher
of the Latin alphabet (see §2.2 and §3.4 above), the perceived inferiority of

Plate 2
The Ballymorereagh Ogam stone with cross (170)
QENILOCI MAQI MAQI-AINIA MUC. . .

which when compared with its model was such that it was assumed that anyone possessed of an ability to use the latter would be unlikely to employ the former in any practical capacity. The exclusive use of Ogam and of the Irish language is thus turned into an argument in favour of the aloofness of the two cultures, and since it is acknowledged that the inscriptions fall within the Christian period, the scenario of a two-tier system of native Irish and imported Christian Latin learning is envisaged, each equipped with its appropriate writing system and firmly fixed on the one or other side of a religious divide. But if this argument were brought to its logical conclusion the Ogam alphabet would never have been invented, since its very invention presupposes a familiarity with Latin which its users, in accordance with this theory, are being denied. It does seem somewhat *ad hoc*, moreover, to concede the presence of Latin at the time of the creation of the script and to deny such presence thereafter.[40] What is more, the traditional 'nativist' view of a segregated two-tier system of learning has come under some heavy fire in recent years, and it is now being argued that the Irish learned classes had already embraced Christianity and Christian Latin learning by the sixth century.[41] If so, the pagan school's portrayal of the Ogamists becomes increasingly difficult to credit.

The notion of the writing system as the hallmark of a particular intellectual or religious environment is clearly evident in this context in the case of the Inchagoill stone (1 **LIE LUGUAEDON MACCI MENUEH**), the inscription on which, though grammatically akin to the Ogams and not bearing any specific Christian sentiment, is automatically accepted as Christian owing to its use of the Latin alphabet. The bilingual inscriptions of Britain, however, completely undermine any such compartmentalization and show the true alignment as being between Ogam and the Irish language on the one hand and Latin and the Latin language on the other, without reference to any particular intellectual tradition or religious persuasion. This, indeed, is what one would expect, since as we have seen (§3.12) there is good reason to believe that the Ogam alphabet was designed specifically as a vehicle for the Irish language, not as a cipher to the Latin alphabet, and its design was executed under the influence of Latin learning. To appreciate the position of the Ogam inscriptions of Ireland *vis-à-vis* the contemporary inscriptions of Britain, to which they stand in a very close relationship, one need only assume that to the Irish mind the Ogam alphabet was considered the appropriate vehicle for recording Irish names on stone, and Irish names were most naturally written in their Irish form.[42] There is nothing inherently improbable in the hypothesis that the Ogam and Latin alphabets could have coexisted side by side in complementary capacities, the one serving like Roman capitals as a monument script, the other essentially a book script used exclusively for Latin writing in the early period but gradually extending to Irish with the development of literacy in the vernacular. Certainly ignorance of the Latin alphabet is not a prerequisite to account for the Ogam inscriptions, not only because the British monuments confirm the opposite but also because the very concept of a restricted literacy embracing Ogam only is difficult to conceive of. One does less violence to the evidence available by seeking the equivalent of the Christian inscriptions of Britain in the Ogam corpus than by asserting the uniqueness of the latter and trying to account for it with a set of highly improbable circumstances. After all, if the dearth of Christian inscriptions in Ireland in the early Christian period were itself a problem requiring explanation, an outbreak of pagan inscriptions coinciding with the spread of Christianity would surely constitute a far greater one. We must not lose sight of the fact that if our dating criteria are not completely off the mark the cult of the Ogams dates in the main from the fifth and sixth centuries. It did not 'survive into' the Christian period, it began in it.

It is not being claimed here that all the Ogam inscriptions in Ireland commemorate Christians. That would be as unverifiable a claim as those of the pagan school, particularly in view of the fact that the identity of the people recorded on the stones is unknown to us. It would be equally rash to assert that the contemporary inscriptions of Britain were exclusively Christian. What is being argued is that the British and Irish inscriptions belong to the same genre and that there is nothing in the nature of an Ogam memorial which precludes the possibility that the subject of its inscription was Christian, or that those commissioned to execute it belonged to a learned class which embraced both Irish and Latin learning.[43] This is evident, for example, in the case of the Arraglen stone (145), which commemorates the 'priest' Rónán in a traditional formula written in Ogam characters and complemented by two fine crosses. As a priest Rónán can scarcely have been ignorant of Latin – the word for 'priest' is itself a Latin loanword (see below) – and it is improbable that those who commissioned his memorial would have turned to a class of professionals diametrically opposed in their outlook and training to Rónán himself. And while the Irish evidence may in most cases be quite ambivalent, that of the British Ogams, which are contemporary with and not a late offshoot of their Irish counterparts (see §5.33), points to an easy cohabitation of the two scripts which belies any strict separation of them and makes nonsense of any suspicion of dark druidic associations with Ogam. It is the misfortune of Ogam studies that the unusual character of the script has too often been seen to demand unique sets of circumstances both for its creation and its employment. Once this difficulty is overcome and Ogam is considered no more and no less than the Irish equivalent of Roman monumental script the need for such forced argumentation disappears.

To sum up, then, the witch-hunt for MUCOI formulae, the disinfecting of perfidious inscriptions with Christian symbolism and the general aversion to Ogam as an embodiment of a pagan past all make colourful, not to say sensational, reading but are probably as divorced from reality as is the impression to which they give rise, that of Christianity and its literary vehicle, the Latin alphabet, supplanting a pagan writing system. We have seen that the inspiration for Ogam probably came from Latin itself, and the cult of inscribing Ogam memorials flourished during the early Christian era. It does seem a little forced, therefore, to argue that an innovation in Ireland dating in all probability to the late fourth or early fifth century, using an alphabet deriving ultimately from Latin and observing a custom found in contemporary Gaul and western Britain, could have been the brainchild of an isolated and backward-looking class which found the trappings of Roman culture distasteful if not offensive.[44]

These views on the pagan character of the Ogam inscriptions notwithstanding, the overtly Christian element in the *Corpus* has probably been exaggerated. The only reliable case is 145 (QRIMITIR RON[A]NN MAQ COMOGANN)

with its Latin loanword *qrimitir* (gen., nom. *\*qrimiter* ⟨ *\*qremiteras*) deriving
from Latin *presbyter* through a form *\*praebiter* or *\*praemiter* (McManus, 1983,
46. n60). On 100, which Macalister regards as the memorial of the 'abbot'
Ulcagnos (with rather bad grammar) the AB is best ignored, as in Macalister's
earlier reading. Similarly, the interpretation of 127 as the work of an
iconoclastic Bishop Maqil, that of 193 as a ' "scholastic" essay', of 263 as bearing the equivalent of *vici episcopus* (BIGA ISGOB), and the retrogressively read
SAŋTI of 189 (on which see McManus, 1986, 21) are all extremely doubtful. A
number of Latin names, however, are attested and point to contact with the
Roman world (see §6.20).

§4.10 Unlike their counterparts in Britain the Irish Ogams are seldom accompanied by an inscription in Latin letters and never by an equivalent in Latin.
This, as we have seen, has been put down to unfamiliarity with Latin, but such
a conclusion is quite unnecessary. Circumstances in Ireland were different to
those obtaining in Britain, where the Irish colonists would naturally have felt
the urge, if not the need, to adapt to the customs of their immediate neighbours.
The bilingual Gaulish/Latin Todi inscription (see §4.6) near Rome is an
interesting parallel from the continent (see Lejeune's comments, 1970/71,
389-90). The most famous and at the same time most baffling Latin letter
inscription accompanying an Irish Ogam is 19 **IVVEn/rE DRVVIDES** which
was turned into an Ogam CELI TURLEGETTI by Macalister in a flight of
interpretative fancy. Uncertainty regarding the fifth letter makes the interpretation of the first word difficult but the second might be a Latin or Primitive Irish
nom. pl. of the word for 'druid'. The relationship of this to the Ogam OVANOS
AVI IVACATTOS, however, is quite unclear.[45] 176 bears a half-uncial inscription read as **FECT CUNURI** by Macalister, who thought it the work of a busy-
body; Schaffs (1923) reads **FEC** (or **FET**) **TVVNVRI** treating it as a gloss cor-
recting a faulty Ogam TUNURI to CONURI. The half-uncial **SCI FINTEN** (or
**INTEN**, the **F** is no longer visible) is clearly unrelated to the accompanying
Ogam EQO(?)DD on 186, while the **FECT QUENILOC** which Macalister reads
on 170 would appear to be imaginary (O'Kelly, 1945, 152). Far more interesting
is the Inchagoill stone (1 **LIE LUGUAEDON MACCI MENUEH**) already
referred to. Macalister believes this is a transliteration of an original Ogam but
there is no evidence to support this contention. The stone is unique in bearing
the formula word with final -**I** (on the spelling **MACCI** see §5.18) in Latin letters
and can probably lay claim to being the oldest surviving Irish 'text' written in
the Latin alphabet.

§4.11 Of the forty relatively well preserved Ogam inscriptions in Britain[46] nine
(345, 405, 426, 439, 496, 501-4) bear Ogam characters only, two (368, 427) have
independent Ogam and Latin inscriptions (the first inscription on 409 is also
independent of the Latin), on one (422) the relationship between the Ogam and
Latin is unclear owing to the condition of the latter[47] and the remaining twenty-
eight can be described loosely as bilingual. On eleven of these (341, 362, 399,
430 (as reconstructed), 446, 449, 456, 466, 484, ?489 and 500) the Ogam and
Latin echo one another more or less exactly, allowance being made for minor
spelling variations and morphological adjustments (e.g. 362 **AVITORIA FILIA**

**CVNIGNI**, AVITTORIGES INIGENA CUNIGNI (see further §6.25), 449
**SAGRANI FILI CVNOTAMI**, SAGRAGNI MAQI CUNATAMI; on the mor-
phological adjustments involving Latinization see §6.22). In the remainder the
Latin inscription is invariably longer than the corresponding Ogam, sometimes
only in the addition of the phrase **HIC IACIT** (e.g. 428 **TRENEGVSSI FILI
MACVTRENI HIC IACIT**, TRENAGUSU (an error for -O?) MAQI MAQI-
TRENI), more often in bearing an indication of filiation which is absent from
the Ogam (e.g. 353 **TRENACATVS IC IACIT FILIVS MAGLAGNI**,
TRENACCATLO, leg. -CCATO?, see also 380, 431, 450, 470), or in the addition of a title or qualifying word (e.g. 358 **MEMORIA VOTEPORIGIS PRO-
TICTORIS**, VOTECORIGAS, see also 409, 445). These differences
notwithstanding, both inscriptions normally commemorate the one person, as
one would expect, the only exception being 488 (**DOBVNNI FABRI FILII
ENABARRI**, ENABARR) the Ogam on which seems to be a generation older
than the Latin. On 342 (**CVNOCENNI FILIUS CVNOGENI HIC IACIT**,
CUNACENNI [A]VI ILVVETO) the same person appears to be recorded with
different formulae.[48]

§4.12 The importance of these inscriptions cannot be overstated. They con-
stitute valuable contemporary evidence for the existence and distribution of
Irish settlers in western Britain in the fifth and sixth centuries of our era
(Richards, 1960, 140ff.). In this they are complemented by a number of non-
Ogam inscriptions bearing Irish names (e.g. 326 **HIC IACIT MACCV-
DECCETI**, see also 319, 364, 370, 440, 457, 462, 472, 492) as well as by some
features which may stem from Irish practices, such as the X son of Y formula,
the preference for the genitive construction and the vertical disposition of
inscriptions on memorial stones.[49] Great importance attaches to them also in
that they provide irrefutable contemporary proof of the values of most of the
Ogam characters, thus confirming many but not all of the details of the later
manuscript record, and because the accompanying contemporary Latin inscriptions have the added advantage of providing a dating criterion in the form of
their palaeography, Ogam 'palaeography' being relatively useless in this regard
(see below §5.2 and §§5.31ff.). The British Ogams, too, form an important and
obvious link between their Irish counterparts and Gallic funerary customs, most
apparent in the appearance of the **HIC IACIT** formula (which originated in
Italy in the fourth century A.D., Nash-Williams, 1950, 8) on an Ogam stone,
and their very existence shows that many of the arguments of those who would
assert the unique and pagan character of the Irish monuments are quite unreal.
Bu'lock (1956) has argued quite rightly that all of the fifth-seventh century
inscriptions of Ireland, Wales, Devon/Cornwall, the Isle of Man and Scotland
are expressions of the same common idea, and the Christian character of many
of the Welsh monuments bearing Irish names has been noted by Richards (1960,
144). Nash-Williams points out (1950, 8) that in Wales the Irish colonists must
have been Christianized early if they were not Christian already on arrival.

§4.13 The presence of a Latin equivalent apart, there are some important differences between the British and Irish Ogams which are worth noting. With the
exception of 327 and 409, for example, which attempt to reproduce a Latin *p* in

Ogam, the supplementary characters are unknown to the former. The absence of the first of these in particular is noteworthy in view of its increasing popularity among the Irish epigraphists who used it with two separate values (see §5.3). Of greater significance, however, is the fact that the relative frequency of formulae is also quite distinct in both areas. There is only one example of MAQI MUCOI in Wales (426) and two elsewhere[50] and the KOI, ANM and CELI formulae do not occur. X MAQQI Y is attested but there is a marked preference for single-name inscriptions, even when the accompanying Latin bears the equivalent of X MAQQI Y, viz. **X FILI(I) Y**. Drawing attention to some of these differences and making the comparison in particular with the Waterford inscriptions in Ireland, to which one might have expected the Welsh Ogams to bear closest similarity, Mac White (1960/1, 301-2) suggested that the discrepancy could be accounted for by regarding the Welsh Ogams as a late or aberrant offshoot of their Déisi counterparts. The former of these alternatives, however, will not fit the linguistic evidence. The language (or at least the orthography) of the British Ogams is quite conservative by comparison with that found in Ireland (see §§5.32-3) and will not permit the hypothesis that such differences as there are between the two groups could be explained by regarding the British Ogams as later. They must be put down to the special circumstances obtaining in Britain, in particular to the pressure on the colonists to assimilate to a socio-linguistic environment very different to that in contemporary Ireland.

If some scholars have regarded the Latin inscriptions accompanying the Ogams as secondary in nature, designed for the benefit of native Britons who could not read the Ogam script, the single-name Ogams with more detailed Latin legends appear to suggest that the opposite was in fact the case, i.e. that the Ogam was considered secondary and complementary and might be abbreviated or modelled on the Latin. Since no such influence was present in Ireland, where as we have seen there was no epigraphic tradition in Latin, many of the discrepancies between the two groups can be accounted for in this way. In the case of 466, for example, the highly irregular Ogam IGENAVI MEMOR with its Latin loanword (in the nominative, see §§6.25, 6.27) and preposed genitive is clearly dictated by and reproduces the primary Latin **INGENUI MEMORIA** in Irish, and the same is probably true of 341 (**MACCV-TRENI SALIGIDUNI**, MAQI-TRENI SALICIDUNI) and 399 (**SIMILINI TOVISACI**, S[I]B[I]L[I]N[I] [TO]VISACI), neither of which bears a traditional Ogam formula word; the Ogam reproduces the honorific epithet in the case of the latter and the (?)territorial agnomen of the former. 362 is exceptional by Ogam standards but not by those of the Latin inscriptions of Britain in general (see 401, 402, 419, 451) in commemorating a woman, and it may be significant that her father's name is British, not Irish, in form (viz. **CVNIGNI**, the Irish equivalent being *Cunagnī* gen. of *Cunagnas*, *Conán*, see further §6.12). The primacy of the Latin in this case too may be reflected in the disposition of the Ogam, which appears to be designed to have the name AVITTORIGES adjacent to its Latin equivalent **AVITORIA**, and in the imitation of the Latin **FILIA** with the Irish nominative INIGENA (see §6.25). A similar arrangement is found on 378 **BIVADI AVI BODIBEVE**, AVVI BODDI[BA] BEVVE (Macalister's reading, which should be emended to BEVVU. . . (for BIVV. . .) AVVI BODDIB. . .),[51] a stone on which the Ogam can be shown to be subsequent to the Latin.

Such examples show that the Ogamists in Britain were not free agents in the way that their counterparts at home were. For stone 362 see plate 1.

**§4.14** The extent to which Irish colonists in Britain continued to speak their language and retain Irish names and traditions will have varied no doubt from place to place and from family to family, and some indications of the varying trends are recoverable from the inscriptions. The paucity of MUCOI and AVI type formulae, for example, suggests that these typically Irish types of nomenclature were not as fashionable abroad as they were at home, for whatever reason. A decline in tribal feeling among the colonists would be an obvious explanation, together with the influence of patterns of nomenclature among the indigenous population. The number of Latin names recorded in Ogam is significantly high (e.g. 327 **TVRPILLI**, TURP[I]L[LI]; 409 **PVMPEIVS**, P[.]P; 430 **ETTERNI FILI VICTOR**, ETTERN[I MAQI VIC]TOR; 445 **VITALIANI**, VITALIANI; 466 **INGENVI**, IGENAVI; 470 **LATINI**, LA[TI]NI and 484 **IUSTI**, [?]USTI) and reflects intermarriage with the British population among whom, as Jackson points out (1950, 208), Latin names were common. And while some colonists had assimilated to the extent of adopting Latin names yet retained Ogam as a memorial script, others bearing Irish names have epitaphs in Latin only. This is the case, for example, with *Vlcagnus* (Latinized form of Irish *Ulcagnas*), whose memorial (370 **HIC IACIT VLCAGNVS FI[LI]US SENOMAGLI**), though relatively early in date (the latter part of the fifth century, Jackson 1950, 210), shows complete assimilation not only in the choice of Latin and the Latinization of his name but also in the 'correct' (see n4.53) use of the nominative with **HIC IACIT**. Similarly, *Ēnabarras*, whose name is Irish, is recorded in Ogam (488), but his son has a double name[52] and was commemorated in Latin only on the same stone in the middle of the sixth century **(DOBVNNI FABRI FILII ENABARRI)**. The inscriptions also throw interesting light on the use of Irish among the colonists, and it is significant that those in Latin, once the Latinization has been recognized (see further §6.22), are more instructive in this regard than the Ogams, which tend to be quite conservative (see §§5.32-3). Thus, 364 **QVENVENDANI FILI BARCVNI** (Macalister's accompanying Ogam with its impossible Irish form BARCUNI for *BARCUNAS is imaginary) bears Irish names in Latin only, but their form shows that the language was still being spoken, as both have undergone syncope (on which see §5.17), the final -**I** in each case being a Latinization. A similar Latinization of an Irish name occurs on the Wroxeter inscription (xxi **CVNORIX MACVS MAQVI-COLINE** which also shows a very interesting delabialization of /k$^w$/ before a back (**MACVS** for **MAQVS**), but not a front, (**MAQVI-**) vowel (see §5.18). By contrast, the bilingual memorial to *Trēnagusus* (428 **TRENEGVSSI FILI MACVTRENI HIC IACIT**, TRENAGUSU MAQI MAQI-TRENI) combines bad grammar[53] in the Latin with remarkably conservative Irish in the Ogam, preserving pre-syncope and pre-apocope forms on an early seventh-century inscription (see further §§5.32-3). All of these factors add considerably to the interest of the British Ogams and highlight the need to take the special circumstances of the environment in which they were produced into account when considering their form *vis-à-vis* that of their Irish counterparts.

## APPENDIX 2

Inscriptions in Macalister's *Corpus* the readings of which I can confirm or in which differences between Macalister's reading and mine are minimal are (low case indicates uncertainty with regard to the reading): 4 LUGADDON MAqi LuGUDEC, DDISI MO. . .CQU SEL; 17 MUCOI MUCC. . .; 30 NAV-VALLo AVVI GENITTAC. . .; 46 SEDAN. . . .TABBOTT AVVI DERC-MASOC; 69 GIRAGNI; 70 CUNAGUSOS MAQI MUCOI VIRAGnI; 81 CaSSITTa/oS MAQI MUcoI CALLITI; 88 BRANAN MAQI oQOLI; 89 BOGAI MAQI BIrAC. . . (leg. -I); 90 CRONUN MAC BAIT; 92 ACTO MAQI . . . . MAGO; 93 ERCAIDANA; 102 DILOGONN; 103 CARRTTACC MMAQI MU CAGGi; 107 CUNAGUSSOS MA. . .; 113 VEQIKAMI MAQI LUGUNI; 119 DALAGNI MAQI DALI; 128 DOVETI maQi LOCARENAS, Celi MaQi CULiDOVI, 137 ANM VEDLLOIGGOI MACI SEDDOINI (in each case OI = seven vowel scores which could be read OI, UE etc.); 145 QRIMITIR RONaQQ MAQ SOMOGAQQ (= RONaNN MAQ COMOGANN); 146 LuGuQriT MAqi QRITTi; 147 MOINENA MAQI OLACON; 148 DUBONIRRAS MAQQI TENACi; 149 MAqQI QETTIa MAQQI CUNITTI m..; 151 BROINIONAS; 155 AKEVRITTI; 156 MAQQI IARI kOI MAQQI MuCCOI DOVVINIAS; 157 DOVETI MAQQI CATTINI; 158 SUVALLOS MAQQI DUCOVAROS; 159 MAQI DECCeDA MAqi GLASICONAS; 160 TRIA MAQA MAILAGNI, CURCITTI; 161 INISSIONAS; 166 COIMAGNI MAQI VITALIN; 170 QENiLOCI MAQI MAQI-AINIA MUc. . .; 181 TALAGNI MAc/q; 188 MARIANI; 190 GOSSUCTTIAS; 191 GAMICUNAS; 192 QENILOCGNI MAQI D. . .; 195 CURCI MAQI MU (mounting covered remainder); 196 ERCAVICCAS MAQI CO. . .; 197 DEGOS MAQI MOCOI TOICAKI (S added later); 198 MAQI-RITEAS MAQI MAQI-DDUMILEAS MUCOI TOICACI (an S inserted prematurely at the first E was erased by the lapidary); 199 CUNACENA; 200 MAQI-TTAL MAQI VORGOS MAQI MUCOI TOICAC; 203 MAQI-DECEDA MAq..; 216 GOSOCTEAS MOSAC MAKINI; 217 NOCATI MAQI MAQI-REC. . . MAQI MUCOI UDDAMI; 218 LaGoBB. . .MUCO TUCACAC; 223 ANM VINNAGiTLET. . .; 252 DUMELI MAQI GLASICONAS NIOTTA COBRANoR. . . .; 253 GALEOTOS; 254 MAQI RECTA; 256 ANM TEGANN MAC DEGLANN; 263 LUGUDECCAS MAQ. . . ..COI NETA-SEGAMONAS DOLATIBIGAIS-GOB. . .; 265 AMADU; 268 CATTUVIR; 353 **TRENACATVS IC IACIT FILIVS MAGLAGNI** TRENACCATLO; 358 **MEMORIA VOTEPORIGIS PROTICTORIS** VOTECORIGAS; 362 **AVITORIA FILIA CVNIGNI** AVIT-TORIGES INIGENA CUNIGNI; 364 **QVENVENDANI FILI BARCVNI** (no Ogam); 368 **BARRIVENDI FILIVS VENDVBARI HIC IACIT** MAQI M. . . dUMELEDONAS; 399 **SIMILINI TOVISACI** Sib/miLiNi [TO]VISACI; 422 VENDOGNi (accompanying Latin for the most part illegible); 423 . . . AQ. . .QA. . .GTE; 430 **ETTERNI FILI VICTOR** ETTERN. . . . . .TOR; 432 **TIGERNACI DOBAGNI** DOVAGNI; **VITALIANI EMERETO** VITALIANI; 446 **MAGLOCVNI** (sic leg.) **FILI CLVTORI** MAGLICUNAS MAQI CLU-TARi; 449 **SAGRANI FILI CVNOTAMI** SAGRAGNI MAQI CUNATAMI; 450 **HOGTIVIS** (leg. -NIS ?) **FILI DEMETI** OGTENAS; 456 **GEndiLI** GENDILI

To these can be added the following confirmed by O'Kelly in his review of
the *Corpus* (I exclude those already referred to): 143 TAQMAQ; 165 dROGNO;
286 CUNAMAQI LUGUDECA MUCoi CUNEA; 290 MAQI E. . .; 132
LACAVAGNI is confirmed in O'Kelly, 1952, 38. n24. Harvey (1987) confirms
135 MINNACCANNI MAQI AILLUATTAN though he concedes considerable
difficulty, particularly with the vowels. Of the inscriptions in the Isle of Man
Kermode's (1907) readings confirm 501 CUNAMAGLI MAQ. . .; 502
. . .MAQ LEOG. . .; 503 DOVAIDONA MA. . . .QI DROATA and 504
BIVAIdoNAS MAQI MUCOI CUNAVA. . . .

In the case of the following Irish inscriptions I had greater difficulty reading
one or more letters (indicated in low case) but I would hesitate to reject
Macalister's reading: 29 BRaNiTTaS MaQi DuCriDDA; 32 maqi ERACiasS
maqi . . . DiMaQa MUCo.. ; 41 COVAGNi MAQi muCoi LUGuNi; 63
BRuSCo [maqi] DOVALESCi, COLOMAGNi. . .V. . .D. . . ; 71 COiMAGNi
MAQI MOCOI G. . .; 85 griLAGNi MAQi SCILaGni; 86 CLIUCoANAS
MAQI MAQI-TrEni; 94 Do/u/e/MM. . .MACi. . .ERI; 98 CoRBAGNi K..
. . .COI cOROtANI; 99 SACATTiNi; 114 GRi. . .GN. . . CERC..; 116
BRANI MAQQI MUC. . .; 120 BROINIENAS KOI NETA TTRENALuGos;
136 ctn. . .qla; 150 grAVICAS MAQI MUCO. . .; 154 cuNAMAQQI CORBBI
MAQQ. . .; 163 NeTTA-LAMINACCA KOI MAQQI MUCOI DO. . . .; 164
VOEnaCUnAs; 171 DUGeNNGGi mAQi Ro-eDDoS, 172 TOGITTACc MAQi
SAGARET[tos] (third piece of stone bearing last three letters missing); 176
SOQUQEVV MANI SOQe/iRI = CONUNETT MAQI CONe/iRI); 178 ERC
MAQI MAQI-ERCIAs mu DOVInIA; 180 BRUSCCOS MAQQI CALiACi
(ignore the letters after CALIACI in Macalister); 182 GANICc(a?); 187 ANM
Anm MAiLE iNbIR MACI BROCANN; 202 NIoTTVRe/iCC MAQi . . . .gNi;
241 B. . .AGN..maqI ADDiLoNA, NaGuNiMuc/qo BaiDaN. . ., AMIT
BAIDAGNI NIR***MNIDAGNIESSICONIDDALA; 262 ERCAGNI MAq/ci
. . . .; 285 BIVODON MUCOI ataR. O'Kelly in his review has similar comments regarding 144 DITAV (I exclude reference to those I have mentioned
myself) and in 1952, 38. n24 on 131 LITUBIRI MAQI QECIA (he confirms
LITUBIRI but the rest is faint) and 133 VAITEVIA (described as faint). In this
book I follow Macalister's readings with regard to these.

The readings of a number of inscriptions in the *Corpus* are largely correct but
require reappraisal in respect of some, often important, points. 26: Of the
second E in Macalister's NETTAVRECC only the first two notches are visible
and it appeared to me that there was enough space remaining for an E or an
I, which would give a more plausible reading VROECC or VROICC.
Macalister's sketch is more accurate than the accompanying reading with regard
to the last name on the inscription. 83: I cannot confirm the MAIC which
Macalister read, with some hesitation, before the last name. My reading was
LAMADo/uLICCI MAC . . . CBRO[C] (the final letter was not clear owing to
the way in which the stone has been erected). 95 MEDDOGENI: from a personal examination I think it possible that the intended composition vowel here
was U and Harvey (1987) too confirms MEDDUGENI as a possible reading.
100: The AB which Macalister reads some distance before the name ULC-
CAGNI is not very deeply cut and there is ground for considerable doubt as to
whether it should be considered part of the inscription. 117 COLLOS:

My reading was COLLI (see also Harvey (1987) ). 162: The CUNAMAQQI is problematical (I read CUb/miMAQQI). 204: My reading was ANM MAGANN MAQI N?DAd/t. . . and it is highly unlikely that the symbol between the N and the D of the last name should be read as an otherwise unattested epigraphical *forfid* with the diphthong value *úa*. 342: Nash-Williams' sketch of this is more accurate than either his or Macalister's transcription, particularly in regard to the -NIVI of the first name, which poses considerable difficulties. I accept Jackson's suggestion that CUNACENNI [A]VI was probably the original reading. 378: My reading was BEVVu. . . AVVI BODDIB. . . (there are only four scores in the first vowel though there is room for five and I suspect BIVV. . . was the intended reading). 426: I read slECI for the final word but both Macalister and Nash-Williams read BR- and this may be correct). 431: I read DoVaTuCIS but Nash-Williams' D[O]V[A]TUCEAS is preferable, -EAS being what Macalister's sketch has and though only one vowel notch was visible after the T there was room for three. 433 Nash-Williams' reading is closer than Macalister's but the latter is not likely to be wrong in view of the accompanying Latin.

Similarly, doubt with regard to readings will be found in Harvey (1987) in the case of 83 (the first name), and 152 (LU[BB]IAS possible) and Gippert (1990, 292) corrects 244 CORBBI to CORBI. O'Kelly (O'Kelly / Kavanagh, 1954, 108) has also corrected 211 RITTUVVECC to RITTAVVECC and 250 RITUV-VECAS to RITTAVVECAS (Macalister's earlier reading) and in his review of the *Corpus* O'Kelly points out that the final -I in 186 and 84 does not exist, the MAQI of 287 should be MAQ, 64 should be read LADIMANI, 79 TULENA MU[C. . . and 82 MAILAGURO MAQ[I. . .]LIL. . . . The reader's attention should also be drawn here to my comments on a number of stones in my 1986 paper.

Some inscriptions which I examined were in an extremely bad condition and I would query the readings given in the *Corpus*: 28: Macalister's sketch is upside-down. The tombstone in front of the stone made a satisfactory reading impossible. The only letters of which I could be certain were the MUC of MUCOI and the MAC of MACORBO. 34: My reading was [..]LL[..][. . . .]MAQQ[..]m[..]C[. . .]. 112: The MI- of the first name was not clear and I could only read L and N with certainty in the second, though no.113 would support the reading LUGUNI. 193: I would be very sceptical about anything after the initial ANM COL. 327: My reading was TURPiLli [. . .] LuNi (i.e. closer to Nash-Williams than Macalister). 409: I read Pa/oP. . . on one angle and could not read the vowels on the other. Nash-Williams' reading of this angle is more accurate. 439: I read I?[..]SS?[. . . .]ASOg/v/s/n/. . . . The ? stands for symbol 13, probable in the first case, certain in the second. Macalister's restoration of this as INGEN SANGKTA SEGNI has been described, not unfairly, as 'preposterous' by some reviewers.

Similarly, Gippert (1990, 303-4) points out that only parts of the letters can be made out in 87 and he reads QENO[ ]EN QIt/c/q G[ ]Th/d/t/c/q for 2. See also Jackson's comments on the Scottish Ogams (above §4.2)

Finally I should mention my policy in this book with regard to inscriptions I have neither seen nor read confirmation or rejection of. If Macalister's earlier reading (in *Studies in Irish epigraphy*) corresponds to that of the *Corpus* I have

generally adopted it without question. If there is a significant difference, however, or if there is an indication in Macalister's discussion of a given stone that
there was serious difficulty with all or part of the reading I try to reflect this
by placing a question mark before the inscription or relevant part of it quoted.
Restored inscriptions such as 36, 55, 105 and the restored Ogams of 349, 364,
376, 404, 434, 473 and 478 are not trusted.

Inscriptions discovered since the publication of vol. i of the *Corpus*:

### (i) Macalister (1949, no. 1082)

From a souterrain in Ballybroman, near Tralee, Co. Kerry. No information
is supplied regarding the circumstances of discovery. The reading is given by
Macalister from a transcript by Dr. Raftery and a rubbing by Capt. O'Connell,
R.N. as GLANNANI MAQI BBRANNAD with no suggestion as to whether it
is incomplete or not. The first name looks like a diminutive of GLAN- (OI *glan*
'clean, pure' see further §6.12), the second clearly contains the element BRAN-
'raven' (see §6.6) and if incomplete might have read BBRANNADOVI (see v
below, OI *Brandub*), or BBRANNADI (cp. *brandae* 'raven-like' and see
§6.13(b) for the suffix).

### (ii and iii) Macalister (1949, no. 1083)

These inscriptions, one of which was published by Macalister in 1949 from
a copy supplied by Dr Raftery, were found in a souterrain in Rathkenny, near
Ardfert, Co. Kerry, on land belonging today to Mr. Patrick O'Connor.[1] The
first serves as a lintel in the entrance chamber, the second as a lintel over the
entrance to the passage to the north chamber. A third stone, originally over the
entrance to the passage to the south chamber, has gone missing.

What can be seen of the first stone, the larger of the two, is perfectly legible.
On the north angle the name COMMAGGAGNI can be read without any difficulty and is followed by an M and one vowel score. The stone is embedded
in masonry at this point but a further two vowel scores (they did not feel like
H-series scores, i.e. MAQI) can be felt, suggesting that we have to do with an
X MUCOI Y formula. On the southern angle, reading in the opposite direction,
the letters I SAMM (or G?) NN can be read clearly and the final N appears to
complete the inscription. Nothing can be seen before the I but it is possible, if
not probable, that CO should be read here.

In COMMAGGAGNI we appear to have an earlier form of the name found
on 145, viz. COMOGANN (later nom. *Comgán*, see §6.12). With regard to the
last name I cannot say whether SAMMNN or SAGNN was the intended
reading, though the doubling of M-series scores in the name of the commemorand suggests the former. If -MNN is an error for -MANN, by the omission of a single vowel score, one might compare later *Samán* (< *Samagn*-), but
the appearance on the one inscription of both -AGNI and its later form -ANN
(see §5.16) would be unusual. Alternatively -AMMNN might be a post-apocope
form of -AMNI, compare 125 VALAMNI, in which case we would probably
have to do with a compound name (leg. ISAMMNN = later *Essomuin*?).

The second stone is in a poor condition and I can make no sense of the
reading (from left to right): LiSSe/igvOg. Finbarr Moore kindly supplied me
with his reading of this stone, which was OLSSIgVUG.

(iv) O'Kelly/Kavanagh (1954), O'Kelly (1957/9, 77-87)

Found lying face-down covering human remains in the burial area to the south of the oratory on Church Island, Valencia Harbour, Co. Kerry. According to O'Kelly it is not possible to say whether the site of discovery was necessarily the original site of erection, though the stone certainly did stand upright at one time. The inscription is accompanied by a beautifully formed Maltese type cross which it postdates, as is clear from the fact that some of the scores overlie its head. The cross is so accurately drawn that compasses must have been used in its design, and the exactness of its execution suggests that it is later in date than simpler Maltese crosses drawn with less care (see further n4.29).

The inscription begins on the left-hand front arris and runs in boustrophedon fashion around the top and down the right-hand angle. The first two words, covering the left-hand arris and finishing just at the top are beyond any doubt BECCDINN MACI. An R occupies the top angle and is followed immediately by an I, the last notch of which has been damaged. The next two letters are VV but there is a light tentative score-like mark opposite the first score of the first V indicating, according to O'Kelly, that the lapidary had begun to write a letter of the H-series but failed to complete it (or changed his mind about it). The second V is followed by two clear vowel notches (= O), then by a lightly executed X (= E or C) on top of which two further vowel notches have been imposed (on the face, not the arris), apparently by way of correction. These are so spaced that taken with the preceding two vowel notches they would read E, one of the values of X. The last two letters are clearly SS.

According to O'Kelly the name might be read RI[T]VVOESS, RI[T]VVESS, RI[T]VVEESS, RI[T]VVUEASS, RI[T]VVUCASS, RI[T]VVECSS or RI[T]VVOCSS depending on how one interprets the four vowel notches and the X, though as he admits, none of his proposed readings finds a parallel elsewhere. In his contribution to both papers Kavanagh restores it as RI[T(T)A]VVECASS, suggesting somewhat despairingly that the lapidary did not have a clear knowledge of the name or a close acquaintance with it, whence the mistakes. To some obvious objections to such argumentation, however, can be added the all-important point that a form RITTAVVECAS occurring alongside what appears to be a post-syncope BECCDINN (see below) would be an otherwise unparalleled anachronism.

The simplest interpretation of the confusion at the point between the second V and the first S would be that the lapidary intended to write E and began the traditional way but changed his mind, writing X, and then superimposed two vowel notches on the X to insure that E be read and not OC or OE.[2] A degree of hesitation is also indicated by the light score opposite the first score of the first V which, as already noted, suggests that he initially intended to write on the H-side of that arris. If we assume that the turn of the stone confused him (see §5.2) a perfect parallel will be found in the famous Arraglen stone, the intended reading of which was undoubtedly QRIMITIR RONANN MAQ COMOGANN, but QRIMITIR RONAN/Q MAN SOMOGAQQ ( / indicates the turn of the stone) is what was actually written. In this case the mistake is confirmed by MAN, which analogy suggests must be read MAQ. If the lapidary of the Church Island stone made the same error, and it is easily made, the intended reading would have been RITTECC, a far more easily explained form than RIVVESS not only onomastically but also morphologically and orthographically as there is no reliable evidence for a Primitive Irish case-ending -ESS on the inscriptions nor is a final double SS attested elsewhere.

I take RITTECC to be the intended reading and consider this an Early Old Irish form of Primitive Irish *Ritavicas* corresponding to gen. *Rethech*, later *Rethach* > *Ráthach* as in *Uí Ráthach*, dat. *Íbh Ráthach*, Anglicized *Iveragh* (see Bergin, 1932a, 138-9), the name of the barony in which the stone was found (cp. 211 RITTAVVECC and 250 RITTAVVECAS in the neighbouring baronies of Dunkerron North and Trughanacmy respectively). The attested EOI form *Rethech* (see Bergin, 1932a, 141 and O'Brien, 1962, 287 = 158, 44) has the expected vocalism of the first syllable but the retention of unlowered I in the initial syllable of the Ogam spelling, if not simply due to error (see §2.2), is analogous to that found in 211 and 250, in each of which the I of the original penultimate syllable has already been lowered, and can hardly constitute an argument against the equation (see further n5.39, but compare no. viii below). On the significance of the loss of the post-syncope post-consonantal V see §5.34.

The name of the commemorand is less clear. Kavanagh takes it to be a compound containing the forerunner of either *bécc* 'cry' or *becc* 'small', both of which are attested in Irish nomenclature, the former as a B (i) type (see §6.11), the latter as both A (§6.3ff.) and B (i) (cp. *Bécc* and *Becc*, *Becairle*, *Becenech* etc. O'Brien (1973, 222, 224), *Cenél mBécce* = Kinalmeaky, a barony in Co. Cork). As the name BECCDINN appears to be either of the A or B (iii) type the element is more likely to be *becc* 'small', though the spelling with CC is not what one would expect in orthodox Ogam (OI *becc* < *biggo-*, whence an Ogam *BEGG-*). There can be no doubt, however, that the form is post-syncope.

## (v) O'Kelly/Kavanagh (1954a)

Found standing upright in a souterrain in the townland of Gearha South, near Sneem, in the barony of Dunkerron South, Co. Kerry. The stone was not incorporated into the stonework of the walls of the structure, nor did it act as a support for the roof. It appears to have been smoothened in advance in preparation for the inscription which was executed in sharp shallow knife-cuts and is in good condition, owing in some measure to the protection from weathering afforded by its location. The final part, however, has been lost. O'Kelly considers this the result of deliberate mutilation in ancient times, supporting Macalister's views on the destruction of the MUCCOI formula (see however §4.9). The reading is BRANADDOV MA MAQI QOLI MUCOI DOVI. . ., restored somewhat tentatively by Kavanagh as BRANADDOV[INIA] MA[QI] MAQI-[O]QOLI MUCOI DOVI[NIA].

A name BRANADOVINIA would be very unusual as would be the suggested abbreviation. As DOV is a reasonably common element in personal names (see §6.29(c) ) both on the inscriptions and in later Irish, however, it does seem appropriate to make a division after V, in which case the name BRANADDOV could be regarded as a post-apocope form of *Brandub* (earlier *Branadoví*, cp. 128(-)CULIDOVI, also an *o*-stem and see Uhlich, 1989, 130 and §6.29(c) below). If so the following MA, which must be separated from the ensuing MAQI, would have to be an abbreviated form of MAQI, and an abbreviation of this kind before a MAQI- name is understandable (see n4.12). The alternative is to read BRANADDOV MMAQI .. and to ignore the A. Kavanagh restores MAQI-[O]QOLI on the basis of 88 BRANAN MAQI OQOLI, which is a possibility, but if one takes Q as an error for C,[3] postdating the confusion of /k/ and /kʷ/ (see §5.18), one could equate the name with the later *Mac-Cuill*. The last name can be restored without doubt as DOVINIA or DOVINIAS, and it is worth noting that all other examples of this tribal name are found on stones in the barony of Corkaguiney (*Corcu Duibne*, see §6.18).

### (vi) Fanning/Ó Corráin (1977)

Discovered in 1975 built into the side of a nineteenth-century burial vault or tomb in the southwest corner of the ancient church at Ratass near Tralee, barony of Trughanacmy, Co. Kerry. The inscription is disposed on the left-hand arris and the incisions are clear, regular and unweathered though the first N is somewhat worn owing apparently to the use of the stone as a knife-sharpener, and chipping and polishing may have removed an O or an A from the end of the inscription at the top of the stone. There is a simple Latin cross composed of double grooves on the opposite face to the Ogam which Fanning considers secondary to the inscription as the latter would have been turned upside-down when the stone was *in situ* as a cross-inscribed pillar, and there is some evidence that the use of the stone for sharpening knives took place before it was turned into a cross-slab. The reading as recorded by Fanning is NM SILLANN MAQ FAT-TILLOGG (the transcription with F rather than V possibly due to the suggested late date of the inscription, see below) with the very strong likelihood that an A is missing from the beginning, viz. leg. ANM, and the possibility that an O or an A is gone from the end (leg. -LLOGGO or -LLOGGA).

Ó Corráin identifies the commemorand as *Sílán m. Áedloga* m. Domungein of the Uí Angáin who, he suggests, could be placed in the eighth or early ninth century but could not possibly be earlier than the seventh century on genealogical evidence. If so, he points out, a Cíarraige Ogam – which this would be if the identification were correct – could not occur at Ratass earlier than the late seventh or early eighth century.

It would be very difficult, however, to equate VATTILLOGG with Old Irish *Áedlogo*. The latter might be expected to appear on an Ogam inscription as AIDULUGOS, AIDU/OLOGO, AIDLOGO etc. (in each case with or without the I (see §6.28) and with single or double consonants (§6.30(d) ), but the closest one can get to this is to read MAQV (cp. 104 MAQVI) ATTILLOGG[O] and assume TT is an error for DD. The identification, therefore, must remain doubtful.

If an -O is missing from the end of the inscription we can be reasonably certain that the second element in the compound is the divine name *Lug* (see §6.5 and n6.12). The first element, VATTI, appears to be an *i*-stem and is probably identical to the second element in 11 CUNOVATO.

The name of the commemorand is better equated with later *Sílán* than with *Sillán* if the latter is from *Sinlán*, diminutive to *Sinell*.

### (vii) Rynne (1962, 155, no. 272)

Found in the townland of Brookhill, Barony of Dunkerron North, Co. Kerry, among stones from a demolished field-fence. It is a fragment of an apparently carefully dressed stone which, according to Rynne, appears to have been broken off in antiquity. The reading is fragmentary: . . .A MAQ LUG. . . .

(viii)

This stone, now in the Heritage Centre (Láthair Oidhreachta) in Ballyferriter, Co. Kerry, was discovered in 1989 embedded in the gable wall of an outhouse belonging to Mr. Eogan Ó Grifín of Com, near Annascaul.[4] The angle facing outwards was trimmed in the appropriation taking away the final part of the inscription. The opposite angle and the top of the stone are intact, however, and the reading on these is clear and beyond doubt: RETAGIN MAQI DOV. . . . The V is followed by three vowel scores (= U) but the inscription breaks off at this point.

The elements in the name of the commemorand are clear but do not occur together elsewhere in the corpus. RETA- is very likely a form of the divine name RITTA-, found in 250 RITTAVVECAS, 211 RITTAVVECC and iv RITTECC (see §6.5). If so, it is interesting in that it is clearly post-affection and is precisely the form one might have expected in all other attested examples (see n5.39). The element -GIN is attested elsewhere (see §6.7) in the forms -GENI, -GINI, -GEN and ?-GINN, but never, in the Ogam inscriptions at least, following a divine name. To my knowledge the name is not attested later. Its Old Irish form would be nom. *Rethgan (cp. Éogan).

If the inscription *ended* with an I after the V we would have an example of the adjective later attested as *dub* 'black' as a personal name of the B(i) type (see §6.11, later *Dub*, gen. *Duib*). For DOV as an *o*-stem compare 128 (-)CULIDOVI and see the discussion of v above as well as §6.29(c). DOV(E)- or DOV(I)-, however, (hardly DOVU in view of Uhlich's theory, see §6.29) could equally well be the first part of a compound or B (iii) type name (on which see §6.13). DOV[INIAS] is an improbable restoration as the inscription does not bear the MUCOI formula.

This stone is a classic example of a secondary appropriation damaging the final part of an inscription (see the discussion of the supposed early destruction of MUCOI formula inscriptions, §4.9).

(ix, x and xi) O'Kelly/Shee (1968)

These three inscriptions were discovered in 1967 on stones acting respectively as a jamb, a lintel and a roof-slab in a souterrain near Dunmanway, Barony of East Carbery, Co. Cork. All three are incised in fine knife-cuts, a technique common in Cork, and the readings of the first two are beyond doubt. The third is a little less clear but is for the most part certain, according to O'Kelly. (ix) MOESAC or SACEOM (depending on the direction of the reading, but the first is the more probable), (x) MOUNIN, (xi) [A?]DARUN M[A]CI COLAL[I?].

MOESAC is compared by O'Kelly to the second word in 216 GOSOCTEAS MOSAC MAKINI and to the second in Macalister's reading of 327 TURPILI MOSAC TRALLONI (accompanied by **TVRPILLI IC IACIT PVVERI TRILVNI DVNOCATI**; for the Ogam Nash-Williams, 1950, 69 reads TUR-PIL[LI MAQI? TRIL]LUNI), a word to which he gives the meaning 'boy' in the sense 'attendant' rather than 'son' (cp. Lat. **PVVERI**). Both the reading and the interpretation of the latter, however, are very doubtful and a word with this meaning appearing on its own on an inscription would be most peculiar, though it does appear to be in formula-word position on 216. If MOUNIN (with its otherwise unattested OU, see §6.28) is an error for MININ it might be a diminutive of the element found in 1 **MENUEH** (i.e. ⟨ *Min* + *-igni*) but this is doubtful. If [A]DARUN is for ODARUN one might compare *Odorán*, *Odrán* with a different vocalism in the suffix (see §6.12) but this too is very tentative.

(xii) Raftery (1969, 105, no. 96)
This stone was found in the surface soil of an earthwork, possibly a ringfort, in the townland of Kilgrovan, Barony of Decies Without Drum, Co. Waterford. A portion of the stone was broken off in antiquity so that the beginning of the inscription is missing, and the end is chipped and uncertain. The reading recorded is:. . . U MAQI CUMOGODUU MUCO. . . . The name may contain the first two elements found in *Comgán* (⟨ *com-ag-agnas* see §6.12) in which case the final -DUU may be for -DI or -DIA (⟨ -DIAS, see §6.13d).

(xiii) Raftery (1960, 33, no. 126)
This stone was found on the surface of a field in the townland of Keel West, Co. Mayo. All surfaces are weather-worn and the inscription cannot be read with certainty.

(xiv) Pilsworth (1972, 70, see plate 3)
This stone was discovered by G. Doyle in 1969 by the bank of a small tributary to the river Nore (no further information is supplied regarding the site of discovery[5]) and has since been erected against an arch at the entrance to the now largely demolished chancel of Thomastown Church, Co. Kilkenny. It measures approx. 146 cm high, 31 cm wide and 20 cm thick. The scores are very deeply cut and the inscription is in extremely good condition. It reads up the left-hand arris across the top and down the right in boustrophedon fashion and continues on the left-hand-side rear arris. The reading is (/ indicates the turn of the stone) VEDDELLEMETTO MU/CI/ LOGIDDEAS / AVVI MUNICCONA.
A very light mark on the B side before the first V is unlikely to be part of the inscription and there is only one L in LOGIDDEAS (the reading in Pilsworth is LLOGIDDEAS). The scores of the U at the top of the first angle are somewhat longer than those of the vowels lower down and they look a little like H-series characters but the following C confirms that they are not. The reading at the top of the stone is certainly CI, not the expected COI of MUCOI. The -S of LOGIDDEAS is about two-thirds way down the right-hand angle and the area below it is slightly damaged but nothing followed here. In the first N of MUNICCONA the initial score is separated from the remainder by a greater distance than they are from each other, but the space is not as great as that between the two Vs of the preceding word and BS can hardly have been the intended reading. There is no trace of any scores on the right-hand rear angle.
If MUCI is an error for MUCOI, not MAQI/MACI, and this is suggested both by the U and the C, the formula recalls that of (the hitherto unique and isolated) 124 ANAVLAMATTIAS MUCOI [..]OELURI AVI AKERAS (East Muskerry, Co. Cork) in placing the tribal affinity before that of the sept (see n4.15). In that case the O of LOGIDDEAS might be taken as the variant of the

Plate 3
The Thomastown Ogam stone (xiv)
VEDDELLEMETTO MUCI LOGIDDEAS AVVI MUNICCONA

diphthong OI (see §6.28) and the equation with the *Corcu Loígde* would suggest itself.[6] The Corcu Loígde dominated Munster in the very early period (Ó Corráin, 1972, 29) and there is evidence to suggest that the Osraige, in whose territory the inscription was found, had once been ruled by Corcu Loígde kings (Byrne, 1973, 180); their patron saint, St. Cíarán of Saigir, belonged to the Corcu Loígde. This might well explain the location of this particular inscription which, linguistically, appears to belong to the first half of the sixth century (see §5.26 and §5.30). It should be stressed, however, that there are several difficulties with this equation.

The name of the commemorand is undoubtedly an early form of *Fedelmid/ Feidlimid*, an *i*-stem derivative of the female name *Fedelm* (Latinized and Anglicized *Fidelma*). The third E of VEDDELLEMETTO, therefore, may be erroneous (as *Fedelm, Fedelmid* cannot come from *\*Vedelem-*, which would have given *\*Feidlem*, with lenited *m*) or, as Jürgen Uhlich has suggested to me, we may have to do here with a svarabhakti vowel (see n6.28). The name is also attested in 206 TELEDMEV.. which is almost certainly inverted and to be read VEDELMET[TO]).

The sept name AVVI MUNICCONA (*\*Uí Muinchon?*) is not recorded to my knowledge. One might consider the possibility that the N is an error for R (cp. *Muirchú*).

(xv)

Found acting as a gate-post between Bennettsbridge and Thomastown, Co. Kilkenny,[7] this stone is now standing together with no. 35 beside the round tower in the graveyard at Tullaherin. It measures approx. 156 cm high, 51 cm wide and 26 cm thick. The face of the stone has been spalled away both at the top and bottom removing any scores which might have been present here, and the arris on both sides is fractured and rugged, making an accurate reading of vowels impossible. On the left angle 39 cms from the bottom and just above the lower spalled area a consonant D (reading upwards) can be read and is followed by a T 11 cms further up. Nothing else can be read with certainty on this side. On the right-hand angle 66 cms from the bottom M and what might be a vowel score can be made out (again reading upwards) followed by a gap of 11 cms, then a C (originally MUCOI ?). There then follows another gap of 33 cms followed by what might have been an R, though the part of these scores on the face of the stone can only be made out clearly for the first. A further 13 cms above this there follow two scores, apparently of the M-series, i.e. G.

There is little point in attempting to restore the inscription.

(xvi)

This stone was found in Shankill, Co. Kilkenny, and was presented by Capt. M. Doyle (see the *Old Kilkenny Review*, 21, 1969, 101, entry 60/6) to the museum at Rothe House in Kilkenny, where it is on view.[8] It is remarkably small, measuring approx. 57 cm high, 14 cm at its widest point and 5½ cm thick, and is mounted in a wooden base in such a way as to obscure the final consonant on the first angle. The inscription is on three angles reading downwards (owing to the way in which it was mounted) as follows: left angle MAQI CUNALIG. . .; right angle MAQI COILLI; right rear angle MUCOI COSCIS/N.

The transcription in the museum (which appears to have been made before the stone was mounted) reads -GIN at the end of the first angle but only one vowel notch is clear after the G and another just before the last consonant. Of the latter only two scores (of the B-series) are visible above the mounting. In view of 275 CUNALEGEA, therefore, one wonders whether the reading was CUNALIGIAS or CUNALIGEAS, but this cannot be verified. The C of CUNA looks more like DD, the spacing being similar to that found in the LL of the second angle, but C is probably the intended reading. If the commemorand is recorded on this angle we must take the name as belonging to the C type (see §6.14), i.e. MAQI-CUNA-.

COILLI looks like the gen. of the name later attested as *Cóel, cóel* 'thin, slender' (a B (i) type name, see §6.11). The last notch of the I of COSCIS/N is unclear and four scores of the final letter can be read with certainty, a fifth being debatable owing to damage below the letter. If the intended reading was -IAS (see the discussion of the first name above) or -EAS, COSCIAS/COSCEAS might be gen. of a fem. *ā*-stem *\*Coscā* (cp. the *Coscraige,* ⟨ *Cosc* + *-raige*?, who belonged to the Déisi, O'Brien, 1962, 257 = 155a 12).

As already noted this stone is unusually small and one cannot help thinking that, in its present size at least, it would have constituted something of an embarrassment as a memorial. Unless it can be shown that it was part of an originally larger stone, therefore, one might entertain some doubt as to its authenticity.

(xvii)

Found in a souterrain in Ballybarrack, Co. Louth, this stone is now in the National Museum in Dublin. The top has been broken off, probably as part of the appropriation for use in the souterrain (see §4.5). Though incised very finely the consonants are legible but the vowel notches were not cut very deeply and many are uncertain (indicated here by lower-case or a dot). The inscription reads up both angles as follows:

Left angle: MAQI CORaBiR MaQi? TAN.b/l. . .
Right angle: NeTa SaLaGIa MAQi MuCoi. . .

The first name is probably *Mac-Coirpri* but the remainder is doubtful. As the gen. NETAS is not attested (see §6.15) the S following NeTa probably belongs to the following word.

(xviii, xix, and xx)

During recent excavations three Ogam stones were discovered in a souterrain in Nobber, Co. Meath.[9] These are on the first capstone in the entrance passage and on the third and fourth in the passage to the left of the T-junction at the end of the main passage. Owing to the difficult conditions within the souterrain and to the fact that the stones have been reincorporated into the renovated structure I cannot offer reliable readings. I can only confirm that they are Ogam inscriptions as the formula word MAQI can be read on all three.

(xxi) Wright/Jackson (1968)

Discovered in 1967 just *inside* the defences of the Roman town at Wroxeter (*Viroconium*), this stone may commemorate an Irish *foederatus* who settled at

Wroxeter in the late fifth century. The inscription is roughly pecked in three horizontal lines of crude Roman monumental capitals on the face of the stone reading:

**CVNORIX**
**MACVSMA**
**QVICOLINE**

The **Q**, **L** and **N** of the third line are damaged almost beyond recognition but are very likely to be the intended readings.

Jackson takes the inscription to be a partially Latinized Primitive Irish form of what in Old Irish would be *Conri* (nom.) *macc Maic-Cuilinn* (PI *Cunarīs maqqas Maqqī-Colinī*) and if the reading is correct this interpretation can scarcely be doubted. On epigraphic grounds he says the inscription could be dated to between the beginning of the fifth and the middle of the sixth century but on linguistic evidence he assigns it to between the middle and the later part of the fifth, revising his earlier dating of the delabialization of /kʷ/ before back vowels in the first half of the sixth century (1953, 143) to the second half of the fifth on the evidence of **MACVS** (see §5.18). In the chronology in chapter 5 of this book it would belong to the early pre-affection inscriptions (see §5.24 and §5.30) with a reservation regarding the final -**E** for an expected -**I**, though the endings in general in the inscription are Latin, not Irish.

The Wroxeter stone is clearly of considerable importance both linguistically and socio-linguistically. The Latinization (-**X** for PI -*ss* ‹ -*ks* ‹ -*gs*, the **O** in **CVNO**- for Ogam A, the -**VS** in **MACVS** for Ogam AS, the **QV** in **MAQVI** for Ogam Q, see further §6.22) is relatively superficial and unlike the Christian inscriptions of Wales does not extend to replacing the Irish word for 'son' with Latin *filius*. It also differs from the bulk of the British inscriptions in using the nominative rather than the genitive of the name of the commemorand, and given the doubts regarding the authenticity of the Silchester stone (see §4.2) the site of its discovery makes it unique in the corpus of Irish inscriptions from the period. The inscription also provides clear proof that the delabialization of /kʷ/ took place earlier before back than before front vowels (**MACVS** as opposed to **MAQVI**) and if Jackson's appraisal of the -**E** (for an expected -**I** ‹ -*ī*) were correct it would confirm what one must otherwise deduce from historical phonology, namely that long unstressed vowels in absolute final position in Primitive Irish underwent shortening (and consequent confusion) earlier than those protected by -*s* (**COLINE** ‹ *\*Colinī* but **CVNORIX** preserving *i*, see §5.13). Against this interpretation, however, is the fact that the inscription is pre-affection.

# CHAPTER FIVE

# The Ogam Inscriptions: Dating

**§5.1** Dating the Ogam inscriptions is a particularly difficult task, somewhat simplified in the case of the British stones by the accompanying Latin. For the Irish inscriptions we do not have a single secure anchor point at an archaeological, palaeographical, historical or linguistic level. Absolute dating is beyond our reach as the identity of the people commemorated on the inscriptions is unknown (see §4.7) and explicit indications such as consular dating of the kind found on inscriptions in Gaul, and once on those in Britain (396 **IN TE[M]P[ORE] IVST[INI] CON[SVLIS]** and see Jackson, 1953, 163), are of course wanting. Indeed, the stereotype nature of the formulae and the irregular fluctuation in linguistic forms on the Ogam inscriptions are such that if an inscription which could be dated with certainty in this way were to be discovered, this, while interesting in itself, would not have a significant impact on the problem as a comprehensive series of closely dated stones would be required to establish a pattern on which a general analysis could be based.

**§5.2** Failing absolute dating we are forced to fall back on establishing some kind of relative chronology, but diagnostic criteria susceptible of a general analysis are scarce. Unlike its Latin counterpart the Ogam script has no datable or chronologically significant palaeography. The rectilinear scores of Ogam do not offer much scope for variety, and it can be said in general that the size, section and technique of execution of Ogam characters are not diagnostic for dating purposes. Criteria such as the direction of writing and the disposition of the inscription on the stone are of indeterminate value. Boustrophedon (Macalister's *up-top-down*) is sometimes considered traditional, parallel (*up-up*) writing being regarded as innovative, deriving from the manuscripts, and there may be some truth in this, but it is not *per se* a reliable criterion. 145, for example, is a late boustrophedon, whereas 244, which is clearly earlier linguistically, is parallel. Similarly, the choice of the face of the stone with or without a stemline has been considered a practice of late date and this is certainly the case with the scholastic Ogams in which it is standard, but other factors may have played a part in the decision (see §4.4 above). A fundamental error on the part of the lapidary such as the incorrect orientation of the scores might suggest a waning familiarity with the cult and be considered an indication of late date. Such is the case with 118, 176, 145 (see also the discussion of iv in Appendix 2), all of which are also late linguistically. As a criterion, however, this is clearly of very limited applicability. 215 (ALATTO CELI BATTIGQI, leg. -NI) has a similar error at the turn of the stone but would not appear to be very late.

§5.3 Of the scholastic characteristics - the use of the supplementary characters, of a stemline, of scores rather than notches for vowels and of the feather-mark – the only one sufficiently frequently attested on the orthodox Ogams to be of significance is the employment of the first supplementary character. This is used with two values, consonantal /k/ or /x/ (usually transliterated K) and vocalic /e/ (on which see further n6.38). In the former capacity it is invariably used in the spelling of the formula word KOI (see 22, 34, 38, 48, 120, 156, 163 and the doubtful instances on 26 and 98) and, to judge by the fact that it occurs between vowels, it also has this value on 113, 124, 141, 155, 197, 216, 301 (but not 439), confirmed for 197 TOICAKI by 198 TOICACI and 200 TOICAC. There is nothing in the language of these, however, to suggest that this usage is particularly late. By contrast, when the character is used with its vocalic value (104, 129, 176, 187, ?201, 223, ?230, 235, 239, 256, see also iv), which is standard in scholastic Ogam (see inscriptions 27 (n7.7) and 54 (§7.5i) as well as n7.41), late linguistic features tend to be more frequent and there is a correlation between this usage and that of the ANM formula, which is also symptomatic of late date. It seems clear, therefore, that this was a relatively recent and increasingly popular convention and it may be considered probative for dating purposes. It is conspicuous by its absence in Britain (see §4.13), and it is noteworthy that ANM formula inscriptions and those bearing X with its vocalic value are confined to Cork and Kerry, showing that the south-west remained the centre of the cult to the end.

   For the rest the supplementary characters are too infrequently attested to be of value for dating purposes. In Britain an attempt is made to reproduce Latin *p* with a symbol which does not appear to correspond, in shape at least, to the fourth character of this series in later Irish tradition (i.e. *Pín*, see §7.15) on 327 and 409 (Latin **TVRPILLI** and **PVMPEIVS**; a similar symbol appears on 231). It bears more of a resemblance to the first character and may be no more that a variation on it.[1] Other supplementary characters are identified by Macalister on 7 and 193 (consonantal) and 4, 102, 204, 235, 240 (vocalic), but of these all but 235, an ANM formula inscription with both O (or A, see n6.52) and E written in characters of this series (ANM MOLE-GOMRID MACI VECUMEN), are doubtful.

§5.4 Though they show considerable variety, the evidence of most of the formulae would appear to be quite equivocal on the matter of dating and no definite chronological order of succession can be established for these. The choice between X MAQQI Y, X MAQQI MUCOI Y, single-name inscriptions and so on (see §4.6) would appear to have been entirely at the discretion of the person commissioning the monument – or his purse – and while it is possible that particular families or kin-groups had their own preferences (see for example 197, 198 and 200, 243 and 244), there is neither a strikingly significant

pattern in the geographical distribution of formulae nor an obvious correlation
between particular formulae and early or late linguistic forms, though MUCOI,
AVI and KOI types are uncommon in the later period. The ANM formula, by
contrast, is relatively confined in distribution and characterized by late
linguistic, palaeographical or orthographic features such as post-apocope forms
(187, 204, 219, 229, 235, 255-6 and vi), MACI (on which see §5.18) for
MAQ(Q)I (76, 137, 187, 235), the first supplementary letter with the value *e*
(104, 187, 223, 235, 239, 256), scholastic long scores for vowels (137), the Latin-
looking spelling MAQVI (104, see §6.31) and syncopated INBIR (187). Indeed,
examples of inscriptions of the ANM type with pre-apocope forms (excluding
the stereotyped formula word MAQ(Q)I) are quite scarce (see 75 and 95, 105
being a reconstruction), and the formula word itself is never attested in what
would have been its pre-apocope form, viz. *anmen* (see §6.27). The appearance
of crosses on some of these stones (76, 104, 204, 235 and vi) may be particularly
significant in view of Vendryes' (1955) theory that the formula shows
ecclesiastical influence, being modelled on the use of Latin *nomen*, notably on
Christian inscriptions in North Africa, in the sense 'name' ⟩ 'person' ⟩
'remains' ⟩ 'inscription'.[2] In this last sense ANM may be the only formula word
to survive into manuscript Irish with a specific connection with Ogam in the
phrase *ainm n-oguim* 'an Ogam inscription' (see §8.8).

§5.5 Dating by reference to the crosses which accompany several of the inscriptions is subject to the assumption that both cross and inscription are contemporary which may not be true in all cases, though there are no a priori grounds
for assuming otherwise (see §§4.8-9). It is also hampered by the fact that while
a developmental pattern can be identified in Early Irish cross-types,[3] earlier
forms were not ousted by later ones, so that a number of designs might have
been available to an artist at any given time. To be sure, the more complicated
the design and accomplished the execution the more likely a cross is to be late.
This is the case, for example, with the Church Island stone, the cross on which
has been dated to the seventh or eighth century,[4] the former of which would be
more likely in the present writer's opinion (see below §5.33 and the discussion
of the inscription in Appendix 2, no. iv). The crosses on 145 (see n4.29) and 233
might also be of late date, as are the accompanying inscriptions. In the main,
however, cross typology does not offer great assistance in dating the Ogams,
owing largely to the simple nature of the majority of them.

§5.6 The only really useful criterion available to us is the linguistic one but this
too is more suggestive in nature than absolute. As a guide to relative
chronology, however, it is probably more reliable and certainly more generally
applicable than anything mentioned so far. It should be borne in mind, however, that the inscriptions are the only *direct* evidence we have for the Irish
language in its earliest period, the only back-up being deductions made from
historical reconstruction and the evidence of Latin loanwords. Furthermore,
whereas most of the significant developments which took place in the language
between its Primitive and Old periods are reflected on the monuments, the
inscriptions do not present these in a consistent and chronologically continuous
progression. The very act of writing implies a convention of one kind or

another, and the conservatism of the written *vis-à-vis* the spoken word is a well-known phenomenon. Spellings on the Ogam inscriptions may or may not reflect the spoken word at the time of writing, but it should never be assumed that this was the intention of the epigraphist, otherwise we should have to acknowledge the existence of several linguistically and chronologically self-contradictory inscriptions. Nor should it be assumed that the 'composers' of the inscriptions would have been acting independently of one another. The uniformity of the script throughout the country, the overall agreement in the formulae used and in the orthography cannot be the result of chance, nor is the ability to compose and spell out an inscription likely to have been widespread. We must assume that this was the preserve of a learned class sufficiently mobile to account for the distribution of the monuments and sufficiently well integrated to account for their homogeneity. Thus, to take an obvious example, the fact that the formula word KOI is always written with the first *forfid* whether on the Dingle peninsula (156), in Cork (120), Kildare (22) or Wicklow (48) points to the existence of a conventionalized practice which one would associate with a corporate body of practitioners or professional learned men. So too, formula words in general use would become part of the stock-in-trade, so to speak, of the profession and would tend to become fixed by tradition. It is not surprising, therefore, that these tend to be more conservative and that the most frequently occurring word on the stones, though it is attested in all the forms it passed through from Primitive to Old Irish (MAQ(Q)I, MAQ, MAC, artificial MACI (see §5.18) and a doubtful MAIC on which see §6.30(c) ) did become petrified, as is clear from the occurrence of spellings with -I alongside names in which the old case-ending has been dropped (e.g. 187, 200, 204, 221, 235 and the extreme case in Latin letters, 1 **LIE LUGUAEDON MACCI MENUEH**).[5] The conservatism of a fixed convention, therefore, must always be borne in mind when the forms on an inscription are being considered, and this is imperative in the case of the frequently occurring formula elements.

§**5.7** I use the word conservatism deliberately in reference to the occurrence of early and late looking linguistic forms on one and the same inscription. MacNeill put a somewhat different interpretation on this and related phenomena, and since he used it in support of the isolationist theory discussed above (§4.9) it will be as well at this point to assess his arguments. In 1931 he devoted a paper to 'archaisms' in the Ogam inscriptions in which he presented the view that the composers of the inscriptions- described as professional men of letters as distinct from mere lettered craftsmen (ibid.35) – engaged in deliberate and sometimes misguided archaizing with a view to lending the monuments a semblance of antiquity and learning, thus conferring on them a dignity befitting the honour of the person commemorated. This 'archaizing' involved the restoration of lost vowels and case-endings which MacNeill believed the archaizing scholar could deduce from observing the timbre of consonants in his own day. Pseudo-archaizing such as the duplication of consonants (see however §6.30(d) ) was also practised and the upshot of all this, according to MacNeill, is that the inscriptions cannot be considered reliable as evidence for relative chronology. A criterion such as the presence of case-endings could be deceptive for dating purposes, reflecting not the relative date of the inscription but the degree of archaizing expertise of the composer, and the same might apply in the case of 'restored' syncopated vowels.

MacNeill's views have not been well received[6] and his presentation of them in the context of his discussion of druidic antipathy to the trappings of Roman culture and the 'isolated culture of Ireland [which] became narrowed, perhaps decadent, certainly pedantic, retrospective, therefore archaistic' (p. 34) did little to enhance them. They could be objected to on several grounds but the most important and relevant is the linguistic one. 'Archaizing' is not the only explanation for the occurrence on a given inscription of anachronistic looking spellings. The term implies the existence of a norm which is being ignored or abandoned for an earlier convention. Thus, to take two inscriptions discussed by MacNeill (36-7; 200 MAQI-TTAL MAQI VORGOS MAQI MUCOI TOICAC and 197 DEGO (*sic* in MacNeill) MAQI MOCOI TOICAKI), the spellings -TTAL (for earlier -TTALI) and TOICAC (for earlier TOICACI) show the loss of -I which is preserved in MAQI and MUCOI, and -S is preserved in VORGOS but lost in DEGO (as recorded in MacNeill) on an inscription preserving -I in TOICAKI. For MacNeill the spellings with -I and -S are archaisms not representing the contemporary pronunciation. Those without -I and -S are, by the same token, unadulterated and represent the contemporary norm. Were this so we should have to assume that MAQI and TOICAKI were deliberately chosen alternatives to MAQ/MAC and TOICAK/TOICAC, and MacNeill's explanation of the reasons for this choice might be considered acceptable. The loss of -I in -TTAL and TOICAC in 200 does admittedly suggest that this inscription postdates apocope, the process by which many final syllables were dropped (see §5.15), but this does not mean that the post-apocope spellings are therefore the 'correct' or conventional ones. Contemporary pronunciation is not the measure of accuracy for the spelling of a word or name. This should be measured, rather, by the established convention, and the Ogam inscriptions show that such a convention recognizing the existence of case-endings did exist at one time. Spellings which drop these endings therefore represent a deviation from the norm and are informative by default for the relative date of writing. In the examples under discussion the spellings MAQI, MUCOI, VORGOS and TOICAKI may be taken to represent the convention, while -TTAL and TOICAC are slips of the pen, so to speak, showing the contemporary loss of the relevant sounds. That this is so is suggested by the DEGO of 197 which was actually corrected to conform to the norm by the engraver himself, who placed the S scores omitted in the original on the face of the stone beside the point at which they should have appeared. The 'correct' reading, therefore, is DEGOS, but at the time of writing it is probable that the final *s* had already been transferred across word boundary to the following initial in the form /h/ (see §5.15 and the front cover).

Other suspected examples of 'archaizing' discussed by MacNeill will admit of an explanation along these lines. In the case of 172 TOGITTACC (for an expected TOGETTACC[I], the later nom. is *Toicthech* not *Tuicthech*), for example, the I is not necessarily an incorrectly restored syncopated vowel. Greene (1973, 134) has demonstrated that /e/ and /i/ fell together before the time of syncope so that it is not improbable that the attested spelling is contemporary, reflecting that development (see McManus, 1986, 6-7). Similar confusions, especially of the composition vowel, are found in the Latin inscriptions of Britain (Jackson, 1953, 645) and in Gaulish inscriptions (Schmidt, 1957, 91) and require no special pleading (for further examples in Ogam see §6.26). Pokorny (1918, 423) has suggested that many 'faulty' spellings can be explained by reference to changes actually taking place in the language of the time which destabilized the orthography and these, as we shall see, were numerous. Without a firmly established literary tradition it would have been impossible to maintain a strict standard in the face of such upheaval in the spoken language. Now Ogam comes close to such a standard in its formula words and in recurring morphological elements such as case-endings. But rigid adherence to a convention could not be expected in the spelling of individual names, many of which occur only once in the entire corpus of inscriptions. It is in these, therefore, more so than in the formula words that we should expect to find reflexes of what was going on in the spoken language, and this is the case. Far-reaching implications based on judgments as to the 'correctness' of any given spelling, such as those of MacNeill, are best avoided.

§**5.8** It emerges then that the linguistic forms on any given inscription cannot be interpreted by a mechanical rule of thumb in a chronological investigation. Spellings which on a superficial examination appear mutually incompatible may occur side by side and often involve contrasts between those of conventional formula words and the accompanying names. As inscriptions are contemporary documents and have not suffered at the hands of a modernizing scribal tradition, as have our manuscript sources (see §3.13), the latest spelling on any given stone may be considered decisive as to the relative date of writing, and late spellings of formula words are particularly significant as these show most resistance to change. Early spellings, by contrast, may simply be a measure of the composer's 'literacy' in the norm (as opposed to his ability to archaize), and an inscription bearing no late linguistic feature need not necessarily be old, though the probability is that it is. Any relative chronology of the inscriptions, therefore, is subject to these qualifications, and they should always be borne in mind. Before embarking on such a chronology, however, we must look a little more closely at some of the more important sound changes upon which it will be based.

§**5.9** Primitive, Archaic, Early Old, Old, Middle and Modern Irish are tags used by scholars for successive periods in the history of the language (see n5.25). The progression from any given period to the next did not occur overnight, nor can it be dated absolutely with any degree of accuracy. Arbitrary cut-off points are normally identified as marking the transition from one to the other, and each period is characterized by a set of criteria which may be wide-ranging or restricted, depending on the size of the corpus of material available to us for it. Old Irish, the language of the eighth and ninth centuries, is the earliest period sufficiently well documented to provide for a complete grammar. The manuscript records of Early Old Irish (seventh century) are just enough to whet the appetite, and it was during this period that the cult of the Ogams fell into decline. Our knowledge of Primitive and Archaic Irish (pre-sixth century and sixth century respectively) derives in the main from historical reconstruction and comparative phonology, and the Primitive and Archaic tags are generally used with reference to phonological and morphological criteria. As the only written (and contemporary) sources for these periods the Ogam inscriptions occupy a position of considerable importance in the history of the language, though their evidence is largely corroborative in nature (see §6.23) and they are regrettably barren in accidence, telling us little about the 'grammar' of Primitive Irish. They do not, for example, provide a single instance of a verb, an adjective or a preposition. Nonetheless they furnish a panorama of many of the developments which took place in the language at this time and they throw some light on the relative chronology of the same.

**§5.10** The Irish language underwent several major and minor phonological and structural changes between its Primitive and Old periods. It might be said, indeed, that it changed more during that time than it has ever done since. Words which at the Primitive Irish stage would have had four or two syllables frequently have only two or one respectively in Old Irish. The majority of the old case-endings were lost and replaced by a very different inflectional system, and a series of sound changes which in Primitive Irish were determined entirely by phonetic environment were raised by the Old Irish period to the status of morphophonological mutations and survive as such to the present day. Many of these developments can be seen taking place on the inscriptions, some are not detectable owing to the limitations of the alphabet while others, which belong to the Early Primitive Irish period not covered by the Ogams, had already run their course before the erection of the monuments and appear as a *fait accompli* on them.

**§5.11** To this third category belongs, for example, the loss of *n* before *t* or *k* resulting in the voicing of the latter to the long (or geminated) sounds *dd* and *gg*[7]. A preceding *a* or *e* appears by compensatory lengthening (and a vowel shift in the case of the former) as *ē*: Thus, PI *\*sentus* (Welsh *hynt*) ⟩ PI *\*sēddus* ⟩ OI *sét*[8] 'way, path'; PI *\*kantan* (Welsh *cant*, Latin *centum*) ⟩ PI *\*kēddan* ⟩ OI *cét* 'a hundred'; PI *\*ankus* (Welsh pl. *angeu*, Latin *nex*) ⟩ PI *\*ēggus* ⟩ OI *éc* 'death'; PI *\*tonketas* (Welsh *tynghed*) ⟩ PI *\*toggetas* ⟩ OI *tocad* 'good luck'. That this development had taken place already before the erection of Ogam monuments is clear from spellings such as 66 DECCEDDAS ⟨ *\*Decantos*[9] and 172 TOGITTACC ⟨ *\*Tonketākī*, a name formed from the word for 'good luck' with an adjectival suffix *-ākos* (see further §6.13a).

Other such early developments were the loss of intervocalic *s* (e.g. OI *ïarn* 'iron' ⟨ *\*īsarnon*, Gaulish *Isarno-*, OI *é* 'salmon', gen. sg. *ïach* ⟨ *\*esoks*, *\*esokos*, Gallo-Latin *esox*)[10] reflected in 44 IARNI[11] ⟨ *\*Īsarnī*, but not of final post-vocalic *s* which is still written in Ogam, and the monophthongization of the old diphthong *ou* (⟨ *ou* and *eu*) seen in 190 GOSSUCTTIAS (with *Gōss-* for an earlier *\*Gous* ⟨ *\*gheu-*, later Irish *gúass* 'danger').[12]

The development whereby *o* became *a* in final unstressed syllables (viz. *-os* ⟩ *-as* and *-on* ⟩ *-an*) is not of great significance but is unique in being the only sound change for which the Ogam inscriptions are our sole source of information; it would not be recoverable from historical reconstruction as *o* and *a* have precisely the same effect on neighbouring consonants and the vowels of preceding syllables. This is reflected in the gen. sg. of consonantal stems which are invariably written -AS (⟨ -os see §6.24) in Ogam, e.g. 66 DECCEDDAS above, possibly also in 160 TRIA MAQA MAILAGNI (⟨ *triyon maqqon Mailagnī 'of the three sons of Maílagnas') if this has been interpreted correctly. The development led to the adoption of *a* as the composition vowel of the *o*-stem and consonantal stem nouns (see §6.26), and though there are occasional examples of O in this position on the inscriptions (see §5.23) the change seems to have been well established by the monument period.[13]

If the fourteenth symbol of the alphabet was designed to represent a distinctive sibilant sound (see §3.15 under Z *Straif*) the fact that it is not used on the monuments may suggest that this sound, whatever it might have been, had already been assimilated to *s* between the time of the creation of the alphabet and the period of the monuments. The sound deriving from -*st*- is written S or SS in Ogam (e.g. 70 CUNAGUSOS, 107 CUNAGUSSOS, 121 VERGOSO, all containing the element *guss* 'strength' ⟨ *ghus-tu-s*). Similarly, if symbol six had the value *y* (see §3.15 under H *hÚath*), a sound which was lost at some stage during Early Primitive Irish (e.g. OI *ét* 'jealousy', Welsh (*add-*)*iant* 'longing', Gaulish *Iantu-*, OI *aig* 'ice' Welsh *ia* ⟨ *yagi-*), the fact that the inscriptions never distinguish in spelling between the gen. sg. of *o*-stem and *yo*-stem nouns (see §6.24), where the only original difference was the presence of this sound, may suggest that its loss in initial position (i.e. in the name of the symbol), where it leaves no trace, was earlier than elsewhere.[14]

§**5.12** Of the developments which are not detectable on the monuments owing to the shortcomings of the script the most significant by far is lenition. This has been dated by Jackson to the second half of the fifth century (Jackson, 1953, 143 but see below §5.21) and was one of the most important and far-reaching developments in the history of the language. The process involved a weakening in the articulation of consonants in certain positions, particularly intervocalic and, in the case of stops as well as *m* and *s*, between a vowel and *l*, *n* or *r*, whereby formerly long, intense or geminated stops were reduced to single stops and former single stops passed into their lenited or fricative equivalents.[15] Thus *dd*, *gg*, *bb*, *kk*, *tt* became /d/, /g/, /b/, /k/ and /t/ respectively,[16] while *d*, *g*, *b*, *c*, *t*, became /ð/, /γ/, /β/, /x/ and /θ/. Similarly, the opposition *mm/m* gave way to /m/-/μ/ but it is probable that that of *ll/l*, *rr/r*, *nn/n* respectively continued to be realized by a difference of intensity. The sound *w* was weakened considerably and eventually disappeared by lenition.[17] Original *ss* (and *ss* ⟨ *ks*, *ts*, *ns* and *st*) was weakened to *s* when intervocalic and to /h/ in final position, falling together with original -*s* and the fricatives /ð/, /θ/ and /x/ which were also weakened to /h/ in this position. Single *s* was lost without trace at a very early stage in intervocalic position (see above §5.11.) but at word and morpheme boundary it survived in the form /h/.[18]

An important feature of lenition was the fact that it occurred across word boundary as well as in word interior. Thus, if a consonant at the beginning of a word followed on a word ending in a vowel it underwent the same changes as those operating in the same environment within the word. But because the phonetic environment at the beginning of a word is always subject to variation the lenited sound here remained a variant or 'mutated' form of its unlenited counterpart, whereas in word interior, where the environment was not subject to fluctuation, the lenited sound was fixed. Thus, whereas in Old Irish /t/ and /θ/ in, for example, *catt* 'cat' (/kat/) and *cath* 'battle' (/kaθ/) are distinct and non-interchangeable, *th* at the beginning of a word, e.g. *a thech* 'his house', is no more than a variant, albeit an extremely important one, of the radical *t* in *tech* 'house', conditioned by the preceding *a* 'his'; *thech* has no independent existence as such and can only arise if the preceding word in a phrase conditions it. In Primitive Irish this conditioning factor was a phonological one, the conditioning word ended in a vowel. In Old Irish and indeed right up to Modern Irish it has been raised to a morphophonological level, so that whereas *a* 'his' (⟨ *esyo*) brings about lenition, the phonetically identical *a* 'her' (⟨ *esyās*) and *a* 'their' (⟨ *esyōm*) do not, but are followed by the mutations appropriate to their original auslaut (see §5.15).

The precise chronological relationship between the creation of the Ogam alphabet and lenition cannot be established with certainty. The fact that the alphabet does not have distinctive symbols for lenited sounds might be taken to suggest that its creation was anterior to lenition,[19] but this is not necessarily the case as it is probable that even if lenition were already a feature of the language, the alphabet would have been designed to cater only for *radical initial* sounds. Certainly the acrostic principle operating in the letter names could not cope with anything else, and it would have been uneconomical to do otherwise. The relationship between 'unlenited' and 'lenited' in word anlaut (see above) was such that the lenited sound was always regarded as a variant of its unlenited form and Irish, consequently, never saw the need to represent it with a *distinctive* symbol. In Old Irish, with the exception of the occasional use of *f* for lenited *p* and *lenited s* ( ⟨ *sw*), no radical initial sound has a distinctive character for its lenited counterpart. In fact distinctive symbols would be a nuisance as they would only serve to obscure the relationship between the two. The difference can best be made clear in writing by the use of some means of indicating the feature 'lenited' or 'non lenited' and Old Irish orthography does this by exploiting such devices as Latin *h* (*ch*, *th*, *ph*) and the scribal *punctum delens* (*ḟ*, *ṡ*) on the one hand, and a conventional deployment of tenues and mediae (*c*, *t*, *p*, *g*, *d*, *b*) based largely on the pronunciation of British Latin together with the interchange of double and single consonants (e.g. *mm/m*, *ll/l* etc.) on the other. Of these, the only device available to Ogam was the last (MS *h*, the later value of the sixth character, is conspicuously absent) but while there are numerous examples of the interchange of double and single characters on the inscriptions (see §6.30(d) ) the contrastive possibilities would not appear to have been exploited in a regular way, a fact which is scarcely an argument for a pre-lenition dating since the opposition later realized as unlenited – lenited was at that time precisely of a kind which would have lent itself to a double-single marking system, viz. intense – lax.

The fact is that the majority of Ogam inscriptions do not follow any discernible marking convention for the oppositions and their evidence on the matter is ambiguous, as is that of the alphabet itself. In a form like 70 CUNAGUSOS it is not clear whether the G and final S represent /g/ and /s/ respectively, or /γ/ and /h/, while in 4 LUGUDEC, a form which has clearly lost its final syllable (earlier 263 LUGUDECCAS) and thus must post-date lenition, G, D and C must represent /γ/, /δ/ and /x/ respectively. On the other hand in 46 SEDAN[I] we know that D represents /d/ (⟨ dd ⟨ nt, *Sentanyī) and in 172 TOGITTACC, as we have seen, G represents /g/ (⟨ gg ⟨ nk) and TT and CC must represent /θ/ and /x/ respectively. In Ogam therefore each symbol, irrespective of whether it is written single or double, is capable of representing the unlenited and corresponding lenited sound. That final /s/ or /h/ is still written with *Sail*, therefore, does not prove that the inscriptions belong to a pre-lenition period as *Sail* in both initial and final (but not medial) position can have the value /s/ or /h/. What it does prove, on the other hand, is that *hÚath* cannot have represented this /h/.

§5.13 Irish had inherited a historical opposition between short and long vowels but this was neutralized in unstressed (i.e. non-initial) syllables in Primitive Irish by the elimination of length. The shortening of long vowels in final unstressed syllables ending in /h/ (⟨ /s/, /ss/ etc.) must have postdated that of long vowels in absolute final position as Old Irish shows different reflexes of the two, losing the latter but retaining the former as a short vowel.[20] Otherwise all vowels appear to have been shortened and fallen together with their historically short counterparts. Thus the -ā in PI *tōtā and the a in PI *wiras have both disappeared by apocope in Old Irish *túath* 'tribe' and *fer* 'man', but the ā in PI *tōtās, though shortened, survives as -a in Old Irish *túatha* 'tribes' (nom. pl.). The shortening in non-final syllables is reflected in loanwords such as *ídol/ídal* ⟨ Lat. *īdōlum*, *corann* ⟨ Lat. *corōna* etc. (see McManus, 1983, 59).

This is a process which the inscriptions cannot chart since the alphabet has no mechanism for distinguishing vowel quantity, but it is an important precursor to the next development in Primitive Irish, viz. vowel affection.

§5.14 Vowel affection, or metaphony, was a process whereby short vowels (including those shortened in accordance with §5.13.) in contiguous syllables, usually when separated by a single consonant, underwent partial or complete assimilation in quality. It involved anticipation of the quality of the vowel of a following syllable and would appear to have begun in the stressed (initial) syllable. By 'lowering' the vowels *i* and *u* followed in the next syllable by *o* or *a* became *e* and *o* respectively (e.g. PI *wiros ⟩ *wiras ⟩ *wirah ⟩ *werah, OI *fer* 'man'; PI *widōs (⟨ -ous) ⟩ *wiδōh ⟩ *weδōh, OI *fedo*, gen. sg. of *fid* 'tree'; PI *kluton ⟩ *kluθan ⟩ *kloθan, OI *cloth* 'fame'). By 'raising' *e* and *o* followed in the next syllable by *i* or *u* became *i* and *u* respectively (e.g. PI *medus ⟩ *meδuh ⟩ *miδuh, OI *mid* 'mead' (gen. sg. *medo* ⟨ *medous with *e* retained), PI *mrogis ⟩ *mruγih, OI *mruig* 'farmland' (gen. sg. *mrogo* ⟨ *mrogous with *o* retained). That the process began in the stressed syllable would appear to be clear from PI *olīnā ⟩ *olina ⟩ *ulina ⟩ *ulena, OI *uilen* 'elbow', PI *torīmā ⟩ *toriμa ⟩ *turiμa ⟩ *tureμa ⟩ OI *tuirem* 'act of enumerating' and in particular PI *moniklos ⟩ *munixlah ⟩ *munexla h- ⟩ *munexl ⟩ OI *muinél* 'neck'.[21]

Vowel affection is easily detected on the inscriptions when the etymology of the name in question is known. Examples of forms preceding the development are 85 GRILAGNI, OI *Grelláin*, IVA-, OI *éo-* (259 IVAGENI, OI *Éogain*), -CUNAS, OI *-con* (191 GAMICUNAS), 66 TURANIAS, later *Torna*. Affection has already taken place in 121 VERGOSO (⟨ *Wiragusōs), 74 CONANN (⟨ *Cunagnī), 145 QRIMITIR (⟨ *qremiterī), viii RETAGIN (⟨ *RITAGENI) and in the ending -EAS (⟨ -iyās ⟨ -iās, see §5.15) in 198 MAQI-RITEAS (see further §§5.25-6).

The development of short *u*- diphthongs[22] in stressed penultimate syllables (e.g. OI *fiur*, dat. sg. of *fer* ⟨ *wirū*, OI *neuch* dat. sg. of *nech* 'anyone' ⟨ *nekʷū*, OI *caur* 'warrior' ⟨ *caruts*) and of *u* in unstressed penultimate syllables (e.g. OI *tomus* 'measuring' ⟨ *tomessus*) is a related phenomenon which is not recorded in Ogam (cp. 273 CALUNOVIC[A], the first element of which is probably to be equated with the name *Culann* and 82 MAILAGURO on which see n6.53).

**§5.15** The last significant development associated with Primitive Irish is 'apocope', which involved the shift of word-final *h* and *n* across word boundary to the initial of a following word and the subsequent loss of exposed final short vowels. Exposed long vowels were shortened but not lost. Thus *werah* (⟨ *wiras) ⟩ *wera h-* ⟩ *wer h-*, OI *fer* (nom.); *weran* ⟩ *wera n-* ⟩ *wer n-*, OI *fer n-* (acc. sg.) and *wirī* ⟩ *wiri* ⟩ *wir*, OI *fir* (gen.), but *wirūs* ⟩ *wirūh* ⟩ *wiru h-*, OI *firu* (acc. pl.). Final syllables beginning originally with *y* had become disyllabic and the second of these, together with the *y*, was lost by apocope (e.g. * alyas ⟩ *aliyas ⟩ *aleyah ⟩ OI *aile* 'other' and *alyū ⟩ *aliyū ⟩ * aliuyu ⟩ OI *ailiu* dat. sg. of *aile*).[23]

Since lenition also worked across word boundary there were now three possible mutations at the beginning of a word, (1) lenition of a consonant if the preceding word ended in a vowel, (2) nasalization of a vowel or consonant (expressed as voicing in the case of *t, c, p* (by analogy) and *f*, the nasal merged with *l, n m, r* and *s*) if the preceding word ended in *-n* (⟨ *m*) and (3) the prefixing of *h* to a vowel (the *h* merged with consonants) if the preceding word ended in /h/. The last mutation, however, would be considerably restricted in application to certain hiatus positions in later Irish.[24]

In the Ogam inscriptions pre-and post-apocope spellings can be distinguished for all stem classes except the *yo*-stems, the ending of which is always written -I (which represents pre-apocope *-iyī* or *-ii* and post-apocope *-i*). In the other stem-classes (see further §6.24) apocope can be detected as follows: the loss of -I in the case of *o*-stems (e.g. MAQ(Q)I ⟩ MAQ), -IAS becoming (via -EAS by vowel affection) -EA and eventually -E in the case of *ā*-stems and *yā*-stems (e.g. 178 MAQI-ERCIAS, 198 MAQI-RITEAS, 101 MAQI-ESEA, 106 MAQI-RITE), -OS becoming -O in the case of *i*- and *u*-stems (e. g. 180 BRUSCCOS, 63 BRUSCO) and-AS becoming first -A and then being lost in the case of consonantal stems (e.g. 196 ERCAVICCAS, 250 RITTAVVECAS, 140 LUGUV-VECCA, 221 LUGUVVEC, 1 **MENUEH,** all containing the same second element *-wicas* on which see n6.23). Apocope is taken to mark the end of the Primitive Irish period[25] and is dated to the turn of the fifth and sixth centuries.

**§5.16** Apocope might have resulted in the appearance of awkward consonant clusters in word-final position but this was avoided by the vocalization of certain consonants and the development of a secondary vowel between others.[26] Clusters of the type fricative (deriving from the lenition of stops) + resonant (e.g. /γ/, /δ/ and /x/ before r, l or n, /γ/ before m and /θ/ before l and n) underwent a simplification whereby the fricative disappeared with compensatory lengthening of a preceding vowel. Thus Lat. *signum* 〉 PI *\*signas* (an o-stem) 〉 *\*siɣnah* 〉 *\*seɣna h-* 〉 *\*seɣn* 〉 OI *sén* 'omen'; PI *\*odnas* 〉 *\*oδnah* 〉 *\*oδna h-* 〉 *\*oδn* 〉 *ón/úan* 'lending' (vb. n. of *odaid* 'lends'); PI *\*moniklas* 〉 *\*monixlah* 〉 *\*munexla h-* 〉 *\*munexl* 〉 OI *muinél* 'neck'; PI *\*agm-* 〉 *ám* (vb. n. of *aigid* 'drives'); PI *\*anatlā* 〉 *\*anaθla* 〉 *\*anaθl* 〉 OI *anál* 'breath'; PI *\*etnas* 〉 *\*eθnah* 〉 *\*eθna h-* 〉 *\*eθn* 〉 OI *én* 'bird'. An epenthetic vowel developed after syncope between labial spirants and resonants as well as in the cluster *-thr-* (which behaves like *-dr-* and *-dl-*), e.g. *\*dubnos* 〉 *\*doβna h* 〉 *\*doμn* (by assimilation of the fricative to the nasal) 〉 OI *domun* 'world', *\*atras* 〉 *\*aθrah* 〉 *\*aθra h-* 〉 *\*aθr* 〉 OI *athar*, gen. sg. of *athair* 'father'; compare *\*kantlan* 〉 *\*kēddlan* 〉 *\*kēdla n-* 〉 *\*kēdl n-* 〉 OI *cétal* 'act of singing'.

In the Ogam inscriptions the vocalization of fricatives before resonants is reflected in the replacement of original -AGNI with -AN, often written -ANN (e.g. 467 ULCAGNI (later *Olcáin*), 119 DALAGNI (later *Dalláin*) but 256 DEGLANN (later *Décláin*)[27] and 145 RON[A]NN (later *Rónáin*), all genitives with the suffix *\*-agnas* (on which see §6.12).

One of the important outcomes of the above was the reintroduction to unstressed syllables of long vowels, all of which as we have seen (§5.13) had been shortened earlier.[28] The reduction of these clusters was probably originally confined to final position but spread by analogy (see Greene, 1976, 35). The name *Sárán* 〈 *\*Sagragnas* shows a double reduction, one of which is seen in 449 **SAGRANI** but not in the accompanying Ogam SAGRAGNI. In 488 **ENABARRI**, ENABARR (〈 *\*etno-barrī*) the form which arose in final position would appear to have spread already to the compound just as the composition syllable has adopted the vocalism of the final syllable of the simplex (*\*etnas* 〈 *\*etnos* see §5.11).

§**5.17** Postdating the above was the loss of internal syllables generally denoted by the term 'syncope' and dated approximately to the middle of the sixth century.[29] Syncope brought about a further reduction in the length of words in the language and reintroduced some formerly lost consonant clusters (such as *nt* and *nk*). Short vowels in non-final second syllables were first reduced to /ə/ (〈 *a, o* and *u* before a neutral consonant) and /i/ (〈 *i, e* and *u* before a palatalized consonant) and subsequently disappeared imparting either neutral (with the loss of /ə/) or palatal (with loss of /i/) quality[30] to the resulting consonant group. Thus PI *\*wriggariyan* (〈 *\*writ-garyom*) 〉 *\*wregareya n-* ( *\* wregəre* 〉 *\*wregre* 〉 OI *frecrae* 'answer' (vb. n. of *fris-gair*); PI *\*kʷinutās* 〉 *\*kʷinoθā h-* 〉 *\*kʷinəθa* 〉 OI *cinta* (acc. pl. of *cin* 'fault'); PI *\*aterās* 〉 *\*aθerā h-* 〉 *\*aθira* 〉 OI *aithrea* (acc. pl. of *athair* 'father'); PI *\*togussiyas* (〈 *\*to-gustyos*) 〉 *\*tuɣuseya h-* 〉 *\*tuɣise* 〉 OI *tuichse* 'chosen' (past participle of *do-goa*). Compare further PI *\* Wiragussōs* 〉 *\* Weraɣosō h-* 〉 *\* Werəɣoso* 〉 *Weryoso* (121 VERGOSO), OI *Fergoso* (gen.of *Fergus*); PI *Catubutas* (58 CATTUBUTTAS) 〉 *Caθaβoθ* (46 ?[CAT]TABBOTT) 〉 EOI *Cathboth* (gen. of *Cathub*); PI *\*Lugudikas* 〉 *\*Luɣuδexah* (263 LUGUDECCAS) 〉 *Luɣuδexa h-* (286 LUGUDECA) 〉 *\*Luɣuδex* (4 LUGUDEC) 〉 *\*Luɣiδex* 〉 OI *Luigdech* (gen. of *Lugaid*); PI *\*Tonketākī* 〉 *\*Toggetakī* 〉 *\*Togeθax* 〉 *\*Togiθax* (= 172 TOGITTACC), *Toicthich*, gen. of *Toicthech*.

With some exceptions (such as *do-rigni* beside *do-rigéni*, perfect 3rd sg. of *do-gní* 'does') long vowels which had developed by compensatory lengthening were not syncopated. Thus, the dat. pl. of OI *anál* is *análaib*, not *\*anlaib* and *cenél* 'race' has an acc. pl. *cenéla*, not *\*ceinlea*. In words of five or more syllables the fourth syllable was also lost by syncope. Thus, OI *écsamlai* (nom. pl of *écsamail* 'dissimilar') ⟨ immediate pre-syncope *\*ēgosamali* ⟨ *\*en-kon-samaliyes*. Words which after syncope were still trisyllabic with hiatus in unstressed position have become disyllabic by the OI period by the reduction of hiatus (e.g. *\*tomentiyonas* ⟩ *\*touēdeyona h-* ⟩ *\*touidëon* ⟩ (post-syncope) *\*toudëon* ⟩ OI *toimten* (gen. sg. of *toimtiu* 'thought').[31]

Syncopated forms can be detected with relative ease on the Ogam inscriptions (see VERGOSO above and §5.29). The obscuration of the vowels preceding their loss is also probably reflected in spellings such as 172 TOGITTACC (see §5.7 above and the discussion of the composition vowels in §6.26).

**§5.18** Concurrent with the developments outlined above there was also a gradual erosion of the labial element in the sounds /kʷ/ and /gʷ/ and the palatalization of consonants. The Wroxeter inscription (xxi **CVNORIX MACVS MAQVI-COLINE**) shows that the labial element in /kʷ/ (Q in Ogam) was lost earlier before back than before front vowels and, on the basis of this inscription, Jackson has revised his original dating of its loss in this position from the first half of the sixth century (Jackson, 1953, 143) to the second half of the fifth (Wright/Jackson, 1968, 299-300). The loss before front vowels appears to have been ongoing in the sixth and complete by the late sixth century and Jackson (1953, 140-41) has shown that the delabialization of palatal post-apocope final /(kʷ')kʷ'/ (' indicates palatal quality) to /(k')k'/ was achieved through an intermediate stage breaking up /kʷ'/ into /k'w'/, reflected in the spelling **MAC(C)V-** for **MAQ(Q)I-**. As the complete loss of the labial element postdates syncope (witness post-syncope 364 **QVENVENDANI**), and therefore apocope (cp. Archaic Irish 145 QRIMITIR RON[A]NN MAQ COMOGANN), the -I/**-I** in the Irish spellings MACI/**MACCI** must be artificial and reflect the tenacity of the orthographical convention of writing final I in this formula word.

By the end of the sixth century the labial element can be assumed to have been lost in both /kʷ(')/ and /gʷ(')/ so that these fell together with /k(')/ and /g(')/, leaving the alphabet with two symbols each for these sounds (see §3.13 and §3.15 above). The delabialization is reflected in Q ⟩ C in spellings such as MAQ(Q)I ⟩ MAC(I), 358 VOTECORIGAS (= **VOTEPORIGIS**, British *p* corresponding to PI /kʷ/, not /k/) as well as in hyper-correct Q for C such as 3 QUNACANOS for CUNA- (see §6.29).

**§5.19** Palatalization of consonants[32] occurred at several stages during the Primitive and Archaic periods of the language. It involved the anticipation of a following front vowel (*i* or *e*) in the articulation of a consonant by raising the front of the tongue towards the hard palate. Eventually the palatal quality was invested in the consonant itself irrespective of the fate of the following vowel – which might be lost (by apocope or syncope) or obscured (see §5.20(5) below) – and the opposition palatal/neutral arising from the second palatalization came to play a very important role in the inflexion of the noun (e.g. nom. *ball*, gen. *baill*, nom. *gabál*, dat. *gabáil* etc.).

The first palatalization took place in the Primitive Irish period after vowel affection in stressed syllables and operated on single consonants followed by *i* and *e*, though there were several exceptions. The second was caused by *e* and *i* in final syllables before they were lost by apocope, and the third has been mentioned under the discussion of syncope. Thus, the *r* in *tuirem* 'act of enumerating' ⟨ *torīmā* was palatalized by the first, the *-ll* in *baill* 'limbs' (nom. pl. of *ball*) ⟨ *ballī* by the second, and the *rt* in *cairtea* 'friends' (acc. pl. of *carae*) ⟨ (pre-syncope) *karēda* ⟨ *karantās* by the third. The difference between the first (which did not palatalize consonant clusters) and the second is quite clear in, for example, OI *gabálae* (gen. sg. of *gabál* 'taking') ⟨ *gabaglyās*, but *gabáil* (dat. sg.) ⟨ *gabagli*, and *Ercae* ⟨ *Ercyās* (gen. of a fem. *ā*-stem) but *Eirc* ⟨ *Ercī* (gen. of a masculine *o*-stem). Compare further *tigirn* ⟨ *tigernī* (gen. sg. of *tigernas* 'lord') and *tigernae* (⟨ *tigerniyas*) 'sovereignty, lord'.

Palatalization is not written in Ogam though it must have been present in the language in the sixth century. When apocope takes place in the word MAQQI it is written either MAQ or MAC, as compared with the standard *maicc* (with *i* indicating the palatal quality of the *-cc*) of the manuscripts. Similarly -AGNI becomes -AN(N), not * -AIN (MS -*áin*). It is for this reason that 83 MAIC, is quite exceptional and questionable (the reading is doubtful). The result of this is that genitive forms often have the appearance of nominatives and Macalister was mislead by this in the case of 145 QRIMITIR RON[A]NN MAQ COM-OGANN, which he describes as a (Christian) 'signature' as opposed to a (pagan) 'epitaph' (see further §6.25). Here RON[A]NN, MAQ and COMOGANN have the deceptive appearance of nominatives but QRIMITIR with-IR, not -ER, is quite clearly genitive.

§5.20 Syncope marks the end of Archaic Irish and the beginning of Old Irish, the first stage of which (seventh century) may conveniently be referred to as Early Old Irish though its distinctive characteristics are often labelled 'archaic' from the standpoint of 'Classical' Old Irish, the language of the eighth and ninth centuries. The seventh century saw the vernacular establish itself as a literary vehicle but texts dating from this time are mostly preserved in manuscripts of a much later date in which a modernizing scribal tradition has generally erased most of the distinct phonological features of the period. Nonetheless, many of these features are known to us, mainly from the spelling of Irish personal and place names recorded in early Latin texts dating from the end of the seventh century, though incorporating materials from earlier sources,[33] and from texts such as the *Cambray Homily* and the *prima manus* of the Würzburg glosses.[34]

Among the features which distinguish the language of this period from that of Classical Old Irish are (1) the retention of *é* and *ó*, diphthongized to *ía* and *úa* respectively in Old Irish (e.g. EOI *fédot*, OI *fíadat,*, EOI *Tóthail*, OI *Túathail*), (2) the continued separation of the diphthongs *aí* and *oí* which are confused in Old Irish, (3) the exclusive use of *-o* in the gen. sg. of *i*- and *u*-stems (Old Irish also has *-a*), (4) the retention of post-consonantal /w/ arising from syncope (e.g. EOI *Conual, Bresual*, OI *Conall, Bresal* ⟨ *-walos*) and in particular (5) the retention of *e* and *o* between neutral consonants in closed unstressed syllables where Old Irish has *a*, reflecting an important obscuration of short vowels in this position (e.g. EOI *Fechreg*, OI *Fíachrach*, EOI *fédot*, OI *fíadat*). Some of these features can be used as criteria in examining the latest of the Ogam inscriptions (see §5.34).

§**5.21** While there is general agreement that the developments outlined above as belonging to Primitive and Archaic Irish took place in the sequence in which they have been presented, allowance being made of course for a degree of overlap, the absolute dating of these, and consequently of the inscriptions in which they are reflected, is not so straightforward a matter. This is probably not quite so surprising when one considers the extent of disagreement on what one might have thought a more tractable matter, that of the floruit of the national apostle, St. Patrick. Sound changes are more elusive than saints, and particularly so when the contemporary record is as meagre as it is in the present case.

Jackson's framework (1953, 142-3), which places lenition at the beginning of the latter half of the fifth century, apocope around A.D. 500 and syncope in the middle or second half of the sixth century, has become the standard though by no means universally accepted chronology. O'Rahilly believed syncope was still operative in the early part of the seventh century (1946, 464 and 1950, 396), while Thurneysen on the evidence of the poems ascribed to Colmán mac Lénéni (1933, 207) thought it complete already by the end of the sixth. At the earlier end of the chronology the discrepancies are considerably greater. Jackson points out (1953, 139. n1) that Thurneysen did not make a clear statement on the date of lenition but seemed to have believed it to be ancient. For his part Jackson considered the evidence of the earliest Christian Latin loanwords in Irish, which he associated with the missionary activity of 'St. Patrick and his fellows between 432 and 461', conclusive proof against a remote date for lenition – as these words undergo the same developments as the native vocabulary – and he assigned it to the second half of the fifth century to accommodate this evidence. Against this it has been argued that the framework beginning with lenition and ending with syncope telescopes major developments in the phonological structure of the language into a very short period and the authenticity of the borrowing *Cothraige* ⟨ *Patricius*, which underpins Jackson's dating, has been challenged.[35]

As lenition does not figure as a dating criterion in the Ogams (see §5.12) the issue of its date need not concern us here. It will suffice to say that it could have been considerably earlier than Jackson thought; its appearance in the earliest loanwords (McManus, 1983, 49-51) would then have to be explained as due to adaptation to already existing phonetic patterns. Vowel-affection, apocope and syncope, on the other hand, all of which are found in the Latin loans, are less likely candidates for such adaptation and one has to assume that these were taking place during the borrowing period. In the chronology below, therefore, I propose to take Jackson's chronology with regard to these features as a rough guide.

§**5.22** On the basis of the characteristic criteria of successive periods in the history of Early Irish outlined above it is now possible to attempt to establish an outline relative chronology of the Ogam inscriptions. It should be emphasized again, however, that such a chronology will have all the shortcomings inherent in treating the written word as evidence for the spoken variety, in regarding what may have been overlapping developments as consecutive, and in assuming that they proceeded at the same pace throughout the country. Absolute consistency, therefore, cannot be expected and is generally found only at the extreme ends of the period (e.g. 66 MAQI-DECCEDDAS AVI TURANIAS as opposed to 256 ANM TEGANN MAC DEGLANN). The inner strata show a considerable variety of inconsistency and irregular fluctuation, making the establishment of a pattern that much more difficult.

§**5.23** Of the developments outlined vowel affection (§5.14) is the earliest offering contrastive possibilities for a relative dating of the inscriptions, those preceding it in time being either undetectable or already complete and thus providing no contrast. The occasional appearance of O as composition vowel for the commoner A (⟨ o in o-stems and consonantal stems, see §6.26) is not diagnostic as a criterion for early date (i.e. preceding the development of o to a in this position, see §5.11) as the falling together of /o/ and /a/ in this position as /ə/ before syncope (see §5.17) could give rise to this spelling (cp. for example 303 CATABAR with CATA- ⟨ CATO- ⟨ CATU- by lowering), and inscriptions on which it is found are not characterized by strikingly early linguistic features. It is noteworthy that it often occurs in the vicinity of a labial sound (e.g. 11 CUNOVATO, for the more common CUNA- and 269 IVODACCA for IVA-) and we may have to do here with a rounded vowel of no particular significance for dating purposes (see Hamp, 1953/4, 284 and for further examples see §6.26). In Britain Ogam A usually corresponds to Latin **O** (e.g. 342 CUNACENNI, **CVNOCENNI**, 446 CLUTAR[IGAS?], **CLVTORI** and see also 370 **SENOMAGLI**, 457 **DVNOCATI**), so that 380 ICORIGAS (**ICORI**) and 422 VENDOGNI (the accompanying Latin is uncertain) might be due to British influence. In 488 **ENABARRI**, ENABARR the influence worked in the opposite direction.

§**5.24** A substantial proportion of inscriptions show no trace whatsoever of vowel affection or, in default of vowel affection sequences, of any of the developments postdating it in the outline above. These may be considered the oldest in the corpus and they could in theory be assigned to a very early period.[36] The earlier one dates them, however, the greater the vacuum in time between this and the following category which is post-affection and probably belongs to the second half of the fifth century. For this reason and because no Early Primitive Irish features are recorded on the stones (see §§5.10-11) it is unlikely that they are much older than the fifth century and they may belong to the first or early part of the second half of it, though some could possibly date from the late fourth century. On the questionable Ogam of the Ballinderry II Crannóg bone die as an unreliable basis for inference as to the possible date of our earliest inscriptions see §7.4.[37]

To this category belong inscriptions such as: 19 OVANOS AVI IVACATTOS, 44 IARNI (⟨ *Ísarní, see §5.11), 47 NETA-CARI NETA-CAGI, 56 SAGITTARI, 66 MAQI-DECCEDDAS AVI TURANIAS, 69

GIRAGNI, 70 CUNAGUSOS MAQI MUCOI ?VIRAGNI, 81 CASSITTAS
MAQI MUCOI CALLITI, 85 GRILAGNI MAQI SCILAGNI, 119 DALAGNI
MAQI DALI, 120 BROINIENAS KOI NETA-TTRENALUGOS, 125 MAQI-
ERCIAS MAQI VALAMNI, 156 MAQQI-IARI KOI MAQQI MUCOI DOV-
VINIAS, 157 DOVETI MAQQI CATTINI, 158 SUVALLOS MAQQI
DUCOVAROS, 160 TRIA MAQA MAILAGNI,[38] 161 INISSIONAS, 162
?CUNAMAQQI AVI CORBBI, 180 BRUSCCOS MAQQI CALIACI, 188
MARIANI, 190 GOSSUCTTIAS, 191 GAMICUNAS, 246 CORBAGNI MAQI
BIVITI, 251 VELITAS LUGUTTI, 258 MAILAGNI MAQI GAMATI, 262
ERCAGNI MAQI-ERCIAS, 300 CUN[A]NETAS MAQI MMUC[OI] NETA-
SEGAMONAS, 307 MODDAGN[I] MAQI GATTAGN[I] MUCOI LUGUNI.
A number of damaged inscriptions would appear from what remains to belong
here also, e.g. 5 ALLATOS MAQI BR. . ., 58 CATTUBUTTAS MAQ. . ., 107
CUNAGUSSOS MA. . ., 124 ANAVLAMATTIAS MUCOI [..] OELURI AVI
AKERAS, 154 CUNAMAQQI CORBBI MAQQ. . ., 164 VOENACUNAS
M. . . (on the OE see §6.28), 179 . . .ETORIGAS, 181 TALAGNI MAQ. . .,
196 ERCAVICCAS MAQI CO. . ., 228 . . .MAQI BROCI.

§5.25 In the next category vowel affection begins to appear but the case-endings
remain intact, e.g. 198 MAQI-RITEAS (⟨ -iās) MAQI MAQI-DDUMILEAS (⟨
-iās) MUCOI TOICACI, 244 COILLABBOTAS (⟨ -butas) MAQI CORBI
MAQI MOCOI QERAI. In 71 COIMAGNI MAQI MOCOI GA. . . the U of
MUCOI has been lowered to O, the only case for the feature in what remains
of the inscription, and this is true also of 197 DEGO[S] MAQI MOCOI
TOICAKI, the final S in the first name of which was inserted later by the
lapidary (see §5.7), suggesting that the process of apocope had already begun.
In fact most inscriptions with lowered or raised vowels show the workings
of apocope in one form or another and belong to the next stage in the
sequence.

§5.26 The earliest post-apocope inscriptions show a variety of fluctuation with
regard to the retention or loss of final consonants or syllables. Among the possible combinations are:
     (a) The consonantal stem gen. ending -AS appearing alongside -A (⟨ -AS),
and -A (⟨ -AS) alongside the complete loss of the syllable, e.g. 147 MOINENA
(⟨ -as) MAQI OLACON (⟨ -cunas), 159 MAQI-DECCEDA (⟨ -as) MAQI
GLASICONAS (⟨ -cunas), 266 COLLABOT (⟨ -butas) MUCOI LUGA MAQI
LOBACCONA (⟨ -cunas).
     (b) -I already gone in inscriptions preserving -AS (or -A ⟨ -AS) or -OS, e.g.
20 MAQI-DDECCEDA (⟨ -as) MAQI MARIN (⟨ -inī), 172 TOGITTACC (⟨
-etācī) MAQI SAG(A)RETTOS, 200 MAQI-TTAL (⟨ -tālī) MAQI VORGOS
MAQI MUCOI TOICAC (⟨ -ācī), 250 CATTUVVIR (⟨ -wirī) MAQI
RITTAVVECAS[39] (⟨ -wicas) MUCOI ALLATO (⟨ -ōs).
     (c) -I dropped in one name but not in another, e.g. 40 MAQI-CAIRATINI
AVI INEQAGLAS (⟨ -glasī), 166 COIMAGNI MAQI VITALIN (⟨ -inī), 88
BRANAN (⟨ -agnī) MAQI OQOLI, ii COMMAGGAGNI MU[CO]I
SAMMNN, v BRANADDOV MA MAQI QOLI MUCOI DOVI. . ., viii
RETAGIN MAQI DOV. . . .

(d) -I preserved but -S dropped, e.g. 63 BRUSCO (⟨ -ōs) MAQI DOVALESCI, 101 MAQI-ESEA (⟨ -iās) MAQI DOMANEQI.

(e) -OS preserved but -AS dropped, e.g. 211 RTTTAVVECC (sic leg. ⟨ -wicas) MAQI VEDDONOS.

Other examples in this category are: 11 CUNOVATO (⟨ -ōs),[40] 21 ..MAQQI ?COLLABOTA (⟨ -butas), 134 ASSICONA (⟨ -cunas), 170 QENILOCI MAQI MAQI-AINIA (⟨ -iās) MUC.., 175 MAQQI-ERCCIA (sic leg., ⟨ -iās) MAQQI MUCOI DOVINIA (⟨ -iās), 178 ERC (⟨ Ercī) MAQI MAQI-ERCIAS MU DOVINIA (⟨ -iās), 184 MAQQI-DECEDDA (⟨ -as) MAQQI CATUVIR (?sic leg. ⟨ -wirī), 215 ALATTO (⟨ -ōs) CELI BATTIGNI, xiv VEDDELLEMETTO (⟨ -ōs) MUC[O]I LOGIDDEAS (⟨ -iās) AVVI MUNICCONA (⟨ -cunas).

The delabialization of /kʷ/ before back vowels had already begun by this stage (see the Wroxeter stone xxi **CVNORIX MACVS MAQVI-COLINE**, and the resulting confusion with /k/ may be reflected in a spelling like 3 QUNACANOS, if the first element is the otherwise well attested CUNA-. Before front vowels, however, Q continues to hold its ground. All inscriptions mentioned so far retain both the Q and the pre-apocope -I in the formula word MAQ(Q)I, and MUCOI also tends to be fixed in form though it occasionaly shows lowering of the u to o.

§**5.27** To the next category may be assigned inscriptions in which endings which were dropped are gone from all names but retained in formula words (excluding ANM), e.g. 4 LUGADDON (⟨ -donas) MAQI LUGUDEC (⟨ -decas), 94 DOMMO MACI VEDUCERI (assuming the latter to be a yo-stem), 104 ANM CORRE (⟨ -iās?) MAQVI UDD[. . .]METT ( ⟨ -tas?), 106 -OT (⟨ -utas?) MAQI MAQI-RITE (⟨ -iās) [. . .] COI CORIBIRI, 169 MAQI-LIAG MAQI-ERCA (on the ending -A see §6.24), 176 CONUNETT (⟨ *Cunanetas) MOQI CON-URI, 204 ANM MAGANN (⟨ -agnī) MAQI N?DAD/T. . . (on Macalister's reading of the last name as NUADAT, see below §5.34), 243 MAQI-RITTE (⟨ -iās) MAQI COLABOT (⟨ -butas) . . . .(compare 244 in §5.25 above and see §4.7), 235 ANM MOLE-GOMRID (⟨ -iās and -dī or -tī, see §6.28 and n6.70) MACI VECUMEN (⟨ -nī or -nas?), 255 ANM VURUDDRANN (⟨ -agnī) MAQ[I] DOLIGENN (⟨ -egnī or -nas?), 285 BIVODON (⟨ -donas) MUCOI ATAR (⟨ -rī or -ras?).

The ANM formula is now becoming more common, the oldest examples of it being a little earlier (75 ANM CASONI [MAQ]I ?RODAGNI, if the reading is correct, and 95 ANM MEDDOGENI, for which one might read MEDDU-; 105 ANM NETACUNAS is a rash reconstruction). From 94 and 235 it will be apparent that the delabialization of /kʷ/ before front vowels is also beginning to show itself and as MACI is an artificial spelling (see §5.18) these two inscriptions might in fact belong to §5.28. The vocalization of fricatives before resonants can also be seen in 88 BRANAN, and 255 VURUDDRANN. There are no reliable examples of -GN(N) ⟨ -GNI (60 MAILAGN[I] and 307 MOD-DAGN[I], GATTAGN[I] appear to have had the final vowel originally) and -AN(N)I for -AGNI is uncertain (7 CERAN[I] has a preceding [MA]Q, 241 BAIDANI is a doubtful reading as is 288 ?DEBRANI and 317 MAGLANI (cp. 353 ?MAGLAGN[I]) is a reconstruction; possible examples are 135 MINNAC-CANNI, 75 CASONI and i GLANNANI). Spellings in Britain such as 449

**SAGRANI** (accompanied by Ogam SAGRAGNI) are not reliable as examples of vocalization before apocope as the -**I** in these is the Latin ending (cp. the post-syncope 364 **QVENVENDANI** and **BARCVNI** with -**I**, and see below §6.22). As the next category shows this vocalization complete all inscriptions of the -AGNI type might belong at the latest at this point.

§5.28 Inscriptions in which all endings are lost but which do not show the reduction brought about by syncope may be placed next in the chronological sequence. In these the word for 'son' tends in general to be written MAQ, occasionally MAC, and -AGNI is always -AN(N): 90 CRONUN MAC BAIT (assuming the inscription is complete as such), 112 ?MICANAVVI MAQ LUGUN[I] ( -I, confirmed for the latter by 113, in each case the *yo*-stem gen. ending), 145 QRIMITIR RON[A]NN MAQ COMOGANN, 219 ANM CRUNAN MAQ LUQIN, 239 ANM GATTEGLAN, 256 ANM TEGANN MAC DEGLANN, 303 CATABAR MOCO VIRI-CORB, vi [A]NM SILLANN MAQ VATTILLOGG

§5.29 The next contrastive criterion in the chronological sequence is syncope. It should be noted, however, that late inscriptions not bearing sequences susceptible to syncope cannot be dated by this criterion and may be younger than some included in this category. This is particularly true of inscriptions bearing MAQ and MAC spellings as MAQI is still possible on post-syncope inscriptions. An asterisk indicates the point at which a vowel would appear to have been dropped: 10 MAQ CORRB*RI MAQ AMMLLO. . .TT, 46 SEDAN. . . . . .TABBOTT AVI DERC*MASOC, 73 DOMN*GEN, 103 CARR*TTACC MMAQI MU CAGG. . ., 118 VEQ*REQ MOQOI GLUN*LEGGET, 121 VER*GOSO MACI LLOMINACCA, 187 ANM MAILE-IN*BIR MACI BROCANN, 221 CAT*VVIRR[41] MAQI LUGUVVEC, 227 OTTINN MAQI VEC*[R. . .], 233 ?TIDONN[A?] MAQ DOMN*GINN, iv BECC*DINN MACI RITT*ECC. To this group also belongs the Inchagoill Latin alphabet inscription **LIE LUGUAEDON MACCI MEN*VEH** (⟨ *Minawicas*). On 235 MOLE-GOMRID (§5.27) see n6.52 and on 4 LUGADDON (§5.27, ⟨ *Luguaidonas*, cp. 1 **LUGUAEDON**, later MS forms such as *Lugadon* do not show syncope) which is accompanied by non-syncopated LUGUDEC see §6.26.

§5.30 Thus far the contrastive criteria have been exploited to produce an outline relative chronology and it will be apparent that inscriptions bearing the relevant sequences can be broadly classified into distinctive categories. Owing to the fragmentary nature of many inscriptions it is impossible to give exact figures but the bulk appear to belong to the Late Primitive Irish period with a substantial but decreasing proportion in Archaic Irish and a very small number in Early Old Irish. No orthodox Ogam inscription bears diagnostic criteria which would assign it either to the Early Primitive Irish or to the Classical Old Irish periods (see further §5.34). To attempt a more minute chronology in absolute terms is a tentative exercise subject to all the qualifications mentioned above, in particular the uncertainty attaching to the absolute dating of sound changes and the conservative nature of the written word. If one were to follow Jackson's chronology, however, and allow for a period of time between the development

in speech and its appearance in writing, inscriptions in §5.24 would belong to
the fifth century (with no mechanism for establishing a lower limit), those showing vowel affection alone (§5.25) might be dated towards the end of the fifth
century, those in which apocope begins to show itself (§5.26) to the first half
of the sixth, those in which it is attested in all names (§5.27) to the middle or
second half of the sixth century and syncopated forms (§5.29) to the late sixth
or early seventh century. If so the main period of the Ogams should be placed
in the fifth and first half of the sixth century with the possibility that some date
from the late fourth. The cult would appear to have been waning in the latter
half of the sixth century and to have died out in the early seventh.

§5.31 The British Ogams accompanied by an equivalent in the Latin alphabet
can be dated by reference to the palaeography of the latter, in particular by the
progressive intrusion of uncial and half-uncial letter-forms on the older Roman
capitals. Using this method Jackson (1950, 205) has worked out a chronology
of these inscriptions which places the bulk of them in the period from mid-fifth
to the mid-sixth century. This would appear to corroborate the results of our
survey of the Irish Ogams but a comparison of both series presents a rather con-
fusing picture. Few of the developments which provide contrastive evidence for
dating the Irish Ogams are attested on their British counterparts, and it is
noteworthy that Jackson's evidence for the persistence of Irish as a spoken
language in Britain is taken in the main from inscriptions in the Latin alphabet.
    Examples of British inscriptions as arranged chronologically by Jackson
are:

Mid. to later fifth century:
445 **VITALIANI EMERETO** VITALIANI
446 **MAGLOCVNI** (*sic leg.*) **FILI CLUTORI** MAGLICUNAS MAQI
                                                  CLUTAR[IGAS?]
467 **[HI]C IACIT VLCAGNI** ULCAGNI

End of fifth to beg. of sixth century:
341 **MACCV-TRENI SALIGIDVNI** MAQI-TRENI SALICIDUNI
353 **TRENACATVS IC IACIT FILIVS MAGLAGNI** TRENACCATLO
362 **AVITORIA FILIA CVNIGNI** AVITORIGES INIGENA CUNIGNI
432 **TIGERNACI BOBAGNI** DOVAGNI
442 **MACCV-DICCL FILIVS CATICVVS**[42]
449 **SAGRANI FILI CVNOTAMI** SAGRAGNI MAQI CUNATAMI
466 **INGENVI MEMORIA** IGENAVI MEMOR
500 **AMMECATI FILIVS ROCATI** [AM]B[I]CATOS M[A]QI
                                          ROC[A]T[O]S[43]

Earlier part of sixth century:
342 **CVNOCENNI FILIVS CVNOGENI** CUNACENNI [A]VI ILVVETO
378 **BIVADI AVI BODIBEVE** BIVVU[. . .] AVVI BODDIB[. . .]
433 **ANDAGELLI IACIT FILI CAVETI** [A]NDAGELLI MACV CAV[ETI]
431 **DOBITVCI FILIVS EVOLENGI** D[O]V[A]TUCEAS (*sic leg.* see §5.32)

Mid-sixth century:
358 **MEMORIA VOTEPORIGIS PROTICTORIS** VOTECORIGAS
488 **DOBVNNI FABRI FILII ENABARRI** ENABARR


Later sixth century:
364 **QVENVENDANI FILI BARCVNI** (no Ogam)
380 **ICORI** ICORIGAS
489 **FANONI MAQVI RINI** SVAQQUCI MAQI QICI[44]


End of sixth or beg. of seventh century:
484 **IUSTI** [?I]USTI


Early seventh century:
428 **TRENEGVSSI FILI MACV-TRENI** TRENAGUSU MAQI MAQI-TRENI
      **HIC IACIT**


§5.32 Apocope and the first stage in the delabialization of /(kʷ')kʷ'/ are reflected in the spelling **MAC(C)V-**[45] (Ogam MAQI-) on inscriptions dating from the end of the fifth and beginning of the sixth century (341 **MACCV-TRENI**, 442 **MACCV-DICCL**), early to middle sixth century (326 **MACCV-DECCETI**) and early seventh century (428 **MACV-TRENI**), but 341 and 428 have the Ogam spelling MAQI-TRENI. In fact the only example of a corresponding spelling in Ogam is 433 MACV (early sixth century), a spelling which is never found in Ireland. Similarly, the vocalization of /γ/ before *n* is reflected in 449 **SAGRANI** (late fifth or early sixth century), but not in the accompanying Ogam SAGRAGNI, and the same is attested together with syncope in 364 **QVENVENDANI FILI BARCVNI** (⟨ *Qennavindagnī* and *Barracunas* with Latin genitive endings in each, late sixth century). In Ogam vowel affection is reflected in 431 D[O]V[A]TUCEAS (*sic leg.* for Macalister's DOVATACIS, early sixth century, ⟨ *-iās*) and possibly in 362 INIGENA (⟨ *eni-*, end of fifth to beg. of sixth century), but not in 467 ULCAGNI and 446 MAGLICUNAS MAQI CLUTAR. . . (both mid. to late fifth century), 342 CUNACENNI (early sixth century), 358 VOTECORIGAS (mid-sixth century), 380 ICORIGAS (late sixth century) and 428 TRENAGUSU (? for -O, early seventh century). This does not tally at all with the Irish evidence. Similarly, apocope is found in 466 MEMOR (end of fifth to beg. of sixth century) and 488 ENABARR (mid-sixth century) but -I is still written in 428 MAQI-TRENI (early seventh century), and while -S has been dropped in 353 TRENACCATLO (end of fifth to beg. of sixth century, for -CCATO) and 342 ILVVETO (early sixth) it is still written in 358 VOTECORIGAS and 380 ICORIGAS. The delabialization of /kʷ/ is found only in 358 VOTECORIGAS (the first stage is seen in 433 MACV), the vocalization of /γ/ before *n* is unrecorded in Ogam, and there is not a single spelling in the British Ogams corresponding to the syncope category in Ireland. Even the early seventh century 428 TRENAGUSU shows no syncope though the accompanying Latin **TRENEGVSSI** does show obscuration of the composition vowel (on which see further §6.26).

**§5.33** As a dating criterion palaeography is of course inexact as the choice of a particular type of letter might be subject to factors other than the time of writing. Nonetheless, even if allowance be made for that fact, a striking and puzzling contrast still emerges between the two series and it will be clear that the British Ogams cannot be considered a late offshoot of their Irish counterparts (see §4.13 above). The character of the language of the British Ogams might be explained in terms of conservatism, a well-known feature of 'colonial' varieties of language (Jackson, 1950, 206), or of the influence of British and Latin, the latter in particular in the case of the retention of -**I**, or both. The discrepancy between the two series could alternatively be resolved by assuming that the younger forms on the Irish Ogams bear witness to a longer life-span of the cult in Ireland than in Britain, and by revising the chronology of the Irish inscriptions accordingly. That the cult would have survived longer in Ireland than elsewhere is perfectly understandable and precisely what one might expect, and the ANM formula together with the use of the first supplementary character with its vocalic value, both of which are characteristically late in Irish, could then be explained as innovations which came too late for the British series. If so Irish inscriptions with the spellings MAQ and MAC and those with syncopated forms would be considerably later than the beginning of the seventh century if MAQI-TRENI and TRENAGUSU (for -O) are typical for that time (but note the syncope in 364 and the apocope in 466 and 488) and if 358 (VOTECORIGAS, with its Primitive Irish -RIGAS showing neither vowel-affection nor apocope) is correctly dated to the mid-sixth century (see §4.7) this might allow Irish inscriptions of the earliest type to be placed as late as the beginning of sixth century. But an upward revision of the chronology of the Irish Ogams on this scale would present considerable difficulties within Irish itself if the *Amra Choluim Chille* and the poems ascribed to Colmán mac Lénéni are works of the late sixth century (see Greene, 1977, 13 and Thurneysen, 1933). If Thurneysen is correct in arguing that the post-syncope character of these poems is not prejudicial to such an early dating, pre-syncope inscriptions must surely belong to the sixth century at the latest, particularly in view of the fact that the language of Irish poetry is not characteristically innovative. It might be argued of course that with a history of approximately two centuries behind them funerary inscriptions could draw on a traditional orthographical convention in a way in which this new departure in Irish letters could not, so that while late sixth century poetic compositions might avail of the language of the day, funerary inscriptions could and probably would continue to use standard conventional forms. This, no doubt, is the explanation for the -I in MAQ(Q)I and in particular in MACI/**MACCI** (see §5.18) on late inscriptions. But if pre-syncope Ogam spellings were common in the seventh century one might have expected to find more of them in the forms of Irish names recorded in Latin texts written towards the end of the century (but drawing on earlier sources) especially as there is a partial overlap here with Ogam orthographical conventions (see §6.30). In these, however, syncope is the all but universal rule and such pre-syncope spellings as are attested probably derive form earlier sources contemporary with the events or people they record.[46] The upshot, therefore, would seem to be that a revision of the tentative chronology above would present as many difficulties as it would solve.

§**5.34** Post-syncope inscriptions together with some not bearing sequences susceptible to syncope (e.g. 90 CRONUN MAC BAIT, and 256 ANM TEGANN MAC DEGLANN) can be placed in the seventh century without hesitation, and those in which all endings are lost are no doubt the latest of all. Earlier forms of formula words survive, however, and are sometimes accompanied by very late spellings overlapping with the MS record of Early Old Irish. The VEQREQ of 118 (which MacNeill described as the latest form he had noted on the inscriptions, 1931, 42) overlaps with EOI *Fechureg*, *Fechreg* and *Fechrech*, the use of the same symbol for both guttural sounds being particularly significant (McManus, 1986, 2-4), and if RITTECC is the correct reading of the last name on iv (earlier RITTAVVECAS, RITTAVVECC, nos. 250, 211), the form has not only undergone syncope but has lost the post-consonantal /w/ still retained in 221 CATVVIR, 1 **MENUEH** and in some EOI manuscript spellings such as *Bresual* and *Conual* (< *Bressawal-* and *Cunawal-*).[47] There are, however, no orthodox Ogam inscriptions which can be safely placed in the Old Irish period by reference to the criteria mentioned above in §5.20, in particular the diphthongization of *é* and *ó* (see § 6.28) and the obscuration of *e* and *o* in closed unstressed syllables (§6.28). The NUADAT of 204, therefore, were this the correct interpretation of what is on the stone, would be quite exceptional, given its Old Irish *úa* and *a* in the second syllable together with its final T for Ogam D (see §6.30). Jackson (1950, 201) describes it as being at least two hundred years later than the preceding MAQI, but my own examination of the stone and of the supplementary characters in general (see §§7.13ff.) leave me in considerable doubt as to the veracity of Macalister's interpretation.[48]

## CHAPTER SIX

# The Inscriptions: Nomenclature, Morphology, Phonology and Orthography

§**6.1** Apart from their value as a contemporary source for the study of Primitive and Archaic Irish the Ogam inscriptions also constitute our earliest corpus of Irish personal and tribal names[1] and are of intrinsic importance to the study of Irish onomastics. Many Irish names make their first, some their only, appearance in history on the Ogam stones and the inscriptions are a valuable source of information on the relative frequency of name types[2] and on the location of some tribal states in the early period. They also provide useful, though limited, corroborative information on the historical morphology of the noun and on some aspects of historical phonology, and their orthography, the earliest devised for the Irish language, is of considerable interest in its own right.

### NOMENCLATURE

### IRISH PERSONAL NAMES

§**6.2** The personal names in the Ogam corpus, almost all of which appear in the genitive case (see §6.25), can be classified broadly into three types: (A) compounded dithematic names (German *Vollname*), (B) uncompounded monothematic nouns and adjectives with or without a suffix (German *Kurz-* and *Kosename*) and (C) uncompounded dithematic names of the structure inflected noun + dependent genitive or attributive adjective. Of these category (A) appears to have been the most popular, closely followed by (B), which can be further subcategorized into (i) suffixless nouns and adjectives, (ii) diminutives, and (iii) nouns and adjectives with miscellaneous suffixes. In category (C) names containing *Maqqas*-, gen. MAQ(Q)I- as first element are the most frequently attested. This type was very popular at a later date, outnumbering type (A) by a hundred to one,[3] but it seems to have become fashionable rather late in Ogam terms, from about A.D. 600, at a time when, as we have seen, the custom of erecting Ogam stones was already in decline.

As the German term *Kurzname* (lit. 'short-name') implies, the monothematic name is often considered a shortened and derivative form of the compounded dithematic type, though the once generally held theory that the Indo-European name was typically compounded has been challenged.[4] On the Ogam inscriptions, as in Irish nomenclature in general, the categories are not exclusive with regard to name elements, some being found in all three (e.g. ERCA: (A) 196 ERCAVICCAS, (B, i) 178 ERC, (B, ii) 262 ERCAGNI, (C) 175 MAQQI-ERCCIA), others in two (e.g. BRAN: (A) 39 BRANOGENI, (B, i) 116 BRANI, (B, ii) 88 BRANAN). In the following the categories are discussed individually with illustrations for each.

## (A)

§6.3 In compound names some elements may appear in either first or second position, others in one or other of the two. To the former belong two of the most commonly occurring elements in these names, viz. CUNA-, -CUNAS (OI *n*-stem, nom. sg. *cú*, gen. *con*, 'dog, hound'[5]) and CATU-, -CATOS (OI *u*-stem nom. *cath*, gen. *catho*, 'battle'). Examples are:

CUNA- (also CUNO-, CONU-, **CVNO**-): 342 CUNACENNI, **CVNOCENNI**, 199 CUNACENA (for -I?, *Conchenn, Conchand*, Welsh *Cyngen*), 107 CUNAGUSSOS (*Congus*), 3 CUNALEGI, 275 CUNALEGEA, see also xvi CUNALIG. . .? (*Conlang?*), 501 CUNAMAGLI (*Conmál*), 154 CUNAM-AQQI (*Conmac*), 300 CUN[A]NETAS, 176 CONUNETT (*Conda* for *Conne*, gen. *Connath, -ad*), xxi **CVNORIX** (*Conri*, gen. *Conrach*, Welsh *Kynyr, Kynri*), 449 **CVNOTAMI**, CUNATAMI (Welsh *Cyndaf*), 504 CUNAVA[LI] (cp. 468 **CVNOVALI**, Welsh *Cynwal*, EOI *Conual*, later *Conall*), 11 CUNOVATO. ?Cp. also 3 QUNACANOS.

-CUNAS (also -CONAS, -CONA, -CON, -**CVNI**): 134 ASSICONA (*Assiucc*[6]), 86 CLIUCOANAS (?leg. -CUNAS), 191 GAMICUNAS, 159, 252 GLASICONAS (*Glaisiuc*, gen. *Glaschon*), 266 LOBACCONA, xiv MUNIC-CONA (?leg. MURI- = *Muirchú*), 446 MAGLICUNAS, **MAGLOCVNI** (*sic leg.*, Welsh *Meilic, Maelgwn*), 147 OLACON (*Olchú*[7]), 126 VEDACU[NA] (gen. *Fíadchon*), 164 VOENACUNAS. Cp. also 363 **BARCVNI** (*Barrchú*).

CAT(T)U- (also CATA-, CAT-, **CATO**-): 303 CATABAR (*Cathbarr*), 425 **CATOMAG[LI]** (*Cathmál*), 58 CATTUBUTTAS, 46 ?[CAT]TABBOTT (*Cathub*, gen. *Cathboth*, later *Cathbad*), 250 CATTUVVIRR, 268 CAT-TUVIR, 221 CATVVIRR, 184 CATUVIQ (?leg. -R and see Macalister's comments on 250), (*Caither*).

-CAT(T)OS (also -C(C)AT(T)O, -**CATI**): 500 [AM]B[I]CATOS, Latinized **AMMECATI** (*Imchad*, see §6.21), 327 **DVNOCATI** (*Dúnchad*), 19 IVACATTOS (gen. *\*Éochada*[8]), ?496 EBICATO[S], 500 ROC[A]T[O]S, Latinized **ROCATI** (*Rochad*), 353 TRENACCATLO (leg. -CCATO, cp. the accompanying **TRENACATVS**, nom.).

§6.4 Other elements attested in both positions are: BARR (OI *o*-stem *barr* 'top, head, hair of the head'). In first position this does not appear in Ogam but see 363 **BARCVNI** (a Latinization of a post syncope form of *\*Barracunas*,

*Barrchú*; Macalister's Ogam BARCUNI is a reconstruction and an impossible Irish form) and 368 **BARRIVENDI** (son of **VENDVBARI**, a name containing the same elements in reverse order, *Barr(f̣)ind* and *Findbarr*). In final position the element is found in: 303 CATABAR (*Cathbarr*), 488 ENABARR, **ENABARRI**, 298 VEDABAR; BIVA (OI *béo* 'living, alive', Latin *vivus*): 504 BIVAIDONAS, 285 BIVODON (*Béoáed*); 378 BODDIB. . ., **BODIBEVE** ⟨ -**BIVI**?[9] (*Búaidbéo*); DOV (OI *dub* 'black', see further §6.29(c) ): 503 DOVAIDONA (*Dubáed*), 63 DOVALESCI (*Duiblesc*); v BRANADDOV (*Brandub*), 128 (M[A]Q[I]-) CULIDOVI (*Cúldub*); GLAS (OI *glas* 'light green'): 159, 252 GLASICONAS (*Glaisiuc*); 40 INEQAGLAS (*Enechglas*); MAGL[10] (OI *mál* 'prince'): 446 MAGLICUNAS, **MAGLOCVNI** (Welsh *Meilic, Maelgwn*[11]), 427 ?MAGL[I]DUBAR,501 CUNAMAGLI (*Conmál* with the same elements as in 446 reversed). Further examples are 425 **CATOMAG[LI]** (*Cathmál*), and 349 ?**BROHO[MAGLI]** (Welsh *Brochfael*), **VENDVMAGLI** and **ARTHMAIL** (Macalister, 1948, nos. 1028 and 1024) ; VIR (OI *fer* 'man'): 121 VERGOSO (⟨ \**Wiragusōs, Fergus*), 268 CATTUVIR etc. (*Caither*).

§**6.5** In initial position divine names are relatively common: ERCA- (OI *Erc*, gen. *Eirc, Erce*): 93 ERCAIDANA, 196 ERCAVICCAS; RITTA- etc. (OI gen. -*Rithe*): 250 RITTAVVECAS, 211 RITTAVVECC, viii RETAGIN, iv RIT-TECC (EOI gen. *Rethech*, OI *Rethach*); LUG[12] (OI *Lug*, gen. *Logo*): 1 **LUGUAEDON**, 4 LUGADDON (*Lugáed* gen. *Lugedon* etc.), 263 LUGUDECCAS, 286 LUGUDECA, 4 LUGUDEC (*Luguid*, gen. *Luigdech*), 68 LUGUQRIT. . . also 146, ?207 (*Luccreth*), 140 LUGUVVECCA, 221 LUGUV-VEC (gen. *Lugech, Lugach*, see Bergin, 1938a, 235. n1}. Cp. further 279 DENAVEC[A], 1 **MENUEH** (⟨ \**Minawicas*).

§**6.6** Other elements found in initial position are: BRAN (OI *bran* 'raven'): 39 BRANOGENI (*Brangen*), v BRANADDOV (see also i, *Brandub*); QENN- (OI *cenn* 'head'): 2 ?QENUVEN. . . (? = 364 **QVENVENDANI**, *Cenannán*), 192 QENILOC[A]GNI (*Cennlachán, Cellachán*), 170 QENILOCI (*Cellach*); IVA-(OI *éo* gen. *í* 'tree, yew tree'): 19 IVACATTOS (gen. \**Éochada*), 269 IVODACCA, 259 IVAGENI (*Éogan*); TREN- (OI *trén* 'strong'[13]): 353 TRENACCATLO (leg. -CCATO), 428 TRENAGUSU (for -O) **TRENEGVSSI**, 120 TTRENALUGOS (or NETA-TTRENALUGOS, see §6.15, *Trianlug*).

§**6.7** The most frequently occurring elements in final position are: -AIDONAS[14] etc.: 504 BIVAIDONAS, 285 BIVODON (*Béoáed*), 503 DOVAIDONA (*Dubáed*), ?368 DUMELEDONAS, 16 DUNAIDONAS, 93 ERCAIDANA (for -DONA, Thurneysen, 1946, 59 compares *Hercaith*), 4 LUGADDON, 1 **LUGUAEDON** (*Lugáed*): -BUTAS[15] etc.: 58 CATTUBUTTAS, 46 ?[CAT]TABBOTT (*Cathub*, gen. and nom. *Cathboth, Cathbad*), 244 COILLABBOTAS, 21 ?COLLABOTA, 243 COLABOT (*Cóelub*, gen. and nom. *Coílboth, Cóelbad*[16]); -DECAS[17] etc.: 263 LUGUDECCAS, 286 LUGUDECA, 4 LUGUDEC, 108 LUGUDUC for -DEC? (*Luguid*, gen. *Luigdech*); -GENI[18] etc.: 39 BRANOGENI (*Brangen*), 342 **CVNOGENI**[19], 73 DOMNGEN, 233 ?DOMNGINN (*Domungen*), 259 IVAGENI (*Éogan*), 95

MEDDO/UGENI (*Midgen*), viii RETAGIN, 126 SOGINI (gen. *Sogain*); -GUSOS[20] etc.: 70 CUNAGUSOS, 107 CUNAGUSSOS (*Congus*), 428 TRENAGUSU, **TRENEGVSSI**, 121 VERGOSO ( ⟨ *Wiragusōs, Fergus*, gen. *Fergoso*); -RIGAS[21] etc.: 446 CLUTAR[IGAS?], **CLVTORI** (cp. Irish *clothrī* 'famed king', Welsh *Clodri*), xxi **CVNORIX** nom. (*Conri*, Welsh *Kynyr, Kynri*), 380 ICORIGAS, **ICORI**, 118 VEQREQ, 227 VEC[REG/C] (*Fíachri*), 358 VOTECORIGAS, **VOTEPORIGIS** (Gildas voc. *Vortipori*, Old Welsh *Guortepir*); -VALI[22] etc.: 504 CUNAVA[LI], 468 **CVNOVALI** (*Conall*, Welsh *Cynwal*) 375 **TOTAVALI** (*Túathal*, Welsh *Tudwal*), see also *Cathal*, Old Welsh *Catgual*, Gaulish *Catuwalos* and *Domnall*, Old Welsh *Dumngual* (with *Catu-* and *Dubno-* 'world' as first elements); -VICAS[23] etc.: 273 CALUNOVIC[A][24], 279 DENAVEC[A], 196 ERCAVICCAS, 140 LUGUVVECCA, 221 LUGUV-VEC (gen. *Lugech, Lugach*), 1 **MENUEH** (⟨ *Minawicas*[25]), 250 RITTAV-VECAS (*sic leg.*), 211 RITTAVVECC (*sic leg.*), iv RITTECC (gen. *Rethech* ⟩ *Rethach* ⟩ *Ráthach*).[26]

**§6.8** As might be expected, the less frequently attested the elements in compound names in the Ogam corpus the greater the degree of difficulty in explaining them. In 46 DERCMASOC, for example, we appear to have the name later attested as *Dercmossach, Dercmaisech*, but the vocalism of the Ogam is unusual.[27] Given the likely equation 307 GATTAGN[I] = *Gáethán* (cp. *Gáethíne*), with the A variant of the diphthong AI (see §6.28), it is tempting to take 239 GATTEGLAN as a compound of *gáeth* 'wise' + *glan* 'pure', viz *Gáethglan*, though this name is not attested later to my knowledge and the E for the composition vowel is unusual in Ireland (but see §6.26). 131 LITUBIRI may be a compound of *lītus* 'festival, luck' (later *líth*, cp. Gaulish *Litugenus, Litumarus*) and *beryos*, an agentive derivative of *berid* 'carries' (i.e. 'luck-bringer') but one would have expected -BERI (but see 126 SOGINI for -GENI). MacNeill's equation (1909, 357, 358 and 1931, 39, see also Thurneysen, 1946, 192-3) of 124 ANAVLAMATTIAS with *Anblomath*, gen. *Anfolmithe* looks very convincing but his identification of the first element with later *anbal* 'shameless', *ainble* 'excess' is problematic on several grounds if, as seems likely, *anbal* is correctly explained as *an* (negative prefix) + *fíal* 'seemly'. This should appear in Ogam as ANVEL- and one would expect a palatal consonant group on the syncope of the *e* (cp. *ainble*).[28] 94 VEDUCERI is equated by MacNeill (1909, 357, with the reading VEDUCURI) with later *Fidchuire*. If so we might expect the reading VIDUCORI or the like but note VED- in 298 VEDABAR, 126 VEDACU[NA], 408 **VEDOMALI** (or **VEDOMAVI**, Jackson, 1953, 180. n3). MacNeill (1909, 357) equates 302 VALUVI with the later gen. *Fáilbi* but Ogam V for later Irish *b* (= /β/) is restricted to very specific cases (see §6.29(c)) of which this is not one. The equation of 84 ERACOBI with later *Ercbe* (⟨ *Erc* + *bios*, an agentive derivative of *benid* 'strikes', see MacNeill, 1931, 38 and Meyer, 1912a, 800-801 and compare *Lugbe*) is very tempting, but the A here and in the accompanying name ERAQETA, if this contains the same element (§6.19), presents a problem which MacNeill hardly solved with his theory on the archaizing insertion of non-syllabic vowels. These are but a few of many compounds in the Ogam corpus which present difficulties of varying degrees.

§**6.9** Compound names can be classified according to the grammatical category of their respective elements and their relationship to one another. In this classification those of the structure noun + noun are the most common, but noun + adjective, adjective + noun, adjective + adjective and prefix (usually a preposition) + noun are also attested. Examples from the inscriptions are:

(a) noun + noun: 39 BRANOGENI ('raven' + 'he who is born of', or 'son'), 107 CUNAGUSSOS ('hound, wolf' + 'vigour'), 250 CATTUVVIRR ('battle' + 'man'), 73 DOMNGEN ('world' + 'son'), 191 GAMICUNAS ('winter' + 'wolf'), 19 IVACATTOS ('yew' + 'battle'), 259 IVAGENI ('yew' + 'son'), 95 MEDDO/UGENI ('mead' + 'son'), 121 VERGOSO ('man' + 'vigour') and numerous others.

(b) noun + adjective: 378 **BODIBEVE**, BODDIB. . . ('victory' + 'living, alive'), v BRANADDOV ('raven' + 'black'), 128 (M[A]Q[I]-) CULIDOVI ('(hair of the ) back of the head' + 'black'), 46 DERCMASOC (see n6.27), 40 INEQAGLAS ('face' + 'grey, wan'), 2 ?QENUVEN.. (? = 364 **QVENVEN-DANI**, '(hair of the) head' + 'fair' + diminutive suffix). Cp. 368 **BAR-RIVENDI** the reverse of the accompanying **VENDUBARI** ('top, head, hair of the head' + 'fair').

(c) adjective + noun: 504 BIVAIDONAS ('alive' + 'fire'), 503 DOVAIDONA ('black' + 'fire'), 159 GLASICONAS ('grey' + 'wolf'), 353 TRENACCATLO, **TRENACATVS** (? 'strong' + 'battle'), 428 TRENAGUSU, **TRENEGVSSI** (? 'strong'+ 'vigour'). Cp. also 368 **VENDUBARI** ('fair' + 'head').

(d) adjective + adjective: 63 DOVALESCI ('black' + 'sluggish'?), 239 GAT-TEGLAN (? 'wise' + 'pure' see §6.8).

(e) prefix + noun: 500 [AM]B[I]CATOS, **AMMECATI** (Gaulish **AMBICATVS**, *Imchath*, OI *im* 'around'[29], + 'battle'), 500 ROC[A]T[O]S, **ROCATI** (*Rochad*, OI *ro* intensifying prefix + 'battle'), 97 VORRTIGURN, 297 VORTIGURN ( *Foirtchern*, OI *for* 'on, over' + 'lord', Welsh *Gwrtheyrn*), 225 VORUDRAN, 255 VURUDDRANN (*Furudrán*, OI *for* + *odor* 'dun' + -*án* dim. suffix). To this category also belong compounds with the prefixes SO-/SU- and DO-/DU- (OI *so-* 'good', *do-* 'bad') e.g. 126 SOGINI ('good' + 'born one'), 175 DOVINIA (*do-* 'bad' + *bhw-* 'to be' + -*īnyā*, cp. *Suibne* and see Uhlich, 1989, 131). Other possible examples are 281 ?SOVALINI, 158 SUVALLOS, 158 DUCOVAROS, 29 DUCR[I]DDA, 63 ?DUCURI, 171 DUGENNGG[I].

§**6.10.** With regard to the interrelationship of the elements in compounds, including compound names, and their overall meaning a number of constructions can be identified. In Dvandva (or copulative) compounds[30] (noun + noun or adjective + adjective) the two elements are coordinated and the compound can be decomposed into its constituent elements and connected by 'and' (e.g. Irish *sall-c[h]arna* 'bacon and fresh meat', *úacht-gorta* 'cold and hunger' *brat-biad* 'raiment and food', *find-chass* 'fair and curly'; Gaulish *Ollo-dagus* '(he who is) great and good', *Dago-marus* '(he who is) good and great', Irish *Finten* ⟨ *\*windo-senos* '(he who is) fair and old', *Findchóem* '(he who is) fair and beautiful', *Cóemfind* 'beautiful and fair'). In Tatpuruṣa (or determinative) compounds the last member is defined more exactly by the first which stands semantically in an oblique case relationship to it. The first member is a noun, the second a noun or an adjective (e.g. Irish *ár-mag* 'field of slaughter, battlefield', *teglach* 'household', Gaulish *Cingeto-rix* 'king of heroes', Gaulish *Litugenus* 'son (he who is born) of the feast' (or 'luck'), *Litumarus* '(he who is) big in luck'). The descriptive determinative type, Karmadhāraya, is similar to the Tatpuruṣa in that the second element is defined by the first, but here the relationship of the latter to the former is that of a predicate (see below). Bahuvrīhi (or possessive) compounds are adjectival in nature and their final element is a substantive (Irish *nocht-chenn* 'having a bare head', *clár-ainech* 'having a flat face', Gaulish *Carro-tala* 'he who has the forehead of a waggon', *Dubno-tali* 'he who has a deep forehead', Irish *Findbarr* 'he who has a fair head of hair'). In Celtic these elements often appear in inverted position, whence the term 'inverted Bahuvrīhi' (German 'umgekehrtes Bahuvrīhi'), e.g. Irish *bél-remur* 'having a thick mouth (or thick lips)', *folt-lebor* 'having long hair', Gaulish *Penno-vindos* 'he who has a fair head of hair', Irish *Bronnfind* 'she who has a fair bosom'. All of these types are attested in the Ogam corpus, e.g. (a) Dvandva: 63 DOVALESCI '(he who is) black and sluggish', 239 GATTEGLAN '(he who is) wise and pure'; (b) Tatpuruṣa: 501 CUNAMAGLI 'prince of wolves', 300 CUN[A]NETAS 'champion of wolves', 303 CATABAR 'head ('chief') in battle', 250 CATTUVVIRR 'man of battle', xxi **CVNORIX** 'king of wolves'. These might also be classified as Karmadhāraya, viz. 'prince/champion/king like a wolf'; (c) Bahuvrīhi: 107 CUNAGUSSOS '(he who has) the strength of a wolf', 121 VERGOSO '(he who has) the strength of a man', 368 **VENDVBARI** '(he who has) a fair head of hair'; (d) Inverted Bahuvrīhi: 40 INEQAGLAS (eponym *Bresal Enechglas*) 'having a grey face', 368 **BARRIVENDI** '(he who has) a fair head of hair', 46 DERCMASOC '(he who has) an elegant/filthy eye' etc.

The elements which make up personal names give us some insight into the predilections of the society, or the particular class of the society (see n6.2), which produced them. In the case of Celtic they reflect a particular interest in the martial arts, deities, trees and animal life.[31] To any discussion of the lexical content of names, however, one must add the rider that the function of a name is to act as a tag for identifying individuals, and they can perform this function quite satisfactorily without reference to the dictionary meaning of their constituent elements. In this connection Pulgram has noted (1947, 201) that to interpret German *Haduwolf* ('Battlewolf') as 'Like a Wolf in Battle' may be poetic, 'but it is more than questionable that an ancient German gave the meaning of the combination a second thought.'[32] The same is probably true of Irish names and applies as much to (B) and (C) type names as to the compounds.

### (B)

§6.11 B (i): Suffixless nouns and adjectives are quite common in the inscriptions. Examples are: 92 ACTO (*Acht*, related to *aigid* 'drives' ?), 5 ALATTOS, 215 ALATTO (gen. *Alta*, OI *allaid* 'wild'), 90 BAIT (*Báeth, báeth* 'foolish'), 43 BARI (*Barr, barr* 'top, head'), 277 BIR (*Berr, berr* 'short-haired'), 116 BRANI (*Bran, bran* 'raven'), 228 BROCI, 83 BROCC (*Brocc, brocc* 'badger'), 180 BRUSCCOS, 63 BRUSCO (Latinized *Bruscus, brosc* ? 'thunder'), 67 CARI (cp.

47 NETA-CARI = gen. *Nadcaeir*, §6.15, *Car*, gen. *Cair*, related to *caraid* 'loves' ?), 154 CORBBI (*Corb*, related to *corbaid* 'defiles'³³), 104 CORRE (*Corr*, gen. *Corrae, corr* 'heron'), 195 CURCI (*Corc, corc* 'heart' or related to *corcaid* 'reddens, burns'), 119 DALI (*Dall, dall* 'blind'), 197 DEGOS, 122 DEGO (*Daig*, gen. *Dego, daig* 'flame, blaze'), 94 DOMMO (gen. *Domma*), 31 ?DRUGNO, 167 DROGNO (*Drón* gen. *Dróna*³⁴), 178 ERC (*Erc* masc. and fem., gen. *Eirc* and *Ercae*, a divine name, *erc* 'heaven' or *erc* 'cow' ?), 44 IARNI (*Iarn, ïarn* 'iron'), 12 MEDVVI (*Medb* masc. and fem. related to *mid* 'mead'), 171 ?RODDOS (*Rúad* ?, *rúad* 'red' or REDDOS, gen. *Ríata* ?), 57 TRENU (leg. -I?, *Trén, trén* 'strong' or *Trian*³⁵), 206 TIGIRN (*Tigern, tigern* 'lord'), 200 VORGOS (*Fuirg*, gen. *Forgo*), 12 VRAICCI (*Fróech, fróech* 'heather').

§**6.12** B (ii): Diminutives in -AGNI ⟩ -AN(N) (nom. -*agnas*, OI -*án*, gen. -*áin*, see n6.18) formed from both nouns and adjectives are particularly common and this is the most frequently used suffix in these names: 241 BAIDAGNI (*Báetán*),³⁶ 88 BRANAN (*Branán, bran* 'raven'), 316 BROCAGNI, 187 BROCANN, cp. also 372 and 478 **BROCAGNI** (*Broccán, brocc* 'badger', Welsh *Brychan*), 7 CERAN[I] (*Cérán* ⟩ *Cíarán, cíar* 'dark'), 71, 166 COIMAGNI, 434 **COIMAGNI** (*Cóemán, cóem* 'dear, precious'), 63 COL-OMAGNI (*Colmán, colum* 'dove'³⁷), ii COMMAGGAGNI, 145 COM-OGANN, (*Comgán, com-* 'with' + *ag* 'leads', Gaulish *Comagus*), 74 CONANN (*Conán, cú* 'hound, wolf'), 98, 246 CORBAGNI (*Corbán, corbaid* 'defiles'), 41 COVAGNI, ?507 CRON[A]N (*Crónán, crón* 'brown'), 441 **CVRCAGNI** (*Corcán, corc* 'heart' or *corcaid* 'burns') 282 ?DAIMAGNI, 119 DALAGNI (*Dallán, dall* 'blind'), 256 DEGLANN (*Déclán*³⁸), 432 DOVAGNI, **DOBAGNI** (*Dubán, dub* 'black'), 262 ERCAGNI, 376 **ERCAGNI** (*Ercán*, divine name *Erc*), 307 GATTAGN[I] ( *Gáethán* ?, cp. *Gáethíne, gáeth* 'wise'; cp. 239 GATTEGLAN = *Gáethglan* ? and see §6.8), 69 GIRAGNI (*Gerrán*, ?*gerr* 'short (-haired ?)'), i GLANNANI (*Glanán* ?, *glan* 'pure'), 85 GRILAGNI (*Grellán*), 139 ?LAIDANN (cp. 138 LADDIGNI diminutives of OI *laíd* 'poem'?), 236 LOSAGNI, 204 MAGANN, 60, 160, 258 MAILAGNI (*Máelán, máel* 'bald', 'cropped'), 135 MINNACCANNI ((*Huí*) *Mincháin*), 307 MODDAGN[I] (*Múadán, múad* 'noble'?), 61 ?OLAGNI (cp. 147 OLACON ?), 192 QENILOC[A]GNI (*Cennlachán, Cellachán*), 75 ?RODAGNI (*Ródán* ⟩ *Rúadán, rúad* 'red'), 145 RON[A]NN (*Rónán, rón* 'seal'), 449 SAGRAGNI, **SAGRANI** (*Sárán*), 85 SCILAGNI (*Scellán*), vi SILLANN (*Sílán*), 181 TALAGNI (*Tálán, tál* 'adze'), 28 ?TASEGAGNI, 256 TEGANN (*Tecán*, see n6.36), 467 ULCAGNI, **VLCAGNI** (*Olcán, olc* 'evil'), 70 ?VIRAGNI (*Ferán* ?, *fer* 'man' or *Fírán* ?, *fír* 'true'), 304 ?VOCAGNI (*Fúaccán* ?).

A different vocalism is found in the initial syllable of the diminutive suffix in the following (cp. later -*án*, -*ón*, -*én*, -*éne* etc.:³⁹ -IGNI (-INN ?): 215 BAT-TIGNI (*Báethíne, báeth* 'foolish'), 6 QASIGN[I] (*Caissín, Caissíne, cas* 'curly'), 362 CUNIGNI, **CVNIGNI** (Welsh *Cynin* corresponding to Irish *Conán*, 74 CONANN), 138 LADDIGNI (see 139 ?LAIDANN above), 220 ?LLATIGNI (or leg. SATTIGNI?), 287 NISIGNI, 227 OTTINN.

-OGNI (-ONI, -UN, all doubtful): 422 VENDOGNI (*find* 'fair'; the O here could, however, be due to Latin influence, see §5.23), 75 CASONI (*cas* 'curly' but note the absence of G, see §5.27), 90ʹ CRONUN (*crón* 'brown', if not an error for CRONAN).

§**6.13** B (iii): Miscellaneous suffixes to nouns and adjectives.
   (a) Guttural
   -AC (*o*-stem): This is one of the most prolific suffixes in Irish personal names (O'Brien, 1973, 223). An extended form -TAC developed from words ending in *t*: 89 BIRACO (leg. -I, *Berach, Berrach*[40]), 180 CALIACI (*Cailech*), 103 CARR-TTACC (*Carthach*), 30 AVVI GENITTAC[I?] (*Uí Gentig*), 135 MINNAC-CANNI (cp. *Uí Mincháin*, with the suffix expanded by a diminutive), 148 TENAC[I] (cp. *Uí Thenaich*), 172 TOGITTACC (*Toictech*, Macalister, 1949, no. 774 **TOICTHEG**), 198 TOICACI, 310 ?VOBARACI. Cp. 448 **RINACI**, 432 **TIGERNACI**, 399 **TOVISACI** [TO]VISACI.[41]
   -TUC (masc. *ā*-stem and *o*-stem): 431 D[O]V[A]TUCEAS (*sic leg.*, **DOBITVCI**, cp. Macalister, 1949, no. 1022 **DO[BI]TAUCI**), 37 DOVATUCI (*Dubthach, Dubthoch*).[42]
   -OCT (*ā*-stem): 190 GOSSUCTTIAS, 216 GOSOCTEAS, 283 GOSOCTAS (EOI *Gósacht, gúas* 'danger').
   (b) Dental
   -IT(T), -ET(T) (*i*-stem):[43] 10 AMMLLO..TT.. (*Amlongid*?), 317 DOTETTO, 168 IRCCITOS (leg. E-, *Ercaid* or gen. *Irchada*), 172 SAGARETTOS (?leg. SAGR-, *Sáraid* ?), xiv VEDDELLEMETTO, 206 VEDELMET[TO] (*Fedelmid*). If 29 BRAN[I]TTAS and 81 CASSITTAS are to be so read and not with -OS they appear to be consonantal stems (nom. -*its*, gen. -*itos*).
   -IT(T) (*yo*-stem): 155 AKEVRITTI, 246 BIVITI (Latinized *Bitheus*), 81 CALLITI (*Caílte* ?, but see n6.57), 149 CUNITTI, 160 CURCITTI (*Cuircthe*), 231 LOGITTI (cp. 251 LUGUTTI, cp. the derivative *Luigtheg* gen. *Luigthig* with the suffix in (a) above added and see Bergin, 1938a) ). Cp. also 433 CAV[ETI], **CAVETI**, 128, 157 DOVETI.
   -AD, -OD (*yo*-, *yā*-stem): 378 BIVVU. . ., **BIVADI** (*Béodae* ?), i BBRAN-NAD (for -ADI?, *brandae*), cp. 366 **ECHADI**, *Echdae*). Cp. also xiv LOGID-DEAS (*Loígde* ?).
   (c) Nasal
   -IN, -AN (*yo*-stem and *ā*-stem): 153, 157 CATTINI (*Caitne*), 216 MAKINI, 156 DOVVINIAS etc. (*Duibne*). Cp. also 41, 112, 113 LUGUNI (*Luigne*), 46 SEDAN[I] (*Sétnae*), 66 TURANIAS (*Tornae*), 129 VEQOANAI (*Fíachnae* ?).[44]
   -(I)AM (*o*-stem ? and *n*-stem): 185 ?VLATIAMI (*Flaithem*[45]), 300 NETA-SEGAMONAS (*Nad-Segamon*[46]).
   (d) *r*-suffixes (or compounds with *ar* 'before' + the agentive suffix -*yos* ):
   -(U)RI (*yo*-stem): 176 CONURI (my reading was CONe/iRI, *Conaire*), 10 CORRBRI, 106 CORIBIRI (*Coirpre, Cairbre*).

## (C)

§**6.14** Of this category of name the most commonly attested in the inscriptions is the type with MAQ(Q)I- (**MAQVI-, MAC(C)V-**) as its first element. MAQ(Q)I- does not denote a filial relationship to the second element – often a dependent genitive of a divine name or the name of a tree or a word associated

with a trade – but probably originally had the meaning 'devotee' or the like.
MAQ(Q)I-X names can be distinguished from the patronymic MAQ(Q)I X type
either by appearing first on the inscription (e.g. 40 MAQI-CAIRATINI AVI
INEQAGLAS) or by being preceded by MAQQI or some other formula word
(e.g. 170 QENILOCI MAQI MAQI-AINIA MUC. . .). In Britain MAQ(Q)I-
differs from MAQ(Q)I in that the former is not translated by **FILIUS/FILI** (see
§6.22). Examples are: 170 MAQI-AINIA,[47] 40 MAQI-CAIRATINI, 230
?MAQI-CARATTINN (*Mac-Caírthinn, cáerthann* 'rowan tree'), xxi **MAQVI-
COLINE** (*Mac-Cuilinn, cuilenn* 'holly-tree'), ?128 M[A]Q[I]-CULIDOVI (if
the preceding word is a formula word), 66 MAQI-DECCEDDAS, 20 MAQI-
DDECCEDA etc., 440 **MACV-DECETI** etc. (*Mac-Deichet*), 198 MAQI-
DDUMILEAS (gen. *Duimle*), 178 MAQI-ERCIAS, 175 MAQQI-ERCCIA etc.
(*Mac-Erce*), 156 MAQQI-IARI (*Mac-Iair*), 169 MAQI-LIAG (*Mac-Liac, lie,*
gen. *liac* 'stone'), 149 MAQQI-QETTI, v MAQI-QOLI (*Mac-Cuill* ?, *coll*
'hazel-tree'), 198 MAQI-RITEAS, 106 MAQI-RITE (*Mac-Rithe*), 87 ?MAQI-
RODAGNI (*Mac-Rúadáin*), 200 MAQI-TTAL (*Mac-Táil*, Latinized *Mactaleus,
tál* 'adze'), 86 ?MAQI-TRENI, 341 **MACCV-TRENI**, MAQI-TRENI etc.
(*Macc-Tréin, -Tréoin* ?).

§**6.15** MacNeill discussed both NIOTA and NET(T)A in his 1909 paper
(369-70) and took them as the reflexes of two distinct words which fell together
in later Irish, the former meaning 'nephew', 'sister's son'(< nom. *\*nepōts*, gen.
*\*nepotos*, Latin *nepos*), the latter 'champion' (< nom. *\*neit-s*, gen. *\*neit-os*).
Thurneysen (1912, 185) suggested the possibility that the two were in fact one
etymologically, taking NET(T)A as an early contracted form of *\*ne(p)otos*, and
NIOTA as a later variant influenced by the vocalism of the nominative (*\*nius*
< *\*nepōts* or *\*nios* < *\*nepots*). This view was rejected by Pokorny (1915a, 405)
who pointed out that such contractions are younger than apocope and that
NIOTA is continued in the later form *nioth*.
Certainly most of the expected forms of two etymologically distinct words are
attested in Irish but it is difficult to make a hard and fast semantic distinction
between them. From *\*nepōts* and *\*nepotos* we can derive the forms *nio* (= *nïo*
nom. for an expected *\*nïu* < *\*nëūs* < *\*ne(p)ōts*) and *nioth* (= *nïoth*, EOI gen.)
respectively. From *\*neit-s, \*neit-os* come nom. *né, nía*, and gen. *néth* (EOI) >
*níath/níad* (OI), and *nath/nad* in proclitic position (< *neth* < *néth*).[48] Pokorny
attributes the falling together of the two to a functional interchange as elements
in personal names once their original meanings had been obscured in that
capacity (1915a, 407), but in his excellent discussion of the avunculate in early
Irish literature Ó Cathasaigh has demonstrated (1986, 141) that there was an
existing semantic overlap between 'sister's son' and 'champion' which would
have been a strong contributory factor to the confusion.
As for the status of these words in the Ogam inscriptions, NET(T)A generally
occurs in first position (26, 47, 163, 261, 271 and 426) or after the formula word
MUCOI (263, ?292 and 300) or CELI (109). From this one can deduce (see the
comments in §6.14 on MAQ(Q)I- as opposed to MAQ(Q)I that it must stand
in an (A) or (C) name-type relationship to the following element, and the fact
that it is never written NETAS (the full genitive as opposed to the compositional
form) would suggest the former construction. As it happens, however, later

forms of attested names show that the construction is generally of the (C) type, e.g. 426 NETTA-SAGRI (*Nad-Sáir*), 300 NETA-SEGAMONAS (see also 263, ?292, *Nad-Segamon*), 109 NETTA-SLOGI (*Nad-Slúaig*), 271 NETA-VROQI and 26 NETTA-VRECC (-VROECC or -VROICC are possible readings, *Nad-Froích*). In these the proclitic form *Nad-* shows that NET(T)A cannot have had the full stress of the first element in the (A) construction [49] and is therefore best rendered NET(T)A-. Again 47 NETACARI would appear to correspond to the later gen. *Nadcaeir* (for *-cair*, riming with *lindglaein*, for *-glain*, Ó Riain, 1985, 187) demonstrating that it too should be read NETA-CARI. The balance, therefore is in favour of reading 163 NETTA-LAMINACCA and 261 NETA-CUNAS, though in the case of the latter the existence of an (A) type compound with the same elements reversed (300 CUN[A]NETAS, gen. *Connad*, nom. *Conda* for *Conne*, MacNeill, 1909, 349) suggests the possibility that we have a compound of that type here (cp. 446 **MAGLOCVNI**, MAGLICUNAS, Welsh *Meilic, Maelgwn* and 501 CUNAMAGLI, *Conmál*) and it may be continued in *Niadchú*, Ó Riain, 1985, 296, s.n. *Maicnia*). In the case of 47 NETA-CARI NETA CAGI and 120 BROINIENAS KOI NETA TTRENALUGOS the position of NETA (the second in 47) is different to that of the other inscriptions but the balance of probability is in favour of taking it as forming an (A) or (C) type name with the following element (i.e. NETACARI or NETA-CARI and NETATTRENALUGOS or NETA-TTRENALUGOS, the latter alternative in each case being followed in this book). This leaves these inscriptions devoid of a formula word and they must therefore be regarded as possessive genitive types (see §4.6).

Only two forms are attested with the -IO- vocalism, viz. 202 NIOTTVRECC MAQI . . .GNI and 252 DUMELI MAQI GLASICONAS NIOTTA COBRANOR[. . .]. Of these the former bears an obvious similarity to 26 NETTA-VRECC (possibly -VROECC or -VROICC) as well as to 271 NETA-VROQI and all may be variants of an expected *NETA(S)-VROIC(I), (*Nad-Froích*). In the case of 252 it has been suggested (see Charles-Edwards, 1971, 120 and Ó Cathasaigh, 1986, 144-5) that the NIOTTA has the status of a formula word and serves to indicate the kindred membership of *Dumel(i)as*[50] who, as son of a *cú glas* (witness the name GLASICONAS), an immigrant from outside Ireland,[51] would have belonged to the kindred of his mother's brother. The theory is an attractive one though the equation of GLASICONAS with *cú glas* is tentative and the construction is isolated.

§**6.16** The remaining initial components in (C) type names in the inscriptions are: MAILE- (⟨ *mailyās*, ⟩ OI *Máel-*, gen. *Maíle-* 'cropped'). This element is extremely popular later in the names of clerics and it may be significant that the Ogam examples are late): 187 MAILE-INBIR, 235 MOLE-GOMRID (*Máel-Gemrid, Máel-Gaimrid*[52]) and 82 MAILAGURO.[53] VIRI- (OI *Fer-*): 303 VIRI-CORB (*Fer-Corb*).

## GENTILIC NAMES

§**6.17** Tribal and sept or kindred names are introduced in the inscriptions by the formula words MUCOI (or MAQ(Q)I MUCOI) and AVI respectively.[54] The former survives in the manuscript tradition in the form *mocu*, *maccu*, though it would appear to have gone out of use by the beginning of the eighth century, the latter in the form *Aui*, *Uí (H)í* (nom. pl.) + X is typical for septs arising in historical times. The MUCOI/*mocu* formula is followed in the genitive by the name of the eponymous ancestor of the *túath*, the tutelary god or goddess of the tribe, AVI/*Aui* in later times by the name of the historical ancestor of the kindred in the genitive (e.g. *Uí Néill*) but the proportion of feminine eponyms following this element in the early period led MacNeill (1909, 368-9) to suspect that it denoted a remote mythological ancestor, and that it had a religious rather than a genealogical significance (1911, 82-3).

Names following MUCOI and AVI can be of any one of the three types discussed above. Of those which can be identified in later records the AVI type appear in the expected form *Aui* + X while MUCOI names may appear as *mocu/maccu* + X but are more often found in the shape *Corcu* + X, *Dál* + X or X-*r(a)ige*, X-*ne* or X-*acht* . Examples are:

(MUCOI) 250 ALLATO (*mocu Alta/Altai*, *Altraige*[55]), 426 BRIACI/BRECI (*Brecraige*[56]), 81 CALLITI (*Calraige* ?[57]), 106 CORIBIRI (*Dál Coirpri*[58]), 504 CUNAVA[LI] (*Conaille* ⟨ *Conailne*), 156 DOVVINIAS (see also 163, 175, 178, v, *Corcu Duibne*), xiv MUC[O]I LOGIDDEAS (*Corcu Loígde* ?) 41, 307 LUGUNI (*Dál Luigni*), 28 ?MACORBO (see also 272, 283, *Dál Maic-Cuirp* ?[59]), 279 MEDALO (*Dál Mo Dala* ?), 298 ?ODR. . .REA (*Odrige* ?), ?243, 244 QERAI (*Cíarraige*), 57 QRITTI (*Crothrige* ?, see however McManus 1983, 47. n61 on the vocalism of OI gen. *crotho*), 277 ROTTAIS (*Rothrige*[60]), 126 SOGINI (*Corcu Sogain*[61]).

(AVI) 124 AKERAS (*Hí Aicher*), 162 CORBBI (*Uí Chuirbb*), 46 DERC-MASOC (*Uí Dercmossaig*), 30 GENITTAC. . ., (*Uí Gentig*), 40 INEQAGLAS (*Uí Enechglais*), 66 TURANIAS (*Uí Thorna*).

§6.18 Some of the above stones are found in areas corresponding more or less to the location of the relevant tribe or sept in later records. Thus, the *Corcu Duibne* (eponym *Corc Duibne mac Cairpri Músc*, see O'Brien, 1962, 378) occupied territories on the Dingle and Iveragh peninsulas in Kerry and gave their name to the former (Corkaguiney). With the exception of v, which is on the Iveragh peninsula, all DOVINIAS stones are in fact in Corkaguiney. Similarly, the *Altraige* occupied north Kerry and the *Cíarraige* (whence the name Kerry), with whom they were closely associated, were just to the south of them extending as far north as Tralee (see Ó Corráin in Fanning/Ó Corráin, 1977, 17 and 1969, 27). Stones 250 and 243/244 in the baronies of Trughanacmy and Magunihy respectively reflect this geographical alignment. The *Sogain*, a subject people of the Uí Maine in Connacht are located in Galway, Meath and Fernmag (Byrne, 1973, 236-7) but the *Corcu Sogain*, who may have been related, are found among the Benntraige in Co. Cork (O'Rahilly, 1946, 465-6) and it is probable that stone 126 in the barony of East Muskerry in Co. Cork commemorates one of their members. Similarly, as MacNeill points out (1911, 72. n4), the *Conaille* in Muirthemne, Co. Louth, were adjacent to the Isle of Man, where stone 504 is located, and the *Corcu Loígde* were probably present if not dominant in Osraige territory in the Ogam period, and may be recorded on stone xiv. On the other hand the *Luigni* are associated mainly with Connacht

and Meath while inscription 307 is in the barony of Middle Third in Co. Waterford, though 41 in the barony of Upper Kells, Co. Meath, is well located for
the *Luigni* of Meath. So also, whether one equates CALLITI with the *Cailtrige*
(in Connacht) or the *Calraige* (in Westmeath, Longford, Roscommon, Mayo
and Sligo, O'Rahilly, 1946, 81) neither suits the location of stone 81 in the
barony of Kilnameaky, Co. Cork, and the *Dál Coirpri* were one of the primary
divisions of the Lagin whereas stone 106 is in East Muskerry.

The situation is somewhat similar with regard to the sept names. Thus, stones
30 and 124, commemorating members of the *Uí Geintig* (Osraige, see O'Brien,
1962, 114 = 130a30) and the *Uí Aicher* (Éoganacht, see MacNeill, 1911, 83)
respectively are located appropriately in the baronies of Gowran, Co. Kilkenny
and East Muskerry, Co. Cork. On the other hand the *Uí Thorna*, who may
originally have been the leading group among the Cíarraige, occupied the territory between Slíab Lúachra and the sea (. . .*obsides nepotum Torna, que gens
est in medio regionis Chiaraigi, a monte Luchra usque ad mare*, Plummer, 1910,
I, 174) and gave their name to Abbeydorney (Mainistir Ó dTorna) just north
of Tralee, but stone 66 is in the barony of Bear in Co. Cork, and the *Uí Dercmossaig* were a Leinster sept located at Dublin (*hic/oc Áth Cliath* O'Brien,
1962, 44 = 121a24, 69 = 124a13) while stone 46 is in the barony of Shelburne
in Co. Wexford. Similarly, the *Uí Enechglais* are located on the east coast of
Co. Wicklow, near Arklow, a considerable distance from Painestown in the
barony of Duleek Lower, Co. Meath, where stone 40 was found, though in this
case it has been argued (Byrne, 1973, 138 and 142) that the relegation of the *Uí
Enechglais* to the politically insignificant area of the Wicklow coast may have
been relatively recent.

Further examples of gentilic names unidentified as such are:
(MUCOI) 285 ATAR, 98 ?COROTANI, 286, 289 ?CUNEA, -IA, 306
DONM[A], 118 GLUNLEGGET, 269 IVODACCA, 266-7 LUGA, 309
?MEUTINI, 263 NETA-SEGAMONAS (see also ?292, 300, *Nad-Segamon*,
*-Segamain*), 34 ?RINI, ii MU[CO]I SAMMNN, 55 ?TEMOCA, 197 TOICAKI
(see also 198, 200), 26 ?TRENALUGGO, 218 ?TUCACAC (?leg. TUCACI =
TOICACI), 217 UDDAMI, 302 VALUVI, 70 ?VIRAGNI, 303 VIRI-CORB
(*Fer-Corb*).

(AVI) 7 ?ATHECETAIMIN, 43 BARI (*Barr*), 378 **BODIBEVE**, BODDIB
(*Búaidbéo*), 282 ?DAIMAGNI, 230 ?DALAGNI (*Dallán*), 63 ?DUCURI, 19
IVACATTOS      (gen.      *Éochada*),      xiv      MUNICCONA,      270
?NEAGRACOLINEA, 288 ?OGATOS, 275 QVECI, ?3 QUNACANOS, 37
TULOTANAGIA, ?185 ?VLATIAMI.


§6.19 In early Irish nomenclature the custom of father and son having the same
name was avoided (see MacNeill, 1910, 83. ngg) but an element in the father's
name might be repeated in that of his son and this is found quite often in the
genealogies (e.g. *Fer-Corp m. Cormaic m. Coirpri*, all names containing the element *corb*, O'Brien, 1962, 630). Examples in the inscriptions are: 500
[AM]B[I]CATOS M[A]QI ROC[A]T[O]S, **AMMECATI FILIVS ROCATI**,
176 CONUNETT MOQI (leg. MA-?) CONURI, 342 **CVNOCENNI FILIVS
CVNOGENNI**, CUNACENNI [A]VI ILVVETO (see §4.11), 119 DALAGNI
MAQI DALI, 84 ERACOBI MAQI ERAQETA (*sic leg.*, for ERC-, ERQ-?),

262 ERCAGNI ?MAQI-ERCIAS, 4 LUGADDON MAQI LUGUDEC, 146 LUGUQRIT MA[QI] QRITT[I], 47 NETA-CARI NETA-CAGI (see §6.15). The same is found with AVI names in 3 CUNALEGI ?AVI QUNACANOS (if QUNA- = CUNA and AVI is correct) and 378 **BIVADI AVI BODIBEVE**, BIVVU. . . AVVI BODDIB . . . .

## LATIN NAMES

§6.20 As might be expected Latin names are more common in the British inscriptions than in those in Ireland but a significant number are recorded in the latter. In the following all inscriptions numbered above 317 are in Britain: 265 AMADU (*Amatus*), 430 **ETTERNI**, ETTERN[I] (*Aeternus*), 466 **INGENVI**, IGENAVI (*Ingenuus*), 484 **IVSTI**, [I?]USTI (*Iustus*), 470 **LATINI**, LA[TI]NI (*Latinus*), 16, 188 MARIANI (*Marianus*), 20 MARIN (*Marinus*), 404 **MARTI** (*Martius*, the relevant part of the accompanying Ogam is missing), 409 **PVMPEIVS**, P[.]P (*Pompeius*), 56 SAGITTARI (*Sagittarius*, see §3.2), 399 **SIMILINI**, S[I]B/M[I]L[I]N[I] (*Similinus*), 327 **TVRPILLI**, TURP[I]L[LI] (*Turpillius*), 430 **VICTOR**, [VIC]TOR (*Victor*), 445 **VITALIANI**, VITALIANI (*Vitalianus*), 166 VITALIN (*Vitalinus*). Note also the name 63 COLOMAGNI (but not 193 COLMAN which is a very doubtful reading) which appears to be a derivative through British (see n6.37) of Latin *columba* 'a dove' (whence *Colmán*, *Columbus*, *Columbanus* etc.).

## BRITISH NAMES

§6.21 Owing to the structural congruence of British and Primitive Irish it is sometimes difficult to establish whether a given name is British or Irish in origin or belongs independently to both. An example is 500 **AMMECATI**, [AM]B[I]CATOS (Gaulish *Ambicatus*), the Primitive Irish form of which would be *Imbicatōs* (gen.). Jackson notes (1953, 173. n1) that there is no room on the stone for the restoration of I and suggests British influence in the vocalism of the initial syllable (viz. *am* for *im*). This influence, however, clearly does not extend to the cluster -mb- which became -mm- early in British (whence the spelling **AMM**-, see n6.37) but later than the Ogam period in Irish (whence the B of the Ogam). 342 **CVNOCENNI** and CUNACENNI (Welsh *Cyngen*, Irish *Conchenn*) is also indefinite in this regard as are 446 **CLVTORI**, CLUTAR[IGAS?] (Old Welsh *Clodri*, Irish *clothrī* 'famed king', a cpd. containing *clutan*, Welsh *clod*, Irish *cloth* 'fame') and 468 **CVNOVALI**, 504 CUNAVA[LI] (Welsh *Cynwal*, Irish *Conall*).

A number of names, on the other hand, would appear to be British rather than Irish in form. 446 **MAGLOCVNI** (*sic leg.*), MAGLICUNAS appears in Welsh in two forms, *Meilic* (< nom. *Maglocū*) and *Maelgwn* (< gen. *Maglocunas*), but not in Irish though the same elements in reverse order are attested in *Conmál* (501 CUNAMAGLI and see §6.15 and MacNeill, 1910, 155. nw). Similarly 362 **CVNIGNI**, CUNIGNI is a diminutive of the word for 'hound, wolf' reflected in Welsh *Cynin* but not in Irish where the vocalism of the dim. suffix was -*agnas* (*Conán*, 74 CONANN), and 449 **CVNOTAMI**, CUNATAMI is continued in Welsh *Cyndaf* but not in Irish.

§**6.22** It should be noted that both Irish and British names generally undergo Latinization in respect of their case-endings when they appear in the Latin alphabet. This is not obvious when the name belongs to the *o*-stem class as the ending -*ī* was shared by all three languages. In 488 ENABARR, however, which appears to be a generation older than the accompanying **DOBVNNI FABRI FILII ENABARRI** it is clear that the -I in the latter must be explained as due to Latin, since it has been dropped in the earlier Ogam. Similarly as 364 **QVENVENDANI** has undergone syncope the final -**I** is unlikely to be Irish and cannot be in the case of the accompanying name **BARCVNI** (see below). More obvious examples are those involving names belonging to other stem-classes in Irish and British which are Latinized with -**I**, irrespective of the nature of the native ending. Examples are *i*-stems, Irish gen. -O(S), 500 **AMMECATI, ROCATI**; *u*-stems, Irish gen. -O(S), 428 **TRENEGVSSI** (the accompanying TRENAGUSU is probably an error for -O); consonantal stems, Irish gen. -(A)(S), 446 **MAGLOCVNI**, 364 **BARCVNI**, 440 **MACV-DECETI**, and the numerous examples of -**RI** for Irish -RIGAS, 446 **CLVTORI**, 380 **ICORI** together with -**RIGIS** in 358 **VOTEPORIGIS** etc. In view of this it would be inadvisable to take xxi **CVNORIX** as evidence for the persistence of the group *chs* (⟨ -*gs*) in Primitive Irish. This too is probably a Latinization, which does not extend to the vowel preceding the ending (cp. **VOTEPORIGIS** not -**REGIS**).

The Irish word for 'son' is almost invariably replaced by **FILIUS, FILI(I)** and the fact that MAQ(Q)I- in (C) type names is not so translated (e.g. 440 **MACV-DECETI** not *__FILI-DECETI__, see §6.14) is clear evidence that it was not felt to have that meaning. Exceptions to the translation of MAQ(Q)I are xxi **MACVS**, albeit with a Latin case-ending, and 489 **FANONI MAQVI RINI**, and as already noted (nn4.48 and 51), Irish AVI was borrowed into the Latin in 378 **BIVADI AVI BODIBEVE**.

## MORPHOLOGY

§**6.23** The parallels between the morphology of the Irish noun and its counterparts in other Indo-European languages have been obscured considerably by the workings of apocope (§5.15), which resulted in the loss or reduction of many final syllables. With the aid of the comparative method, however, it is possible to reconstruct those endings by working backwards from Old Irish. By observing the timbre of final consonants, the quality of preceding vowels and the effects on a following word one can establish with reasonable certainty what, in any given case, the original ending in Primitive Irish was. Thus, given the root *wir-* (Latin *vir* 'man') and the OI nom. sg. *fer* 'man' with its final neutral consonant, its *e* lowered from *i* and the fact that it neither lenites nor nasalizes a following closely connected word, it is possible to reconstruct its PI form as either *__wiros__ or *__wiras__ and the Old Latin second declension nom. sg. ending -*os* (Classical Latin -*us*) together with Greek -*os* and Continental Celtic -*os* confirm the former, though as we have seen (§5.11) this would have become -*as* in Primitive Irish. Similarly, the OI gen. sg. *fir*, which has a palatal final consonant, retains the root vowel *i* unchanged and lenites the initial of a following closely connected word must go back to PI *wiri*, *wirī* or *wire* and the gen. sg.

*cuill* (nom. *coll* 'hazel' ⟨ PI *collas* ⟨ *coslos*) shows by its *u* that *-e* must be excluded. A comparison with Latin *virī* again confirms one of our possible reconstructions and it is confirmed also by Ogam -I. Thus, even without the evidence of the Ogam inscriptions, which are our only written source for pre-apocope Irish, the morphology of the Irish noun can be reconstructed and compared with its Indo-European counterparts, but it is useful and encouraging to find our reconstructions confirmed on stone, especially with more troublesome case-endings than the ones cited above.

§6.24 Celtic (with the exception of Celtiberian) and Latin generalized *-ī* as the gen. sg. ending of *o*-stems at the expense of IE *-os(y)o*, reflected in Sanskrit *-asya*. The ending- *ī* was shortened in PI to *-i* and after vowel-affection it, together with *-e*, brought about the second palatalization (§5.19) before being lost by apocope. No merger of *-i* and *-e* before apocope comparable to that posited before syncope (see §5.17) is reflected in Ogam[62] where the ending appears as -I or has disappeared completely, e.g. -AGNI ⟩ -AN(N), MAQ(Q)I ⟩ MAQ ⟩ MAC etc. The ending has been lost in 103 CARRTTACC, 303 CATABAR, 268 CATTUVIR, 73 DOMNGEN, 233 ?DOMNGINN, 145 QRIMITIR, 200 TOICAC, 206 TIGIRN etc.

The *yo*-stem gen. sg. ending differed from that of the *o*-stems only in the presence of *y*, viz *-yī* which became *-iyī* in Primitive Irish (see §5.15). That the distinction between the two was always maintained is clear from the fact that they have different reflexes in Old Irish where the *yo*-stem ending appears as *-(a)i* as compared with the complete loss of original *-ī*. In Ogam, however, where both are written -I, this distinction is never brought out except inasmuch as post-apocope *yo*-stem forms retain -I, and Kim McCone has suggested to me that the explanation may be that *-ī* had first become *-i* (by shortening in accordance with §5.13) and then *-iyī* ⟩ *-ī*, which survived in the same was as an original long vowel followed by /h/ (§5.13). Examples of *yo*-stems are (MS equivalents are in the gen.): AVI (*aui*), 215 BATTIGNI (*Baíthíni*), 246 BIVITI (*Bíthi*), 10 CORRBRI (*Coirpri*), 160 CURCITTI (*Cuircthi*), 113 LUGUNI (*Luigni*), 46 SEDAN[I] (*Sétnai*) etc.

The expected PI gen. sg. of *ā*-stems would be *-ās*, which would give *-a* in Old Irish, not the attested *-(a)e*. In Latin *-ās* was abandoned for a hybrid of the *ā* of the stem and the *-i* of the *o*-stem genitive in the form *-ai* (Classical Latin *-ae*) and the identity of the Old Irish gen. sg. of *ā*-stems and *yā*-stems (e.g. *túaithe*, gen. of *túath* 'tribe' and *guide* gen. of *guide* 'prayer') points to a merger of the two in Primitive Irish involving the adoption by the *ā*-stems of the *yā*-stem ending *-yās*, reflected in Ogam -IAS (⟩ -EAS ⟩ -EA ⟩ -E). Examples from the *ā*-stems are: 431 D[O]V[A]TUCEAS (*Dubthach* gen. *Dubthaige*), 190 GOSSUCTTIAS (*Gúasacht* gen. *Gúasachtae*), 125 MAQI-ERCIAS (*Mac-Erc(a)e*, nom. *Erc*), 198 MAQI-RITEAS (*Mac-Rithe*) 187 MAILE-INBIR (*Maíle-*, nom. *Máel-*). Among *yā*-stem genitives are: 170 MAQI-AINIA (*Mac-Áine*?, nom. *Áine*), 156 DOVVINIAS (*Duibne*, gen. *Duibne*), xi LOGIDDEAS (*Loígde*, gen. *Loígde*) etc.

In accordance with the observed treatment of long vowels followed by *s* in final unstressed syllables (see §5.13 and §5.15), the ending *-yās* should have yielded *-ea* after a palatal consonant (*túaithea* ⟨ *tōtiyās*) and *-a* after a neutral one (*Erca* 〈 *Erciyās*) in Old Irish (see n5.23). The ending -A is in fact attested in Ogam (e.g. 169 MAQI-ERCA and 82 MAILAGURO as analysed by Meyer[63]) and -AS is found in 283 GOSOCTAS as compared with 190 GOSSUCTTIAS and 216 GOSOCTEAS, but it would be unwise to base any inferences on these in view of the overwhelming testimony of Old Irish and Ogam in general. As noted already no difference in the treatment of long and short vowels in final syllables is recoverable when these were preceded by *y*.

In Old Irish the *i*-stems and *u*-stems have the same gen. sg. ending -*o* and -*a*, the former of which is the older and must derive from Primitive Irish -*ōs*. This can be explained in the case of the *u*-stems as deriving from -*ous* or -*eus* (cp. Latin gen. *manūs*, with -*ūs* 〈 -*ous*) but it is unlikely that an *i*-stem gen. ending -*ois* or -*eis* would have given Primitive Irish -*ōs*, so that one must assume borrowing from the *u*-stems. The ending appears in Ogam as -OS, 〉 -O.[64] Examples are : *i*-stems: 215 ALATTO (*Allaid*, gen. *Alta*), 197 DEGOS (*Daig*, gen. *Dego*), xiv VEDDELLEMETTO (*Fedelmid*, gen. *Fedelmeda*), 200 VORGOS (*Fuirg*, gen. *Forgo*); *u*-stems: 180 BRUSCCOS, 63 BRUSCO, 70 CUNAGUSOS (*Congus*, gen. *Congusa*), 121 VERGOSO (*Fergus*, gen. *Fergoso*), 120 TTRENALUGOS (gen. *Trianlugo*).

The IE consonantal stem gen. sg. ending -*os* is reflected in the neutral quality of the final consonant in Old Irish (e.g. OI *ríg*, later *ríogh* 〈 *\*rīgos*, *con* 〈 *\*kunos* etc.). In Primitive Irish -*os* became -*as* (see §5.11) and the ending appears in Ogam as -AS, which becomes -A and then disappears by apocope. Examples are: Lenited guttural stems: -VICAS 〉 -VECAS 〉 -VEC 〉 -EC: 196 ERCAVICCAS, 250 RITTAVVECAS, 211 RITTAVVECC, 1 **MENUEH**, iv RITTECC; -DECAS 〉 -DECA 〉 -DEC: 263 LUGUDECCAS, 286 LUGUDECA, 4 LUGUDEC; -RIGAS 〉 -REC: 380 ICORIGAS, 118 VEQREQ. Unlenited guttural stems: 169 MAQI-LIAG. Dental stems: -BUTAS 〉 -BOTAS 〉 -BOTA 〉 -BOT: 58 CATTUBUTTAS, 244 COILLABBOTAS, 21 ?COL-LABOTA, 243 COLABOT; NETA- (〈 *\*neitos*): 426 NETA-SAGRI, 300 NETA-SEGAMONAS etc., also 300 CUN[A]NETAS. Other examples are 251 VELITAS, 81 CASSITTAS, 29 BRAN[I]TTAS if the last two are not for -OS. Unlenited dental stems: 66 MAQI-DECCEDDAS. Nasal stems: -CUNAS 〉 -CONAS 〉 -CONA 〉 -CON: 191 GAMICUNAS, 252 GLASICONAS, 134 ASSICONA 147 OLACON etc.; -DONAS 〉 -DONA 〉 -DON: 504 BIVAIDONAS, 503 DOVAIDONA, 4 LUGADDON. Cp. also 151 BROIN-IONAS (= ? 120 BROINIENAS), 161 INISSIONAS, 147 MOINENA, 450 OGTENAS, 300 NETA-SEGAMONAS. Stems in *r*: 124 AKERAS?[65]

An exceptional ending -AI, -AIS is found in a number of names: 89 BOGAI, 115 ?CULRIGAI, 152 LUBBAIS, ?243, 244 QERAI, 311 QETAIS (cp. 248 . . .QET[IA?]S, 274 [QE]TTEAS), 277 ROTTAIS, 129 VEQOANAI. See also 281 . . .NAI and 36 . . .TT[AI]S, and note that 84 ERAQETAI is corrected to ERAQETA by O'Kelly in his review of the *Corpus*). Gray (1929) takes -AIS as deriving from -*ois*, the IE gen. sg. of *i*-stems transferred to *yo*-stems, but this seems highly unlikely and the evidence is too fragmentary to justify assuming the existence of a distinctive case ending. Harvey (1987, 60) has pointed out that 152 LUBBAIS can be read LU[BB]IAS and it is possible that the other cases of -AI, -AIS are errors for -IA(S) (on which see MacNeill, 1931, 38, 42).

**§6.25** In Britain several Latin inscriptions bear the commemorand's name in the nominative and the nominative of the formula word is reproduced in Ogam in the case of 362 AVITTORIGES INIGENA CUNIGNI (**AVITORIA FILIA CVNIGNI**) as the expected gen. sg. of the word for 'daughter' would be *INIGENIAS (Latin **FILI(A)E**). AVITTORIGES, on the other hand, cannot be nominative and Jürgen Uhlich has suggested to me that it is probably an error for -EAS (gen. see §2.2). If so, as he points out, the syntactical error might be explained as due to the lapidary imitating the Latin formula having already used the traditional genitive in the commemorand's name. That he was influenced by the Latin inscription is clear from the disposition of the inscription on the stone (see §4.13 and for a syntactical error involving the genitive with the **HIC IACIT** formula, see n4.53). Similarly, in the case of 466 IGENAVI MEMOR, **INGENVI MEMORIA** the Ogam reproduces the Latin nominative together with its preposed genitive. The nominative is also found, as already noted, in the case of the Wroxeter stone (xxi **CVNORIX MACVS MAQVI COLINE**) but there are no diagnostic examples of this practice from Ireland. Macalister takes 145 QRIMITIR RON[A]NN MAQ COMOGANN, which he considers a Christian 'signature' rather than a pagan epitaph, to be a nominative construction but this is out of the question in view of the -IR of the first word, which would be -ER in the nominative. The other words are not diagnostic as palatalization, the only means of distinguishing the genitive from the nominative in this instance, is not indicated in Ogam (see §5.19). A possible case of the nominative in Ireland is 265 AMADU (the Latin name *Amatus*) and the word ANM, of course, is nominative in form (the genitive would be *ANMES or *ANME). Otherwise the genitive is the rule (23 MAQV[A]S is very doubtful and 3 CUNALEGI is a genitive not an *i*-stem nominative). In 160 TRIA MAQA MAILAGNI we appear to have an instance of the gen. pl. (-*om* ⟩ -*an*; -*an m*- ⟩ -*am m*- ⟩ -*a mm*- written -A M-, see n5.38).

**§6.26** The following expected forms of the composition vowel are found in Ogam:

A in *ā*-stems (⟨ *ā*[66]), *o*-stems and consonantal stems (⟨ *o*): 196 ERCAVICCAS, 250 RITTAVVECAS; v BRANADDOV, 40 INEQAGLAS; 107 CUNAGUSSOS, 3 CUNALEGI etc.

U in *u*-stems: 58 CATTUBUTTAS, 250 CATTUVVIRR, 263 LUGUDECCAS, 131 LITUBIRI, 115 ?MENUMAQ[I] (see Uhlich, 1989, 132. n11).

I in *i*-stems: 378 **BODIBEVE**, BODDIB. . ., 191 GAMICUNAS, ?vi VAT-TILLOGG[O].

The composition vowel A is regularly elided before a following vowel: 504 BIVAIDONAS (⟨ *Biwa-aidonas*), 16 DUNAIDONAS (⟨ *Dūna-aidonas*) 93 ERCAIDANA, for -DONA (⟨ *Erca-aidonas*). In this position one might have expected U to become /w/ (cp. 1 **LUGUAEDON**, = /Luɣwaiδon/?) but it appears to have been dropped (or subsequently lost as in iv RITTECC ?) in 4 LUGADDON (⟨ *Lugu-aidonas*, gen. *Lugadon*, *Lugedon* etc.). See further the remarks on DOV- for *Dubu-* (§6.29(c)).

Owing to its weak unstressed position the composition vowel became obscured and this is reflected in a number of spellings, most of which point to difficulty with the sound /ə/ (< /a/ or /o/, including /o/ < /u/). Examples are:

O for A (= /ə/ or rounded /ə/, see §5.23): 39 BRANOGENI, 273 CALUNOVIC[A], 98 ?COROTANI, 11 CUNOVATO, 84 ERACOBI (? for ERCOBI), 179 . . .ETORIGAS, 129 EQOD.., 186 EQODDI?, 269 IVODACCA, 141 O]GGODIKA, 313 ?OVOMAN[I], 129 VEQOANAI. In 285 BIVODON (cp. 504 BIVAIDONAS) we may have a rounding of the first element of a diphthong (viz. = *Biwoidon < *Biwa-aidonas with O for OI, see §6.28) or a reduction of AI to /ə/ as is probably the case in 4 LUGADDON (see §6.28).

O for U (= /i/): 95 MEDDOGENI, though there is a possibility that U should be read here. *Dubu- appears to have undergone thematicization to dubwo-, dubwa-, whence DOV(A)- (see Uhlich, 1989 and below §6.29(c) ).

I for A (= /ə/): 128 (-)CULIDOVI, 446 MAGLICUNAS (**MAGLOCVNI**), 427 ?MAGL[I]BUBAR, 192 QENILOC[A]GNI, 170 QENILOCI. In 134 ASSICONA the later form *Assiucc* appears to suggest that the I is correct and this is probably the case too in 159, 252 GLASICONAS (*Glaisiuc*). Note also 368 **BARRIVENDI**, 341 SALICIDUNI, 130 ?SECIDARI, 113 VEQIKAMI.

E for A (= /ə/): 239 GATTEGLAN. Cp. also 400 **SENEMAGLI**, 428 **TRENEGVSSI** (TRENAGUSU) and 368 DUMELEDONAS with E for AI (= /ə/ ?, see §6.28).

U for A (= /ə/): 176 CONUNETT, 2 ?QENUVEN. . . . The readings 211 RITTUVVECC and 250 RITUVVECAS have been corrected to RITTAVVECC and RITTAVVECAS (O'Kelly/Kavanagh, 1954, 108). Cp. further 368 **VEND-VBARI**.

A for O (= /ə/, lowered from U): 303 CATABAR, 46 [CAT]TABBOTT.

Similar confusion is also found as already noted (§5.7) in weak unstressed non-composition syllables, e.g. 145 COMOGANN (for COMAGANN, cp. ii COMMAGGAGNI, *Comgán* < *com-ag-), 30 GENITTAC. . . (later gen. *Geintig* not *Gintig), 172 TOGITTACC (later nom. *Toicthech* not *Tuicthech), xiv LOGIDDEAS (for *Loigadeas, Loígde ?).

## FORMULA WORDS

§6.27 ANM is the apocopated nom. sg. of PI *anmen, gen. *anmēs, OI *ainm*, gen. *anm(a)e* (neuter *n*-stem) 'name' cognate with Latin *nomen*, Sanskrit *nāma* etc. (Pokorny, 1959, 321). For its use in Ogam and parallels in Latin see Vendryes (1955). In later Irish the phrase *ainm n-oguim* is used of an Ogam inscription bearing a personal name (see §8.8).

AVI is the gen. sg. of PI nom. *awiyas (> *auweyas > *auwe > OI *aue* > óa/úa, Ó, gen. awiyī > *auwiyi > OI aui > uí, Í, yo-stem) 'grandson, descendant' cognate with Latin *avus, avia* 'grandfather, grandmother' (see Pokorny, 1959, 89 and Ó Cathasaigh, 1986, 137ff.). The meaning 'grandson' cannot be confirmed (e.g. by association with a related inscription) for any instance in Ogam and the proportion of feminine eponyms following AVI lead MacNeill to suppose that it denoted a remote descendant, probably from a mythological ancestor (1909, 368-9) and had religious rather than genealogical significance (1911, 82-3). Certainly we appear to have a difference in usage between Ogam and later Irish as membership of a sept (as distinct from the surname *Ó X*) in the later period is indicated by a plural genitive or dative construction, not by the singular genitive. MacNeill indeed proposed interpreting AVE QVECEA as gen. pl. but this reading is corrected in the *Corpus* to (275) AVI QVECI, which appears to be sg.

CELI is the gen. sg. of PI *cēlias* (OI *céle*, gen. *céli* 'companion, client', *yo*-stem) which must be cognate with Welsh *cilydd* 'fellow, companion' though the vocalism of the latter, if it derives from **keilios* (Pokorny, 1959, 539-40) presents a problem. On the use of *Céle* in (C) type names in later Irish see O'Brien (1973, 230).

INIGENA is attested only once (362; 439 INGEN should be ignored) and is the PI nom. sg. of the regular Irish word for 'daughter' (OI *ingen*, gen. *ingine*, *ā*-stem) deriving from **eni-genā* 'she who is born within' (compare the Gaulish personal name *Enigenus*, Evans, 1967, 206 and see Pokorny, 1959, 312 s.v. *en* etc. 'in' and 375 s.v. *gen* etc. 'born'). The form has undergone raising and renders the Latin nominative FILIA (see §6.25).

KOI, which is invariably written with the first supplementary character and is alone among formula words in not being attested later, has been explained as a word defining locality, 'here', analogous to **HIC IACIT** in the British inscriptions though it is never used in these. Marstrander (1911) takes it to be an old adverbial locative from the pronominal stem **ke*, **ko*, standing in the same ablaut relationship to later Irish *cé* 'here' (⟨ **kei*) as Latin *hūc* (⟨ **ghoi-ce*) to *hīc* (⟨ **ghei-ce*). See further n4.13.

MAQ(Q)I (MAQ, MAC, MACI, **MACCI** etc.), the most frequently occurring word on the inscriptions, is the gen. sg. of PI **maqqas* (the nom. in Latinized form is found in xxi **MACVS**, 23 MAQV[A]S is a doubtful nom.), OI *macc* gen. *maicc* (*o*-stem), the standard Irish word for 'son', cognate with Welsh *mab* (earlier *map*) 'son' and differing from it only in the (hypocoristic?) gemination of the /kʷ/ (*macc* ⟨ **makʷkʷos*, *map* ⟨ **makʷos*). Pokorny (1959, 696) relates the word to **maghos*, **maghu-*, whence OI *mug* 'slave'.

MEMOR, like INIGENA, is attested only once (466 **INGENVI MEMORIA**, IGENAVI MEMOR; in 358 **MEMORIA VOTEPORIGIS PROTICTORIS**, VOTECORIGAS it is not rendered in the Ogam) and is a loanword from Latin *memoria* in the sense 'memorial, tombstone' used in Christian Roman epitaphs in Italy and North Africa (see Nash-Williams, 1950, 10). It appears to be nominative (see §6.25) and if the final -R is palatal, a quality not indicated in Ogam (see §6.30(c) ), it would correspond in form to Old Irish *mebuir* 'memory' (with *b* (= /β/) ⟨ *m* (= / =μ/) by dissimilation), though semantically it is closer to *mem(m)ra* 'a monument over the dead, a tomb' (see McManus, 1983, 39. n45).

MUCOI (*mocu*, *maccu*) is exceptional among formula words in being confined in later Irish (i.e. up to the end of the seventh century, when it appears to have died out) to the stereotype sequences *X mocu Y* and *mocu Y* (on the latter see MacNeill, 1909, 367), that is it does not occur independently. Owing to the tendency of words in this position to undergo reduction[67] and to the fact that *mocu*, *maccu* is indeclinable[68] it is not possible to say with certainty whether *mocu* continues Ogam MUCOI – which one assumes is a genitive – as a petrified form, or derives from an original unattested nominative. MacNeill (1909, 367) regards *mocu* as a collective term, taking it as a partitive genitive when it follows a personal name, and his original contention (1907, 44) that *mocu* continued MAQI MUCOI (or *maq(as) mucoi*) in contracted form is repeated by O'Brien (1956, 178 and 1973, 218) though MacNeill himself had already revised this view in 1909 (367. n2).

If *mocu* derives directly from MUCOI and the spellings MUCOI, MOCOI (197), MOCO (303) represent the line of development MUCOI would appear to have been a trisyllabic form which underwent lowering of the U and apocope of the final -I. If so -OI can hardly have represented a diphthong, whether *oi* or *ōi*, and this conclusion is supported by the known reflexes of these in Irish (cp. the *o*-stem nom. pl. *fir* ⟨ PI *\*wiri* ⟨ *\*wiroi* and the *o*-stem dat. sg. *fiur* ⟨ PI *\*wirū* ⟨ *\*wirūi* ⟨ *\*wirōi*). The etymology of MUCOI is unknown[69] but there can be little doubt that it serves to indicate membership of a *túath* or gens and is followed by the name of the eponymous ancestor (cp. Adamnán's use of the word *gens* in *Lugbeus gente mocu Min* beside *Lugbeus mocu Min* and see MacNeill, 1907, 42). The formulae X MUCOI Y and X MAQI MUCOI Y appear to be equivalent in value., viz. 'X of the posterity of Y' and 'X son (i.e. member) of the posterity of Y' (see MacNeill, 1909, 367).

NIOTA On the possible formula status of this word see §6.15. NIOTA is from PI *\*nëotas* with *e* raised to *i* in hiatus (Thurneysen, 1946, 50) ⟨ *\*nepotos* (root *nepot-*, Pokorny, 1959, 764), later *nio*, *nía(e)* etc. 'nephew, sister's son'.

## PHONOLOGY

§6.28 The phonology of the Irish of the Ogam inscriptions differs in a number of important respects from that of MS Irish. In the vocalic system five short vowels are found as in Old Irish but in the earliest inscriptions these have not undergone lowering and raising by metaphony (see §5.14) nor have short vowels been lengthened by compensation in the sequences vowel + fricative + resonant (see §5.16). Even in the latest Ogams short vowels in closed unstressed final syllables have not undergone the reduction to /ə/ reflected in Old Irish orthography where original /o/ and /e/ are both written *a* (see §5.20). Here /o/ and /e/ are still distinguished as in Early Old Irish (e.g. 285 BIVODON, 46 [CAT]TABBOTT, 266 COLLABOT, 46 DERCMASOC, 4 LUGADDON, 466 MEMOR etc. and 176 CONUNETT, 221 LUGUVVEC, 1 **MENUEH**, 118 VEQREQ, iv RITTECC etc.). Before a final palatalized consonant, however, I does appear for historical /e/ (see McManus, 1986, 9-10) in 233 ?DOMN-GINN, (cp. 73 DOMNGEN), 187 MAILE-INBIR, 145 QRIMITIR, 126 SOGINI, 131 LITUBIRI and 206 TIGIRN, viii RETAGIN, and exceptionally for historical /a:/ [70] in 235 MOLE-GOMRID. An exceptional U for E/I is found in 97 VORRTIGURN and 297 VORTIGURN which Pokorny (1918, 423) suggests might reflect a change of suffix but it could also be due to error (see §2.2), as is likely to be the case in 108 LUGUDUC for -DEC.·

Ogam Irish presents a similar picture to that of Early Old Irish in respect to long vowels (in stressed syllables) in that the two deriving from the diphthongs *eu/ou* and *ei*, viz. /o:/ and /e:/ have not yet undergone the diphthongization to /uə/ and /iə/ found in Old Irish (e.g. 378 BODDIB. . ., **BODIBEVE**, *Búaidbéo*, 307 MODDAGN[I] *Múadán*, 75, ?RODAGNI *Rúadán*, 109

NETTA-SLOGI *Nad-Slúaig*, 190 GOSSUCTTIAS *Gúasacht* (cp. also 375 **TOTAVALI**, *Túathal*) and 244 QERAI, *Cíara*; 7 CERAN[I], *Cíarán*, 118 VEQREQ *Fíachrai*. On 204 NUADAT, *Núadat* see §5.34. 242 BRRUANANN, therefore, may be an error for BRRENANN (*Brénainn* or *Brénán*) and 135 AILLUATTAN for -LETAN ( = -*lethan* ?).

With regard to diphthongs Ogam Irish presents us with a stage postdating the monophthongization of IE *eu* (309 ?MEUTINI is hardly a trustworthy counter-example), *ou*, *au* and *ei* but predating the rise of the rich variety described by Greene (1976), leaving only two possibilities, viz. *ai* and *oi*. As in Early Old Irish these are normally kept distinct and are written with *i* as the second element, viz. AI and OI (e.g. 241 BAIDAGNI, 90 BAIT, 504 BIVAIDONAS, 40 MAQI-CAIRATINI, 503 DOVAIDONA, 16 DUNAIDONAS, 93 ERCAIDANA (for -DONA ?), 160 MAILAGNI, 187 MAILE-INBIR; 151 BROINIONAS, 244 COILLABBOTAS, 71 COIMAGNI, 147 MOINENA, 198 TOICACI. E appears exceptionally for I as second element in 1 **LUGUAEDON** and 164 VOENACUNAS (see also 124 ?[. . .]OELURI) and the diphthongs are confused, again exceptionally, in 12 VRAICCI for VROICCI (cp. 271 NETA-VROQI below) and in 235 MOLE-GOMRID (for MAILE-) if the supplementary character here is correctly read as O (see n6.52).

The diphthongs AI and OI may also be written with no second element, i.e. as A and O,[71] e.g. 215 BATTIGNI (*Baíthíne*, cp. 90 BAIT, *Báeth*), 230 ?MAQI-CARATTINN (cp. 40 MAQI-CAIRATINI, *Mac-Caírthinn*), 307 GATTAGNI (see §6.12), 239 GATTEGLAN (§6.12), ?138 LADDIGNI (cp. 139 ?LAIDANN); 243 COLABOT, 266 COLLABOT, 21 ?COLLABOTA (cp. 244 COILLABBOTAS), xiv LOGIDDEAS ( = *Loígde* ?), 271 NETA-VROQI (*Nad-Froíc*, cp. 460 **VROCHANI** = *Fróechán* ?). In view of this it is not clear whether 4 LUGADDON and 285 BIVODON represent LUGAIDON and BIVOIDON (for BIVAIDON with rounded first element) or reflect the reduction of the diphthong in unstressed position to /ə/ (cp. MS *Lugedon*, *Lugadon*, *Cinadon* etc. and see §6. 26), which is probably more likely. A similar reduction may also be found in 368 DUMELEDONAS (for -AIDONAS) though this is earlier and may simply be an erroneous spelling for AI. In 26 NETTA-VRECC -VROECC or -VROICC is a possible reading but 202 NIOTT-VRECC is most peculiar with IO for an expected E in the first element and E for an expected OI in the second.

§**6.29** The undetectable nature of lenition and palatalization apart, there are also some significant differences between the consonantal systems of Ogam and manuscript Irish. Among the more important of these are:

(a) Historical *s*, which in later Irish survives as such only in initial position, is preserved in word-auslaut in Ogam -OS and-AS, but there are no examples of its preservation in intervocalic position within the word. The fact that -S is so written, however, does not mean that it was still pronounced /s/ at the time of the inscriptions (see §§5.11-12).

(b) The labialized guttural /k$^w$/ (British *p/b*), which by the period of MS Irish had merged completely with /k/, is preserved in Ogam, e.g. MAQ(Q)I (Welsh *mab*), 40 INEQAGLAS (Breton *eneb* 'face'), 2 ?QENUVEN. . . (Welsh *pen* 'head'), 57 QRITTI (rel. to *cruth* 'form', Welsh, *pryd* 'form'), 129

EQOD[I] (*ech* 'horse', Welsh *ebol* 'colt') etc., though the spellings C for Q and Q for C show that the falling together of these sounds (see §5.18) was within the Ogam period (e.g. MAQ(Q)I ⟩ MAC(I), 358 VOTECORIGAS beside **VOTEPORIGIS** and note 271 NETA-VROQI beside 12 VRAICCI, *Fróech*, Welsh *grug* 'heather', 3 QUNACANOS for CUNA-?, *cú*, Welsh *ci* 'dog', 118 VEQREQ (= /rex/) ⟨ *-REC ⟨ *-REG ⟨ -RIGAS), 184 CATUVIQ (for -VEC if not for -VIR, which is more likely), v MAQI-QOLI (for -COLI). Since the history of /gʷ/ (⟨ *gʷh) was similar to that of /kʷ/ we can assume that it too existed in the Ogam period and it has been argued elsewhere in this book (see §3.15) that the alphabet had a symbol for it, though the sound is not reliably attested on the inscriptions.

(c) By the Old Irish period historical /w/ had become /f/ in initial position, had merged with lenited *b* after certain consonants (*r*, *l*, *n*, *d*), and had either been lost in intervocalic position or merged with a preceding vowel as the second element of a diphthong. In Ogam it is retained (e.g. 200 VORGOS, *Fuirg*, 12 MEDVVI, *Medb*, AVI, *aue*, 259 IVAGENI, *Éogan*, 268 CATTUVIR, *Caither* etc.). When as a result of the syncope of a preceding vowel it became post-consonantal it survived for a time (e.g. 221 CATVVIRR, EOI *Conual* etc.) but eventually disappeared, as in iv RITTECC (for EOI *Rethech* ⟨ *Ritawicas). The sound /w/ arising from the composition vowel *u* before a vowel is found in 1 **LUGUAEDON** but lost in 4 LUGADDON.[72]

Ogam V for an expected B has been explained by Jackson (1949, 108-9) as an attempt to provide an adequate representation of the sound of lenited *b*, and by the present writer (McManus, 1986, 12. n17) as due to the confusion between historical /w/ and /b/ as /β/ in certain post-consonantal positions. In his excellent study of Ogam DOV(A)-, however, Uhlich (1989) has provided a much more satisfactory interpretation of the evidence which explains not only the consistency with which V appears instead of B in the name-element DOV-, -DOV- (for an expected *DUBU), but also the other two irregularities associated with it, namely the O (for U) and the composition vowel A (for U). Uhlich has shown that -*bu*- would regularly become -*bw*- before a vowel (e.g. 432 DOVAGNI, **DOBAGNI** ⟨ *dubwagnī ⟨ *dubu-agnī, 503 DOVAIDONA ⟨ *dubwaidonas ⟨ *dubu-aidonas) and points to the confirmation of Ogam V as a spelling for this sound in DOVINIAS (⟨ *du-bhw-īnyās). In view of this he proposes that *dubu- was thematicized to *dubwo-, whence *dubwa- ⟩ *dobwa-, = DOVA- in 63 DOVALESCI, 37 DOVATUCI, 431 D[O]V[A]TUCEAS, **DOBITUCI** etc., and gen. -DOVI, post-apocope -DOV, ⟨ *dubwī, in 128 (-)CULIDOVI (possibly also in viii MAQI DOV[I] but see the discussion in Appendix 2) and in v BRANADDOV. He acknowledges, however, that later spellings such as *Duiblesc*, gen. *Duibleisc* do show reflexes of the original *dubu- ( nom. *Dovalescas ⟨ *dubwalescas should have given *Doblasc). A consequence of this is that MacNeill's (1909, 345) equation of 302 VALUVI with gen. *Fáilbi* must be rejected as it is based on a presumed interchange of V and B which Uhlich's theory shows is not the case. LUGUVVE = gen. *Lugbi* is also invalid not only for this reason, but more particularly in view of the reading in the *Corpus*, 140 LUGUVVECCA.

# ORTHOGRAPHY

**§6.30** In his 1909 paper (336ff.) MacNeill assessed the differences between Ogam and MS orthography and argued that they were 'as distinct and separate as if they belonged to two unrelated languages.' His informative discussion erred in the present writer's view (McManus, 1986, 7-13) in its emphasis on the distinctiveness of each, due in no small degree to his contention that the Ogam tradition was pagan to the last, that of the manuscripts Christian from the first (333 and see §4.9 above). Such differences as there are, and MacNeill's discussion includes some which are quite unreal, would be very significant if it were possible to demonstrate that the two conventions actually coexisted and were complementary. But this is not the case. We have, rather, an evolving orthography with a degree of continuity from Ogam to manuscript, though the MS convention does represent a new beginning in some respects. The convention of Ogam Irish was established at a time prior to many of the developments to which the salient features of MS Irish were a response (an obvious example is palatalization, lenition is a possible one) and the orthodox Ogam period comes to an end, as we have seen, in the early seventh century while the MS materials which formed the basis for MacNeill's comparison date from the eighth century and later. The intervening period is something of an orthographic melting pot which has some points of contact with the earlier period and some with the later. If we had manuscript sources predating the seventh century, or orthodox Ogams – the scholastic Ogams follow manuscript conventions (see §7.3) – from the eighth or ninth, the overlap of which we find important traces would probably be complete. In this connection it is unfortunate that the Inchagoill inscription (1 **LIE LUGUAEDON MACCI MENUEH**), which has obvious contacts with Ogam and is our earliest contemporary Irish text in the Latin alphabet, does not contain any diagnostic sequences for comparison.

(a) The most important difference between the two is in the representation of non-initial /d/, /g/ and /b/, which appear in Ogam as D, G and B respectively (e.g. 241 BAIDAGNI and 265 AMADU = *Amatus*, 172 TOGITTACC, 10 CORRBRI), in MS as *t*, *c* and *p* (e.g. *Báetán*, *Toicthech* and *Coirpre*). In this instance the MS convention derives from British Latin, in which intervocalic /t/, /c/ and /p/ became voiced as in British to /d/, /g/ and /b/ but continued to be written the traditional Latin way. Latin loanwords borrowed into Irish with this pronunciation were probably the vehicle for the introduction of this convention which was already established by the end of the seventh century to judge by Adamnán's spellings of Irish names (e.g. *Baitan*, *Beccan*, *Coirpre* etc.). The traditional, or Ogam, convention does appear, albeit exceptionally, in the manuscript tradition (e.g. *agaldemathacha* for later *ac(c)-* in the Donatus gloss, Thurneysen, 1933, 208, *roslogeth* and *adobragart* in the *prima manus* of the Würzburg glosses, see McManus, 1986, 11). There are no certain examples of the MS convention in Ogam: 204 NUADAT for an expected NODOD has already been noted as unreliable (§5.34). Macalister sees the hypocoristic suffix -*óc*, which is very common later, in 194a LLONNOCC (see also Harvey, 1987, 64-5) but the name might equally contain later -*ach* (cp. 46 DERCMASOC). If the first element in iv BECCDINN corresponds to Old Irish *becc* its spelling resembles that of MS Irish, but the name is unclear (see the discussion in on the inscription).

(b) MS Irish with its *h*, its *punctum delens* and its lengthmark has a means of distinguishing the lenited sounds *th, ch, ph, ṡ* and *ḟ* from their unlenited counterparts *t, c, p, s* and *f* as well as long from short vowels but as these devices were not available in the Ogam alphabet we cannot speak here of differing conventions but rather of the use of different resources. Again, however, there are traces of a significant overlap in the case of lenited *t* and *c* (*p*, of course, is not attested in Irish Ogams). Just as intervocalic /t/ and /c/ became /d/ and /g/ in British and British Latin with the result that *t* and *c* adopted the values /d/ and /g/ in this position, so too in Irish the development of these to /θ/ and /x/ would lead us to expect a traditional notation of these sounds as *t* and *c*. This is what we find in Ogam (e.g. iv RITTECC = gen. *Rethech*, 103 CARR-TTACC, *Carthach* etc.) and in a significant number of early manuscript spellings (e.g. *rígteg* ⟩ *rígthech*, *Findubrec* ⟩ *Findabrach* etc. see McManus, 1986, 11).

(c) In MS Irish we find a convention developing whereby the quality of consonants (i.e. whether palatal or neutral) comes to be indicated by the use of glide vowels, *i* before and *e* or *i* after a consonant to mark palatal quality (e.g. *maicc* gen. as opposed to *macc* nom., *aithrea* for an earlier *\*athra* with palatal *-thr-*, *toimtiu* for an earlier *\*tomtiu* with palatal *-mt-*, *súili* alongside *súli* with palatal *-l-* etc.) and *a* after a consonant to mark neutral quality (e.g. *cumachtae*, earlier *cumachte*, with neutral *-cht-*, *cnámai*, earlier *cnámi*, with neutral *-m-* etc.). The system is by no means fully developed in Old Irish and post-consonantal glides are particularly uncommon in Early Old Irish (Kelly, 1979, 243, 245, 247), but pre-consonantal *i* is seldom omitted before a final consonant, probably because of the crucial grammatical role it played (*maicc* is different from *macc* at a grammatical level in a way in which *súili* is not different from *súli*) and it is regular before a palatal consonant group arising from syncope (e.g. *aithrea*, *toimseo* etc., Thurneysen, 1946, 55-57 and 61-2). This, therefore, is the only glide which offers a legitimate basis for comparison with Ogam and there are clear differences between the two systems. Ogam inscriptions present us with either the pre-apocope and pre-syncope forms in which the need for the glide does not arise, or with the immediate post-apocope and post-syncope forms in which the convention of writing it had not yet developed. Thus in Ogam we find either MAQ(Q)I or MAQ/MAC (83 MAIC is exceptional and questionable) for MS *maic*, though there may be an attempt to render the slender sound with post- rather than pre-consonantal -I/-I in the spellings MACI, **MACCI** (see §5.18 and McManus, 1986, 10. n14). Further examples of the non-indication of palatal quality are 103 CARRTTACC for MS gen. *Carthaich*, 268 CATTUVIR, 221 CATVVIRR for MS *Caither* (nom.), 466 MEMOR (see §6.27) and 10 CORR-BRI for MS *Coirpre*. Similarly we find -AN(N) for MS *-áin* and ANM for MS *ainm*. As already noted, however, I does appear for E before a palatal consonant in 145 QRIMITIR etc. (see §6.28).

(d) The frequency with which an apparently meaningless duplication of consonants occurs in the Ogam inscriptions constitutes a remarkable extravagance, less because of the absence of a phonetic basis for it than because of the very investment in time and energy required to produce it on stone. The contrast with the thrift of the Scandinavian runemasters, who studiously avoided doubling even to the point of allowing a single consonant serve both the auslaut and anlaut of two juxtaposed words (Page, 1962, 897-8), is quite striking. Noting the non-phonetic nature of the phenomenon MacNeill thought (1909, 340-2) that it might have been inherited from an earlier period in which it could have had some such basis – one thinks of pre-lenition Irish in which an opposition geminate/single obtained – and he put its survival down to an archaizing tendency on the part of epigraphists eager to make a parade of learning. Later, however, he appears to have taken a more mundane view of the matter, suggesting that it might be no more than a fraud perpetrated by Ogamists on unsuspecting clients obliged by contract to pay by the score (Macalister, 1945, xvi)!

If the phenomenon had been inherited from an earlier period of geminate/single consonant oppositions one might have expected it to be more common in earlier than later inscriptions and statistically more frequent in the case of consonants in which an opposition tense/lax survived after lenition (viz. *l*, *n* and *r*). This, however, is not the case. Doubling is as frequent in later as it is in early inscriptions, more so indeed if one includes the examples of -ANN for -AGNI, and LL and RR are not particularly common while NN occurs mostly in final position for original -GNI, a case in which the intense feature was not present to judge by later -*án*, *áin*. My own approximate figures for frequency (which differ from MacNeill's) are T56, C33, N30, D24, L17, V (including AVVI) 16, R13, G10, B8, S8, M5, Q (excluding MAQQI) 3. If one includes examples of MAQQI under Q and omits those of NN ⟨ GN under N, the consonants of the H series (excluding H of course) are the most frequently doubled, a fact the significance of which is not clear.

The capricious nature of the phenomenon can be illustrated by the following pairs, which are not intended to be exhaustive: 83 BROCC, 228 BROCI; 180 BRUSCCOS, 63 BRUSCO; 266 COLLABOT, 243 COLABOT (see 244 COILLABBOTAS); 263 LUGUDECCAS, 286 LUGUDECA; 100 ULCC-AGNI, 467 ULCAGNI. That it is as frequent, if not more so, in later Ogams as early ones will be clear from 250 RITTAVVECAS, 211 RITTAVVECC; 250 CATTUVVIRR, 268 CATTUVIR, 221 CATVVIRR; 504 -AIDONAS, 4 -ADDON etc. as well as from post-syncope spellings such as 103 CARRT-TACC, 10 AMMLLO. . .TT, iv BECCDINN, RITTECC. The distribution of inscriptions with one or two duplicated consonants follows the overall pattern, those with three or more being confined, according to Mac White (1960/61, 298-9), to West Cork and Kerry. The Thomastown stone (no. xiv) with its six double consonants, therefore, is quite exceptional.

Duplication would not appear to be restricted to any particular part of a word or name, being attested in absolute internal intervocalic position, in final post-vocalic position, at the beginning of the second element of a compound and of a (C) type name (e.g. 140 LUGUVVECCA, 20 MAQI-DDECCEDA), and in both pre- and post-consonantal position. Though not unknown it is, however, quite infrequent in absolute anlaut (e.g. 103 MMAQI, not GAQI, 121 LLOMINACCA, 153 CCICAMINI, 177 ?CCILARI, 194A LLONNOCC, if not for SONNOCC, 220 ?ANM LLATIGNI, 300 MMUC[OI], not GUC[OI]) and Harvey has suggested (1987a, 4-6) that this may be due to the influence of Latin conventions.

On a cursory examination there would not appear to be any obvious correlation between duplication and geminate or unlenited sounds. In fact a consideration of some spellings would suggest the opposite. Thus, of four examples of the name related to OI *allaid* with geminate *ll* and a lenited dental only one (250 ALLATO) has LL and the others (215 ALATTO, 5 ALATTOS and 224 ALOTTO) have TT. Similarly, the name corresponding to MS *Mac-Deichet* with lenited *ch* and unlenited formerly geminate *-t* (= /d/) is written twice (66 MAQI-DECCEDDAS, 184 MAQQI-DECEDDA) with DD but three times (20 MAQI-DDECCEDA, 159 MAQI-DECCEDA, 66) with CC and in one of these (20) the initial D, which is lenited, is also doubled. In names containing the element corresponding to MS *Erc*, with unlenited *c*, this is written once (175 MAQI-ERCCIA) with CC but otherwise (ten times in all) with C. In his detailed survey of the phenomenon in the first two hundred inscriptions in the *Corpus*, Harvey's (1987, 65) figures reflect this in the high number of instances of duplication in the case of lenited sounds, but he points out that there is a very strong bias in favour of duplication as opposed to single representation in the case of non-lenited sounds when not in initial position, and he questions the notion that duplication might have been a device to indicate lenition (on which see Carney, 1978-9, 419 and 421).

The MS tradition presents a contrast (though see Harvey, 1987, 69) in that whereas a capricious interchange of single and double consonants is found, doubling is exceptional in lenited sounds (Kelly, 1979, 244). Again, however, an overlap with the Ogam convention is found in Early Old Irish in the spellings of Irish names in the Book of Armagh (e.g. *Coimmanus*, *Roddanus* etc, see Carney, 1978-9, 419 and McManus, 1986, 9). Similarly, the pre-syncope spelling *Commogellus* (see n5.46) has *-mm-* as in Ogam for lenited *m*.

It is worth noting that the post-apocope forms of the formula word MAQQI, in which we have a clear case of duplication correlated with a geminate sound, are MAQ and MAC, not MAQQ and MACC.

§6.31 The extent to which Ogam orthography might have been influenced by that of Latin has never been fully investigated, probably because of the prevailing separatist view which dictated that such influence could not have been present (see §4.9). A cursory examination of some features suggests as little deference to a potential Latin model as was shown by the framers of the alphabet to their alphabetic prototype. Thus, in the spelling of the diphthongs /ai/ and /oi/ Ogam does not follow the *ae* and *oe* of Latin orthography (which replaced earlier *ai* and *oi*), but as these diphthongs had long since been monophthongized in Latin, giving rise to confusion of **AE** and **E** as well as **OE** and **E**, this model was hardly a suitable one. As already noted (§6.28) there are occasional examples of OE and the **AE** of the Inchagoill stone may be significant, but the Ogam convention is clearly AI, OI with the possibility of omitting the final element. Similarly, though the Latin convention of writing **QV** is found in Irish names in the Latin alphabet (e.g. xxi **MAQVI-COLINE**, 364 **QVENVENDANI**, 462 **QVENATAVCI**) and in the Irish word for 'son' when it is borrowed into the Latin (489 **MAQVI**), examples of this from Ireland are very scarce (275 QVECI, 104 MAQVI, 23 ?MAQV[A]S) and the artificial rule later expanded for this symbol by the MS Ogamists (see McManus, 1986, 15-16 and §3.13 above) clearly did not apply during the period of the inscriptions when the convention was to write Q or QQ but not QV. Again, it was customary in Latin to write -II for the gen. sg. of *io*-stems (though -I was a recognized alternative) and this practice would have suited the needs of Primitive Irish to keep this class distinct from the *o*-stems. But -II is never found, and the general avoidance of doubling vowels is interesting when compared with the willy-nilly duplication of consonants. As for the paucity of examples of consonant doubling in word-initial position, Harvey's suggestion (1987a, 4-6) that the influence of written Latin may have acted as a deterrent in this regard has already been noted.

The significance of these Ogam conventions for establishing the presence or absence of a knowledge of Latin must, however, remain indeterminate. In the case of AI, OI, for example, we cannot reject the presence of Latin as a hypothesis since this spelling is standard in Early Old Irish, the corpus of which is made up in considerable part of Irish names in Latin texts. On the biliteral inscriptions of Britain Q is standard in the Ogam as it is at home, despite the obvious Latin presence, and though the British Ogams differ in a number of ways from those in Ireland (see §4.13) this does not extend to any significant degree to orthographic conventions (apart of course from the survival of early conventions in late inscriptions, see §§5.32-3). The matter, therefore, must remain *sub judice*.

§**6.32** To conclude this survey, then, one may say that the orthographical convention of the Ogam inscriptions represents the earliest attempt to write Irish words and names. The period of the inscriptions saw enormous changes taking place in the language and the orthography responded to these as best it could with the devices available to it, but it did not succeed in coming to terms with them all (the role of varying consonant quality as a substitute for the old case-endings being an obvious example). The earliest forms of MS Irish show a continuation of some of the characteristic features of Ogam orthography, a fact which makes a hard and fast cleavage whether social, religious or otherwise unreal, but a major overhaul of the orthography was taking place in the seventh century introducing the influence of British Latin based orthography and updating spelling conventions to reflect the spoken word more accurately. If these developments did not find general currency in Ogam inscriptions it is not because the latter belonged to a tradition apart, but because the cult of the inscriptions had already in large part run its course.

# CHAPTER SEVEN

# The Later Tradition (1): Scholastic Ogams and the Revisions of the Alphabet

**§7.1** At some time in the seventh century Ogam fell into decline in its capacity as a monument script and, from the eighth century on, was replaced by conventional script in the form of the Irish semi-uncial book-hand with its manuscript contractions, rather as the monument capitals were replaced by manuscript minuscule in Britain at the same time (see Jackson, 1950, 204). This development is not to be seen in simplistic terms as the mere abandonment of one script for another; the funerary inscriptions in semi-uncials do not continue the Ogam tradition in a superficially modified guise. They represent a new beginning, differing from the Ogams not only in script and orthographical convention but also in distribution and in the general choice of recumbent slabs as opposed to the more common standing pillar of the earlier period. In their formulae there is a partial overlap with the Ogam inscriptions in the use of the name in the genitive type; otherwise there is again a new departure in the incorporation of the genitive governing word **LEC** 'stone' (compare the **LIE** on the Inchagoill stone), in the use of the nominative with or without an indication of parentage and/or occupation and in particular in the ever increasing stereotype request for a blessing or a prayer. Unlike the Ogams these grave slabs tend to occur in clusters associated with particular ecclesiastical sites such as Clonmacnoise or Gallen and they bear ornamented crosses much more frequently than do their earlier counterparts though, again, there is some degree of overlap between the cross types on both.[1]

It is, of course, tempting to see the demise of Ogam and the rise of the semi-uncials in black and white terms. The contrastive features of both genres together with the obvious Christian character of the later one make the hypothesis of a Christian triumph over a pagan cult all too attractive, but apart from the fact that such a 'triumph' would be taking place rather late in the history of Irish Christianity, the evidence, as pointed out above (§4.9), will not support such clear-cut distinctions. The change was probably more one of fashion than anything else and while greatly facilitated by increasing literacy in the vernacular was probably inspired by that same spirit of innovation which one finds in Irish ecclesiastical architecture and sculpture at the same time. Whether the contemporary demise of the *moccu* type names was a related symptom of this change is unclear.[2]

§**7.2** From the seventh century on the centre of gravity in Ogam studies shifts in the main from the epigraphic to the manuscript record and the position of the script relative to the Latin alphabet would be analogous thenceforth to that occupied today by Roman numerals alongside their Arabic counterparts. Knowledge of the script never died out, however, nor was it likely to as long as the letter name sequence to which it marked position – the *Beithe-luis-nin* – was being memorized, and as this had made a place for itself in the training of the *filid* (see below §7.12) its survival was guaranteed at least until the seventeenth century.[3] The appearance of Ogam alphabets of various kinds in eighteenth and nineteenth century manuscripts, moreover, testifies to continued familiarity with the system right down to the dawn of modern research into it, though whether Ogam memorial inscriptions of the nineteenth century represent an authentic survival of an archaic tradition, as suggested by B. Raftery (1969, 162-3), is doubtful (see below §7.5.v).

§**7.3** Post seventh-century examples of the use of the Ogam script are generally classified as scholastic, a potentially misleading term in that it might be understood to imply that the orthodox inscriptions were not the product of a scholarly tradition, a view which, in the present writer's opinion at least, is untenable. In general scholastic may be understood to mean that the grammar and orthographical convention (in particular the use of *hÚath* with the value *h*) together with some features of the outward appearance of these Ogams – such as their use of a stemline, of long scores of equal length to the consonants for vowels, the frequent use on hard materials of the first supplementary letter for E (but not for K), the appearance of an arrow-head to indicate the direction of writing and to separate words or names – derive from MS usage and do not continue the earlier genre in a direct line. Scholastic Ogams, therefore, are the counterpart in the Ogam script to the semi-uncial inscriptions in the Latin alphabet.

§**7.4** Non-MS scholastic Ogams occur on a variety of portable objects as well as on tombstones and date from the Old Irish period right up to the nineteenth century. A find from the Ballinderry Crannóg No. 2, were the conventional explanation of it correct, might have a claim to being one of the earliest examples of a non-orthodox use of Ogam. This is one of two bone dice found on the site, each of which bears the appropriate amount of dots to represent the numbers 3, 4 and 6, the number 5 being represented in this conventional way on the one, whereas on the other a sequence of three parallel vertical (or horizontal, depending on the way one looks at it) scores appear in place of the expected five dots (O'Neill Hencken, 1942, 54, fig. 22, nos. 17 and 45). Hencken's suggestion that these represent the third character of the Ogam alphabet (viz. V) with its Roman numerical value has been accepted by most commentators and, together with Raftery's second-century dating of the find,[4] has opened up new possibilities for the antiquity of the Ogam alphabet which are explored by MacWhite (1960/1, 301-2) and Carney (1975, 56). Such a use of an Ogam character, however, would be a peculiar aberration even if one were to go as far as B. Raftery (1969, 161) in positing a familiarity with the script among the general body of the people, which is unlikely. Furthermore, if for want of a

better explanation we concede the possibility that it is an Ogam character, the
fact that no stemline is present makes it impossible to choose with certainty
between the third symbol (*Fern*), with its orthodox (i.e. non-scholastic) pre
seventh-century value *V*, and the eighteenth symbol (*Úr*) with the scholastic
value it bears in the Berne manuscript (see below §7.8) where it stands for Latin
consonantal *v*. All in all, therefore, the Ballinderry die is an unreliable basis for
inference regarding either the antiquity of the Ogam alphabet or the uses to
which it might have been put in the early period.

§7.5 Among scholastic Ogams recorded on stone are:

i (Macalister, 1945, no. 54; Marstrander, 1930; Olsen, 1954, 181-2): The stem
of a cross found built into the wall surrounding the Cathedral enclosure in
Killaloe. A runic inscription is inscribed on the face reading **ThURKRIM RISTI
[K]RUS ThINA** 'Thorgrimr raised this cross' and is accompanied by a damaged
scholastic Ogam inscribed on the side reading BENDACHT (E written with the
first supplementary character) . . . TOROQR. . . which can be restored with
reasonable certainty as BENDACHT FOR TOROQRIM 'a blessing on T.'. The
first O in the Ogam spelling of the man's name is correct; the runic Fuþark in
use on the stone had no symbol for this sound and uses the U-rune instead (see
Kermode, 1907, 85 on the same in the Isle of Man, and Page, 1987, 21 and 54).
Ogam Q appears to be a transliteration of the K-rune used for the sound /g/.
The alignment of the Ogam and the vertical disposition of the runes are reminiscent of the bilingual inscriptions of Britain, though the Killaloe stone is
obviously much later. Marstrander (1930, 398ff.) dates it to the eleventh century
and assesses its importance as a contribution to the history of the Norwegian
colonization in the Shannon and Limerick districts.

ii, A and B (Macalister, 1945, 483 on A; Kermode, 1907, no. 115 and no. 104;
Olsen, 1954, 202, 215-17; Page, 1983, 140-41, Maughold I and Kirk Michael
III): The first of these is a broken slab of slaty stone from Maughold in the Isle
of Man. It bears a runic inscription reading **[I]UAN + BRIST + RAISTI +
ThISIR + RUNUR** 'John, the priest, carved these runes', together with a
fifteen-letter runic Fuþark and an incomplete (owing to the break) Ogam
alphabet, the first two *aicmi* being all that remain. The Irish connection is
indicated by a related runic inscription also from Maughold inscribed by the
same man (Kermode, 1907, no. 114 and p. 77, Olsen, 1954, 202-5 and Page,
1983, Maughold II). This reads + **KRISTh : MALAKI : OK BAThRIK :
AThANMAN x [II]NAL. SAUThAR. IUAN. BRIST. I KURNAThAL** translated by Kermode as 'Christ, Malachi and Patrick [and] Adamnan! But of all
the sheep is John [the] priest in Corndale', an invocation to Christ and three
Irish saints, the first of whom (Malachy = Máel-Máedóc Úa Morgair, see Kenney, 1929, 764-7) ) died in 1148, thus giving a *terminus post quem* for the
inscription. B, also from the Isle of Man (Kirk Michael), is a slab bearing a
decorated cross with sculptured figures on each side of the shaft below which
there is a complete Ogam alphabet in which the ends of the scores of each letter
are joined by straight lines as found in the Pictish Ogams. The rear face of the
slab bears two runic inscriptions, three of the names on the first of which are
Irish (**MAL : LU/YMKUN : RAISTI : KRUS : ThENA : EFTER : MAL :
MURU/Y : FUSTRA : SINE : TOTIR TUFKALS : KONA : IS : AThISL : ATI**

+ 'Máel-Lomchon erected this cross to the memory of Máel-Mura his foster [mother], daughter of Dubgal, the wife whom Athisl had' (Kermode's translation but see Page, 1983, 137-8) and **[B]ETRA : ES : LAIFA : FUSTRA : KUThAN : ThAN : SON : ILAN** + 'Better is it to leave a good foster [-son] than a bad son'). These are accompanied by an Ogam inscription which cannot be made out with certainty (see Kermode, 1907, pages 100-102).

The custom of inscribing alphabets on stone and other hard materials, possibly for purposes of instruction, is well known in runic tradition, and it is significant that these unique examples of the same in Ogam occur on Scandinavian inscriptions.[5] The appearance of Norse and Irish names side by side on these and other monuments from the Isle of Man is reminiscent of that of Roman, Irish and British names on the Ogam inscriptions of Wales, Devon and Cornwall (see chapter six) at an earlier time and points to a similar mixture of cultures. In Man, however, the formulae, language and writing system employed are predominantly Scandinavian, though grammatical irregularities and solecisms appear to point to a bilingual situation with language interference (Kermode, 1907, 77 and Page, 1983, 137-8, 142-4 and 1987, 59).

iii (Macalister 1949, no. 749, 1902, no. 121) This slab from Clonmacnoise is recorded as missing by Macalister but has since been refound (Lionard, 1960/61, 98). It bears the name **COLMAN** in conventional script beneath which there is an inverted scholastic Ogam on its own incised stemline reading BOCHT 'poor' in the opposite direction to that indicated by the arrow-head. As Macalister points out this is the only example of Ogam in the large collection of inscriptions from Clonmacnoise (see further the quatrains below in §8.9).

iv Recent archaeological investigation of the East Tomb Chamber at Knowth (site I in Eogan, 1986) has revealed two Ogam inscriptions of the scholastic type, the one in the left recess on the corbel above orthostats 41-42, the other from orthostat 56 in the right recess. The readings, for which I am indebted to Professor Eogan, are (B)IEQB(H)IE/S and ETLLORZGANAU/O respectively. As the chamber was occupied in the ninth to eleventh centuries (Eogan, 1986, 35) when Knowth was an important political centre (Byrne, 1968) it is probable that these inscriptions date from this period. What they mean, however, is quite unclear.

v (B. Raftery, 1969, 162-4) A tombstone in the graveyard of Ahenny, Co. Tipperary bears simple decoration together with an inscription in English recording the death of Mary Dempsy in 1802 and an Ogam reading FA AN LIG SO 'NA LU ATA MARI NI DHIMUSA O MBALLI NA GCRANIBH 'Under this stone lies Mary Dempsy from Ballycranna.' The stone is a product of one of several regional schools of craftsmen who specialized in tomb carving in the eighteenth and nineteenth centuries but it is difficult to agree with Raftery who regards it as a 'living archaism' of orthodox Ogam tradition. Macalister (1945, 256) refers to it as one of several inscriptions of its kind written with 'much more zeal than discretion' and inspired by the publication of the Mount Callan Ogam in 1780, a view shared by de hÓir in her excellent discussion of the latter forgery in which she notes (1983, 49-50) that the Ahenny inscription echoes that of Mount Callan, viz. FAN LICSI TA CONAN COLGAC COS-FADA 'Under this stone lies (lit. is) C. C. C.'). This renewed interest in Ogam brought its complement of forgeries executed by 'scouts' ever willing to meet the enthusiasm of unwary antiquarians for new finds with fakes if the real thing were not to hand. The Mount Callan stone itself, though it served the useful purpose of arousing widespread interest in the subject, was the most notorious of these forgeries.[6]

For further examples of scholastic Ogams on stone see 72, 183, 246b and 247 in Macalister (1945), and B Raftery (1969, 162) on a portable altar-stone bearing the name of Father Laurence Hartnett (Nat. Mus. Reg. No. 1941, 1117). The fragments of the Hackness cross in Yorkshire (Macalister, 1945, 478; Brown, 1930, 52ff. and Derolez, 1954, 140ff.) bear three Latin inscriptions, a runic inscription made up of standard runes and *Hahalruna* and a fifth inscription in a scheme similar to that of Ogam but using the shape of the characters rather than position relative to a stemline to distinguish the groups. Whether it is directly related to Ogam or not is unclear.

**§7.6** Of the scholastic Ogams on hard materials other than stone the most impressive by far must be those of the Ballyspellan silver pennanular brooch, dated to about the ninth century (Macalister, 1945, no. 27). The Ogams are written in four lines, each with arrow-heads indicating the direction of writing and separating the words as follows: (1) 〉 CNAEMSECH 〉 CELLACH, (2) 〉 MINODOR 〉 MUAD, (3) 〉 MAEL-MAIRE, (4) 〉 MAEL-UADAIG 〉 MAEL-MAIRE. These appear to be personal names in the nominative (the forms are Old Irish or later)[7] and it has been suggested that they may record successive owners of the brooch. The Ogams, however, seem to be the work of one man.

Two scholastic Ogams are found on a bronze hanging bowl (Macalister, 1949, no. 1086, Raftery, 1966, 30ff., Nat. Mus. Reg. No. 1945, 80) discovered in a bog called Clounacilla in the townland of Kilgulbin East, Co. Kerry. The unusual shape of the bowl suggested to Raftery the possibility that it might date from around 400 A.D., though in that case the Ogams would have to be considered secondary. These are inscribed along the upper surface of the rim and on one of the escutcheons respectively reading BLADNACH COGRADEDENA (Macalister COGRACETENA) and BLADNACH CUILEN. The word common to both is probably a personal name and this may be true also of the CUILEN of the latter (Old Irish *cuilén* 'pup, whelp', *Cuilén*, O'Brien, 1973, 228). The second part of the inscription on the rim, however, is quite unclear. Recognizable forms are Old Irish in date or later.

Ogam-like characters of indeterminate significance have been found also on the bone of a sheep (together with zig-zag ornament, Macalister, 1945, no. 52), on an amber bead (ibid. no. 53), on a wooden weaver's sword (B Raftery, 1969, 162, Nat. Mus. Reg. No. 1954, 7) and on a knife-handle from Norfolk (Clarke, 1952). The inscription on the so-called Conyngham patera, a bronze age cupped bracelet found in Co. Mayo, was shown by Graves (1847) to be a forgery.[8] Each of the five letters has its own stemline and the reading is usually given as UOSER (leg. SERVO ?).

**§7.7** Manuscript Ogams may be classified according as to whether the choice of the script is dictated by context – in tabulations and/or discussions of alphabets in general or Ogam in particular – or by the whim of the scribe. The latter includes single words, signatures etc., differing from the usual marginalia in Irish manuscripts only in script. The best-known examples are those of Codex

Sangallensis 904, a ninth-century manuscript containing the Latin text of the first sixteen books of Priscian's Grammar heavily glossed in Old Irish. The bulk of the marginalia, both Irish and Latin, are written in conventional script and are of the usual type, i.e. indications of the day or time of writing, complaints about the cold, the parchment or the ink, invocations to saints for favour or the reader for patience etc. (Stokes and Strachan, 1903, xx-xxii). The marginalia in Ogam are usually brief but are not distinguished by content. They are as follows: fol. 50 FERIA CAI HODIE 'today is the feast-day of Gaius'; fol. 70 FEL MARTAIN 'feast-day of (St) Martin'; fol. 170 MINCHASC 'Little Easter (Low Sunday)'; fols.193, 194, 195 COCART 'correction'; fol. 196 A COCART INSO 'this is their correction'. The most interesting and amusing however is the scribe's apology for any shortcomings in his work expressed in a single word written LATHEIRT in Ogam on fol. 204 and *lathæirt* in conventional script on fol. 189. In Cormac's glossary (Meyer, 1912b, 68, no. 820) the word is etymologized and explained as follows: *Lait[h]irt .i. lait[h] ort .i. lait[h] ron-ort [.i.] ōl cormæ* 'Laithirt i.e. ale [+] killed i.e. ale has killed us [i.e.] ale-drinking.' This together with other contexts shows the basic meaning to be 'excessive ale-consumption' with the logical extensions 'excessive drunkenness' and 'massive hangover', the last probably the meaning intended in the Priscian Ogams.

The best-known signature in Ogam is that of the scribe of the Stowe Missal, the oldest surviving missal of the Irish church, dated to around 800 AD (Warner, 1915, xlii and plate viii). The scribe introduces himself in his conventional request that the reader bear him in mind in his prayers: *Rogo quicumque hunc librum legeris ut memineris mei peccatoris scriptoris .i.* SONID[9] *peregrinus Amen. Sanus sit qui scripsit et cui scriptum est Amen.* Folio 14 of Harleian 432, a sixteenth century vellum manuscript containing material from the *Senchas Már*, also bears a scribal signature in Ogam written across the upper margin, viz. GILLA NA NAEM O DEORAIN SOND.

In the Annals of Inisfallen under the year 1193 (Rawlinson B 503, fol. 40c, MacAirt, 1951, 318) three stemlines were drawn to accommodate the following observation in Ogam which occupies only the first two: NUMUS HONORATUR SINE NUMO NULLUS AMATUR. One is reminded of the following marginalium from Codex Sangallensis 904, fol. 203 *maraith sercc céin mardda aithne, a Máellecán* 'love remains as long as property (lit. deposits, gifts) remain, O Máellecán.' Harleian 432 (see above) also bears the following obscure piece in three types of Ogam[10] across the upper margin of fol. 4: BEICH MAIDNE / MARCACH IS / A LOCHT SO TIS FAM COSAIB BA HI AS COMAIRTHI (word division is mine).

The Ogams above may be described as functional, as opposed to the illustrative or theoretical kind to be discussed below, but the fact that they occur only sporadically is indicative of the marginal status of Ogam *vis-à-vis* conventional script from the eighth century on. With regard to their form it is worth noting that they eschew all but the first of the supplementary characters and that even this is a hard material feature. Thus whereas all Es on both the Ballyspellan brooch (assuming CMAEMSECH be an error for CNAIMSECH, see n7.7) and the Kilguibin East hanging bowl are written X, as is the single E of the Killaloe cross, there is not one instance of this character in the manuscript Ogams discussed above. On the supplementary characters see further below (§§7.13-14).

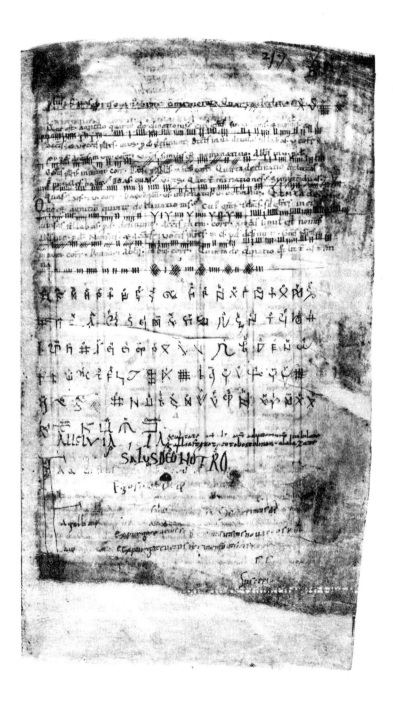

Plate 4
Codex Bernensis 207 fol. 257r
(courtesy of the Burgerbibliothek Bern)

§**7.8** Of the illustrative type of Ogam the bulk of examples are to be found in Irish manuscripts containing texts dealing specifically with Ogam and dating from the fourteenth century or later (though of course the texts are much older), but two instances from continental manuscripts are particularly important as the earliest examples of this genre, viz. Codex Bernensis 207, fol. 257r and Bibliotheca Apostolica Vaticana MS. Reg. Lat. 1308, fol. 62v.[11]

The first of these (see plate 4) has been discussed in detail by Derolez (1951, 3-11, see also Derolez, 1954, 174-5 where the manuscript is dated to the eighth-ninth centuries). The folio on which the Ogams are found is given over entirely to alphabets of various kinds but the upper third, which the Ogams occupy, has been overwritten with part of a Latin grammar. Luckily only the first line of the seven lines of Ogam suffered in this secondary appropriation (the Latin text is written *between* the following lines) and the nature of its contents make it possible to restore what has been erased with reasonable certainty. The first line presents a Latin alphabetic sequence of Ogam characters, the remaining six a syllabary arranged in the Latin sequence as follows BA BE BI BO BU, CA CE CI CO CU . . . ZA ZE ZI ZO ZU (line 2 has B C and D, 3 F G H, 4 K L M, 5 N P Q, 6 R S T, 7 V Z).

These Ogams are particularly important not only because of the date of the manuscript but also because unlike, for example, the Priscian Ogams, the nature of the material ensures a full, or almost full, complement of symbols and their arrangement in the Latin alphabetic sequence (compare the runic alphabets as opposed to the runic Fuþarks) makes their values reasonably certain. They show that the assignment of the values H to *Úath* (lines 1 and 3) and Q (and K) to *Cert* (lines 1, 4 and 5) had already taken place by the Old Irish period (the Priscian Ogams show this only for *Úath*). Some doubt or hesitation with the new values appears to be indicated, however, by the use of *Gétal*, not *Gort*, for Latin G (lines 1 and 3) and by the use of a doubled *Straif*[12] (similar to the doubled *Coll* in *Emancholl*) for Latin Z (lines 1 and 7). That Latin F should be rendered by *Fern* (lines 1 and 3) is precisely what one would expect from the seventh century on, and the natural consequence of this shift in the value of the Ogam character was that *Úr* should be used for Latin consonantal V (lines 1 and 7). Latin P is rendered by a Y-like symbol (lines 1 and 5) unattested elsewhere.

Following *Úr*, for Latin consonantal V, on the first line there are four symbols, the last of which (doubled *Straif*) appears to serve the purpose of completing the Latin sequence, as it does in line 7. The third is *Emancholl* ( = Latin X, see below §7.15) which is unusual in being written below the line and with only three horizontal strokes. The first two characters are the *Ébad* and *Ór forfeda* (the latter with the angular shape it has in the Book of Ballymote copy of *In Lebor Ogaim*, see below §7.13), and do not appear to be designed here to represent characters of the Latin alphabet but rather to fill out the complement of Ogam symbols in what precedes. Unlike the other characters these four have their values written above them in conventional script as follows *ae*, *oe* or *oo*, *ach* and *rr*.[13]

Derolez has argued (1951, 10) that there is no reason for doubting that the Ogam fragment was written at the same time as the rest of the manuscript, which has been described as a vade-mecum of liberal culture and must have been the product of a centre with strong and direct Irish influence.

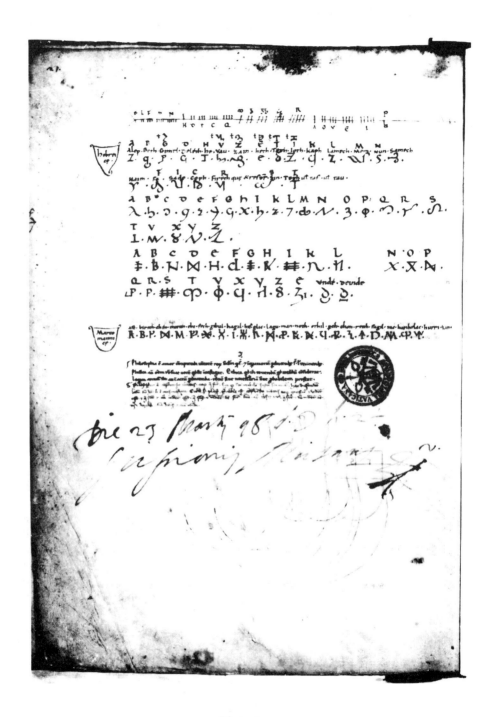

Plate 5
Biblioteca Apostolica Vaticana MS Reg. Lat. 1308 fol. 62v
(courtesy of the Biblioteca Apostolica Vaticana)

The Ogams of the Vatican manuscript (see plate 5) occupy the first line of fol. 62v and are followed by four alphabets, the first and last of which are named as Hebrew and Marcomanni, the middle two being unidentified but having characters in common with alphabets below the Ogams in the Berne manuscript and with the 'Egyptian' and 'African' alphabets in *In Lebor Ogaim* (see Derolez, 1951, 13ff. and 1954, 355ff. on the Marcomanni and below §7.11 (h) on the foreign alphabets in *In Lebor Ogaim* ). The Ogams are made up of the standard twenty character alphabet with accompanying transcription (*Gétal* being rendered GG as in the *Bríatharogam* texts (see McManus, 1988, 136) not NG as in the *Auraicept na nÉces* and the Ogams of *In Lebor Ogaim*) and a single supplementary character (*Pín/ Iphín*) transcribed P (on which see §7.15). This alphabet is unique in that if the scholar responsible for it was familiar with the other *forfeda*, as is likely, he chose to ignore all but the single character required to write Irish, viz. *Pín*. This economy is the very antithesis of the spirit in which the *forfeda* were created (see §7.16).

§7.9 The main body of manuscript Ogams is to be found in three Irish texts which deal in part or exclusively with Ogam, viz. *Auraicept na nÉces* 'The Scholars' Primer', *De dúilib feda na forfid*, a short tract dealing with the values of the supplementary characters, and *In Lebor Ogaim* 'The Book of Ogam' or 'The Ogam Tract'.[14] The contents of the first and third of these, insofar as they relate to the origin of Ogam, will be discussed below (§§8.3-4). For the moment it will suffice to refer to the use of the Ogam alphabet itself in them.

In the *Auraicept na nÉces* and its extensive Commentary the Ogam alphabet is used only sparingly and all examples are designed to be illustrative of the particular topic being discussed. Text itself is not written in Ogam.[15] A full twenty-five character alphabet is given at 1138/4229 following the alphabets of the three *prímbélrai* 'principal languages', Hebrew, Greek and Latin. Elsewhere Ogams tend to be confined to the *forfeda* (sometimes as at 952 to the *feda*, i.e. the 'vowels', viz. *Aicme Ailme* together with the *forfeda*, as opposed to the *táebomnai* 'consonants') and the three *foilchesta* of Ogam,[16] i.e. the tenth, thirteenth and fourteenth characters of the alphabet with the values Q, NG and Z respectively. These illustrations are usually designed to show the growth of the *forfeda* class (1141ff./4239ff.), how to distinguish their use from that of the vowels of *Aicme Ailme* (see e.g. 1290ff./4387ff.), and the correct use of *Cert*, *Gétal* and *Straif*, here modified to *Queirt*, *nGétal* and *Zraif* (e.g. *Queirt* when *c* occurs before *u* in conventional script as in *cuing* = QUING, 2894; *nGétal* when *n* occurs before *g*, e.g. *cengid* = QENGID; and *Zraif* when *s* occurs before *t*, e.g. *stán* = STAN 2899).

The concentration on these particular symbols is dictated largely by the uncertainty regarding their use (whence the need for illustration) arising from the fact that they do not correspond to single distinctive characters used for writing Irish in conventional script. They may also be cited as examples of the 'superiority' of Ogam over other alphabets (especially Latin) which do not have corresponding symbols e.g. 1055ff./4011ff.: *Cach son dona airnecht cairechtaire isna aipgitribh ailibh ol chena ar-richta carechtaire leosumh doibh isin Beithi-luis-nin in Ogaim* 'every sound for which a (distinctive) character was not found in the other alphabets, characters have been found by them (the inventors of Ogam) for them in the Beithe-luis-nin' (the characters cited being the *forfeda* 1057, or *nGétal* and the last three *forfeda* 4013; see also 1077ff./4073ff. where Irish/Ogam is described as being *leithiu* 'broader' than Latin in words, meanings and letters).

**§7.10** In *De dúilib feda na forfid* (Calder, 1917, 5416-5463) all the supplementary characters are given in Ogam with their diphthong values together with a series of examples, in conventional script, of words in which they might be used. Thus, *Ébad* is prescribed for *éo, féoil, béoir* etc., *Ór* for *óen, roí, gnoí* etc., *Uilen* for *úair, fúar, búaid* etc., *Iphín* for *íar, fíal, fían, fíad* etc. and *Emancholl* for *áed, baí* but also *baill, baile* etc. (see further §7.13 on these).

**§7.11** The largest collection of manuscript Ogams is to be found in The 'Book of Ogam' or 'Ogam Tract', *In Lebor Ogaim*, which contains in excess of one hundred 'alphabets'.[17] For the most part these have no practical capacity and do not occur outside of this context. Dismissed by Zimmer as 'wertlose Spielerei' this material adds little to our knowledge of Ogam. To the modern reader these 'alphabets' have all the appearances of being the creations of idle schoolboys, but they seem to have been taken more seriously in medieval times (see §7.12). They may be classified broadly as follows:

(a) Ogam alphabets superficially (and often rather absurdly) varied in appearance from standard Ogam form the bulk of the material in this collection. The name given to each of these 'alphabets' is usually descriptive of the device employed for variation on the norm and may be further qualified by association with some individual, often a character from Irish saga. Occasionally the latter alone serves as the name. Examples are: (1) *Aradach Find* 'The ladder-like [Ogam] of Finn [mac Cumaill]', an Ogam alphabet in which each character appears on its own vertical stemline, those of *Aicme Ailme* having the appearance of a ladder. (4) *Tredruimnech* 'Three ridged', the alphabet arranged along three horizontal stemlines. (13) *Ebadach Ilaind* 'The *Ébad*-like [Ogam] of Iland', an Ogam alphabet in which each character appears separately on or through the lines of its own *Ébad* (first supplementary character). (14) *Ogam Bricrenn* 'The Ogam of Bricriu', an alphabet in which the grouping principle of Ogam is abandoned, each letter being represented by the number of strokes or dots corresponding to its numerical position in the sequence (see n2.10 above). In the Book of Ballymote this entry is followed by a quatrain, elsewhere ascribed to Flann mac Lonáin, in Ogam Bricrenn (see Meroney, 1947). (19) *Crad cride ecis* 'torment of a poet's heart', in which squares, rectangles and rhomboids are disposed in standard Ogam orientation above, below or through the stemline, the characters being distinguished by the number of scores projecting from these. (45) *Ogam leni* (leg. *léime*) *da reib* (leg. *dar réib*) 'Jump over stripe Ogam', is a standard alphabet with a *ríab* 'stripe' between each letter. (61) *Taebogam Tlachtga* 'Side-Ogam of Tlachtga' has all characters drawn below the stemline, the groups being distinguished by the angle. In (73) *Ogam airenach* 'Shield-Ogam' each character is curved like the boss of a shield. (48) *Coll ar guta* 'C for a vowel', a standard Ogam alphabet in which, however, the vowels are represented by one to five Cs. The *Ogham Coll* of later manuscripts, a cipher in conventional script in which vowels are written with one to five *c*s (see Hyde, 1932, 170-1), is based on this. To these variations belong also the (74) *Rothogam Roigni Roscadhaigh* 'Wheel-Ogam of R. R.', the (75) *Fege Find* 'Finn's ridge-pole [Ogam]' and (76) *Traigsruth Fercheirtne*[18] 'Ferchertne's foot-stream?', arrangements of Ogam in a wheel or on the lines of five and four concentric circles and squares respectively.

(b) Ogam alphabets in which the standard sequence is varied though each character retains its own value. For example: in (44) *Ogam ind co ind* 'End to end Ogam', the first character is followed by the last, the second by the second-last etc., i.e. BILEFU. . . In (46) *Ogam sesmach* 'Standing Ogam', the third and fourth groups are placed first followed by the second and first reversed internally so that it is read from the end to the middle and then from the beginning to the middle *ar is ina medon ata forba na ceithri n-aicme* 'for it is in its middle that the end of the four groups is.' (47) *Gort fo leith*[19] (? *sic leg.*, see Thurneysen, 1928, 302) 'Distinctive field (i.e. orientation) [Ogam]' is an arrangement of the alphabet placing the first letters from each group together followed by the second etc. to avoid consecutive letters on the same side of the stemline.

(c) Ogam alphabets in which a variation on the sequence as in category (b) above serves as a cryptic device, the characters taking on new values dictated by the arrangement. Thus, (35) *Ogam buaidir fo-ranna* 'Ogam of confusion which subdivides'[20] is an arrangement of the characters as in *Gort fo leith* (see (b) above), but in this case while *Beithe* has the value B, *hÚath* has the value L, *Muin* F etc. (33) *Cend ara n-aill* (*sic leg.* see Thurneysen, 1928, 302) 'Head before the other' (i.e. back to front) an arrangement in which the character sequence in each *aicme* is reversed so that *Nin* has the value B, *Sail* L etc. (42) *Ogam imarbach* 'Deceitful[21] Ogam', the second group takes on the values of the first and vice versa, the third those of the fourth etc. (36) *Rind fri derc* 'Point against eye [Ogam]' the first group with the values of the fourth and vice versa, the second with those of the third etc. (60) *In diupartach* 'The defrauding [Ogam]', the alphabet is defrauded of its first letter so that *Luis* has the value B, *Fern* L etc.

(d) Other cryptic devices such as (15) *Ogam uird* 'Ogam of order' in which the letters of the name to be written in Ogam appear in their alphabetic sequence, e.g. BNRA for BRAN. (18) *Gle[s] selge* 'The hunting arrangement' in which the words or names to be written in Ogam are written through one another so that the matching parts have to be 'hunted out'. (31) *Ogam ro mesc Bres* 'The Ogam which confused Bres [mac Elathan]' (whose half-brother Ogma is said to have created Ogam, see §§8.4-5), a device in which, to judge by the example, the name of the letter is written for the letter itself.[22] (32) *Ogam dedenach* 'Final Ogam', the last letter of the name is written for the letter, thus E for *Beithe*, S for *Luis* etc.

(e) (10) *Osogam* 'Stag-Ogam', (20) *Armogam* 'Weapon-Ogam', (30) *Mucogam* 'Pig-Ogam', (83) *Ogam n-eathrach* 'Boat-Ogam', (88) *Ogam cuidechtach* 'Company-Ogam'. These belong to the category of subject-indexed alphabetic word-lists discussed below under (i).

(f) (27) The standard Ogam letter name sequence followed by the standard alphabet (28). The supplementary characters are not named but their values are given. No. 26 is a sequence of *Crannogam*, i.e. a word-list of tree-names of type (e) above retaining some but not all of the standard Ogam letter names which denote trees.

(g) Series of *foraicmi* 'supplementary groups of characters' and *deich* (pl. of *deach* 'syllable, verse-foot', here apparently meaning sigla or contractions for syllables) which an Ogamist is obliged to know *air ni cumaing bus Ogmóir*[23] *lasna biat a deich ┐ a foraicme ┐ a forbethi* (23) 'for he cannot be an Ogamist who does not have (i.e. know) its *deich* and its *foraicmi* and its *forbethi* ( = *forbaidi* 'accents'?).' These are found at 23-25 and again at 77-81 where they are named *forfeda*.

(h) Foreign alphabets:[24] (84) Hebrew, (85) Egyptian, (86) 'African', (91) Scandinavian (called *Ogam Lochlannach*) and (92-3) *Gallogam* 'Viking Ogam' i.e. a Fuþark together with the names of the runes. In H.3.18 these are accompanied by series of Hebrew, Greek and Syrian number-words together with a concordance of Greek letter names and their numerical values.

(i) To these varieties of 'Ogams' belong a further twenty-seven which precede the tabulation of alphabets beginning with *Aradach Finn*.[25] Of these the last three detail cryptic (or short- and long-hand) ways of writing. In *Cend a muine* 'head in a bush (?)'(5810) the letter alone is used for the letter name when the latter reproduces the initial part of the word or name being written, as in CLE for *certle*.[26] *Cend fo muine* 'head under a bush (?)' (5817) does the same for the last part of whatever is being written, e.g. MAEL R = *Máel-Ruis*, and in *Nathair imceann* 'two-headed snake' (5821; see Carey, 1990, 37-39 on *imchenn* 'two-headed') a name is written forwards and backwards from a central point, e.g. HCALLAECEALLACH = *Ceallach*.[27] *Macogam* 'Boy-Ogam' (5773) is explained as a method of divining the sex of an unborn child by 'dividing' the mother's name (i.e. the letters of her name) in two, an uneven division indicating a boy, and both *Cossogam* 'Foot-Ogam' (5779) and *Sronogam* 'Nose-Ogam' (5786) are described as finger-spelling forms of Ogam using the shin-bone and nose respectively as stemlines. The bulk of these, however, is made up of alphabetic sequences of words of a particular subject category indicated in the name, e.g. *Enogam* 'Bird-Ogam' (5692), a list of twenty names of birds arranged alphabetically beginning *Besan*, *Lachu* etc., *Ogam tirda* 'Agrarian Ogam' (5724), a list of tools used on the farm, *Næmogam* 'Saint-Ogam' (5791), a list of saints, *Danogam* 'Craft-Ogam' (5797) a list of crafts etc. In many of these the list contains only four subject-words, each representing an *aicme* and said to be doubled, trebled etc. to fill the remaining slots in the group, e.g. *Boogam* 'Cow-Ogam' (5759): *Lilgach* 'milch cow' for *Aicme Beithe*, two milch cows, three etc.; *Gamnach* 'a stripper', *Samaisc* 'a three-year old heifer' and *Dairt* 'a yearling heifer' for the remaining three. This is the case with all of those listed in (e) above.[28]

§7.12 In text II of *Mittelirische Verslehren* (Thurneysen (1891, 32. 2 and 34. 9, 12) the training of the first three years of the *fili* is said to include, among other subjects, (1) *Coeca ogum im certogum* 'Fifty Ogams including *Certogam*', (2) *L ogum im ogum n-uird* 'Fifty Ogams including *Ogam Uird*' and (3) *L ogum im ebadaig n-Ilmain* 'Fifty Ogams including *Ébadach Ilmain*' (leg. *Ilaind*).[29] Though it falls short of listing one hundred and fifty varieties of Ogam, even if one includes the *Bríatharogam*, it is clear that reference is being made here to

the material of *In Lebor Ogaim*. This is confirmed further by the following difficult piece of verse which appears, fittingly, at the end of the tabulation of
Ogams in all manuscripts.[30] It appears to be an address (by Morann?) to Nere[31],
quintessential judge of Irish poets, informing him that he (the addresser) has
studied the Ogams prescribed for primary study and feels confident of having
mastered them:[32]

1 Mo Nere nemnig núallbrethaig,[33]
2 dia n-ogam n-idan n-imráide(a),
3 ro sluindi[u] díri[u]g díanindscib
4 cach [n]-irlunn [n]-ogaim anaichnid,
5 hi cestaib có(i)rib comairci.[34]
6 Ar is crann fo lóch[35] lercherdach
7 tri cóecat n-ogam n-ilardae,
8 do-rata fri húair [n]-irscrútain.[36]

1 O splendid famous-judging Nere,
2 if you treat of pure Ogam,
3 I can name straight-off in rapid words
4 every unfamiliar parallel (i.e. variation) of Ogam,
5 of which you inquire in fitting questions.
6 For he (i.e. Nere) is a multi-skilled luminary
7 of thrice fifty varied Ogams
8 which have been set at the time of primary study.

What practical benefits the *fili* could have derived from learning these
'alphabets' is not immediately clear. The only 'Ogams' which one could imagine
a poet having recourse to in the exercise of his craft are the subject-indexed
alphabetic word-lists with full complements of words. A substantial number of
these committed to memory so that they could be rimed off, as the text puts it,
*díriug díanindscib*, would have put an extensive conveniently classified
vocabulary, including rare words, at his fingertips. These, however, form a
small percentage of the total number of 'Ogams' in this material. For the rest,
the fact that these were considered worthy of study is an indication of the
fascination of the medieval mind with cryptic varieties of alphabets. That this
became an obsession in Ireland was probably due in no small part to the nature
of the Ogam script, which lent itself to variation in this manner.

## THE *FORFEDA*

§7.13 The main importance of the Ogams of the *Auraicept* is that they highlight
the *foilchesta* and the *forfeda* as a category apart and in doing so provide some
insight into the later history of the alphabet and the revisions it underwent.
These can be best illustrated by an examination of the *forfeda* in the three tracts
referred to above.

The texts tabulate the *forfeda* and their values as follows (A = *Auraicept na
nÉces*, B = *De dúilib feda*, C = *In Lebor Ogaim*:

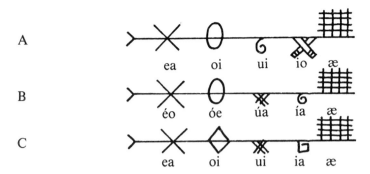

In all three traditions there is agreement with regard to position in the sequence in the case of the first, second and fifth characters (*Ébad*, *Ór* and *Emancholl*). In A, however, characters three and four (*Uilen* and *Iphín*) appear in reverse order to that of B and C though the values themselves are not reversed. In the Book of Ballymote C shows a preference for straight lines, so that *Ór* and *Iphín* are angular in this tradition but round in A and B.[37] The position of the characters relative to the stemline, however, is the same in all.[38]

With regard to the values there is agreement in all in the case of the fifth character, which represents the diphthong *ae* written with the ligature æ. There is, however, a marked difference between B on the one hand and A and C on the other in the case of the first four *forfeda*. All agree in having E, O, U and I as the first vowels respectively in each value. In the A and C traditions these characters are made to correspond to the digraphs of conventional script used in the case of front vowels before neutral consonants (*ea* and *io*) and back vowels before palatal consonants (*oi* and *ui*). In B, and in all three traditions in the case of *Emancholl*, on the other hand, the values are those of the diphthongs in which *é*, *ó*, *ú*, *í* and *á* respectively are the first elements. The B tradition is the most successful in establishing the *forfeda* as a distinctive homogeneous group, but there is an overlap between the two inasmuch as the term *défoguir*, which the *forfeda* are said to represent, may be used both of diphthongs and digraphs. Nonetheless at 1296ff./4396ff. the *two* (leg. *deudha* as in 4396 for *trega* at 1296) reasons for bringing the *forfeda* into the alphabet are stated to have been that they should correspond to *défoguir* and serve to distinguish soft from hard vowels.

That the diphthong values which the B tradition assigns the *forfeda* are distinct from the five principal vowels goes without saying. The values of the A/C tradition look a little more artificial, but in both Irish grammar and prosody the difference between a vowel followed on the one hand by a palatal consonant or on the other by a neutral consonant was very important. In grammar it usually meant a different case of the noun, in prosody it was crucial to rhyme. To distinguish *e* + palatal consonant[39] from *e* + neutral consonant by the use of distinctive names, therefore, could prove useful for purposes of instruction in metrics and the *forfeda* letter names – not the symbols themselves, as the script was by now largely redundant – were pressed into service to this end.[40] In writing, however, these distinctions are best made by the use of digraphs (whether in conventional script or Ogam) and it is difficult to believe that the *forfeda* would have been created with them in mind.[41] The benefits to be derived

from such an innovation would have been far outweighed by the complexities
to which it would have given rise. These traditions, therefore, make the best use
possible of a series of superfluous characters and their names but tell us nothing
of why these were created in the first place.

§7.14 That the *forfeda* were not created with the values of these traditions in
mind is shown by the letter names themselves. *Ébad* and *Ór* are distinct from
*Edad* and *Onn* in having long initial vowels, not diphthongs or digraphs (though
*Ébad* came to be written *Éabhadh* and *Ór* was modified to *Óir* to generate a
*défogur*). *Emancholl* has an identical initial to *Edad* and did not originally function on the acrostic principle at all but was brought into line with it by modification to *Æmancholl*.[42] In *Iphín* the initial *i* is followed by a palatal consonant and
is less appropriate to the value *io* than the principal vowel *Idad*. What is more,
the alternative form of the name, *Pín*, does not begin with a vowel at all. In fact
the only *forfid* with a name the initial of which matches a value in one of these
traditions is *Uilen*. It will be clear, therefore, that in the majority of cases the
names of the *forfeda* presuppose a set of values which cannot be reconciled with
the traditions outlined above. They are closer to yet another tradition in the
*Auraicept* which appears to be associated with Munster.

In a passage at 1359ff./4501ff., said to be taken from the *Auraicept Muman*
'*Auraicept* of Munster', it is indicated that the addition of the *forfeda* to the
alphabet took place in two stages. *Ébad* and *Ór* were added first, whence *na
secht feda* 'the seven vowels' of Ogam,[43] and the remaining three were incorporated later. The *Auraicept Muman* names these *Iphín* with the value of a
*défogur* 'diphthong, digraph', *Pín* with the value P and *Emancholl* with the
value X. *Uilen* is not mentioned here but the passage immediately following this
(1367ff./4422ff.) points out that the correct value of *Iphín* is P, that of *Emancholl* X, that of *Uilen* Y and it assigns *Ébad* and *Ór* the values É and Ó.

§7.15 Since there is evidence of a desire on the part of later Ogamists to have
the supplementary characters fit into the Ogam scheme by having them all
represent a similar type of sound, it will be clear that a version which has some
of them functioning as vowels and others as consonants must constitute the
*traditio difficilior* and have considerable claim to authenticity. That this is so
is further confirmed for some of the characters by their names and shapes, and
by the evidence of some manuscript Ogams. The name *Emancholl*, for example,
does not operate on the acrostic principle. It is descriptive of the actual shape
of the character 'double *Coll* (C)' and was clearly inspired by Latin X and Greek
*Chī* and designed *for foimtin na focul nGrecda no Laitinda do thabairt isin
nGaidelg* 'in readiness for the adoption of Greek and Latin words into Irish' as
pointed out at 1370-74/4427-30.[44] In alphabets 32, 33 and 35 of the Book of
Ogam the symbol is given the values *cc* (based on the name) and *ach* (the
fricative value of Greek *Chī*) as alternatives to *æ*, and in the Berne manuscript
it has the value *ach* as already noted.[45] The value P is confirmed for the fourth
character of this series by the Vatican Ogams (see §7.8) and by alphabet (33)
in the Book of Ogam. Its shape in both of these, moreover, clearly betrays its
origin; it is no more than an inverted P written in an angular fashion. The name
*Pín* (‹ Latin *pinus*), which is likely to be original in view of the later perceived

requirement that each supplementary symbol have a name beginning in a distinctive vowel, also confirms this value. Whether *Iphín* is a perfunctory modification of *Pín* designed to generate a name beginning in *i*, or is an authentic variant of *Pín* representing the Greek fricative *Phī* is not clear. Thurneysen (1928, 297) thought it original and suggested that both its shape (in its rounded form) and name derived from the the *hyphen* of the grammarians.

Given that this tradition records *Emancholl* as having been created to accommodate Latin and Greek words in Irish (= Ogam) it is highly probable that *Uilen* was intended for the same purpose and was in fact based on Latin Y (Greek *Upsīlon*), as indicated in the passage referred to above. This is the only explanation which will accommodate the acrostic principle and allow for the coexistence of *Uilen* and *Úr*. The initial *ui* in *Uilen* was not designed to represent a sound in Irish distinct from that represented by *Úr*; it simply reproduces the name of the letter Y in medieval Latin, viz *ui* (Thurneysen, 1928, 297), whence English *wy*. This is confirmed by the use of the symbol *y* in Irish manucripts for *ui*.

Finally, in the tradition which gives the last three *forfeda* the values Y, P and X the first two are said to stand for the long vowels *é* and *ó*, values which are consistent with the application of the acrostic principle to their names *Ébad* and *Ór* (< Latin *aurum*).[46] These are confirmed elsewhere in the *Auraicept* by transcription with *ee* and *oo* (1141) and are probably the values intended in the Berne Ogams (see n7.13). The shape of *Ór*, moreover, is also reminiscent of Latin O (cp. the remarks on *Pín* above, both names being Latin loanwords) and is consistent with this interpretation.[47] That the inspiration for the long-vowel values came from without, as we saw was the case with the last three *forfeda*, is hinted at in *Auraicept* 2872 where they are said to be *seichimh nGreigda* 'in imitation of the Greek [alphabet]' (i.e. of Greek *Ēta* and *Ōmega*) and it is probable that the seven vowels of Greek suggested the *secht feda* of Ogam in the *Auraicept Muman*.

Thus, the *traditio difficilior*, which has the greatest claim to authenticity, presents a heterogeneous set of values for the *forfeda*, each of which can be reconciled with its letter name either on the acrostic principle or as a term descriptive of its shape, and can be accounted for as inspired from without, not by any need for it to write Irish. These values and/or names are also what underlie the Old Irish kennings which, as I have pointed out in a different connection, arc the oldest, least contaminated and most trustworthy source of information on the Ogam letter names in general (McManus, 1988, 129-30, 136-7, 165-6).

§7.16 The twenty-five character alphabet of the manuscript tradition, then, may be described as a revised and enlarged edition of the original. The revision involved rescuing *Úath*, *Cert*, *Gétal* and *Straif* from redundancy by assigning them foreign, cosmetic values reflected in the modified forms of their names (*hÚath*, *Queirt*, *nGétal*, *Zraif*) and identifying *Ébad* with Greek *Ēta*. The enlargement involved the addition of the remaining *forfeda*. Of these nine symbols the only one which was identified with a character in Irish conventional script was *hÚath*. The remaining eight were problematic (*foilchesta*) or supplementary (*forfeda*) and formed a category which required elucidation, whence

the Ogams of the *Auraicept*. Irish had no need of these and the objectives of
the Ogamists responsible for them differed markedly from those of the original
framers of Ogam, who were concerned to create an alphabet specifically for
Irish. This first revision took place after Ogam had ceased to be used in a practical capacity and had nothing to do with writing Irish. It was inspired by a comparison of Ogam with the Latin and Greek alphabets and was designed to
generate an alphabet which would be capable of catering for words borrowed
from these languages. The result gave Ogam a status which, measured in terms
of its letters, was, in the opinion of these revisors at least, equal if not superior
to that of its classical counterparts. The redundancies in the inherited alphabet
and its deficiencies *vis-à-vis* Latin and Greek had been seen to reflect badly on
Irish letters, and were made good in a purely cosmetic way.

§7.17 The first revision was followed by a second which was very different in
inspiration. This too had nothing to do with Ogam as a script, but it had
everything to do with the Irish language, not foreign alphabets. The comparison
of Ogam with the Latin and Greek alphabets had secured a central role for it,
not as a writing system but as a framework for the study of Irish, and Ogam
terminology formerly associated with the script now passed into the vocabulary
of instruction in Irish grammar and metrics. Reflecting this new status the word
Ogam would eventually develop the meaning 'written Irish' as opposed to
'spoken Irish', and the letter names, still memorized in their old sequence, now
came to function as an inventory of sounds in the Irish language. In this scheme
of things a role was found for twenty-three of the twenty-five names; the only
two which would remain redundant, but would continue to be learned, were
*Queirt* and *Straif*.[48] *Úath*, now modified to *hÚath*, was equated with the *nota
aspirationis* of Latin grammar, and a verbal-noun formation *húathadh* 'h-ing'
was coined to denote Irish 'lenition'. The modification of *Gétal* to *nGétal* had
produced an Irish equivalent to Latin and Greek *Agma* and this letter name,
later developing to *Níatall*, was now used to denote the sound /ŋ/, which in the
classification of Irish consonants for metrical purposes belonged to the 'heavy'
(*teann*) group.

As a group the *forfeda* differed from others in having no internal consistency
and little or no relevance to Irish. These two irregularities were resolved by making them represent a distinctive class of vocalic sounds. To this end a modification in the names was undertaken, rather as *Úath*, *Cert* etc. had been modified
earlier, to generate five distinctive initial vowels. The vowels *e*, *o* and *u* were
catered for by *Ébad* (> *Éabhadh*), *Ór* (modified to *Óir*) and *Uilenn* (> *Uillionn*).
*Pín* was abandoned for *Iphín* (> *Ifín*) giving *i*,[49] and *Emancholl* was first
modified to *Æmancholl* then to *Amharcholl* to generate an initial *a*. Each of
these names was now pressed into service to denote a diphthong or a digraph
beginning with its initial vowel and was thus distinguished from the corresponding letter name in *Aicme Ailme*, which denoted the pure vowel. This is the
scheme we see developing in the *Auraicept* and culminating in later Bardic
tradition (see Mac Aogáin, 1968, 4 and Bergin, 1915, 5) where *Éabhadh* is
said to have four values (*ea*, *eu*, *eo* and *eoi*), *Óir* one (*oi*), *Uillionn* three (*ua*,
*ui* and *uai*), *Ifín* five (*ia*, *io*, *iu*, *iai* and *iui*) and *Amharcholl* four (*ao*, *ae*, *ai* and
*aoi*).[50]

Evidently, then, the manuscript tradition presents us with a contemporary modified form of the Ogam alphabet, not the original preserved in cold storage. This is in fact precisely what one might expect, and the recognition of this clearly undermines any attempt to identify the prototype of Ogam using this material (see §3.13).

# CHAPTER EIGHT

# The Later Tradition (2): Medieval Theories on the Origin of Ogam and Ogam in Early Irish Saga and Law

**§8.1** As we have seen in the last chapter the first revision of the Ogam alphabet was inspired by the study of the Latin and Greek alphabets and a desire to effect a status for the native system which put it on an equal footing with its classical counterparts. This revision was not an isolated phenomenon. Latin grammar was only one of several subjects on the curriculum of the Early Irish *literati*, which ranged from 'scriptural exegesis, canon law and computistics to the inherited native law, legend and genealogy' (Ó Corráin, 1985, 52). Of all of these the study of scripture was the most revered and biblical exegesis was to have a profound effect on Irish scholarship, expressed in Irish law, saga, history and genealogy.[1] In the domain of aetiology in particular the Bible, as the authoritative origin-legend of mankind, could not be ignored and the Irish *literati* set about securing a place for their own nation in this scheme of things by recasting their history and, as Ó Corráin has pointed out (1985, 55), by splicing their genealogical superstructure to the scriptural one. It is in the context of the Latin learning which provided this world view and the revisions to which it gave rise, and which was also probably the inspiration for the creation of standard Old Irish as an efficient literary instrument, that the elaboration of the Ogam alphabet as discussed in the last chapter should be seen, and the fact that the exposition of the origin of Ogam by these revisors has a biblical setting serves only to confirm this. This is the doctrine found in the *Auraicept na nÉces* and it contrasts with what in view of the current idiom in Early Irish textual and sociological analysis may be labelled the 'nativist' tradition, that of *In Lebor Ogaim*. Before discussing these a few words on the *Auraicept* itself will not be inappropriate.

**§8.2** The reception of the *Auraicept* by modern scholarship has in general been less than enthusiastic, though recent studies have led to a more appreciative assessment of it. For Bergin (1938, 207) it was 'an attempt to construct an Irish grammar on the model set by the Medieval Latin grammarians' which 'led nowhere' and 'was abandoned'. That this cannot be a fair or accurate evaluation of it must be evident from the fact that, to judge by its extensive manuscript tradition (Ahlqvist, 1982, 22ff.), it was one of the most widely read and commented upon texts in medieval Ireland. Like the works of the Latin grammarians the *Auraicept na nÉces* 'The Scholars' (or Poets') Primer', as its title shows, was read as a propaedeutic to the study of metrics and was prescribed for the trainee *fili*'s first year of study.[2] The *Auraicept* was not the first expression of linguistic analysis in the history of Irish letters – that honour must be reserved for the creation of the Ogam alphabet – nor is it entirely Latin-based. Watkins has shown (1970, 8) that it contains a basic purely native Irish doctrine of poetic learning.[3] That it was not 'abandoned' as Bergin puts it is clear from Ó Cuív's demonstration (1965, 154ff.) that the Bardic grammarians drew heavily on it in matters of terminology and it is referred to in the introduction to the later Bardic Grammatical Tracts where its doctrine on the origin of Irish is reproduced. There is, however, an important difference in emphasis between the *Auraicept* and the later tracts. They concentrate on Irish as a vehicle for poetic composition and present us with a prescriptive grammar of the language for that purpose. The *Auraicept* on the other hand is decidedly reactionary in spirit and assesses the analysis of the Irish language *vis-à-vis* that of Latin. Its authors'[4] main concern was to compare Irish in as favourable a light as possible with the language of the Western Church.

   To this end, just as the Latin and Greek grammarians looked to the Latin and Greek alphabets as the descriptive framework for the study of their languages, so the compilers of the *Auraicept* (and the later grammarians following their lead) looked to Ogam, or more correctly the *Beithe-luis-nin*, for the study of theirs. This was due both to the authority vested in Ogam by its antiquity and to the fact that, though moribund as a script, the salient features of the system – its inventory of letters, their sequence and their names – were considered peculiarly Irish and suited to Irish requirements. These provided the Irish grammarians and prosodists with a sufficiently distinctive framework for comparison with Latin and part of the considerable importance which attached to the *Auraicept* as a primer for the trainee *fili* must have lain in its self-confident assertion of the right of the vernacular to equal consideration alongside the three *prímbélrai* or *linguae sacrae*, especially as some were apparently content to dub it a 'worldly speech' read only by the 'uncouth'.[5] The compilers of the *Auraicept* were not apologetic in their assessment of Irish *vis-à-vis* Latin, notwithstanding the enormous prestige attaching to the latter. They observed the maxim that attack was the best form of defence and this is particularly evident in their exposition on the creation of the Irish language and its alphabet.

§**8.3** In brief, *Auraicept* teaching on the origin of Irish and Ogam is as follows: Fénius Farsaid, a learned man in the three principal languages (Latin, Greek and Hebrew), journeyed together with Goídel mac Ethéoir, Íar mac Nema and a retinue of seventy two scholars from Scythia to the Plain of Shinar with the intention of studying the languages confused at Nimrod's Tower (the Tower of Babel).[6] Finding that these had been dispersed throughout the world he sent forth his scholars to study them, staying on at the tower himself co-ordinating the enterprise and supporting his scholars with food and clothing. Having completed their investigations the scholars returned after ten years and requested that Fénius select for them from all the languages of the world one which no-one else would know but they alone. Fénius agreed and created *in Bérla tóbaide* (or *teipide*), 'the selected language' which he called *Goídelc* 'Gaelic' after Goídel mac Ethéoir. At the same time he also created the super-additions of *Goídelc*, namely *Bérla Féne* (called after Fénius Farsaid), *Íarmberla* (after Íar mac Nema), *Bérla n-etarscartha*, *Bérla na filed* and *Gnáthbérla* together with the *Beithe-luis-nin*.[7] 'And what was best of every language and what was widest and finest was cut into Irish and every sound for which a sign had not been found in other alphabets, signs were found for them in the *Beithe-luis-nin* (1053ff./4010ff.). And there were twenty-five scholars of the school who were most noble and their names were given to the vowels and consonants of Ogam' (1135ff./4236ff.).

This tale has been dismissed by Bergin as 'fabulous' (1938, 207) and by Graves as 'clumsy fiction . . . embodying no authentic information with respect to the history of Irish letters' or as an 'absurd legend' containing 'no single element of truth' (1876, 453-4). But if it may be summarily dismissed in this fashion so too surely may the fictional biblical narrative (Genesis 11, 6ff.) which underlies it, as this equally tells us nothing 'authentic' about the origin of languages. Indeed to expect the Irish *literati* of the Old Irish period to be able to tell us anything authentic about the origin of the Irish language or Ogam would be a tall order. Their legend is a typical product of its time and is important not as a record of 'authentic' history but rather as a document expressing the attitudes and aspirations of its framers. Their confident challenge to the supremacy of the three principal languages, expressed in the argument that *Goídelc* was created *after* them by selection of the best from them, is clearly the response of the Irish *literati* to the enormous prestige of Latin and establishes the equal right to consideration of the vernacular. This was indeed the *de facto* position of Irish at the time of composition, for though Ireland was at the time a major centre of Latin learning the Irish language continued to be the vehicle of intellectual thought in the important domains of law and history and particularly in those closely associated with the *filid*, saga and poetry. The *Auraicept* aetiology is a statement of this status, a charter of rights for Irish, a fact which explains in part why it was prescribed reading for the aspiring *fili* in the first year of study.

Notwithstanding its 'mythical' nature, moreover, the broad thrust of the origin of the Irish language as outlined in the *Auraicept* is not wide of the mark as a statement on the origin of Ogam itself. We have seen, for example, that Ogam was a once-off *creation*, not the result of an evolution over a period of time. Its creators were undoubtedly familiar with Latin and possibly also with Greek, just as Fénius Farsaid was a sage in the three principal languages, and the system was created specifically for Irish, rather as *Goídelc* was created for the exclusive use of the scholars of Fénius' school. There is a sense too in which Ogam might reasonably have been regarded as a refinement of its alphabetic forerunners, in that it gives graphic representation to the distinction between vowels and consonants of which Latin and Greek grammarians speak, but which is not reflected in their alphabets. One wonders further whether the process of creating Irish as described in the *Auraicept*, i.e. by selection of the best from other languages, might not be interpreted as a statement on the genesis of standard Old Irish. We know little about how this standard was fixed but if the process resembled the establishment of the Classical Modern Irish standard, for which see Ó Cuív (1973a, 131), the result could reasonably have been labelled *in bérla tóbaide/teipide*, i.e. a form of Irish 'selected' or 'abstracted' from regional varieties in the spoken language. Examined in this light, then, the legend would be fictional only in a superficial sense, and anything but clumsy!

§**8.4** An alternative version of the origin of Ogam is to be found in *In Lebor Ogaim*, a tract dealing specifically with Ogam and containing in the main the varieties of 'Ogams' discussed above (§7.11) together with the *Bríatharogam*, both dating from the Old Irish period.[8] The prologue, which is somewhat later, opens with the frequently used 'What is the place, time, person and cause' formula, here in reference to the invention of Ogam, and answers these questions with an account which owes nothing to the Bible and differs from *Auraicept* doctrine in locating the creation at home. The inventor here is Ogma mac Elathan who is said to have been skilled in speech and poetry and to have created the system as proof of his intellectual ability and with the intention that it should be the preserve of the learned, to the exclusion of rustics and fools. 'Ogam is from Ogma according to sound and from *ōg-úaim* ('perfect sewing', or 'alliteration' but see below §8.6) according to matter. The father of Ogam is Ogma and his hand or knife is its mother. And the first thing ever written in Ogam was [a message containing] seven *b*s in a single switch of birch sent as a warning to Lug mac Ethlenn: "your wife will be carried away from you seven times to the *síd* ('otherworld') unless the birch protect her." And this is why *Beithe* ('birch') is the first letter in the alphabet, because it was first written on birch' (5481ff.). This serves as a lead-in to a discussion of the theory that the Ogam letter names were in origin the names of trees and the *Auraicept* teaching to the effect that they were called after twenty-five scholars in the school of Fénius Farsaid is cited as an alternative. The *Bríatharogam* texts, the main source of information on the meaning of the letter names, then follow.

The exclusivity of Ogam is highlighted here once again, though in this case it is probably no more than a statement of the *de facto* situation with regard to literacy, which cannot have been very widespread at the time. The explanation of the word *ogam* is a typical example of *bérla n-etarscartha* i.e. Isidorian-type etymology, based here, if the rendering *ōg-úaim* is correct, on the word *Ogam* in the sense 'written Irish' to judge by the ensuing explanation (5479-81) *.i. og-uaim do-berait na filid forsin filideacht trid, ar is fri fedaib toimsither Gædelg icna filedaib*: 'i.e. perfect alliteration which the poets apply to poetry through it, for it is by reference to the letters that Irish is measured by the poets' (for an alternative suggestion see below §8.6). The reference to the first use of Ogam is interesting and will be discussed below. Here it will suffice to say that the message sent to Lug is more akin to tally notation than alphabetic writing. The idea that the letter names were all names of trees is a medieval fancy as shown by the ensuing *Bríatharogam* and hinted at by a commentator in the *Auraicépt* (1147-9) who, following a reference to this alternative to *Auraicept* doctrine, points out that 'some of these trees are not known today.' But of all aspects of *In Lebor Ogaim* teaching on the origin of Ogam the qualities which it ascribes to its inventor, Ogma, and the nature of the relationship between his name and the word *ogam* present the greatest difficulties.

§**8.5** Ogma mac Elathan is known to us from other sources, in particular from the famous tale of mythic history *Cath Maige Tuired* 'The [second] Battle of Mag Tuired' (*CMT*) which recounts the epic contest between the gods of pagan Ireland, the Túatha Dé Danann, and their supernatural enemies, the Fomóiri.[9] In *CMT* he is known variously as Ogmae mac Ela(u)than (§138), Oghmae mac Ethlend (§59) and Oghmai mac Ethnenn (*sic leg.* for MS Etnae?, §36) and is half-brother to Bres mac Elathan – whose reign as king of the Túatha Dé Danann ushered in a period of chaos – on his father's side and to Lug mac Ethlenn/Ethnenn – who successfully led the Túatha Dé Danann into battle (and was the first to use Ogam) – on his mother's. Ogma's role in *CMT* is that of a Túatha Dé Danann warrior (*trénfer*) whose considerable strength (§§72, 105) is diminished only by undernourishment during the reign of Bres when he is made to perform the menial task of fetching firewood (§25). As Thurneysen noted (1937, 195) he is not distinguished in *CMT* for the quality of eloquence with which *In Lebor Ogaim* credits him and there is no indication whatsoever that the author of *CMT* was familiar with the ascription to him of the important role of inventor of a writing system. Indeed in the capacity of firewood fetcher he is not far removed from the 'rustics' expressly excluded from the benefits of his invention, but this portrayal of him is clearly to be interpreted as a reflection of the chaos of Bres' reign. In the Dumézilian scheme Ogma's appropriate function is that of martial force.

Given that the Ogma of *CMT* does not fit the bill as alphabet inventor it would be tempting to assume that the choice of him by the authors of the *In Lebor Ogaim* doctrine was dictated in part by a desire, well attested elsewhere, to secure a divine origin for a writing system but in the main by both the accidental suitability of his name, Ogma, which removed the need to invent an eponym of the Fénius Farsaid type, and the appropriateness of his patronym mac Elathan (*elatha* gen. *elathan* 'art, science'). In that case we should be obliged to assume that the description of him as 'a man skilled in speech and in poetry' was fabricated to meet the requirements of the new role he was being made to play, one which is some distance from that which he plays in *CMT*. This line of argument, however, is undermined by evidence from what in the circumstances is a rather unusual source, the second-century A.D. Greek rhetor Lucian.

In his account (Harmon, 1913, 62ff. = *Lucian, Heracles* 1ff.) Lucian points out that Heracles (Hercules) was known to the Gauls as *Ogmios* and he describes a picture of him in which though equipped like Heracles – dressed in lion's skin and bearing a club, a quiver and a bow – he was depicted as an old bald-headed man being followed willingly by a crowd whose ears were tethered by golden chains to his tongue. Lucian was understandably puzzled by this until a learned Greek-speaking Gaul explained that the Gauls identified Heracles, not Hermes, with eloquence because of his superior power and he went on to explain that he was depicted as an old man because 'eloquence shows full vigour in age.' This explanation also quite clearly explained the symbolism of the chains and the fact that the crowd, far from being dragged against their will by Ogmios, were eagerly following him spellbound, so to speak, by his every word.

The significance of Lucian's account to the present discussion will be obvious. If *Ogma* (Old Irish *Ogmae*) and *Ogmios* are one and the same the

*In Lebor Ogaim* description of the former as a *fer ro-eolach a mberla ⁊ a filidecht* (5470) would be consistent with Lucian's informant's explanation and need not be fabricated, while the role of Ogma in *CMT* would be more akin to the orthodox Herculean side of Ogmios' character as expressed in his being depicted with a club, a quiver and a bow. Unfortunately we know too little about both Ogma mac Elathan and Ogmios to allow for certainty of identification but it is difficult to keep them apart, though there are some linguistic problems in the equation and in the relation of both names to the word *ogam*.

The difficulty hinges on the reflex of the intervocalic group *-gm-* in Old Irish. Thurneysen (1937, 196) rejected the derivation of *ogam* from *\*ogmos* on the grounds that the verbal nouns in the phrase *ám [t]hám* (later *áimh tháimh*, compare the parallel *aig taig*) ⟨ *\*agmā*, *\*to-agmā* showed that the treatment of *g* before *m* was identical to that before *n*, i.e. it was lost with compensatory lengthening of the preceding vowel and lenition of the nasal.[10] In that case the expected Old Irish outcome of *\*ogmos*, *Ogmios* would be *\*óm \*Ómae* later *\*úam*, *\*Úamae*, and Ó Corráin (1979, 165) may have confirmed Thurneysen's hypothesis in his identification of the second element in the name *Dar-Óma* (⟨ Old Irish gen. *\*Ómai*) as the Irish reflex of *Ogmios*. If so the only way in which *Ogma* and *Ogmios* can be equated is by assuming that the Gaulish form has undergone irregular syncope (Thurneysen posits a base form *\*ogosmo-* or *\*ugosmo* for *ogam*) or by regarding *Ogma* as a late borrowing of the Gaulish name, a view taken by most scholars following the lead of MacNeill (1919, 170-71). By 'late', however, one would have to assume a date after the loss of *g* before *m* which would make the borrowing very recent in Ogam terms, as the group *-gn-* is retained in Ogam inscriptions. That the Ogam alphabet cannot have been borrowed from the same Gauls will be obvious on these grounds alone.

§**8.6** None of this brings us any closer to an etymology of the word *ogam* and it remains to review the suggestions made in this connection. Richardson's (1943) impossible derivation of it from *Agma* has already been referred to; the very fact that this is a letter name containing the sound it denotes (i.e. /aŋma/) is sufficient to dismiss the derivation not to mention the problem of the initial *a*, the unlikelihood of naming a writing system after a single foreign letter name and the difficulties posed by positing the existence of a symbol for the sound /ŋ/ in the *original* Ogam alphabet (see §3.13). Killeen (1965) draws attention to the Greek and Latin metaphorical uses of words meaning 'furrow' for the 'written line' and suggests a borrowing from Greek *ogmos* 'furrow', a derivation subject to all the difficulties associated with the group *-gm-* and the added problem of the fact that this particular word is not attested in Greek itself with the metaphorical meaning 'writing'.

Given the emphasis on the target language in the creation of Ogam (see §3.12) and the fact that the letter names, with the exception of the two Latin- and Greek-inspired *forfeda Ór* and *Pín*, are all native words, it seems to the present writer at least that it would be reasonable to assume as a working hypothesis that *ogam* is more likely to be an Irish word than a borrowing. If so James Carney's 'half etymology' equating the first syllable with the word *og* 'some part of a sharp weapon, the point (?edge)' whence the meaning 'incising with a point, writing' is very attractive.[11] One is reminded immediately of Latin *putare* 'to cut, lop, reckon' (as on the tally) as well as Greek *gráphein* 'to write', Latin *scribere* 'to write' and English *write*, from roots meaning 'to scratch', 'to cut' and 'to scratch' respectively (see Pokorny, 1959/69, 392, 945-6 and 1163). In this case the etymology *og-úaim* might contain the word *og* (rather than *óg* 'perfect') and mean something like 'point-seam', i.e. a seam made by the point of a sharp weapon (note the reference to *scían* 'knife' as the mother of Ogam), which would be a reasonable description of a line of Ogam writing. The identity of the second syllable in the word, however, (spelled *-um*, *-om*, *-am*) remains a difficulty both in respect to the unlenited *m* and the fact that *ogam* is an *o*-stem. In Irish verbal noun formations containing *m* are *u*-stems, *ā*-stems or *n*-stems (Thurneysen, 1946, 452-3).

As pointed out above (§1.4) the word *ogam* is used in the early period as a generic term for the script, the alphabet itself being referred to as the *Beithe-luis-nin*. The meaning 'something written in Ogam', whence 'inscription' is also well attested (see §8.11) for *ogam*, *ainm n-oguim* being used of an inscription consisting of a name (§8.8). With the adoption of the Ogam alphabet as the framework for the analysis of Irish *ogam* developed the meaning 'written (as opposed to 'spoken') Irish' and is used in this sense in particular in the Bardic Grammatical Tracts in which important distinctions are noted between the way a word is written and its pronunciation for riming purposes.The term *ogam iomagallmha* (lit 'Ogam of conversing') is used here in reference to the twenty-three letter framework (i.e. excluding *Queirt* and *Straif*) required for the discussion of Irish, *Beithe-luis* for the twenty-five letter alphabet. A similar restriction on 'practical' Ogam will be found in the list of verbal nouns said to be arranged *do rér uird aibidreach* 'in alphabetical order' (see Ó Cuív, 1966). In this twenty-one possible initial sounds are recognized, *Queirt* and *Straif* being excluded as in *ogam iomagallmha*, *hÚath* and *nGéadal* on the grounds that they do not occur in initial position.

Outside of the strictly learned milieu the word *ogam* appears to have undergone two distinctive developments, one in form the other in semantics. It became a feminine *ā*-stem (in some dialects with a palatal internal consonant) with a dative singular *ughaim/oidhim/oighim* etc. and developed the meaning 'inference, idea' in Scottish Gaelic *oidheam* and 'intention, purpose' in Irish, whence the phrase *d'aon ogham/oidhim* etc. 'intentionally'. As O'Rahilly has shown (1931, 60-61) Modern Irish *aidhm* 'aim, purpose' is an unhistorical spelling of the word *ogam* in this sense which, he argues, is a development of the meaning 'cryptic writing', comparing *rún* 'secret' ⟩ 'intention, resolve'.

## REFERENCES TO OGAM IN EARLY IRISH SAGA

§8.7 Early Irish saga contains numerous references to a variety of uses of Ogam the relevance of which to a discussion of the origins and original nature of the system is indeterminate. Some scholars have attached great importance to this material, arguing that the sagas refer to a period anterior to the introduction of Roman letters and Christianity and thus constitute a valuable source of information on the antiquity of Ogam and the nature of its uses in the earliest period. On the other hand, early Irish saga *as we know it*, whatever about its possible oral precursors, is the product of the monastic scriptoria and one must always reckon with the possibility that references in it to writing may be no more that projections into the distant past of what was contemporary practice at the time it was written. Recent studies of early Irish literature have highlighted the contemporary relevance of much of its contents and underlined the need for caution in treating it as a 'window on the iron age' (see for example Aitchison, 1987). The best one can do therefore is to attempt to establish what might have been the view of the authors or redactors of these sagas regarding the Ogams they mention in them.

§**8.8** The most frequently occurring single type of reference to Ogam is one which ties in nicely with what *is known* to have been its principal use, i.e. as a vehicle for memorial inscriptions. Accounts of the death of heroes and heroines in Irish saga are often concluded by a description of the burial and attendant ceremonies in a stereotype formula which usually includes the detail that the person's *ainm n-oguim* was engraved on a stone erected above the grave. In recension I of *Táin Bó Cúailnge*, for example, the episode describing Etarcomol mac Eda's death at the hands of Cú Chulainn, *Aided Etarcomail*, is concluded as follows: *Cladar a fert íarom. Sátir a lia. Scríbthair a ainm n-ogaim. Agair a gubae*, 'Then Etarcomol's grave was dug and his headstone was planted in the ground; his name was written in Ogam and he was mourned' (text and translation as in O'Rahilly, 1976, 43, 163). Similarly in *Tochmarc Étaíne*, before leaving to go on a circuit of Ireland Eochaid instructs Étaín to stay by the waning Ailill and, in the event of his death, to 'dig his earthy grave, to raise his standing-stone and his pillar and to inscribe his name in Ogam' (*a anmuimm oghaimm*, Windisch, 1880, 122),[12] and on Fergus mac Léite's death 'his grave was dug, his name was inscribed in Ogam and his funeral games were performed' (*Aidedh Ferghusa*, see O'Grady, 1892, I, 252). The formula occurs again and again[13] with slight variation in the terminology (e.g. *lecht* 'grave' for *fert* 'mound', *coirthe* 'rock' for *lia* 'stone', *ferthair a cluiche caíntech* 'his funeral games are observed' for *agair a gubae* 'his mourning is observed') but the 'engraving' of the inscription is invariably denoted by the verb *scríbaid* and the inscription itself is always referred to as an *ainm n-oguim*.

The term *ainm n-oguim* is clearly being used here in a technical sense denoting a funerary inscription consisting of the name of the deceased, exactly what we find in the orthodox Ogam inscriptions. Whether it represents a continuation of the formula word ANM found on late inscriptions or not is not certain, but there is no reason to suppose that a person's *ainm n-oguim* differed from the name by which he/she was usually known, as Graves believed (1879, 216, 231).[14] The texts do not specify the contents of an *ainm n-oguim* for the simple reason that they are self-evident from the story. When a stone is said to bear an inscription, as opposed to a simple record of the deceased's name, it is referred to simply as an *ogam*,[15] as in the following description of the tomb (*ulad*) of Fothaid Airgtech: *Ata comrar chloche imbi and hi talam. Ataat a di foil airgit ⁊ a di bunne doat ⁊ a muintorc argit fora chomrair ⁊ atá coirthe oca ulaid ⁊ atá ogom isin chind fil hi talam din corthi. Iss ed fil and: Eochaid Airgtech inso. Ra mbí Caílte i n-imaeriuc fri Find* 'He is in a stone coffin there in the ground. His two silver rings and his two arm-bracelets and his torque are on the coffin.

And there is a standing stone at his tomb with an inscription on the end of it which is below the ground. It reads: This is (or 'here lies') Eochaid Airgtech. Caílte killed him in a battle against Finn' (*Mongán ⁊ Aided Fothaid Airgdig* in Best and Bergin, 1929 (= *Lebor na hUidre*, 10991ff.).

From these references one may deduce either that the authors of these tales were familiar with the practice of erecting stones bearing memorial inscriptions in Ogam, though this had long since died out in their own day, or that they are merely projecting into the past the familiar custom of doing the same in conventional script and accommodating to the time-scale of the story by having the inscription written in Ogam, which was known to them to be of considerable antiquity. If the former is the case it is worth noting that whereas one might assume that the Irish *literati* were familiar with orthodox Ogam inscriptions, these are never referred to explicitly (except in the law tracts, on which see below §8.13), nor is an orthodox Ogam inscription recorded anywhere in the literature. As for the nature of these inscriptions, there is no reason to suppose that they were understood to differ in any way from the standard communicative/commemorative type. There is no hint of them serving a magical function or of being cryptic in nature. The case of Fothaid/Eochaid Airgtech, whose *ogam* is said to have been written on the part of the stone buried in the ground, is exceptional. Those who like to emphasize the magical side of Ogam would, no doubt, draw parallels with the Germanic practice of inscribing runes on stones placed *inside* the grave to ward off evil forces or confine the person to his grave (see Elliott, 1980, 69-70). The standard *ainm n-oguim* of Irish tradition, however, will not allow of this interpretation.

§8.9 The stereotype burial formula apart there are other references in the literature which point to the use of Ogam as a memorial script. Thus, Cétchuimnech is said to have been the first person for whom memorials in Ogam were raised in Ireland (*las cetna dernta chumni i n-ogmaib ar tus in hErinn*, Book of Leinster, fol. 320c 27-30), a statement no doubt based on his name. Similarly, the following two quatrains (first and last) from a poem about the battle of Gabair (*Cath Gabra*) attributed to Oisín, whose son Oscar died in the battle, are recorded in the Book of Leinster (fol. 154a 45ff.):

Ogum i llia, lia uas lecht,
bali i téigtis fecht fir,
mac ríg hErend ro gaet and
do gae gand os gabur gil.

In t-ogum út fil isin chloich
imma torchratar na troich,
da mmared Find, fichtib glond,
cian bad chuman in t-ogom.

'An Ogam in a stone, a stone over a grave, in the place where men were wont to pass; the son of the king of Ireland was there slain, by a mighty spear on a white horse's back.'

'That Ogam which is in the stone around which fell the slain, were Finn – with scores of battles [to his credit] – living, long would the Ogam be remembered.' (Windisch, 1880, 158-60 with translation by O'Curry, here slightly modified).

Again the two opening quatrains of the poem by Enoch O'Gillan on the tribes and persons buried at Clonmacnoise describe the cemetery there as follows (Rawlinson B 486, fol. 29, see Petrie, 1872, 5ff.):[16]

Cathair Chiaráin Cluain Mhic Nóis,
baile drúchtsholuis, deargróis;
dá shíol ríoghraidhe is buan bladh,
sluagh fán síodhbhaile sruthghlan.

Atáid uaisle Chloinne Cuinn
fán reilig leacdha leargdhuinn;
snaidhm nó craobh ós gach colainn,
agus ainm caomh cheart-oghaim.

'Clonmacnoise is Ciarán's city, a place dew-bright, red-rosed; it gives (lit. is) lasting fame to its royal seed, the host below the peaceful clear-streamed place.'

'The nobles of Clann Chuinn are [buried] under the brown-sloped flagstoned cemetery; a knot or a branch over every body,[17] and a fair name in *Ceart-ogham*.'

The belief in the power of Saint Ciarán's intercession with God on the Day of Judgment (to which reference is made in the third line of the first quatrain above) was such that Clonmacnoise was a popular burial place for Irish chiefs and the see benefited considerably from the purchase of places of internment (see Petrie, 1872, 4). Only one Ogam inscription, however, has been found on the site, and that of the scholastic type (see §7.5(i)). It will be clear, therefore, that Ogam is here being used either in the looser sense of 'written Irish', or by poetic licence.

**§8.10** There are several references in early Irish saga to uses of Ogam unconnected with memorial inscriptions. In what follows I give an abbreviated summary of the context of the more important of these:

(a) (O'Rahilly, 1967 = Recension II of the Táin, 1068ff.; compare O'Rahilly, 1976, Recension I of the Táin, 710ff.)

In the *Macgnímrada* ('Boyhood deeds') of Cú Chulainn the young hero encounters a pillar-stone on the green in front of the fort of the sons of Nechta Scéne. Around the pillar-stone is an iron ring/withe (*id íarnaidi*), described as a 'ring of heroic deeds' (*id níachais*), with the following inscription in Ogam (*ainm n-oguim* see n8.15) written on its peg (*menoc*): *Gipé tísed in faidche, diamba gascedach, geis fair ar thecht dind faidchi cen chomrac n-óenfir do fúacra* 'If any man came on that green and if he were a warrior bearing arms, it was taboo for him to leave the green without challenging to single combat.' Cú Chulainn pitched the stone and the ring into a nearby pool and the water closed over it.

(b) (O'Rahilly, 1976, 220ff. compare O'Rahilly, 1967, 456ff.)

On another occasion Cú Chulainn writes an Ogam inscription (*ogam*, Rec I, *ainm n-oguim* Rec. II) on the peg of a twisted withe and casts it over the top of a pillar-stone in order to delay the advance of Medb's army to Ulster and to secure time to tryst with his concubine. The withe is first encountered by the scouts Eirr and Inell and they also notice the grazing Cú Chulainn's horses had done on the spot. When the army arrives the withe is given to Fergus mac Róich who reads the inscription as follows: *Ná tíagar secha co n-étar fer ro láa id samlaid cona óenláim, ᚐ óenšlat día tá, ᚐ friscuriur mo phopa Fergus* 'Let none go past till there be found a man to throw a withe made of one branch as it is in the same way with one hand. But I except my friend Fergus.' Fergus then hands the withe to the druids asking them to interpret its 'secret meaning' (*rún*) and they do so, but come up with nothing more than is already known from the inscription.

Fergus then says to the army: 'If ye flout this withe or if ye go past it, though it be in a man's possession or in a locked house, it will go after the man who wrote the Ogam inscription, and he will kill one of you before morning unless one of you cast a withe in like manner.'

(c) (O'Rahilly, 1976, 330ff., compare O'Rahilly, 1967, 560ff.)

To delay the advancing army again Cú Chulainn cuts down a forked branch with one blow of his sword and fixes it in the middle of the stream so that a chariot could not pass it on this side or on that. While thus engaged two warriors, Eirr and Indell, with their two charioteers, Fóich and Fochlam, come upon him and he cuts off their heads and impales them on the four prongs of the forked branch. When the whole army arrives the Ogam inscription (*ogum* in both Recensions but also *ainm ogaim* in Recension I, line 339) is read aloud by *one of them* (*Ar(d)léga fer díb in n-ogum*) as follows: *Óenfer rod lá in gabuil cona óenláim ᚐ ní théssid secce conda rala nech úaib co n-áenláim cenmothá Fergus*, 'One man has cast this forked branch with one hand, and ye shall not go past it unless one of you, but not Fergus, has cast it with one hand'(Rec. I; in Rec. II the text of the inscription is not given but Fergus asks the druids to interpret it and to say who placed the forked branch in the stream and by what means). Ailill marvels at the speed with which the four men were killed but Fergus tells him to marvel rather at the feat of cutting the branch with one hand etc.

(d) (O'Rahilly, 1976, 825ff.)

In another attempt to delay the advance of Ailill and Medb's army Cú Chulainn cuts down an oak tree (*omnae*) in their path and writes an Ogam inscription (*ogum*) in it instructing them that no one should pass the oak until a warrior should leap across it in a chariot. Thirty horses fall in the attempt and thirty chariots are broken there.

(e) (*Tochmarc Étaíne*, Windisch, 1880, 129, § 18)

After Midir's abduction of Étaín Eochaid sends forth his messengers to search for her and he himself seeks her out for a year and a day, but to no avail. He then gives his druid Dallán the task of finding her. Dallán is troubled by her disappearance for over a year and 'he makes four rods of yew and writes Ogam (*oghumm*) in them and it is revealed to him through his keys of science (*triana eochraib écsi*)[18] and through his Ogam (*ocus triana oghumm*) that Étaín is in the *síd* of Brí Léith, having been carried there by Midir.'

(f) (*Baile in Scáil*, see Pokorny, 1921, 373, 26-29)

The following remarks are found in the main manuscript (Rawlinson B 512) at the point at which the *Scál* 'phantom' is about to recite his *díchetal* 'incantation' on the kings of Ireland one after the other from Conn to the end of time: *Ba trom īarum la Cesarnd filid an dīchetail sin do thabairt fri ōinhūair co n-ecmaing tre oghum hi cethēora flescæ iphair. Cethir traigid fichet fott cacha flesci ⁊ ocht ndruimne cacha flesci.* 'Cesarn the poet found it difficult, however, to take (i.e. memorize/record) the incantation in one go and he cut it in Ogam into four rods of yew. Each rod was twenty-four feet long and had eight sides (angles).'

(g) (*Immram Brain*, see Mac Mathúna, 1985, 45)

Returning to Ireland after his journey to the Land of Women, Bran and his comrades arrive at Srúb Brain. One of his comrades leaps from the boat and is turned to ashes on touching Irish soil. Bran decides it is unwise to disembark and relates his adventures from the boat to the crowd gathered at the shore: *ocus scríbais inna rundnu-so tre ogum, ocus celebrais dóib íar sin* 'and he wrote these quatrains in Ogam and he bade farewell to them after that.'

(h) (*Longes Chonaill Chuirc*, Book of Leinster, fol. 287a; Meyer, 1910, 57-8 (= Laud 610) and Dillon, 1977, 9-10)

Corc son of Luguid and nephew of Crimthann mac Fidaig, king of Ireland, is accused by Crimthann's wife of enticing her – he had in fact refused to make love to her – and banished from Ireland. He arrives in Scotland and is befriended by Gruibne, poet to Feradach, king of Scotland. Gruibne sees an Ogam inscription (*ogum*; *ogam fortgithe* 'cryptic Ogam inscription', Laud) in Corc's shield and enquires as to who put it there. Corc, apparently unaware up to this of its existence (or at least ignorant of its meaning), asks what it says. Gruibne explains that it bears an instruction that if he (Corc) should come to Feradach by day he should be killed by night, if he should arrive by night he should be killed by morning.[19] In order to protect Corc, who had saved his life in an earlier incident in Ireland, Gruibne gives Feradach a false account of what has happened and puts a different interpretation on the inscription (in the Laud version he changes the inscription itself), namely that if Corc should arrive by day he should be given Feradach's daughter by evening, and he should have slept with her by morning should he arrive by night.

(i) (*Dauíd ocus Absalón*, see Pokorny, 1921, 177 and compare II Samuel, xi, 14-15)

David desires the wife of one his soldiers and conspires to get rid of him. He sends him to his son, Absalom, with a royal Ogam (*rígogam*) in his shield to give battle to a tribe which opposed David. *Is ed rucad isin scīath, acht co roindlithi in cath, Abisolōn do ēlud as ⁊ in mīlid do fāgbāil* 'And [the message] carried in the shield was, as soon as preparation for battle should have been made, Absalom should escape from it and the soldier should be left [to his death].' The corresponding passage in the Bible, in which Uriah the Hittite is sent to Joab, reads as follows: (14) *Factum est ergo mane et scripsit David epistulam ad Ioab misitque per manum Uriae (15) scribens in epistula ponite Uriam ex adverso belli ubi fortissimum proelium est et derelinquite eum ut percussus intereat.*

(j) (*Sanas Cormaic* entry 1018 = Meyer,1912b, 86-88; see also Dillon, 1932, 48-50 and Binchy, 1978, 2230. 3ff.)

In his discussion of the word *orc* in the phrase *orc tréith* Cormac tells the following story concerning Finn and his fool Lomnae as a background to a quotation containing the word *orc*: While Finn is away on a hunting expedition Lomnae discovers his (Finn's) wife lying in stealth with Coirpre. Wishing to inform his master of her infidelity in a way which would avoid a direct accusation Lomnae hands Finn a four-sided rod (*flesc cetharc[h]uir*) on his return, having cut (*benaid, do-fórni*) the following Ogam inscription (*ogam*; script not specified in the version in Dillon, 1932, where the text is referred to simply as *in liudh sa* 'this accusation') into it: *Cūaille feda / i feilm arguit / ath[aba] i fothracht / fer mnā drūithe / druthlach la fēne foircthi / is fraoch for hÚalann limm Luigne*[20] 'A wooden stake in a fence of silver, hellebore among edible plants, husband of a wanton woman, a cuckold among the well-taught Féni, and heather on Úalann of the Luigne.' Finn understands the implications of this and shows his displeasure to the woman in such a way that she knows she has been betrayed by Lomnae. She avenges herself by having Coirpre kill Lomnae whose decapitated head later speaks the quotation containing the word *orc*.

(k) (*Sanas Cormaic* entry 606, Meyer, 1912b, 49-50)

Here the Irish word *fé* 'woe' is explained as a borrowing of Latin *vae* according to one tradition, or, according to another, as the name of a rod of yew (*flesc idaith*) which used to be kept in pagan graveyards and used for measuring corpses and graves. 'And everyone was afraid to take it in his hands and anything that was hateful to anyone used to be compared to it, or they would write it (lit. 'set it' *do-bertis* or leg. *no-bentis*) on it in Ogam, whence the saying "*fé fris*" has become proverbial, for just as the rod known as *fé* is hateful, so too is any other thing to which it is compared.'

(l) (*Fled Bricrend ⁊ Loinges mac nDuil Dermait*, see Windisch, 1884, 178)

Cú Chulainn has the task of finding the three exiled sons of Duil Dermait. He sees a boat coming to land in the harbour of Dundalk. In the boat is the king of Albu and his followers coming with presents of silk and drinking horns on a visit to Conchobar. Cú Chulainn kills all in the boat but the king, who begs that his life be spared. Cú Chulainn asks him whether he knows what drove the sons of Duil Dermait from their country. The king replies that he does not and adds: '*acht ata murindell lim ⁊ fo-cichertar deit-siu ⁊ rot-bia in curach ⁊ ni foicbea anfis de.*' ' but I have a sea-charm and it will be set for you and you will have the boat and you will not find yourself in ignorance as a result of it.' The text continues *Do-bert Cú Chulaind a sleigin do ⁊ do forne ogum n-ind ⁊ ad-bert fris 'Erich co ro bi im śuidhi-se ind Emain Macha corris'* 'Cú Chulainn gave him his little spear and he cut an Ogam inscription in it and he said to him "go and take my seat in Emain Macha".'

(m) (Calder, 1917, 5483ff. and see §8.4 above)

According to this passage from *In Lebor Ogaim* the first thing written in Ogam (lit. 'through Ogam', *tri ogam*) was a warning sent to Lug mac Ethlenn, consisting of seven *b*s in one switch of birch, to the effect that his wife would be carried away *seven* times from him to the *síd* unless the birch protect her.

§8.11 The following points should be noted with regard to the above:

(1) The Ogam inscription is referred to in most instances simply as *ogam* and exceptionally in the Táin (a) and (b) as *ainm n-oguim*. In (h) the word is

qualified by *fortgithe*, past participle of *for-tuigethar* ' covers, hides', meaning 'hidden' or 'cryptic' (compare *Bérla fortchide na filed* 'the cryptic language of the poets'). When the word *ogam* is not the direct object of the verb 'to write' it is usually introduced by the preposition *tre* 'through' (e.g. (g) *scríbais inna rundnu-so tre ogum*, (h) *scríbtha tria hogum fortgithe*, (m) *roscribad tri ogam*). In these *ogam* has the meaning 'Ogam script' or simply 'writing'.

(2) The verb 'to write' is usually expressed in these references by *scríbaid* (< Latin *scribere*) as in the funerary Ogams. Occasionally a verb meaning 'to strike', 'to cut' etc. is used, e.g. (j) *Benaid didiu Lomnae ogum i fleisc cetharc[h]uir* (*benaid* 'strikes') the variant in this instance being *do-fórni in liudh-sa inti* (*do-foirndea* 'expresses, marks out', a verb containing the element *rind* 'point', compare *ro-rinnad oghmaib* 'it has been engraved in Ogams' below §8.12. The verb *do-foirndea* is used again in (l)). (f) *co n-ecmaing tre oghum* (leg. *condid-ecmaing?*) may contain the verb *ad-cumaing* 'strikes' (if not for *co n-acmaing* 'and he succeeded'). The verb *do-beir* in *do-bertis trie ogham indti* (k) is quite exceptional.

(3) Unlike the memorial inscriptions the material on which these Ogams are written is wood with the exception of (a), which is the only instance of iron. The object on which a given inscription is engraved is variable and dictated largely by the context. In (a) and (b), for example, the withe around the pillar functions as a symbolic prohibition or taboo (*geis*).[21] As the peg (*menoc*) of the withe is the means by which it is locked or released it is appropriate that the inscription, which contains the key to unlocking the *geis*, should be written on it. The forked branch of (c) and the oak tree of (d), on the other hand, are real rather than symbolic obstacles in the way of the army. In (h) and (i) the Ogam, which is designed to seal the fate of a young warrior and a soldier respectively, is appropriately engraved in their shields, while in (l) Cú Chulainn engraves it in his 'small spear' (*sleigín*) as he will require his large one for the expedition he is about to embark on. In the other instances, if specified, it is written in one or more rods *flesc/flesca* usually said to be of yew. The exceptionally large size of these in (f) is dictated by the length of the *díchetal* to be recorded in them, and birch rather than yew in (m) is probably dictated by the conclusions drawn from this 'first Ogam' (viz. that it explains why B is the first letter in the alphabet).

(4) The inscription usually serves to communicate a message; exceptionally it records an incantation (*díchetal* f) or quatrains (*rundnu* g), or is used for purposes of divination (e). The message is once said to be cryptic (h), intelligible only to the sender and the intended recipient (Crimthann and Feradach respectively), but it is intercepted by the poet and Ogamist Gruibne (*ogmaire éccess*) who is able to decipher it. In (i), in which the motif is similar, the soldier presumably could not understand the *rígogam* in his shield. When the text of a message is actually recorded, e.g. (a) and (b), it is generally straightforward. The exception is the rather enigmatic piece inscribed by Lomnae for Finn (j). This is a legal maxim of metaphorical misfits said to be analogous to the bastard son of a man's wife being included among his legitimate sons in the share of his and his family's property. A commentator in a law text describes it as follows: *i. analag so; imtha samlaid na særclanda ⁊ na dærclanda. Ni comhadhuis a cumusg nach a mbreachtra fri macuibh na merdrech* 'This is an

analogy; even so are noble children and base children. It is not fitting to mix them or to speckle them with the sons of harlots' (Binchy, 1978, 1139. 16ff.). By inscribing this maxim for Finn Lomnae succeeds in hinting very strongly at his wife's infidelity without actually accusing her outright, though he might just as well have done so as he paid the ultimate price in the end.

§8.12 Some conclusions which have been drawn from these saga references to Ogam must now be considered. They have been studied by Graves (1879, 214-231) and Vendryes (1941, 90-97, 111-116), both of whom regard them as occult and magical and contrast them with the straightforward strictly communicative and non-cryptic funerary inscriptions. Vendryes goes further and suggests a more fundamental difference between the two. He argues that the Ogam of the funerary inscriptions may be considered to be identical to that known to us from the monuments, i.e. an alphabetical script, but he considers the remaining Ogams to be of a pre-alphabetic kind, a system of conventional mnemonic signs intelligible only to the initiated and representing a method of written communication of the greatest antiquity (1941, 112). These are very considerable claims, but there is little evidence in the texts themselves to substantiate them.

Both Graves and Vendryes draw attention to and highlight the supposed secret and magical character of these Ogams. In the case of (c), for example, Vendryes (1941, 94) considers the role of the druids significant. In Recension I of this instance, however, we are told simply that one member of the army read out the Ogam (Ar(d)-léga fer díb in n-ogum) and it is not inferred, much less actually stated, that it was particularly difficult to understand. In (b) the druids also participate but the message has already been read by Fergus and though he asks them to find the secret meaning (rún) of the withe they can come up with nothing more than what is already known from the Ogam. Their presence here, therefore, is of little consequence to a discussion of the Ogam. As for the magical power of the withe to seek out the man who wrote the Ogam if it were flouted, Bergin (1921) assigns this to the writing on it but it is more probable that it derives from the fact that the withe was formed from *one* branch by *one* man using *one* hand (see Plummer, 1910, I, clxi. n2).

In the case of (f) Vendryes (1941, 95) suggests that the detail concerning the length of the *flesca* shows the importance of wood in the magical functions with which Ogam was associated. There is no magic, however, in this particular case. The poet's inability to cope with memorizing a lengthy incantation is solved by writing it down in rods which are said to be of a size appropriate to the task. There could scarcely be an example of a more mundane and practical use of Ogam and the statement to the effect that the poet was unable to memorize the incantation because of its length is of particular interest in the oral-literacy debate. Again in the case of (h) the fact that Corc did not know the significance of the Ogam in his shield is argued in favour of the secret character of this Ogam (Vendryes, 1941, 96, Graves 1879, 220), but in this instance the Ogam is specified in one manuscript as *fortgithe*, from which one could reasonably draw the inference that *ogam* on its own would have been non-cryptic in the mind of the author. In (i), admittedly, we have a similar case of a person unwittingly bearing his own death warrant without the *fortgithe* specification but it would be dangerous to draw inferences from this as the characters in this story are Biblical and the word *ogam* must be understood in the loose sense of 'writing'. Vendryes may be correct in seeing in (k) a somewhat garbled description of a *defixio* but this would not give Ogam special status as a script capable of establishing contacts with the powers of the Otherworld. *Defixiones* are commonly found in conventional script and their power lay not in the writing on them but rather in their being placed in the grave of the person to be cursed. Again, it is true as Vendryes points out (1941, 96-7) that the message which Lomnae inscribes for Finn (j) is enigmatic, but the enigma here is a means of avoiding a direct accusation and it attaches to the message not to the script in which it is written.

By wrongly identifying the Ogam which Cú Chulainn inscribes in his *sleigín* with the sea-charm which the king mentions Graves (1979, 227-8) sees (l) as an example of Ogam used for purposes of divination. The text is admittedly a little ambiguous but it is more likely that the Ogam on the 'little spear', which Cú Chulainn *gives to* the king, is intended for the latter's benefit when he arrives at Emain Macha to take Cú Chulainn's seat. This explains the choice of the *sleigín* as opposed to the *gáe Bolga*, Cú Chulainn's special magical spear, which he will require on his expedition. In other words the Ogam and the sea-charm are unrelated and the former is of the purely perfunctory message type. In (e) on the other hand we do appear to have an example of Ogam used in divination. This has all the ingredients of druidry, magic and paganism with which some scholars like to associate Ogam and parallels are inevitably drawn (see Vendryes, 1941, 109 and Stokes, 1891, 440) between this and Cicero's notice of the lots used at Praeneste, which were carved in oak in ancient characters, (*in robore insculptas priscarum litterarum notis*, *De Divinatione* § 41, see Falconer, 1923) and Tacitus' description of lot-casting among the Germanic tribes (*Auspicia sortesque ut qui maxime observant. Sortium consuetudo simplex: virgam frugiferae arbori incisam in surculos amputant eosque notis quibusdam discretos super candidam vestem temere ac fortuito spargunt* . . . 'To divination and the lot they pay as much attention as anyone: the method of drawing lots is uniform. A branch is cut from a nut-bearing tree and divided into slips: these are distinguished by certain marks and spread casually and at random over white cloth . . .', *Germania* X, see Hutton, 1970). One can, however, just as readily draw parallels from Christian Irish sources. In *Cáin Adamnáin* (see Meyer, 1905, § 46), for example, the procedure for establishing the guilt of an individual, when more than one is suspected, is described as follows: *scríbtar a n-anman i ndulne; do-ber[r] cach duilend inna ecrus im chrand ⁊ do-bertar na cranna i cailech for altóir. Int-í fora tuit cran[n]char, is é is fíachach* 'Let their names be written upon leaves; each leaf is arranged around a lot, and the lots are put into a chalice upon the altar. He on whom the lot falls is liable.'[22] Lot-casting, then, clearly relies on lots bearing symbols which can be interpreted, whether alphabetic or not, and on divine intervention, whether Christian or not. No inference can be drawn from (e), therefore, regarding specific magical or pagan associations of Ogam, since conventional script can also be used in this way, nor can one infer from the text that the Ogam of *Tochmarc Étaíne* was non-alphabetic, as standard alphabetic Ogam can, as we have seen (§7.11(i) above), be used to divine the sex of an unborn child. Why should we assume that the author of *Tochmarc Étaíne* understood Dallán's Ogam to be any different?

The superstitious belief in the magical powers of writing is a universal phenomenon and is particularly prevalent in societies in which literacy is the prerogative of the few.[23] That we should find Ogam associated with both magic and secrecy, therefore, is without special significance and it would be wrong to base far-reaching theories on the origins of the system on such references. It is quite unnecessary to postulate for these a series of pre-alphabetic or non-alphabetic conventional signs intelligible only to the initiated, when alphabetic characters intelligible only to the literate amount to the same thing and meet all the circumstances of the stories (except (m), on which see below). The distinction drawn between non-cryptic perfunctory Ogams on stone and cryptic magical Ogams on wood is quite unreal and without justification. More importantly, the idea that Ogam is particularly closely associated with magic and secrecy is false and has been wrongly turned into an argument in favour of a genetic relationship with the runes (see §3.6 above and Arntz, 1935, 369-374). In this connection Page's comments (1987, 12) on the runes and magic are particularly apposite and worth quoting: 'Our age shows a lamentable tendency to flee from reason, common sense and practicality into the realms of superstition and fantasy, and runes have been taken up into this. In the view of many scholars this general approach to runes is outdated and nonsensical. Most distinguished Scandinavian runologists now take the view that the Germanic peoples used runes as they would have done any other script (had they known any other), for practical, day-to-day purposes.'

With the notable exception of (m) there is not a single instance in all of the references quoted above in which one could not substitute 'writing' (i.e. conventional script) for Ogam without doing serious violence to the interpretation. Given that this is so one cannot help feeling that the specification that Ogam was used may be no more than an accommodation to the time scale of the sagas (in (i) the *epistula* of the original is accommodated to the Irish version with the term *rígogam*, demonstrating how loosely the word *ogam* can be used). The case of (m) is exceptional not only in that it occurs in a text dealing specifically with Ogam but also in that it specifies and reproduces what was actually engraved in the *flesc*, viz. seven *b*s (in the Ogam character). This is clearly a case of a non-alphabetic script as seven *b*s do not spell any word or message in Irish. It is the *number* of scores carved into the *flesc* which is relevant here and if any importance attaches to this instance it must surely be that it highlights the obvious connection between the Ogam script and tally numerals.

## OGAM IN EARLY IRISH LAW

§**8.13** The practical capacity of Ogam inscriptions is confirmed in particular by Early Irish law. Both in the texts themselves and in the later gloss and commentary reference is made to Ogam inscriptions on stone as evidence of title to land. In the section of the tract *Berrad Airechta* dealing with evidence (*Córus fíadnaisi*), for example, the question *Cid i n-airecar fir la Féniu* 'How is truth (with regard to land ownership) found in Irish law?' is answered *INbat* (leg. *I mbiat*[24]) *la comorbu cuimne, cen ogom i n-ailchib, cen accrus n-aithgnith, cen macu, cen* *ratha (. . .) IT e tiubaithsir fiadain* 'When heirs have [only] memories, without Ogam in stones, without (officially) recognized lot-casting, without *mac* and *ráth* sureties (. . .) it is witnesses who fix truth (leg. *tiudbiat fír)*' (see Thurneysen, 1928a, §59 = Binchy, 1978, 596. 6ff.). The implication is clearly that *ogom i n-ailchib* would be acceptable evidence and this is confirmed by the gloss *amal fíadain he* 'it is like a witness' on the phrase *int oghom isin gollán* 'the Ogam in the pillar stone' (1566. 6-7).[25] At 746. 37ff. an alliterating *rosc* passage listing tokens of lawful inheritance opens as follows: *Comorbus con-raet rathaib / ro rinnad oghmaib / ara-rocet filedaib / fot-ruilled foltaib / fot-ruigled aimsiraib . . .* 'Inheritance has been secured by *ráth* sureties, has been engraved in Ogams, has been pronounced solemnly by poets, has been earned by wealth, has been attested by periods of time [spent in occupation] . . . .' At 754. 39ff. the second of the 'keys which open possessions' (*eochrai aroslaicet selba*, i.e. the means by which lawful possession is secured), is cited as *forgell do thir* 'testifying that it is one's land', and glossed as follows: *.i. a forgell don tuaith conid lais; ł a forgell isinní bis isin thir, int oghum isin gollan* 'i.e. that the *túath* should testify that it is his, or the testimony in that which is in the land, the Ogam in the pillar-stone.' The 'Ogam in the pillar-stone' is mentioned again at 2143. 21-22 alongside the *laíd* 'lay' and *liter* 'letter' as types of evidence which serve as proof of title to land, and at 748. 18-19 it glosses the phrase *comcuimne da crich* 'the mutual memory of two [adjoining] lands', cited as a form of evidence.

At 2199. 8-10 (a text cited in a gloss on *Gúbretha Caratniad*) the 'dead (inanimate) things' (*mairb*) which overswear the living are listed and include the *laid* 'lay', the *litteir* 'letter', the *crich* 'boundary' and the *coirthe* 'boundary stone' and that the latter refers to an Ogam stone is suggested by 2143. 21-2 (referred to above) where in a quotation of the same text the *laid* and the *liter* are followed by *int ogam isinn gollan*. The dead (in the form of writing) overswearing the living in a case of ownership is again referred to in the story 'The decision as to Cormac's sword' (*Scél na Fír Flatha, Echtra Cormaic i Tír Tairngiri ocus Ceart Claidib Cormaic*, Stokes, in Windisch, 1891, 201) in which the name written in the hilt of the sword, albeit not that of the rightful owner, is considered decisive evidence until the discovery of the fraud. In the text edited by Stokes this is expressed with the words *Is andsin rodgella marbh for bíu, i n-agar log don scriband* 'Then does a dead thing testify against a living [person], when advantage is pleaded for the writing' (i.e. when writing is acknowledged as superior testimony). But in a quotation from an earlier version of this law-based tale (see Gwynn, 1940, 34, 226 and Hull, 1967, 8. n8) the text reads: *ann con-sich marbh for bheo, i bhfoirgheall oghaim ógh airibh* 'it is then that the dead constrained the living, in the integral testimony of Ogam against them.' Finally, in the archaic legal poem *Ma be rí ro-fesser* Binchy (1971, 157) translates the words *gaill comlainn, caithigthi astado* as 'stone pillars of contest, fighters who fasten [title]' and explains them as a figure of speech in which Ogam inscriptions are portrayed as 'fighters' in a contest of land-ownership.[26]

It will be clear, therefore, that an Ogam inscription could be used by a person as evidence of lawful title to land of which he was already in possession or to which he was laying claim by hereditary right (see Kelly, 1988, 204). One must assume that in such a case the occupier's or claimant's right was confirmed by his demonstrating that the name recorded on the stone was that of one of his kinsmen or ancestors, and this seems to be implied in the following passage (2143. 39-40): *acht mas e ni fo-gabar ann conid les-sium he, gaibid greim tuinide do* 'but if it be found therein (i.e. in the inscription) that it is his, it (the inscription) has the force of [title of] ownership.' This, of course, presupposes an ability to read the names on Ogam inscriptions and yet it is noteworthy that the text of an inscription is nowhere cited in the legal corpus, nor do linguistic forms of the type found on the earliest Ogam inscriptions occur anywhere in the manuscript record. It is worth noting further that even the earliest law tracts date from a time (seventh century) when the practice of erecting Ogam stones had died out or was in the process of doing so. This may explain why the law tracts do not actually refer to the *practice* of erecting such stones to serve as land charters. In the texts the evidence of these inscriptions is placed alongside 'memory' *cuimne*, in particular the authoritative memory of the *senchaid* 'historian' (751. 5, and see Dillon, 1953, 271-2) 'old (sacred) writing' (*senscribinn deoda*, 751. 5-6 and *scribent .i. senscribent* 776. 13, *liter in senlebair* 2143. 32) and the composition of poets if they have been composing for the family of the person in question for at least three generations (*laig in filed ma thathar aca molad re re trir* 2143. 30 and 749. 2ff.). The reliability of this evidence and its superiority as testimony over the mere word of the claimant attaches to its antiquity and what the law considers its unshakeable form, expressed in the metaphorical term *ail anscuichthe* 'an immovable rock'. The evidence of early Irish law, therefore, is not inconsistent with the dating of Ogam inscriptions in chapter five above.

When Plummer discussed the above evidence (1923) he considered the roles of Ogam stones as memorials and as charters of land ownership unrelated, and he suggested that many of our monuments may never in fact have been sepulchral in nature. Given, however, that territorial boundaries appear to have been defined by pillar-stones[27] and that burial seems to have taken place at the boundary, it is possible that the two functions were complementary. In the Old Irish glosses on *Cáin Fuithirbe* reference is made to an *ogum na creca* 'Ogam of purchase' (776. 13), which suggests that transactions of land could be recorded in Ogam, but even in this case the Ogam is said to be *i llic firt* 'in a tombstone'. The significance of burial on the boundary is highlighted in the procedure to be followed by a person laying claim to a piece of land by hereditary right. In his discussion of this Charles-Edwards (1976, 85) draws particular attention to the requirement that the claimant enter the land over the grave-mound (*fert*) and he suggests that burial on the boundary may have been designed to defend inherited land from the claims of outsiders and could have done so in virtue of pagan beliefs that the dead might 'take an active part in the affairs of the living.' This may or may not have been the case but there is no evidence to support the conjecture that the Ogam inscription could have been considered instrumental in reinforcing the power of the dead in such cases. The texts stress unequivocally the practical capacity of inscriptions to strengthen the claims of the rightful heir. There is no need to romanticize them into something magical. Like Cú Chulainn's withe the gravestone may have had a symbolic function, but the evidence suggests that the inscriptions on both were understood to serve the purpose of communicating information, and to do so in a straightforward way.

**§8.14** In conclusion, therefore, one may say that both early Irish saga and early Irish law point to familiarity with Ogam inscriptions bearing names of individuals and serving in all probability primarily as sepulchral monuments and secondarily as charters of land ownership. Early Irish saga also makes reference to other kinds of Ogam inscriptions, generally on wood, the magical character of which has been greatly exaggerated by modern scholarship. Whether, as is often claimed, these bring us back further in time than the surviving inscriptions to the earliest uses of Ogam is questionable. They certainly tell us nothing conclusive about the earliest *form* of the system and allowance must always be made for the possibility that such references are literary embellishments which the authors adapt to the time-scale of their sagas when they use the term *ogam*.

# Notes

## NOTES TO CHAPTER ONE

1. The representation of vowels as full-length scores drawn at a right angle to the stemline is very uncommon on stone (for an example see no. 137 in Macalister's *Corpus*). This is the standard procedure in the manuscripts and in scholastic Ogams, on which see §7.3ff.

2. On the basis of the name *Beithe-luis-nin* it has been argued (Macalister, 1914, 233) that *Nin* must have once occupied third position in the series, but this does not follow. For a suggestion that the name *Beithe-luis-nin* is based on all five letters of the first group, the middle three represented as LVS (whence *luis*) see MacNeill (1922, 445. n1) and again Mac Eoin in Ó Cuív (1980, 101. n4).

3. The text and translation will be found in Calder (1917, lines 945 ff. and 3887ff.) and Ahlqvist (1982, 51). The latter is reproduced here with minor modifications.

4. On the history of the alphabet see Gelb (1952, 166ff.), Pulgram (1976, 1ff.), Diringer (1968, 145ff.) and Jensen (1970, 450ff.).

5. On Greek see Gelb (1952, 176ff.) and on both Latin and Greek see Diringer (1968, 419ff. and 358ff.) and Jensen (1970, 520ff. and 450ff.). On the runes see Elliott (1980, 1ff.), Moltke (1985, 38ff.) and Page (1987, 6ff.).

## NOTES TO CHAPTER TWO

1. See Macalister (1935, 117; 1937, 19-20 and 1945, v), Binchy (1961, 8), Bergin (1932a, 142), Vendryes (1941, 103), Diack (1931, 86), Thurneysen (1909, 11), Henry (1940, 12) to mention but a few.

2. O'Curry believed (1861, 463ff.) that Ogam was used to record historical events and sustained narrative but his evidence - references in the literature to *taibli* (*támlorga*) *filed* 'tablets of poets' and to writing in tales such as *Baile mac Búain* - was not convincing. In two of the texts discussed later (see §8.10 (f) and (g) ) Ogam is said to be used to record texts but this evidence is hardly trustworthy, given that *ogam* at the time was used in the general sense of 'written Irish'. On MacCurtin's statement to the effect that Ogam was used to record the 'vicious practices' of Irish monarchs see Bergin (1938, 222-3).

3. See Macalister (1914, 232; 1928, 215ff.; 1935, 117ff.; 1937; 19ff. and 1945, vi).

4. See Brennan (1984) and Deuchar (1984) on finger spelling in sign language.

5. For a discussion and edition of the *Isruna Tract* see Derolez (1954, 120ff.).

6. *Iisruna dicuntur quae* i *littera per totum scribuntur, ita ut quotus versus sit primum brevioribus* i, *quae autem littera sit in versu longioribus* I *scribatur.*

7. A few symbols on old runic inscriptions may perhaps be interpreted as *Hahalruna* but the earliest reliable example is the Hackness stone in Yorkshire, which also bears an inscription in a system similar to Ogam (see §7.5) and has been dated to the eighth or ninth centuries (Derolez, 1954, 139ff.).

8. On the history of the tally see Menninger's section on 'Folk symbols for numbers' (1969, 221ff.).

9. As Menninger points out (1969, 240-41, see also Gerschel, 1962, 143) the symbols X and V are among the easiest to carve into wood and were not invented by the Romans. I have chosen to use these for convenience, without prejudice to their origins.

10. For an example of a variant of *Certogam* using position-marking but not grouping see 'alphabet' 14 in *In Lebor Ogaim* (Calder, 1917, 301. no.14 and see §7.11a). This is named *Ogam Bricrenn* 'the Ogam of Bricriu' and is described as follows: *In doimni i mbi in fid isin aipgitir is e lin flesc scribthar ina uath, .i. aen do Beithi, xx do Idad* 'the depth (i.e. numerical position) in which the letter is in the alphabet, that is the number of scores written in its formation, i.e. one for *Beithe*, twenty for *Idad*.'

11. See in particular his explanation of the first two characters of this series as representing the values 10 and 20 respectively (1962, 148-9).

12. An aversion to the 'Herrenvolk' and an urge to demonstrate Germanic character and independence have also been suggested as the stimulus for the runes (see the discussion by Derolez, 1954, xxiii).

13. Diack (1931) attempts to identify the non-alphabetic proto-Ogam on stones in Scotland, but with little success.

14. On the Greek row and alphabetic numerals see Menninger (1969, 268ff.).

15. For a survey of the methods employed see Süss (1923).

16. See Aulus Gellius (*Noctes Atticae* XVII, ix in Marshall, 1968, vol ii) and Caius Suetonius (*De vita Caesarum* I, lvi and II, lxxxviii in Rolfe, 1979, vol i).

17. For a discussion and edition of the *De inventione Linguarum* tract see Derolez (1954, 279ff. and 349ff.). The *Notae Sancti Bonifatii* are mentioned on page 289 and the authorship is discussed on page 378-9, where a date in the first half of the ninth century is suggested. For the account by Aeneas Tacticus see *Aeneas Tacticus* xxxi 'On secret messages' (in Illinois Greek Club, 1923) and see Süss (1923, 142ff.) and for an example of the *Notae Sancti Bonifatii* device in Irish using the Ogam vowel sequence see Ní Shéaghdha (1977, 85) on NLI G 138, 53a.

18. *Cum primam alphabeti literam intimare cupis, unum manu teneto; cum secundam, duo; cum tertiam, tria; et sic ex ordine ceteras. Verbi gratia, si amicum inter insidiatores positum ut caute se agat admonere desideras, iii, et i, et xx, et xix, et v, et i, et vii, et v, digitis ostende; huius namque ordinis literae, 'caute age' significant. Potest et ita scribi, si causa secretior exigat* (Jones, 1943, 181).

19. Macalister (1945, vi) believed that Bede's *manualis loquela* offered his gesture theory a degree of verisimilitude. But once position-marking is conceded as the principle underlying Ogam the need for a *manualis loquela* disappears.

20. For Polybius see *The Histories* X, 43-47 (Paton, 1925) and the discussion by Eisler (1949, n40).

## NOTES TO CHAPTER THREE

1. Graves' enlightened challenge to these views (1876, 446-7; 1888, 242ff.) should have put an end to the pagan theory but it was to surface again in the present century (see §4.9). Note that the numbers accompanying inscriptions refer to Macalister's numeration in his *Corpus Inscriptionum Insularum Celticarum*.

2. Rhys believed that Ireland had been settled by Celts from Britain and that the Irish in Britain who erected the Ogam inscriptions had been settled there from time immemorial. For a rejection of this theory see O'Rahilly (1946, 420ff.).

3. On the supposed Ogam inscriptions from Biere in Saxony see §4.2.

4. Old Irish *óen* 'one' does not and never did begin with /h/ and the /h/ prefixed to it by the particle *a* in counting (Modern Irish *a h-aon, a dó* . . . ' one, two . . .') could not correspond to character six in the alphabet. So too Old Irish *cethair* 'four' and *cóic* 'five' both derive from originals with initial /k$^w$/ (*$k^w$etwores* and *$k^w$enk$^w$e*, Latin *quattuor, quinque*) not /k/ and /k$^w$/ respectively.

5. See for example Hopfner (1919) who has the record of a conversation between a Briton and an Irishman dictating the sequence, and Boyle (1980) for whom the Ogam characters constitute a musical tablature producing a harp-scale (see also Egan's comments, 1983).

6. For others see Graves (1876, 460-1), Macalister (1914, 231ff. and 1928, 227-8) and Rhys (1879, 312ff.).

7. Arntz (1935, 347), for example, is quite right in dismissing Pedersen's observation that the letters L, D, G and O are written with two 'Striche' in both Latin and Ogam.

8. On Kuryłowicz's views regarding the order within *Aicme hÚatha* see McManus (1986, 16).

9. . . . *consonantes a vocalibus discernere ipsasque in semivocalium numerum mutarumque partiri.*

10. On the significance of the word 'should' (*debere*) in this see Gordon (1973, 14, 54 and 61) who argues that without the full context the use of *debere* must be neutral in its implication as to whether Varro is trying to *correct* current practice or is only *confirming* it.

11. On the Greek and Latin letter names see Hammarström (1920, 15ff. and 1930) and Gordon (1973).

12. This however is impossible (see Jackson, 1949, on the fact that /w/ and lenited *b* were kept distinct at all times). On Ogam V for an expected B in the name-element DOV- (= *dub-*) see §6.29(c).

13. *Inter litteram* n *et* g *est alia uis, ut in nomine* anguis *et* angari *et* ancorae *et* increpat *et* incurrit *et* ingenuus. *In omnibus his non uerum* n, *sed adulterinum ponitur. Nam* n *non esse lingua indicio est; nam si ea littera esset, lingua palatum tangeret.* 'Between *n* and *g* there is another value, as in the word *anguis* and *angari* etc. In all of these it is not actually *n* but an adulterated (*n*) which is assumed. For the tongue is evidence that it is not *n.*; for if it were that letter, the tongue would touch the palate.'

14. '. . . which Varro demonstrates in the first book on the origin of the Latin language with these words: as Ion writes the twenty-fifth is a letter which they call *Agma* and which has no [distinctive] form but is a sound common to both the Greeks and the Latins, as in these words *aggulus, aggens, agguilla, iggerunt*. In the same way the Greeks and our Accius write double *g*, others write *n* and *g*, as it is not easy to see the truth (i.e. the appropriate way of writing the actual sound) in this case. Similarly *agceps, agcora*.'

15. In Irish the vowels *e* and *i* are associated with palatal or palatalized quality in consonants, *a*, *o* and *u* with broad or neutral quality (see Greene, 1962 and §5.19).

16. Jackson (1953, 138-9) correctly describes the Ogam alphabet as having been invented for the purpose of spelling the Irish language of its day.

17. For a detailed discussion of these points and the artificiality of the manuscript record see McManus (1986, 13ff.).

18. *In baile i mbi* c *ria* n-u *is queirt is scribtha and,* ut est cuileand 'Where *c* occurs before *u* Queirt should be written, as in *cuileand*' (see Calder, 1917, lines 440-1 and McManus, 1986, 15-16). The name *Queirt*, of course, is no more that an artificial modification of the 'correct' Irish form *Ce(i)rt* (see §7.16).

19. 'How could tradition have preserved the names of the letters, which were completely obscure to the Greeks, so faithfully unless they had been conscientiously committed to memory in the first years of school?'

20. For an example of syllable spelling in Ogam see below §7.8.

21. Compare the following reference to the process of learning off the letters of the alphabet from the Irish Gospel of St. Thomas (see Carney, 1964, 96. qt. 24 and 98. qt. 28): *Ó ro scríb abbgitir dó/ as-bert 'Epir Á'/ cenid frecart macc ind ríg/ ro-fitir ba má. Do-rím Ísu a litre/ doäib ar a súil/ cech aí diib cona dúil/ ocus cona rúin.* 'When he had written an alphabet for him he said "Say A." Though the son of the King did not answer he knew more. Jesus recounted his letters for them before their eyes, each of them with its element (i.e. its *forma*) and with its secret.'

22. See Derolez (1954, xviii, 172), Page (1987, 14) and McManus (1989, 145ff.).

23. See Arntz (1944, 167) and Page (1987, 16) on this phenomenon in the runes and Hammarström (1920, 31-2) for the Latin examples quoted. For a similar practice in Irish see McManus (1989, 147. n7) and §7.11(i).

24. See Derolez (1954, xviii, 173), Page (1987, 16-17) and McManus (1989, 145ff.).

25. Marstrander (1928), who traced the Common Germanic Fuþark to a Celtic alphabetic prototype in the Rhine-Danube area and who described Ogam as a derivative of a Gaulish system of cryptography (183), believed the Celts of Gaul had a homogeneous set of tree-names as letter names for their alphabet and argued that the Germans borrowed the concept of meaningful letter names as well as the 3 x 8 grouping from the Celts (175). His case for a Celtic 3 x 8 grouping, however, rested on very late Irish evidence relating the classification of trees to Ogam characters (in Calder, 1917, lines 5492ff.) and his evidence for Gaulish letter names was based on Gaulish inscriptions like **PERTAE EX VOTO** (identifying *Perta* with a P-Celtic version of the name *Cert*) and on a doubtful derivation of two letter names in the Germanic tradition from Celtic originals (139-41 and 182-3 and see next note).

26. The Anglo-Saxon and Gothic letter names for P and Q (*Peorð, Cweorð* and *Pertra, Quertra* respectively) have been the subject of considerable speculation and dubious theorizing on the relationship between Ogam and the runes. Marstrander (1928, 139-41 and 182-3, see also Carney, 1975, 63) held that they were borrowed from a Celtic alphabet and showed the well-known Continental Celtic opposition of P and Q while Arntz (1935, 358) saw an insular Celtic opposition of Irish /k$^w$/ and Welsh /p/ in them. The rhyming nature of the pairs in each system, however, together with the fact that the Q-rune is not original in the Common Germanic Fuþark and derives its shape in the Anglo-Saxon Fuþorc from the P-rune (Derolez, 1954, 123) suggests that it is much more likely that *Cweorð* and *Quertra* are no more than Latin-inspired modifications of the name of the P-rune. The fact that Q follows P in the Latin alphabetic sequence would have sufficed to dictate the form (see Derolez, 1954, chapters three and four on runic alphabets as opposed to Fuþorcs). To assume borrowing between the Germans and the Celts or the Irish and the Anglo-Saxons on the basis of these names, therefore, is quite dangerous and potentially misleading.

27. I am grateful to Jürgen Uhlich for drawing my attention to this word, which may be attested as a name-element in MAEL-UADAIG on the Ballyspellan brooch (on which see §7.6 and n7.7).


### NOTES TO CHAPTER FOUR

1. The details under (a) are taken from Macalister (1945, referred to as the *Corpus*), (b) are inscriptions discovered in Ireland since the publication of volume one of the *Corpus* (see Appendix 2), and (c) Jackson's figures for Britain (1950, 199). In this and the following chapters numbered references to inscriptions of categories (a) and (c) are to the *Corpus*, those of category (b) being distinguished by Roman numerals referring to the readings given in Appendix 2. Inscriptions in bold type throughout are in conventional script, generally the Latin alphabet.

2. Two further stones from Isle of Man belong to the scholastic type (see §7.5(ii) ).

3. This is the Silchester stone in Hampshire (496). Another inscription from England (Wroxeter, xxi **CVNORIX MACVS MAQVI COLINE**, see Jackson/Wright, 1968 and Appendix 2) bears a very significant partially Latinized Irish name but no Ogam.

4. For a detailed discussion of the Gigha stone see Jackson (1971) and Motta (1982).

5. The distribution of these as recorded in Jackson (1983) is Shetland 7, Orkney 3, Caithness 2, Sutherland 1, 11 from the Pictish heartland between Moray Firth and the Forth and one each from Uist, Argyll and Arran. The inscriptions are studied in Macalister (1940) and their language has been examined by Jackson (1980, 139ff.).

6. See Jackson's discussion and comments on the language which he describes as 'certainly not Celtic, and evidently not Indo-European at all' (1980, 140).

7. These are the inscriptions to which Arntz attached so much importance in his theory on the origins of the Ogam alphabet (see the discussion above §2.4). They are much too late, however, to be of evidential value in that matter.

8. See Krause (1970, 34ff. and 45) and Elliott (1980, 6) and for a more recent discussion suggesting Denmark as the home of the runes see Moltke (1985, 63-4).

9. On the question of the extent of Dalriadic settlement in Scotland before the time of Fergus Mór mac Eirc (approx. 500 AD) see Bannerman (1974, 122-6).

10. Dillon (1977, 3) believed the migration of the Déisi took place at the end of the third century, but on the basis of the Welsh evidence Miller (1977/8, 37) argues for the first quarter of the fifth century while Coplestone-Crow (1981/2, 2) proposes a dual settlement beginning in the late fourth or early fifth century and renewed in the latter part of the fifth or early sixth century. For an illuminating discussion of the Irish evidence and a suggestion that there may have been two migrations from Ireland, one from Waterford and a later from Wexford, see Ó Cathasaigh (1984).

11. On the Todi bilingual inscription see Lejeune (1970/71, 385ff. and 1988, 41-52). On **SEGOMARI** see Evans (1967, 111) and on the use of the patronymic suffix see Evans (1972, 424).

12. See Meyer (1912), Pokorny (1955, 57) and MacNeill (1931, 46-8) but omit 160 TRIA MAQA MAILAGNI; CURCITTI as the last name would appear to be independent of the rest of the inscription. Note that the MAQI- of MAQI-ERCIAS, MAQI-ERCA etc. does not express a filial relationship but is part of the name itself (see §6.14 and §6.22). It may be significant that several of the instances of the omission of the word for 'son' occur before or after the name-element MAQ(Q)I-, -MAQ(Q)I, as in 262 and 154. Compare MacNeill's remarks on a similar feature in the genealogies (1910, 85. nll) and for a possible example of the abbreviation of MAQI to MA before MAQI- see v in Appendix 2.

13. On KOI see Marstrander (1911). Pokorny (1915) suggests that the variant KI may be a pretonic reduced form of KOI but Macalister's original transcription of 156 with an otherwise unattested KI (1897, 13) is corrected to KOI in the *Corpus* and this, to judge by the spacing on the stone, appears to have been the intended reading (see further §6.27).

14. I use the forms MAQQI, MUCOI etc. without reference to the varieties in the spelling of these words on the inscriptions themselves.

15. X MUCOI Y AVI Z (124) and X MUCOI Y MAQQI Z (266) deviate from the standard final position of the MUCOI formula on the inscriptions. For another example of X MUCOI Y AVI Z see the Thomastown stone (xiv).

16. Examples of ANM X MAQQI Y MUCOI Z (55, 220) are very doubtful as are ANM X Y (206, 214) and ANM X CELI Y (a reconstruction of 105).

17. 5(b) is very infrequent and the examples present some difficulties (46, 270, 288). X AVI Y MAQQI Z (185), X MAQQI Y CELI AVI Z (275) and X MUCOI Y AVI Z (124 and xiv) are quite exceptional.

18. KOI occurs very infrequently without an accompanying MUCOI (as in 2 c). The only examples are 38 CORBI KOI MAQI LABRID. . . which is incomplete and 120 BROIN-IENAS KOI NETA-TTRENALUGOS.

19. Most of the CELI inscriptions (105, 109, 123, 128, 142, 215, 275; exclude 19 which is an unwarranted transcription of the Latin) are in bad condition requiring restoration, which is always dangerous. The two most reliable examples appear to be 109 UDDMENSA CELI NETTA-SLOGI and 215 ALLATO CELI BATTIGNI which seem to confirm CELI as a formula word, though the latter could be a possessive genitive type (see §4.6) with the name CELI-BATTIGNI.

20. On the status of NET(T)A and NIOTTA in the inscriptions see §6.15.

21. The equation of VELITAS with Old Irish *filed* presents a difficulty in view of the fact that the acc. and dat. pl. of the word (viz. *fileda* and *filedaib*) do not undergo syncope (see MacNeill, 1931, 45). MacNeill wonders whether a reading VELIADAS is possible but Macalister confirms VELITAS in the *Corpus*.

22. His name appears in the form Guortepir in a Welsh pedigree of the Dyfed dynasty and, in a corrupt transmission, as Gartbuir, Goirtiben (both genitive) in the Irish versions of the same genealogy preserved in the legend of the Expulsion of the Déisi (see Dillon, 1977, 2-3, Ó Cathasaigh, 1984, 18-19 and Richards, 1960, 135, 146). On the form Guortepir see Jackson (1953, 625. nl and 653) and for a suggestion that the **PROTICTORIS** of the inscription mirrors the name see Mac Cana (1961).

23. Mac White (1960/61, 296) mentions a statistical correlation in the occurrence of names found on the Déisi inscriptions and those used in the Déisi genealogies referring to MacNeill

(1910), but no such correlation exists. MacNeill cited from the inscriptions as a whole (see Ó Cathasaigh, 1984, 27).

24. On Amlongaid and the question of his obit see O'Rahilly (1946, 398ff.).

25. The Kilbonane stone (241) presents a number of difficulties which MacNeill attempted to solve in his discussion (1931, 48-53). Bergin (1932) rejected most of MacNeill's proposals including his explanation of ADDILONA, pointing out that *Saidliu is a phantom, the correct form of the name, in the genitive, being Saiglenn with -g- not -d-. The loss of an initial S on the inscription would also be exceptional.

26. One might have expected AIDULUGOS or (post-syncope) AIDLOGO as typical Ogam forms of Old Irish Áedloga. VATTILLOGG, if a form of this name, has an inexplicable initial V, irregular TT for D(D) and an unusual loss of the gen. ending which survives into Old Irish, though it is possible that a final A or O could have been removed from the top of the stone. See the discussion in Appendix 2 (vi).

27. See Carney (1971, 69. n2), Ó Corráin (1971, 98; 1985, 62-3) and Byrne (1973, 137-8).

28. See 8, 32, 34, 45, 76, 135, 146-7, 156, 160-1, 163-4, 171, 180, 184, 188, 194, 197, 204, 217, 231, 233, 235, 265, 269, 298, 311.

29. On early Irish cross types see Crawford (1912 passim) and Lionard (1960/61, 97-8). A discussion and map of distribution of chi-rho inscribed stones will be found in Hamlin (1972, see also 1982, 286ff.) and the Arraglen stone (145) is discussed by Henry (1937, 276 and 1940, 29, where it is described as an imitation of the Brito-Roman type of funerary monument). The Church Island cross is described in detail by O'Kelly/Kavanagh (1954, 103-4) and O'Kelly (1957/9, 80-81), and Henry (1957, 159-60) dates it to the seventh or perhaps the eighth century (see the discussion in Appendix 2 under iv and §5.5).

30. See also Fanning's comments on the cross on vi in Fanning/Ó Corráin (1977, 15). Henry (1957, 77-8 and 160) argues that the fact that the cross on 235 was originally at the top of the stone confounds Macalister's reasoning on this stone and points out that there is no obvious reason to think that the cross and inscription on 233 are not of the same date.

31. Macalister's views were based on a lack of understanding of historical morphology and phonology while MacNeill's were challenged by Thurneysen (1937, 198) and Jackson (1950, 200-1). See also McManus (1986, 4-7) and §5.7.

32. See 31, 32, 116, 150, 170, 220 and 496. Interference is also suspected in the case of 99, 154, 180 (the last twelve letters of which in Macalister's reading do not exist), 191, 192 and 501 though these bear no trace of the formula in question, while 22, 71, 79, 124, 138, 167, 177, 195, 273, 281 and possibly 368 bear MUCOI formulae damaged in one way or another though no suspicion of intent is mentioned (see, however, O'Kelly (1945a, 22) on 79).

33. See MacNeill (1909, 333-4) and Macalister (1945, xvii).

34. For a list of mocu names collected from the manuscript sources see MacNeill (1907, 45-7 and 1911, 75-80).

35. This is the defence of Macalister's view presented in O'Kelly/Kavanagh (1954a, 51-2) but see Byrne (1971, 152-3) who follows MacNeill and explains the demise of mocu names in the seventh century as due to a decline in tribal feeling rather than as a concession to Christian sensitivities.

36. 116, for example, was a lintel stone like 138, 192 and 195 while 181 acted as a jamb-stone in a souterrain. 220 is a very doubtful case, the authenticity of 496 has been called into question, 32 is in a very bad condition generally and the damage on 31 is not unlike that of 10, which does not bear the formula. Macalister's 'prudential aposiopesis' theory (48, 316) as well as his suspicions of camouflage to throw interfering Christians off the scent (19, 103, 118, 176, 178, 300) are quite far-fetched.

37. See MacNeill (1922, 445. n1). Jackson (1950, 207) also believed Latin was unfamiliar 'to those educated in the native learned tradition who set up or could read the Ogams.'

38. See my discussion of MacNeill's polarization of Ogam and manuscript Irish in McManus (1986, 7-13) and §6.30.

39. The dicta occur in the prologue to Auraicept na nÉces (Calder, 1917, lines 46, 49-50) as follows: Cid ara n-abar bescna domunda din Gædhilg? and Cid ara n-eper comad borb fiadh Dia inti legas in Gædhelg? For a discussion rejecting MacNeill's interpretation see Harvey (1987a, 10-12) and see further §8.2.

40. Carney (1978/9, 417) holds that it is unlikely that the Irish would have forgotten the Latin alphabet having used it to create Ogam and Harvey (1987a, 4ff.), accepting this view

as probable, explores a possible case of Latin influence on the orthography of Ogam inscriptions (see further §6.30ff.).

41. See Ó Corráin (1985, 51-2). On 'nativism' see McCone (1990, *passim*, but in particular chapter 1).

42. Compare the comment in the Book of Armagh (Bieler, 1979, 179) in which the failure to translate some passages into Latin is excused on the grounds that they contain a 'great number of Irish names which have no established forms' (*pro habundantia Scotaicorum nominum non habentum qualitatem*).

43. Compare Page (1983, 134) who points out that the Church, far from banning the runes as a pagan type of script, welcomed any method of recording for Christian purposes and rendered runic tradition more fruitful than it might otherwise have been.

44. In this connection I note that de Valera (1979, 26, 146) has suggested that the custom of erecting Ogam inscriptions may have originated among Irish colonists in Wales and spread to Ireland with Christianity, and Hamlin (1982, 285), noting the ecclesiastical association of many Ogam stones, has suggested that some of the sites on which they are found could belong to a very early horizon of the church.

45. See Macalister (1914) and Marstrander (1945) for discussions of 19. Marstrander suggests the reading *juvere druides* or *jubente druide s[acra]/s[acrorum]*.

46. These are 327, 341-2, 345, 353, 358, 362, 368, 372, 378, 380, 399, 405, 409, 422, 426-8, 430-3, 439, 445-6, 449-50, 456, 466-7, 470, 484, 488-9, 496, 500-4. From Jackson's list (1950, 199. n2) I exclude 364 and 404, neither of which bears an Ogam inscription. Of the remaining inscriptions recorded in the *Corpus* as bearing or having once borne Ogams four (328, 348, 423 and 442) have only vestiges, two (329 and 336) are known only from sketches by Llwyd and are also fragmentary, and in the case of eight (343, 349, 376, 401, 411, 434, 473 and 478) it is questionable whether there were ever Ogams present.

47. An earlier transcription made by Edward Llwyd in the seventeenth century suggests that the name in Latin is the same as that in the Ogam, see Nash-Williams (1950, no. 298) and Jackson (1950, 199. n8).

48. Nash-Williams (1950, no. 70) reads the Ogam as CV(*sic* for U)NACENNIVI ILVVETO but his sketch shows that the last letters of the first name are doubtful. Jackson is surely correct (1953, 185. n1) in suggesting the reading -I AVI for -IVI. That the Latin records the name of the father is unfortunate as the word AVI is borrowed into the Latin, not translated, in the only other instance of a bilingual inscription bearing this formula (378, see below n4.51). As is the case with MUCOI, therefore, the bilingual inscriptions provide no contemporary Latin rendering of this word.

49. These are particularly common in South Wales and Devon and Cornwall where Irish influence was strongest, contrasting with North Wales, the centre of Gallic influence, where the **HIC IACIT** formula and horizontally disposed inscriptions are preferred. For a discussion see Bu'lock (1956).

50. 496, the doubtful Hampshire stone, and 504; 501 and 368 are questionable cases, iconoclasm being suspected in the former.

51. See Jackson (1953, 180. n3) who correctly rejects Nash-Williams' (1950, no. 169) transcription of the Latin with **FILI** rather than **AVI**. The supposed ligature of **F** and **I** is most unlike the others conveniently illustrated by Nash-Williams on page 229 and a translation of Irish AVI with Latin **FILI** would be very unusual. See the comments above in n4.48.

52. On double names on these inscriptions see Nash-Willaims (1950, 6, 14).

53. The **HIC IACIT** formula was not infrequently added to the traditional genitive construction with no adjustment for grammatical concord (e.g. 327 **TVRPILLI IC IACIT PVVERI TRILVNI DVNOCATI** and see also 318-20, 326, 329, 331, 342, 344, 354, 368, 386, 388-9, 397, 406, 428). Nash-Williams (1950, 9) suggests these be translated '[The stone of] X [son of Y]. He lies here.' For another suggestion of lack of concord see §6.25.

## NOTES TO APPENDIX 2

1. I would like to express my thanks to Finbarr Moore for his advice regarding these stones and to Mr. Patrick O'Connor for permitting me to examine them.

2. This too is Breatnach's view in his contribution to O'Kelly, 1957/9 (86-7) but he reads RIVVESS, taking this as a gen. of a fem. *ā*-stem *\*Riwā* and comparing the later deity name

*Reo*. There is no reliable evidence, however, for such an ending in the *ā*-, or any other, stem class. On the reading of the -**H** in 1 **MENUEH** as *s* see McManus (1986, 27. n40) and on 362 AVITTORIGES see §6.25.

3. This would, of course, be an unusual error as *Coll* was the name of Ogam C.

4. I would like to thank Professor Pádraig Ó Fiannachta for drawing my attention to this stone and Doncha Ó Conchúir for permitting me to examine it.

5. I have now been informed by Mr. Doyle's son Joseph, whom I thank, that the find was made in the townland of Cloghabrody by the side of a stream separating this from the townland of Columcille. One wonders whether the townland got its name from the stone.

6. If so *Loígde* would have to be analysed as *loíg* 'calf' + adjectival -*de* (see §6.13d), not as an A type compound *\*loiga*- + *dēwā* 'goddess', O'Rahilly's etymology (1946, 3) of the old name of the river Bandon, *Loígde/Lóegda*.

7. I am grateful to Mrs. Margaret Phelan of Kilkenny for drawing my attention to this stone.

8. I would like to express my thanks to Ms. Mary Flood of Rothe House Museum for her assistance in my investigation of this stone.

9. I would like to express my thanks to Professor George Eogan for his advice in connection with my investigation of these stones, and to Mr. Tom Lamb of Nobber for allowing me access to the souterrain.

## NOTES TO CHAPTER FIVE

1. Jackson suggests (1950, 213) that the idea of the late supplementary characters may have arisen from the necessity of representing Latin *p*. On the influence of Latin in the creation of the *forfeda* see §7.16.

2. On the use of *Nomina* in the sense 'relics' or 'remains' in North African inscriptions commemorating martyrs see also Nash-Williams (1950, no. 370).

3. See Lionard's excellent discussion (1960/61, 97ff.) and O'Kelly's comments (1954, 104 and 1957/59, 80).

4. See n4.29 and Henry's interesting work on the cross-slabs of the Caherciveen and Waterville areas of Co. Kerry and their continental models (1948, and 1957, 158-60). In this connection the relatively high incidence of late and ANM formula inscriptions in the baronies of Dunkerron North and South and the barony of Iveragh are worthy of note.

5. Thurneysen's suggestion (1946, 73) that the survival of -I in MAQ(Q)I might be due to proclisis is rejected by Jackson (1950, 201. n3). In the later language words in this position tend to undergo considerable reduction rather than to resist it (see fnn. 6.49 and 6.67).

6. See Thurneysen (1937, 198), Jackson (1950, 200-1) and McManus (1986, 4-7).

7. See Thurneysen (1946, 126-7) for further examples of this development.

8. In Old Irish orthography the sounds /b/, /d/ and /g/ are usually written *p*, *t* and *c* in post-vocalic position, *b*, *d* and *g* in this position representing /β/, /δ/ and /γ/. On Old Irish orthography see McCone (1987, 267-71).

9. Compare British Latinized *Decantae* and see Jackson (1953, 39, 177).

10. On the loss of intervocalic *s* see Thurneysen (1946, 132) and Greene (1976, 27). Greene describes the pattern in Primitive Irish as similar to that of British where, according to Jackson (1953, 313), the loss of non-junctural intervocalic *s* took place in the second half of the first century.

11. O'Rahilly (1942, 119. n4) cites Ogam ISARI (= OI *Iar*) from Macalister (1902, 110) but this is superseded in the Corpus (205) where it is pointed out that the 1902 reading began at the wrong end of the inscription.

12. See Thurneysen (1946, 39-40) and below (§6.28) for further examples of the reflex of this diphthong. The monophthongization is seen already in Gaulish (e.g. *Teutates*, *Marti Toutati*, *Totatigenus* etc.) but Greene has pointed out (1976, 27) that in Irish the levelling of the IE *u*-diphthongs postdates the loss of intervocalic *s*, and therefore belonged to the Early Primitive Irish period.

13. See Thurneysen (1946, 59) and on the spread of this vocalism to the composition syllable see Pokorny (1919, 33) and Hamp (1953/4, 285-6).

14. See Thurneysen (1946, 121-2) and Cullen (1972) on the development of this sound. For a suggestion that it was not lost but merged by contraction with certain following vowels, giving *í*, see Lambert (1979, 209-10).

15. For the details of lenition see Thurneysen (1946, 74ff.) and on lenition as an initial mutation (ibid. 141ff.).

16. See Greene (1956, and 1973, 129) on the reduction of geminates to single stops.

17. On the history of /w/ see Jackson (1949), Hamp (1953/4) and Cowgill (1967).

18. On the development of *ss* and final fricatives see Thurneysen (1946, 109-10), Greene (1973, 129) and McCone (1982, 24. n29). McCone is probably correct in suggesting that the survival of -*h* (⟨ -*s*) as compared with the loss of -*h*- (⟨ -*s*-) may have been due to support from the new -*h* (from -*ss* and final fricatives).

19. Jackson (1950, 202) considers the fact that the Ogam alphabet has no mechanism for writing lenited consonants a consequence of its creation predating the development. For a similar argument see also Ó Cuív (1965, 161).

20. On the requirement that we assume two distinct stages of shortening of long vowels in final unstressed syllables see McCone (1979, 16 and 1982, 25).

21. See Pokorny (1918, 419ff.), Thurneysen (1946, 46-50) and Greene (1972, 233 and 1973, 129-31) on vowel-affection, and McManus (1983, 56ff.) on the same in Latin loanwords.

22. See Greene (1976, 28ff.) on this phenomenon and the later fate of these diphthongs, and (1962) on the concept of '*u*-quality' consonants.

23. See McCone (1982, 25) on the shift of syllable/word boundary and Cullen (1972) on the development of *y* in final syllables. After *y* no distinction in the fate of historically long and short vowels is recoverable. Thus, *\*aliyas* ⟩ *aile* and *\*tōtiyās* (gen. sg.) ⟩ *túaithe*, not *\*túaithea* as one might have expected (see further §6.24).

24. On these mutations in Old Irish see Thurneysen (1946, 140ff.).

25. On the division of the stages of Early Irish used in this book see Greene (1976, 26). It should be noted that the term 'archaic' is often used in Early Irish studies, particularly in editions of early texts, with reference to linguistic features which belong to the period referred to as Early Old Irish in this book.

26. On the reduction of these clusters see Thurneysen (1946, 78-9) and Greene (1976, 34-6).

27. Note that the G in DEGLANN is not a fricative but represents the sound /g/, later written *c* (*Déclán*).

28. This in turn paved the way for the adoption of Latin loanwords with long vowels intact in non-initial syllables. Compare the earlier and later borrowings of Latin *corōna*, viz. *corann* and *coróin* and see McManus (1983, 59).

29. On syncope see Thurneysen (1946, 67ff., 98) and Greene (1972 and 1973, 134-5) and for syncope in Latin loanwords see McManus (1983, 60ff.).

30. Note that an existing consonant cluster is not palatalized by the syncope of a following front vowel (e.g. OI *Colgan*, EOI pre-syncope *Colgion* ⟨ *\*Colgiyonas*, see n5.46 below; OI *daltaib* ⟨ *\*daltiyobis* ; OI *Alban* ⟨ *\*Albiyonas* etc.).

31. In this connection see Greene's discussion of the spelling -*ia*- in early texts (1972).

32. On palatalization see Greene (1973) and McManus (1983, 64-5) for the same in Latin loanwords.

33. On the spelling of Irish names in the Book of Armagh see Kelly (1979) and on those in Adamnán's Life of Columba see Anderson/Anderson (1961, 124ff.).

34. See Stokes/Strachan (1903, xxvi and 244-7) for the Cambray Homily and (1901, xxiii-xxv) on the *prima manus* of the Würzburg glosses. For a discussion of the overlap between Ogam and MS spellings see McManus (1986, 7ff.) and §6.30.

35. See Harvey (1985) for a discussion of the evidence. The derivation of *Cothraige* from *Patricius* is one I find difficult to doubt despite Harvey's assessment. The 'four households' etymology (Harvey, 1985, 6) does not constitute a strong argument against the derivation in view of Breatnach's suggestion (*apud* Koch, 1990, 184) that the glossary word *caí* (.i. *tech*) rather than the word *tech* 'house' itself underlies it. This in fact might presuppose Harvey's starred form *\*Cothairche* (whence the pseudo etymology *cethair* + *caí*).

36. See Jackson (1950, 202-3). MacNeill (1909, 331) has the cult of the Ogams flourishing in the fifth century but in 1931 (33) he assigns the bulk to the sixth, and he points out that no evidence has been found which would enable us to date any inscription earlier that the fifth (1909, 332) or mid-fifth (1931, 33) century. Thurneysen (1946, 10) suggests some

inscriptions are undoubtedly as old as the fourth century and he communicated the view to Arntz (1935, 331) that the beginning of the Ogam period was about 300 A.D.

37. For a discussion of the bone die in relation to the dating of the inscriptions see Mac White (1960/61, 301-2).

38. ⟨ *triyan maqqan Mailagnī* with assimilation of the final nasals to the following initials. One might have expected TRIAM MAQAM MAILAGNI but as Ogam does not use double consonants in a regular way (see §6.30(d) ) the reading as it stands need not postdate the transfer of a final nasal across word boundary. The inscription is accompanied on the other side of the stone by a single name CURCITTI which to judge by the nature of execution of the scores and the direction of writing appears to be unrelated.

39. The fact that the I in RITTAVVECAS has not been lowered though the original I of the third syllable (⟨ *-wicas*) has must be due to the influence of the simplex as suggested by Pokorny (1918, 423). The gen. *Ritiās* (see 198 MAQI-RITEAS) would not have undergone affection in the first syllable. For later examples of the same see 211 RITTAVVECC and the discussion of iv RITTECC in Appendix 2. Inscription viii RETAGIN, on the other hand, shows vowel-affection.

40. Note that in CUNOVATO the final S has been dropped but lowering has not taken place in the first syllable. Compare the spellings with -IA ⟨ -IAS as opposed to -EAS (e.g. 175 -ERCCIA, DOVINIA, 178 DOVINIA in this category but 198 -RITEAS above §5.25).

41. Unless this is a mistake for CATUVIRR. Syncope has not taken place in the accompanying LUGUVVEC.

42. On the dating of 442 see Jackson (1953, 140). The reading of the accompanying Ogam is uncertain (see Nash-Williams, 1950, 195).

43. Jackson (1950, 209) restores the Ogam to the expected [IM]B[I]CATOS and later, having seen the stone (1953, 173. n1), to [AM]B[I]CATOS with British influence in the vocalism of the initial syllable (see §6.21).

44. On 489 see MacNeill (1932, 133-5) who suggests, no doubt correctly, that the reading intended was SVANNUCI MAQI RINI.

45. For a discussion of the spelling **MAC(C)V-** see §5.18 and Jackson (1950, 211-12 and 1953, 140).

46. Examples of pre-syncope spellings are Adamnán's (*Cule-*) *Drebene*, later *Dre(i)bne* (Anderson/Anderson 1961, 224), *Fechureg* (ibid. 240 but *Fechreg*, 508) and *Colgion* (ibid. 278, but *Colcen* 192 and *Colgen* 300) on which see O'Rahilly (1946, 464-5 and 1950, 396). In his Life of Columbanus Jonas has the forms *Commogellus* and *Benechor* for later *Comgellus* (a Latinized form of Old Irish *Comgell/-gall*) and *Benchor* (Krusch, 1905, 158). For further examples and a discussion see Carney (1971, 69 and 1978/9, 422-3), Thurneysen (1933, 208 on the early Donatus gloss with the form *commedes*, later *comtis*), and Ní Dhonnchadha (1982, 200. no. 50) on *Andelaith*, later *Aindlid*.

47. See Thurneysen (1946, 19, 124) and Carney (1978/9, 429) on these Early Old Irish forms. MacNeill's *Cat[h]uer* (1922, 440. n2; leg. *Cathuer*) cited from the Book of Leinster 387a34 is a *varia lectio* of *Cathaīr* (O'Brien, 1962, 5) and therefore a doubtful example of the expected EOI form of *Catuwir-*. Meyer (1912a, 1150) suggests the possibility that Cormac's etymologies of the names *Domnall* and *Nemnall* as *doman-núall* and *nem-núall* point to familiarity with the expected EOI spellings *Domnuall* and *Nemnuall* respectively.

48. My reading was ANM MAGANN MAQI N?DAd/t. . . . The name appears at the top of the angle and I could not be sure as to whether the consonant following the A was D or T, or whether this was the last letter, as there appeared to be at least one vowel score on the top angle. In view, further, of the history of the *forfeda* as outlined in chapter 7 (§§7.13-15) it is highly improbable that the symbol following the initial N (an arrow-head in shape which bears no resemblance to *Uilen*) of the last name is correctly interpreted as the diphthong *úa*. Even functional scholastic Ogams avoid all *forfeda* with the exception of the first (see n7.41).

## NOTES TO CHAPTER SIX

1. On Irish personal names see Pokorny (1955), O'Brien (1971 and 1973), Ó Cuív (1986) and Ó Corráin/Maguire (1981). On Gaulish names see Evans (1967 and 1972) and Schmidt (1957). In this chapter names cited from MS sources are given in the nominative unless otherwise stated. Most examples are taken from the indices to O'Brien (1962 and 1973), Stokes/Strachan (1903), Anderson/Anderson (1961) and Ó Riain (1985).

2. There is, of course, an imbalance in the material in favour of males and of the upper classes of society since it is improbable that many of humbler status would have had the resources to commission an inscription. On the relevance of this latter point to a survey of Indo-European name types see in particular Pulgram (1947, 192ff.).

3. See O'Brien's discussion (1973, 218 and 226ff.). These are sometimes referred to as loose compounds, but they are not compounds in the strict sense. It should be noted that in later Irish the second element is more variable than in the early period and includes place names as well as nouns, adjectives and personal names.

4. See Pulgram's excellent discussion of the limitations of the material available to us (1947).

5. Pokorny (1955, 56-7) suggests the word probably has the meaning 'wolf' in personal names, viz *Cunagusus 'possessing the strength of a wolf' (see also Evans, 1972, 430-1). On the Indo-European word for 'wolf' and its reflex in Irish olc 'bad', Olcán (= 100 ULC-CAGNI, 370 **VLCAGNVS** etc.), Lochán etc. see McCone (1985).

6. One might have expected *Aissiuch but compare Míliucc and drisiuc (acc. pl. driscona) and see Meyer (1912a, 1149) who describes these as pet forms of Mílchú and dris-bard respectively. The appearance of -chú in the nominative of some of these compounds (e.g. Báethchú, Fáelchú, O'Brien 1973, 228) is due to reformation from other cases, as pointed out to me by Jürgen Uhlich.

7. It is tempting to compare the initial element here with Gaulish ollo- (Evans, 1967, 237-8), OI oll 'great, ample', but one would have expected Ollchú in that case. Ogam -L-, of course could represent LL.

8. Bergin (1932a, 140-146) convincingly dismisses MacNeill's equation of IVACATTOS with the later attested gen. Eochada (which he considers an analogical gen. of Eochaid modelled on Labraid, gen. Labrada) and suggests that the Ogam name may be one of the many unidentified names in the inscriptions. Jürgen Uhlich, however, has drawn my attention to the form Eochathān (gen.) cited by Korolev (1984, 164) from the Laud genealogies (see Meyer, 1912c, 296, 13) as a possible instance of the name with the -án suffix, especially in view of the rime with Cathān in the Book of Lecan (54 Rb 38). In the absence of a certain example of the expected reflex of the Ogam name I have asterisked the form *Éochada.

9. If this is the correct interpretation of **BODIBEVE** the -E may be compared with that in xxi **COLINE**) and the first E of -**BEVE** would be due to the vocalism of the nom. *bewah ⟨ *biwas. On Byw in Welsh names see Evans (1972, 427-8) and compare 325 **BIVATIGI[RNI]** (sic leg.?, see Nash-Williams, 1950, 63) and 493 **CONBEVI**. With **BODI**- compare Gaulish Boud-, bod- etc. and the name Boudica (Evans, 1967, 156-8).

10. The element magl is more common in Welsh (mael) than in Irish names in which it interchanges with máel 'bald, cropped' (Conmál, Conmáel, Cathmál, Cathmáel, see O'Brien, 1973, 229 and O'Rahilly, 1946, 360. n2).

11. Cp. Gildas' Maglocune (voc.) = Mailcun, king of Guenedota, who died in 547 (Anderson/Anderson, 1961, 84). The Welsh forms of the name derive independently from the nom. and gen. respectively (*Maglocū and *Maglocunas), cp. Kynyr, Kynri ⟨ nom. and gen. of Cunorīx and Irish Cóelub and Cóelbad below n6.16.

12. On Lugu in Gaulish names see Evans (1967, 219-221). Lug does appear in second position later (see Áedlug, Báethlug etc., O'Brien, 1973, 224) and it may be found in 120 -TTRENALUGOS (see also the doubtful readings in 26 and 348) = (Úa) Trianlugo, (Aui) Trenloco (on which see Grosjean, 1960, 46) and vi VATTILLOGG[O].

13. The equation of TREN with OI trén is doubtful in view of the -ia- in Trianlugo (see last note). The -é- in OI trén derives from compensatory lengthening (⟨ *trekno- ⟨ *treksno-?) and is not subject to diphthongization.

14. This is clearly an n-stem and its inflexion as such is attested later (cp. Adamnán's gen. Nemaidon and Cinedon, Lugedon, Lugadon etc. in the Annals of Ulster, O'Rahilly, 1946,

362. n8). It is probably related to OI *áed* (*u*-stem); gen. *áeda* 'fire', itself the most common of all Irish personal names in the early period (see Ó Corráin/Maguire, 1981, s.n. *Áed*, *Aodh*).

15. This element is probably a derivative of the root \**bhau*-, \**bhu*- 'to strike' (see Pokorny, 1959, 112). With \**bhut-s*, gen. \**bhutos* as a name element one can compare \**wik-s*, gen. \**wik-os* and \**dek-s*, gen. \**dek-os* in LUGUVVECCA, LUGUDECA below. As in these cases the second element of a compound can be a derivative of a verbal stem not attested as a simplex (Pedersen, 1913, 4 citing *trócar*).

16. *Coílboth*, *Cóelbad* are in origin the gen. of *Cóelub* but are attested independently as nominatives. The same is found in *Cathub* gen. and nom. *Cathbad*. Cp. Welsh *Meilic* and *Maelgwn* above n6.11.

17. On -DECAS see Pokorny (1959, 190) and Joseph (1982, 176) where it is related to the root \**dek*- 'to show respect etc.'. Pokorny alternatively suggests the root \**deik*- 'to show', similarly Borgeaud (1971, 41) comparing Latin *iūdex*, in which case Ogam -DECAS would be post-affection for -DICAS. The name *Echuid*, gen. *Echdach* (later analogical gen. *Eochada*, see n6.8) also appears to contain this element (⟨ \**ekwo-diks* or-*deks*, see Bergin, 1932a, 145, comparing *Luguid*, gen. *Luigdech* and Borgeaud, 1971).

18. Cp. Gaulish *gen*- (Evans, 1967, 203 ) and OI *gainithir* 'is born' and note that this element also occurs in the Irish word for 'daughter', OI *ingen*, 362 INIGENA (⟨ \**enigenā*, cp. Gaulish *Enigenus*). In reduced form it is also found in the diminutive suffix -*agnas* etc. see §6.12.

19. The commemorand's name in this instance, **CVNOCENNI**, CUNACENNI, contains the same **CVNO**- element as the father (see §6.19) but -**CENNI**, -CENNI differs from -**GENI** in its C/C and NN/NN and is related to Gaulish *cen*- (OI *cinim* 'I am born', Evans, 1967, 175-7) with hypocoristic gemination.

20. This is OI *gus*, *u*-stem, gen. *goso* 'force, vigour' ⟨ \**ghus-tu-s* ⟨ \**gheu*- 'to pour', Pokorny, 1959, 447-8).

21. Compare Gaulish *reg*-, *rig*-, -*rix*, -*rex* etc. (Evans, 1967, 243-249) and OI *rí*, gen. *ríg* 'king' (⟨ \**rēg-s*, \**rēg-os*), Lat. *rex* etc. On the compounds containing -**RIGIS**, -**RI** in the British inscriptions see Jackson (1953, 624ff.).

22. See Gaulish *val*-, *vall*- from the root \* *wal*- 'to be strong' (Lat. *valeo*), OI *flaith* 'lordship' etc (Evans, 1967, 269-271 and Pokorny, 1959, 1111-1112). The same element may be found in 158 SUVALLOS, 281 ?SOVALINI, 125 VALAMNI (= *Fallomun* ?) and 302 VALUVI.

23. The element -VICAS (nom. \**wik-s*) derives from the root \**weik*- found in Latin *vinco*, -*ere* 'to conquer' and OI *fichid* 'fights' (see Pokorny, 1959, 1128-9). In Gaulish it appears in the names *Brannovices*, *Eburovices* etc. (Evans, 1967, 281-285). It will be noted that in Irish it usually combines with a divine name.

24. CALUNOVIC[A] would appear to contain the name *Culann* best known in the (C)-type name *Cú Chulainn*.

25. On **MENUEH** ⟨ \**Minawicas* see MacNeill (1909, 333), McManus (1986, 27. n40) and Uhlich (1989, 131. n9). The first element may be the same as that found in *mocu Min* (e.g. *Mo-Sinnu mocu Min*), and *Menraige* (MacNeill, 1911, 79).

26. On *Rethech*, *Rethach*, *Ráthach*, (⟨ *Ritawicas*) and *Lugech*, *Lugach* (⟨ *Luguwicas*) see Bergin (1932a, 138-9 and 141, 1938a, 235. n1) and MacNeill (1910, 84. nkk, where the nom. *Lugaei*, suggesting \**Luguwīk-s*, is cited).

27. The former of the later attested forms (*Dercmossach*) seems to contain the word *mosach* 'filthy', the latter (*Dercmaisech*) the somewhat more complimentary element *maisech* ⟨ *mass* 'elegant'. In the Ogam we might have expected DERCMOSSAC or DERCMASSIC.

28. Meyer (1914, 636-7) suggests that we may have examples of a svarabhakti vowel in the second A of ANAVLAMATTIAS and the first I of CORIBIRI. Jürgen Uhlich has suggested to me that the third E of xiv VEDDELLEMETTO may be similarly explained.

29. As *ambi*- may also have intensive force (see Evans, 1967, 134) the names *Ambicatus* and *Rocatus* are synonymous as far as the dictionary meanings of their respective elements go.

30. On Dvandva compounds in Irish see Meyer (1912a, 790-791), Meid (1968), Binchy (1972) and Ó Cuív (1973) who cites perfunctory (i.e. metrically dictated) examples from Bardic poetry such as *úa ChonnChuirc* 'descendant of Conn and Corc'.

31. For a survey of the lexical content of Gaulish names see Evans (1972, 427ff.).

32. Pulgram also points out that in our own times we christen children *Lily, Ernest, Violet* etc. without wishing to call attention to the dictionary meanings of these names.

33. For a discussion of the meaning of the element *corb* in names such as *Corbmac* (= *Cormac*), *Mac-Corb, Cú-Chorb* etc. see Ó Cathasaigh (1977, 43-45) who opts for a connection with *corbaid* 'defiles' (comparing *Corc* etc., *corcaid* 'burns') as against the traditional explanation *corb* = 'chariot'.

34. Cp. the *Uí Dróna* whence the Baronies of Idrone, Co. Carlow, within seven miles of one of the stones which may bear the name (31, Inistioge, Co. Kilkenny).

35. MacNeill (1909, 361) compares the MS gen. *Tréno, Tréna* and suggests reading TRENO, which is possible. Note however 341 MAQI-TRENI which appears to be an *o*-stem.

36. The *Báet* in *Báetán* stands in the same relationship to *báeth* as does the *Túat* in *Túatán* to *túath*. This is described as hypocoristic (i.e. pet) derivation with expressive gemination (Evans, 1972, 425) but it also involves voicing, whence the D in BAIDAGNI. This may be the reason O'Brien includes *Báetán* among borrowed names (1973, 231). Similarly *Tecán* (256 TEGANN), described by Thurneysen (1928, 297) as half-British, half-Irish, presupposes a simplex *tech* cognate with Welsh *teg* 'fair' and found in OI *étig* 'ugly'. One wonders, therefore, whether the suffixes *-acán, -ucán, -ocán* can be explained in this way as deriving from native *-ach* + *-án* etc. rather than from British *-óc* (on which see Thurneysen, 1946, 173-4).

37. One would have expected *\*Columbagnas* (< Lat. *columba* 'dove' + *-agnas*) to give *\*Colbán* in Irish (see Thurneysen, 1933, 209) but *Colmán* is the attested form. The reduction of *-mb-* to *-mm-* reflected in the Ogam spelling may be due to the influence of British, as suggested by Thurneysen. Compare the remarks on **AMMECATI** (§6.21).

38. In connection with the vocalism of the first syllable of this name (on which see Meyer, 1915, 381) it is worth noting that in the inscription in question, 256 ANM TEGANN MAC DEGLANN, the E of the first name, which is known to be short, is written with the first supplementary character, which usually denotes short /e/, whereas that of the second is written the traditional way.

39. On *-án, -én, -ón* etc. see Meyer (1912a, 1148 and 1908/10, 68. n2). The varying vocalism in this suffix arises from its attachment to different stem classes (*o-* (and *ā-*)stems > *-agnas*, *u*-stems > *-ugnas* (> *-ognas*) etc.).

40. Compare Gaulish *Birac[i]* on which see Evans (1967, 311-3).

41. This is the OI word *toísech* (Modern Irish *taoiseach*) 'leader', Welsh *tywysog* 'prince' (< *\*to-wid-tācos*, Pokorny, 1959, 1125-6).

42. For masc. *ā*-stems becoming *o*-stems compare the compounds in *-gal* (O'Brien, 1973, 224).

43. For examples of names with this suffix from later Irish see O'Brien (1973, 224).

44. Compare the names *Fachtnae, Lachtnae, Lugna* etc. (O'Brien, 1973, 223; see also Marstrander, 1910, 376ff. on this suffix in Celtic).

45. On the suffix *-am, -iam* etc. see Watkins, (1962, 182-5). VLATIAMI is a doubtful reading and one might have expected an *n*-stem gen. *\*VLATIAMONAS* (OI *flaithem*, gen. *flaithemon*).

46. For a suggestion that this is the Gaulish name *Segomo* (Evans, 1967, 257) and points to a recent settlement of Gauls in the south of Ireland see MacNeill (1911, 73. n5) and Watkins (1962, 184) on Pokorny. The theory is considered unnecessary by Byrne (1973, 182).

47. It is tempting to see the divine name *Áine* in Ogam AINIA especially in view of the parallel name *Der-Áine* (*Der* 'daughter', cp. *Der-Erce, Mac-Erce*). If so AI must be an error for A as the first syllable does not contain the diphthong *ai* and palatalization is not written in Ogam (see §5.19 and §6.30(c)).

48. The nom. *nia/nio* is found as the second element in compound names (*Flaithnia, Maicnio*) and *Nia*, gen. *Niath* occurs as well as petrified *Nad/Nath* as the first element in (C) type names (*Nia-Corb* etc., O'Brien, 1973, 227-8). On MacNeill's contention (1909, 369) that the *Nia* in *Cairpre Nia Fer* (EOI gen. *Coirpri Nioth Fer*) cannot mean 'nephew' see now Ó Cathasaigh (1986, 143) who points out that *Cairbre* was deemed to have a supernatural father and to have belonged to the human race through his mother (hence 'Cairbre, Sister's Son to Man').

49. Compare the reduction of *Der-* to *Dar-* in proclisis (O'Brien, 1956, 178 and see n6.67 below). The weak position might explain the early loss of final *s* in *Netas-*.

50. Here we appear to have a masc. *o-* or *yo-* stem corresponding to 351 **DALLVS DVMELVS** (Welsh *Dyfel*). The later genitive *Duimle* (Ó Riain, 1985, 150 = 707.747), however, points to either a *yo-* or a (*y*)*ā*-stem and the latter is suggested by 198 -DDUMILEAS, which seems to contain the same element.

51. On the *cú glas* in early Irish law see Kelly (1988, 6, 15).

52. This looks like a post-syncope spelling but there is a gap in the inscription between M and R which Macalister says contains some modern nicking which would make I. The letter transcribed as O (twice) is written with a supplementary character unique in the inscriptions. In view of this one might opt to transcribe it with A rather than O, viz. MALE-GAMRID, representing *Maíle-Gaimrid*.

53. On MAILAGURO see Meyer (1912a, 796-7) who suggests the division MAILA-GURO, taking the second element as the gen. of a *u*-stem adj. corresponding to OI *gor* (*o-/ā*-stem) 'pious' and MacNeill (1932a, 126-7) who compares *Máel-Augrai* and suggests a reading MAILA-[A]GURO together with a change in declension between AGURO and *Augrai*. Compare, however, ALATTO, gen. *Alta*, *Altai*.

54. See MacNeill (1907, 44 ff; 1911, 72ff.) for MUCOI names and (1909, 368; 1911, 82-3) on AVI. A map of distribution of MUCOI inscriptions will be found in Mac White (1960/61) and both Ó Corráin (1972) and Byrne (1973) have maps of distribution of tribal states based on historical sources.

55. Cp. *Brénaind mocu Alta/Altai* (St. Brendan, founder of Clúain-ferta Brénaind, Clonfert) the most famous member of the *Altraige*.

56. On the *Brecraige*, a subject people of the Uí Neill in Co. Meath see Ó Corráin (1972, 23, 31). The stone is in Pembrokeshire in Wales and the reading is uncertain (Macalister MUCOE BRIACI, Nash-Williams MUCOI BRECI). The H surface is damaged at the relevant point and my reading was slECI.

57. This was MacNeill's identification in 1907 (46) but in 1911 (72) he cites the *Cailtrige*. If either is right the equation CALLITI = *Caílte* (§6.13) would be incorrect.

58. See MacNeill (1911, 72. n3). The *Dál Coirpri* were one of the four primary divisions of the Lagin but the stone is in the barony of East Muskerry, Co. Cork.

59. The inscriptions are in the baronies of Gowran, Co. Kilkenny (28) and Decies Without Drum (272, 283) and the *Dál Maic Cuirp* were one of the septs of the Déisi Muman. The equation is MacNeill's (1931, 42) and is based on an assumed reduction of Ogam MAQI-CORB to MACORB, which is unlikely, as well as on an assumption that -CORB is gen. pl. of a word for 'chariot'. See however n6.33 above.

60. MacNeill (1907, 45) ROTTAIS = *Corcu Roíde*, (1911, 74; 1931, 42) = *Rothraige*.

61. Cp. Adamnán's acc. *Silnanum filium Nemaidon mocu Sogin* (Anderson/Anderson, 1961, 330-332).

62. Jackson takes **-COLINE** (for **-COLINI**) to reflect the reduction of *-i* and *-e* to /ə/ but the inscription is clearly pre-affection.

63. See n6.53 above. Meyer (1912a, 796-7) takes the -A of his MAILA-GURO to be the reflex of *-ās* and compares 'archaic' Irish *Máela*.

64. There are no *i*-stem genitives in -IAS. 124 ANAVLAMATTIAS appears later as nom. *Anblamath*, gen. *Anfolmithe* and clearly does not contain the suffix found in *Fedelmid* (Thurneysen, 1946, 192-3).

65. The genitives *Aicher* (cons. stem) and *Aichir* (*o*-stem) are attested later (Thurneysen, 1946, 215).

66. This could also be from *o* as the *ā*-stems in Gaulish have *o* as composition vowel (Schmidt, 1957, 90).

67. Compare also *inghean uí* 〉 *ní*, *mac* 〉 *mhac* 〉 *ac* 〉 *'c* and see MacNeill (1907, 44).

68. See MacNeill (1907, 48) where it is also pointed out that the instances of *mocu* before *t*, *c* and *f* in Old Irish are too few to be decisive as to whether the form took lenition or not.

69. Wagner (1969, 226, 248) connects it with OI *macc*, Welsh *mach* 'surety' pointing out that fellow tribesmen acted *ex officio* as sureties for one another and compares German *Bürge*, *Bürger*. If *corcu*, one of the words which later supplants *mocu*, is not related to *corca* 'oats' but to Welsh *car* 'kinsman', OI *cairde* 'a pact between tribes', we may have a parallel formation in *mocu*, *corcu* but this is very problematical.

70. It is difficult to establish whether the *-red*, *-rad* in *gemred*, *gaimred* 'winter(time)' and *samrad* 'summer(time)' derives from *reto* or *rāto* 〈 *rōto* (Pokorny, 1959, 866 and Thurneysen,

1946, 169), though OI *ráithe* 'a quarter of a year' and Welsh *gaeafrawd* 'the course of winter' suggest the latter. The final -D for an expected -T is also unusual, but see 118 VEQREQ with -REQ ⟨ *-rīgas*.

71. MacNeill (1909, 350) suggests that A and O for AI and OI represent dialectal non-diphthongal varieties comparing later *caorthann* and *cárthann* etc. but Pokorny (1922, 49-53) argues that it is orthographic, pointing in particular to the Rockfield stones 243 and 244 with the spellings COLABOT and COILLABBOTAS respectively probably referring to the same person or at least to members of the same family.

72. **LUGUAEDON** accompanied by post-syncope **MENUEH** and LUGADDON by pre-syncope LUGUDEC present a peculiar state of affairs as LUGADDON has all the appearances of being later that **LUGUAEDON**. See however Uhlich (1989, 131. n9) who explains that formations in *-aidon-* normally appear later in reinterpreted shape.

## NOTES TO CHAPTER SEVEN

1. For an edition of these inscriptions see Macalister (1949) and see Lionard (1960/1) for a very useful survey of the cross-types appearing on them as well as more general remarks on their typology.

2. See Henry (1940, chapter 3) on changing fashions in Irish architecture and Byrne (1971, 153) on the seventh century as the 'end of an era'.

3. See for example the alphabetic list of verbal nouns in Ó Cuív (1966, 287-8).

4. O'Neill Hencken had suggested a seventh-eighth century date for the site (loc. cit., 2) but see Raftery (1959/60, 7) and Mac White (1960/1, 301-2).

5. Compare the Kilmalkedar alphabet stone (Co. Kerry, see Macalister, 1949, no. 913) dated sixth century by Bieler (1949, 271) on palaeographical grounds.

6. On forgeries see further Macalister (1945, pp. iv, 15, 65, 107 and 112).

7. Given that all Es with the exception of the first in CNAEMSECH are written X it is probable that this is an error for CNAIMSECH, cp. gen. *Cnāmsige* (O'Brien, 1962, 111 = 129b54) and *cnáimsech* 'mid-wife' ⟨ *cnáim* 'bone'). MINODOR looks like an adjectival dvandva compound (see §6.10) of *min* 'small' or *mín* 'smooth' + *odur* 'dun'. CELLACH and MUAD may be epithets to the preceding names or independent personal names themselves (with the latter compare 307 MODDAGN[I], *Múadán* (nom.)). The second element in MAEL-UADAIG looks like the gen. of *\*Uadach*, derivative of *\*úad* 'fight' ⟨ *\*yeud-* (cp. *Cathach*), the element found in Welsh *udd* (⟨ *\*yeudyos*) 'lord' (see §3.15 under H *hÚath*).

8. See also Brash (1879, 319-20) who defends its authenticity, Macalister (1945, p.15) and De hÓir (1983, 53-4).

9. The name *Sonid* is unknown and a reverse reading DINOS has been suggested as possible, though this is equally obscure. Graves' view (1879, 242) that *Dinos* might be the 'Ogam name' (*ainm n-ogaim*) of *Dímma*, scribe of the Book of Dímma, is based on the assumption that a person's 'Ogam name' was distinct from his usual name, a misunderstanding of the phrase *ainm n-ogaim* (see §8.8).

10. The first two words are written in the type called *crad cride ecis* 'torment of a poet's heart' in Calder (1917, 302. 19, 303. 19), the second two in *Ogam ad-len fid* 'Ogam which adheres to a letter' (ibid. 302. 17, 303. 17) and the remainder in standard Ogam. On these artificial variations on standard Ogam see §7.11.

11. I would like to express my thanks to Mr Colm Langford for drawing my attention to the Vatican Ogams. The manuscript is discussed in Pellegrin (1978, 163-5) where it is dated tenth century, the alphabets on fol. 62v being an addition of the twelfth.

12. This doubled *Straif* is identical in form, though not in analysis, to the fourteenth symbol in alphabet 64 of *In Lebor Ogaim* (see §7.11) called *Snait[h]i snimach* 'Interwoven thread' in which all symbols are formed by one to five Xs written above, below, across and through the stemline.

13. The *ae* above *Ébad* should probably be read *æ* representing *é*. The second letter in the transcription of the value of *Ór* is unclear but is too rounded to be *i*. According to Derolez *oe*

and *oo* are possible and the latter is the more likely (see §7.15). On *ach* as an early value of *Emancholl* see also §7.15. The symbol for *z* resembles an *r* with a hook above it and is probably what was intended to be read here.

14. All three texts will be found in Calder (1917), to which the line-numbers here used refer: *Auraicept* 1ff./2260ff.; *De Dúilib* 5416-5463; *In Lebor Ogaim* 5465ff. For an edition of the canonical part of the *Auraicept* and details of the manuscript tradition see Ahlqvist (1982). On the title *In Lebor Ogaim* and the manuscripts in which this tract is found see McManus (1988, 132. n21).

15. An exception is 2794ff. where Ogam IA (= *ia* 'a kind of overswearing') and E (= *éices* 'poet') constitute text. The statement, to the effect that the poet overswears *ia*, also occurs in the text on the privileges and responsibilities of poets (Gwynn, 1940, 16. 19-20) where the relevant words are also written in Ogam. I am grateful to my colleague Liam Breatnach for this note.

16. The word *foilchesta* is attested only with reference to these three symbols and never in the singular. At 4358-60 these are said to be the *treidhe is coir do imchisin isin ogam* 'the three [letters] which one should consider (i.e. watch out for) in Ogam' and *foirmcestu* or *imcesta* are cited as the correct designations for them according to another school (*ut dicunt alii*). All three names contain the element *-cesta* which is probably the plural of *ceist* 'question, problem'. If so the meaning of *foirmcestu* and *imcesta* would probably be 'form-problems' and 'great-problems' respectively. The *foil-* in *foilchesta*, however, can hardly be *foil* 'enclosure' or *fail* 'ring', 'spot'. My colleague Liam Breatnach has suggested it might be *fel* 'poetry, science' (compare the *fil, fel, fuil, fail, foil* forms of *attá*). This would make good sense in view of the difficulties which the *foilchesta* presented to the student (*felmacc*).

17. The *Isruna* Tract on cryptic varieties of the runes (Derolez, 1954, 89ff.) is much more restrained. For an analysis of the cryptic schema in these Ogams see Macalister (1937, chapter two) who defends this material as a serious treatise on secret methods of communication.

18. In all manuscripts except G 53 (in which they are not named) the term *Triaigsruth* (*sic* or *Triagsruth*) *Fercheirtne* is applied to this variety of the alphabet with the explanation *.i. u feda in gach snáithi* 'i.e. five characters in each thread'. The same name (written *Traigsruth Fercheirtni*) is also applied to the outline rectangle containing the poem discussed in §7.12. The meaning of the term *traigsruth* (*sic leg.*) is probably 'foot-stream' but the application is not clear.

19. All manuscripts have *lid* or *lidh* in the title and an explanation *arna bet da fid for æn lith* 'in order that no two letters be on one side'. These may contain an old dative of the neuter *s*-stem *leth*. *Gort fo lid* is also the name of a metre (see Thurneysen, 1891, §182).

20. My interpretation of this word as *fo-ranna* 'subdivides' is tentative as the verb does not appear to be attested elsewhere. Calder's rendering 'Ogam of uproar of anger' is based on *forrán* 'violent aggression' but does not describe the variation.

21. Calder's 'combative' would require *immarbágach*. *Imarbach* is a derivative of *immarbae* 'deceit'.

22. The explanation accompanying this variety is that each letter is written *iarsin lin litir bis isin ainm in duine* 'according to the number of letters in the man's name.' For *ainm in duine* one should probably read *ainm ind feadha* 'the letter's name'.

23. The Book of Ballymote's *brogmoir* is a corruption. The best reading is BM Add. 4783 *ar ni cumaing bus ogmoir*. H. 3.18 has *b ogmoir* and G 53 *ni cumaing neach bus ogmóir*.

24. On the 'Egyptian' and 'African' alphabets see Derolez (1951, 11ff.).

25. These in turn are preceded by the *Bríatharogam* on which see McManus (1988) and Appendix 1.

26. The opposite, i.e. writing the letter name for the letter is found as a device in the *Dúil Laithne* (e.g. *Daurun* = *dún*). On this text see Thurneysen (1886) and Macalister (1937, chapter four). On the practice of writing the rune for the name of the rune see above §3.14 and n3.23.

27. The frequency with which the Ogams of *In Lebor Ogaim* are said to be used in writing 'names' is in keeping with the orthodox inscriptions, the contents of which are exclusively onomastic (see §4.6).

28. Gerschel (1962, 157ff.) considers these developments of the primary function of Ogam characters, namely as tally numerals. He compares the 'comptes parallèles' of various tally traditions which use distinctive forms of notation in recording a count of varied stock.

29. In the Book of Ballymote (17a 49ff.) the second of the four divisions of Irish [learning] among the knowledgeable is said to be made up of the thrice fifty Ogams, the declensions (*réimenna*) and the *Dúile Feda*, and is called *gramatach* 'grammar'. The others are (1) *canóin*, (2) *stair* and (3) *rím*.

30. The text is enclosed together with (83) *Ogam n-eathrach* 'Boat Ogam' (see (e) above), to which it bears no relation, in an outline rectangle studded with sigla and named *Traigsruth Ferchertni* (see n7.18).

31. For addresses by Morann to Nere see passages xii and xv edited from the *Bretha Nemed* by Breatnach (1987, 49-50 and 54-57) and the passages beginning *Mo Nere nuallgnaid, diamba brithem* 'O Nere accustomed to fame, if you be a judge' (Binchy, 1978, 2221).

32. Emendations are indicated with square (insert) and round (delete) brackets. There are no significant variant readings in the four manuscripts containing *In Lebor Ogaim* but a considerably modified and extended version of the text is cited in Text III of *Mittelirische Verslehren* (Thurneysen, 1891, 90. no. 118) under the discussion of *Casbairdne*. The corresponding sections in this read as follows: *A mo Nera nemídh nuailbrethaighe, dia molfer nogum nimraite, sluinfet duít ceastaib coraib cudruma breathaib* (v.l. *briathraib*) *dirghib dianinscib . . . ar is crann foloch lercearda* tri *.l. noga*m *nílarda . . . do thorairchim* (v.l. *thorchim*) *ri huair nillsgrudai*n. (v.l. from The Book of Uí Maine, fol. 194(B)/136r, a 30-37).

33. The poem has a regular syllabic count (8³, 8³) and a regular stress pattern (3 stressed words in each line with the exception of line 7 unless one takes *tri* as unstressed, in which case there is connecting alliteration between -*cherdach* and *cóecat*). There is internal alliteration in each line (between all stressed words in 1, 2, 4 and 5) and lines 5 and 6, where there is a natural break, are connected by stressed-word alliteration. Elsewhere connecting alliteration is of a weaker kind.

34. I take *comairci* to be the 2nd sg.pres. indic. prototonic of *con-airc* 'inquires'. The only other attested finite form of the verb is 2nd sg. pres. sub. -*comairser*, on which see Thurneysen (1946, 389), though the verbal-noun *comarc* is well attested. One could read *ro sluinni . . . -comairci[m]* 'You can name . . . of which I inquire' but this is less likely. *MV*'s *sluinfet* 'I will name' supports the reading adopted here.

35. I take *crann fo loch* (reading *lóch*) to be a metrically dictated etymological or descriptive play on the word *lóchrann* (*lócharn*) 'lamp, lantern' in the sense 'luminary'. Compare Colmán mac Lénéni's *ainm gossa fer* (: *ser*) .i. *Fergossa*, (see Thurneysen, 1933, 199).

36. All manuscripts have *irr*- in the initial of this word (see however *MV nillsgrudai*n). On the basis of *irrlund/n* in line 4 (= *airlann*) I take this to be a compound of *air* (v.l. *aur*, *ir*, *ur* ) + *scrútan* 'studying', the *air* having a similar meaning to that found in *Airaicept/Auraicept* 'primer'. I take *airscrútan* to refer to the initial years of study, for which the *Auraicept na nÉces* was also prescribed (see §8.2).

37. The *Ór* in the Berne manuscript and the *Pín* in the Vatican are also straight-lined as in the Book of Ballymote *In Lebor Ogaim*, suggesting that these are the older forms.

38. Note however that in the Berne manuscript *Emancholl* is written below the stemline.

39. Today the distinction is seen to be in the consonants themselves but in traditional Irish grammar it was understood to be in the vowels, whence the dictum *caol le caol agus leathan le leathan* 'slender with slender and broad with broad', used in reference to the vowels flanking consonants.

40. This appears to be the sense of the phrase *do sainigedh foghur forsna fedhaibh* 'to make sound-distinctions in the vowels' (1299). Examples of such distinctions are the prescription that *nem* 'heaven' (later *neamh*) and *sét* 'path' (later *séad*) be written with *Ébad* while *Edad* should be used for *neim* 'poison' and *séitid* 'blows'. Similarly *Iphín* is prescribed for the *i* in *min* 'small' (later *mion*) but *Idad* for that in *min* 'flour' (with palatal -*n*). See 1290ff./4388ff.)

41. As already noted the supplementary characters, excluding the first, are not used in functional scholastic Ogams. The Ballyspellan brooch, for example, has the diphthong *áe* written with *Ailm* and *Ébad* and *úa* with *Úr* and *Ailm* and the Kilgulbin hanging bowl has *ui* with *Úr* and *Idad*. Even in *In Lebor Ogaim* the name element *Máel* is written MAEL with *Ailm* and *Edad* (5820).

42. In the Old Irish period the ligature æ was used for *é* and *e*. In later manuscripts it came to be used for the diphthong *áe* (Thurneysen, 1946, 18).

43. The tradition of the 'seven vowels of Ogam' is also found in *In Lebor Ogaim* where they are referred to as *na secht feda airegda* 'the seven principal vowels' (5508).

44. At 1371-2/4427-8 the decision to represent X with two *c*s is defended on the grounds that *c* is the first of the two letters in X ( = *cs*, its Latin value as opposed to the Greek fricative value indicated by *ach*) but it is more probable that *Emancholl* was dictated by the *shape* of Latin X, viz. *χ*.

45. The value *ach* is also confirmed by the kennings *Lúad sáethaig / Mol galraig* 'groan of a sick person' glossed *ach no uch* (see McManus, 1988, 136-7, 148-9).

46. The manuscript tradition knows nothing of the value /k/ or /x/ which the first supplementary character has on orthodox Ogam inscriptions. In these furthermore the vocalic value which it has is not distinguished from *Edad* by length (cp. 256 TXGANN, *Tecán* accompanied by DEGLANN, *Déclán*). In scholastic Ogams *Ébad* can be used for *e* (Kilalloe BENDACHT), *é* (Kilgulbin CUILEN) and the second element of the diphthong *áe* (Ballyspellan MAEL). The value *é* in this tradition, therefore, appears to be a revised theoretical one.

47. It has already been noted (n2.11) that Gerschel (1962, 148-9) explains the *forfeda* as tally-based symbols and derives the lozenge shape of *Ór* from a combination of two *Ébad*s with the numerical value 20 ( = 2 x 10).

48. In the Grammatical Tracts (Bergin, 1915, 3. 23-26) these are singled out as letters not required for *ogham iomagallmha*, a term rendered 'spelling of current speech' by Ó Cuív (1965, 150 and see further §8.6).

49. The consequence of this was that the sound /p/, which was now well established in Irish, was left without a distinctive letter name of its own and had to make do with surrogate names such as *Beithe bog* 'soft B', *Peithe* and *Peithbog* (see McManus, 1988, 167).

50. See further the *forfeda* category in the list of verbal-nouns published by Ó Cuív (1966).


## NOTES TO CHAPTER EIGHT

1. On the influence of the Bible and Latin learning on Irish law see in particular Ó Corráin, Breatnach, Breen (1984) and Breatnach (1984) and for an analysis of 'Latinist' versus 'nativist' appreciation of early Irish literature in general see McCone (1990).

2. Thurneysen (1891, 32. 2): *Is hi tra cetus foglaím na cetbliadna i. coeca ogum im certoghum ⁊ airacept na n-eicsiné cona broluch ⁊ cona réimendaib . . .* 'First, then, the learning of the initial year is (i.e.) fifty Ogams including *Certogam* and *Auraicept na nÉces* together with its prologue and its declensions . . .'.

3. See for example his discussion of *moth, toth, tráeth* as genuine archaic designations of 'masculine', 'feminine' and 'neuter' and his comments on the doctrine that 'syllable is the origin of all Gaelic except *moth, toth* and *traeth*' (*is ed bunad cacha Gædelge dialt acht mod ⁊ toth ⁊ traeth*, 1236/4570) which he describes as 'a remarkable observation for the native Irish grammarians to have made' (Watkins, 1970, 8-9).

4. The *Auraicept* is divided into four books the authorship of which is stated to be as follows: Book I (the Prologue, 1-734/2260-3492) Cenn Fáelad mac Ailella († 678); Book II (735-1027/3493-3984) Ferchertne Fili, legendary poet to Conchobar mac Nessa, believed to have lived at the time of Christ; Book III (1028-1101/3984-4101) Amairgein Glúngeal; Book IV (1102-1636/4136-4725) Fénius Farsaid, Goídel mac Ethéoir and Íar mac Nema. These ascriptions are, of course, fictitious, but that of the prologue to Cenn Fáelad (*sapiens* † 678) is significant in that his name is associated with the merging of native and foreign learning (see MacNeill, 1922, 14ff.). The statement that Cenn Fáelad lost his 'brain of forgetting' (*a incinn dermait do buain a cind Cind Faelad*, Binchy, 1978, 250. 37-8) might indeed be interpreted to mean that he learned to read and write (see Isidore's comments on writing and the memory in *Etymologiae*, i, iii, 2).

5. See *Auraicept* lines 46ff./2334ff. For MacNeill's view that these criticisms were directed at Ogam see the discussion above (§4.9).

6. The source of information on the three principal languages was probably Isidore (*Etymologiae* ix, i, 13) who also discusses Nimrod's role in the building of the Tower (vii, vi, 2 and xv, i, 4), whence it is named *Tuir Nemrúaid* in Irish.

7. Watkins (1970, 12) compares *tóbaide* 'cut, selected' and *teipide* 'cut, fashioned' in the phrase *in bérla tóbaithe/teipide* to Sanskrit *saṃskṛta-* 'perfected Sanskrit' vs. *prakṛta-* 'la matière brute du langage'. *Bérla Féne* is the professional language, particularly of jurists; *Bérla na filed* is used of an obscure form of poetic language; *Íarmbérla* designates unstressed words in Irish and *bérla n-etarscartha* 'the language of separating' is used of Isidorian-type etymology in which the elements of a word are 'separated' for explanation.

8. On the date of the *Bríatharogam* texts see McManus (1988, 131-2). The date of the 'thrice fifty Ogams' is clearly difficult to fix though some bear indications which point to Old Irish (e.g. 5700 *mbracht* for Old Irish *mbrecht* (later *brecht*) 'variegated' in the slot for *m* in *Dathogam*, see Thurneysen, 1928, 295). The Old Irish verse above (§7.12), however, presupposes their existence.

9. Paragraph references here are to Gray's edition (1982). For a discussion of the tale and its structure see also Gray (1981 and 1982a) and McCone (1989).

10. The phrase *ám [t]hám* is admittedly poorly attested and could be based on a misreading of *áin tháin*, with *áin*, the more regular verbal noun of *aigid*. For a suggestion that the development of the groups *-gm-* and *-dm-* may have depended on their quality see McCone (1985, 170).

11. For Carney's etymology see Stevenson (1989, 140).

12. There is no reference to Ogam in the earlier version of the tale, for which see Bergin and Best, 1938, 164-66, §4.

13. For further examples see Stokes, 1903, 184 (*Aided Crimthainn*), Stokes, 1900, lines 2849, 3103, 3195 and 6748 (*Acallamh na Senórach*), Windisch, 1897, 516 (*Tochmarc Ferbe*) and Van Hamel 1933, 133 (*Aidedh Con Culainn*).

14. Graves' theory is based on the fact that Fothaid Airgtech's name (see the next example) is said to be written Eochaid Airgtech on his memorial. This, however, is probably no more than a confusion of the two names.

15. The term *ainm n-oguim* is used exceptionally in the *Táin* for a non-funerary inscription (see the examples in §8.10).

16. I have restored the text to the Classical Modern Irish standard. The translation is my own.

17. The *snaidhm* 'knot' and *craobh* 'branch' probably refer to the interlacing and decorative ornament often found on these stones.

18. For another example of the use of *eochra écsi* (but not of Ogam) for divination see *Baile in Scáil* (Pokorny, 1921, 372).

19. As noted by Vendryes (1941, 114-5), among others, the parallel with the Bellerophontês episode in Homer (*Iliad* Book vi) is quite striking.

20. The text quoted here is that of Cormac's Glossary. For variants see Dillon (1932, stories ix and xii).

21. On the use of the withe as an inhibitory symbol in early Irish law see Binchy (1973, 78-9. §§3, 5 and 82 note on § 3). Here the placing of the withe is a symbolic gesture which is clarified not by an inscription, as in the sagas, but by formal notice (*apad*) of the complaint.

22. On the practice of wizardry, charms, enchantments and xylomancy ( = *fidlann*?) in eleventh-century Ireland see 'Adamnán's second vision' (Stokes, 1891, §16).

23. On writing and magic see Gelb (1952, 230ff.) and on predicting the outcome of a duel by reference to the sum total of the numerical values of the letters in the combatants' names see Menninger (1969, 266-7). Divining the sex of an unborn child by reference to the letters of the mother's name (see §7.11(i) ) is similar and therefore not exceptional.

24. On the reading *I mbiat* for *INbat* see Bergin (1934, 207. n1)

25. Unless otherwise specified all references are to Binchy (1978).

26. For further examples see 748. 15-16 and 24, 749. 2, 751. 4 (from an Old Irish text, interspersed with later glosses, on prescriptive rights); 776. 14-15 (Old Irish glosses on *Cáin Fuithirbe*); 1280. 18 (*Cóic Conara Fugill*, see Thurneysen, 1926, 27).

27. On the pillar stone as a boundary marker see, for example, the explanation of Faílbe Fálchoirthech's name (Stokes, 1897, 292) and Binchy (1978, 207. 4) where *tir . . . i curtar lia* 'land . . . in which a pillar stone is put' is glossed *.i. in cloch criche* 'the boundary stone.'

# Bibliography

ABBREVIATIONS:

BBCS:    *Bulletin of the Board of Celtic Studies.*
BGdSL:   *Beiträge zur Geschichte der deutschen Sprache undLiteratur.*
CMCS:    *Cambridge Medieval Celtic Studies.*
Corpus   (Macalister, 1945)
EC:      *Études Celtiques.*
JCHAS:   *Journal of the Cork Historical and Archaeological Society.*
JKAHS:   *Journal of the Kerry Archaeological and Historical Society.*
JRHAAI:  *Journal of the Royal Historical and Archaeological Association of Ireland.*
JRSAI:   *Journal of the Royal Society of Antiquaries of Ireland.*
LCS:     *Loeb Classical Series/Library.*
NTS:     *Norsk Tidsskrift for Sprogvidenskap.*
PRIA:    *Proceedings of the Royal Irish Academy.*
RC:      *Revue Celtique.*
Sitz.:   *Sitzungsberichte der königlich preussischen Akademie der Wissenschaften.*
TPS:     *Transactions of the Philological Society.*
ZCP:     *Zeitschrift für Celtische Philologie.*

Ahlqvist, A. (1982): *The early Irish linguist*, Commentationes Humanarum Litterarum 73, Finnish Society of Sciences and Letters.
   (1987): 'An Irish text on the letters of the alphabet', *Studies in honour of René Derolez* (ed. A.M. Simon-Vandenbergen) 3-16.
Aitchison, N.B. (1987): 'The Ulster Cycle: heroic image and historical reality', *Journal of Medieval History* 13, 87-116.
Allen, W.S. (1965): *Vox Latina, A guide to the pronunciation of Classical Latin.*
   (1968): *Vox Graeca, A guide to the pronunciation of Classical Greek.*
Anderson, A.O./Anderson, M.O. (1961): *Adomnan's Life of Columba.*
Arntz, H. (1935): 'Das Ogam', *BGdSL* 59, 321-413.
   (1944): *Handbuch der Runenkunde.*

Atkinson, G. (1874): 'Some account of ancient Irish treatises on Ogham writing', *JRHAAI* 4th Ser., 3, 202-36.

Bannerman, J. (1974): *Studies in the history of Dál Ríada*.

Bateson, J.D. (1973): 'Roman material from Ireland: a re-consideration', *PRIA* 73, 21-97.

Bechtel, E.A. (1909): 'Finger-counting among the Romans in the fourth century', *Classical Philology* 4, 25-31.

Bergin, O. (1915): 'Irish grammatical tracts: Introductory', *Ériu* 8 (supplement).

(1921): 'The magic withe in Táin Bó Cúailnge', *Ériu* 9, 159.

(1932): 'On the Kilbonane Ogams', *Ériu* 11, 107-11.

(1932a): 'Varia', *Ériu* 11, 136-149.

(1934): 'On the syntax of the verb in Old Irish', *Ériu* 12, 197-214.

(1938): 'The native Irish grammarian', *Proceedings of the British Academy* 24, 205-235.

(1938a): 'Varia 1. 25. Luchte', *Ériu* 12, 231-235.

Bergin, O./Best, R.I. (1938): 'Tochmarc Étaíne', *Ériu* 12, 137-196.

Best, R. I./Bergin, O. (1929): *Lebor na hUidre*.

Bieler, L. (1949): 'Insular palaeography recent state and problems', *Scriptorium* 3, 267-294.

(1979): *The Patrician texts in the Book of Armagh*, Scriptores Latini Hiberniae 10.

Binchy, D.A. (1961): 'The background of early Irish literature', *Studia Hibernica* 1, 7-18.

(1971): 'An archaic legal poem', *Celtica* 9, 152-168.

(1972): 'Varia Hibernica, 2 Substantival dvandva-compounds in Irish', *Indo-Celtica, Gedächtnisschrift für Alf Sommerfelt* (ed. H. Pilch and J. Thurow), 38-41.

(1973): 'A text on the forms of distraint', *Celtica* 10, 72-86.

(1978): *Corpus Iuris Hibernici* 6 vols.

Borgeaud, W.A. (1971): 'Hibernica: *Echu-Echach, Echoid-Echdach, Temair*', *Beiträge zur Namenforschung* 6, 40-44.

Brash, R.B. (1879): *The Ogam inscribed monuments of the Gaedhil*.

Breatnach, L. (1984): 'Canon law and secular law in early Ireland: the significance of *Bretha Nemed*', *Peritia* 3, 439-59.

(1987): *Uraicecht na Ríar: The poetic grades in Early Irish Law*.

Brennan, M. (1984): *Words in hand, A structural analysis of the signs of British sign language*, Edinburgh BSL Research Project.

Brice, W.C. (1976): 'The principles of non-phonetic writing', *Writing without letters* (ed. W. Haas), 29-44.

Brown, G. Baldwin (1930): *The Arts in early England*, vol. vi, part i.

Bu'lock, J.D. (1956): 'Early christian memorial formulae', *Archaeologia Cambrensis* 105, 133-141.

Butler, H.E. (1969): *Quintilian's Institutio Oratoria, LCS*.

Byrne, F.J. (1968): 'Historical note on Cnogba (Knowth)', *PRIA* 66, 383-400

(1971): 'Tribes and tribalism in early Ireland', *Ériu* 22, 128-166.

(1973): *Irish Kings and High-Kings*.

Calder, G. (1917): *Auraicept na nÉces*.

Carey, J. (1990): 'Vernacular Irish learning: Three notes', *Éigse* 24, 37-44.

Carney, J. (1964): *The poems of Blathmac son of Cú Brettan*, Irish Texts Society 47.
  (1971): 'Three Old Irish accentual poems', *Ériu* 22, 23-80.
  (1975): 'The invention of the Ogom cipher', *Ériu* 26, 53-65.
  (1978/9): 'Aspects of Archaic Irish', *Éigse* 17, 417-435.
Charles-Edwards, T.M. (1971): 'Some Celtic kinship terms', *BBCS* 24, 105-122.
  (1976): 'Boundaries in Irish law', *Medieval Settlement* (ed. P.H. Sawyer), 83-87.
Clarke, R.R. (1952): 'An Ogham inscribed knife-handle from south-west Norfolk', *The Antiquaries Journal* 32, 71-3.
Crawford, H.S. (1912): 'A descriptive list of early cross-slabs and pillars', *JRSAI* 42, 217-244. (contd. in vols 43 and 46).
Coplestone-Crow, B. (1981/2): 'The dual nature of the Irish colonization of Dyfed in the Dark Ages', *Studia Celtica* 16/17, 1-24.
Cowgill, W. (1967): 'On the fate of *w in Old Irish', *Language* 43, 129-138.
  (1980): 'The etymology of Irish *guidid* and the outcome of *$g^wh$ in Celtic', *Lautlehre und Etymologie* (ed. M. Mayrhofer, M. Peters), 49-78.
Cullen, J. (1972): 'Varia 1: Primitive Irish vowels in final syllables following i̯', *Ériu* 23, 227-229.
de hÓir, S. (1983): 'The Mount Callan Ogham stone and its context', *North Munster Antiquarian Journal* 25, 43-57. (See also vol. 26, 1984, 99).
de Jubainville, (1908): 'Chronique III', *RC* 29, 249-252.
Derolez, R. (1951): 'Ogam, "Egyptian" "African" and "Gothic" alphabets', *Scriptorium* 5, 3-20.
  (1954): *Runica Manuscripta, The English tradition*.
Deuchar, M. (1984): *British sign language*.
de Valera, R. (1979): *Antiquities of the Irish countryside* by P. Ó Riordáin, 5th ed. revised by R. de Valera.
Diack, F.C. (1931): 'The origin of the Ogam alphabet', *Scottish Gaelic Studies* 3, 86-91.
Dickins, B. (1915): *Runic and heroic poems of the old Teutonic peoples*.
Dillon, M. (1932): 'Stories from the law-tracts', *Ériu* 11, 42-65.
  (1953): *Serglige Con Culainn*.
  (1977): 'The Irish settlement in Wales', *Celtica* 12, 1-11.
Dillon, M./Chadwick, N. (1967): *The Celtic realms*.
Diringer, D. (1968): *The alphabet, a key to the history of mankind* (3rd. ed. revised in two vols).
Egan, M. (1983): 'Reflections on Ogham and the Irish harp', *Éigse* 19, 217-229.
Eisler, R.(1949): 'The polar sighting-tube', *Archives internationales d'histoire des sciences* 6, 311-332.
Elliott, R.W.V. (1980): *Runes, an introduction*.
Eogan, G. (1986): *Knowth and the passage-tombs of Ireland*.
Evans, D. Ellis (1967): *Gaulish personal names*.
  (1972): 'A comparison of the formation of some continental and early insular Celtic personal names', *BBCS* 24, 415-434.
Falconer, W. A. (1923): *Cicero De Senectute, De Amicitia, De Divinatione*, *LCS*.
Fell, B. (1978): *America B.C. Ancient settlers in the New World*.

Fulford, M./Sellwood, B. (1980): 'The Silchester Ogham stone: a reconsideration', *Antiquity* 54, no. 211, 95-99.

Fanning, T./Ó Corráin, D. (1977): 'An Ogham stone and cross-slab from Ratass church, Tralee', *JKAHS* 10, 14-18.

Gelb, I.J. (1952): *A study of writing, the foundations of grammatology*.

Gerschel, L. (1957): 'Origine et premier usage des caractères ogamiques', *Ogam* 9, 151-173.

(1962): 'L'ogam et le nombre', *EC* 10, 127-166; 'L'ogam et le nom', *EC* 10 516-557.

Gippert, J. (1990): 'Präliminarien zu einer Neuausgabe der Ogaminschriften', *Britain 400-600 Language and History* (ed. A. Bammesberger and A. Wollmann (Anglistische Forschungen 205) ), 291-304.

Gordon, A.E. (1973): *The letter names of the Latin alphabet*.

Graves, C. (1847): 'On an antique gold ornament . . .', *PRIA* 3, 460-64.

(1876): 'The Ogam alphabet', *Hermathena* 2, 443-472.

(1879): 'On the Ogam Beith Luis Nin', *Hermathena* 3, 208-244.

(1888): 'On Ogam inscriptions', *Hermathena* 6, 241-268.

Gray, E.A. (1981): 'Cath Maige Tuired: Myth and Structure (1-24)', *Éigse* 18, 183-209.

(1982): *Cath Maige Tuired*, Irish Texts Society 52.

(1982a): 'Cath Maige Tuired: Myth and Structure (24-120)', *Éigse* 19, 1-35.

Gray, L.H. (1929): 'The Ogham genitive singular in -AIS', *Language* 5, 251-3.

Greene, D. (1956): 'Gemination', *Celtica* 3, 284-9.

(1962): 'The colouring of consonants in Old Irish', *Proceedings of the fourth International Congress of Phonetic Sciences, Helsinki 1961*, 622-4.

(1972): 'A detail of syncope', *Ériu* 23, 232-234.

(1973): 'The growth of palatalization in Irish', *TPS* 127-136.

(1976): 'The diphthongs of Old Irish', *Ériu* 27, 26-45.

(1977): 'Archaic Irish', *Indogermanisch und Keltisch* (ed. K.H. Schmidt), 11-33.

Grosjean, P. (1960): 'Espoic Branduibh Aui Trenloco Anchoritae', *Celtica* 5, 45-51.

Gwynn, E.J. (1940): 'An Old-Irish tract on the privileges and responsibilities of poets', *Ériu* 13, 1-60, 220-236.

Hamlin, A. (1972): 'A chi-rho carved stone stone at Drumaqueran, Co. Antrim', *Ulster Journal of Archaeology* 3rd ser. 35, 22-28.

(1982): 'Early Irish stone carving: content and context', *The early Church in Western Britain and Ireland* (ed. Susan M. Pearce, BAR British Series 102), 283-296.

Hammarström, M. (1920): 'Beiträge zur Geschichte des etruskischen, lateinischen und griechischen Alphabets', *Acta Societatis Scientiarum Fennicae* 49:2, 1-58.

(1930): 'Die antiken Buchstabennamen. Zugleich ein Beitrag zur Geschichte der griechischen Lauttheorien', *Arctos* 1, 3-40.

Hamp, E. (1953/4): 'Primitive Irish intervocalic *w*', *EC* 6, 281-288.

(1954): (Review of Gelb (1952) ), *ZCP* 24, 308-12.

Harmon, A.M. (1913): *Lucian I, LCS*.

Harvey, A. (1985): 'The significance of *Cothraige*', *Ériu* 36, 1-9.

(1987): 'The Ogam inscriptions and their geminate consonant symbols', *Ériu* 38, 45-71.

(1987a): 'Early literacy in Ireland: the evidence from Ogam', *CMCS* 14, Winter, 1-15.

Henry, F. (1937): 'Early christian slabs and pillar stones in the West of Ireland', *JRSAI* 67, 265-279.

(1940): *Irish art in the early christian period.*

(1948): 'Three engraved slabs in the neighbourhood of Waterville (Kerry) and the cross on Skellig Michael', *JRSAI* 78, 175-177.

(1957): 'Early monasteries, beehive huts and dry-stone houses in the neighbourhood of Caherciveen and Waterville (Co. Kerry)', *PRIA* 58, 45-166.

Holtz, L. (1981): *Donat et la tradition de l'enseignement grammatical.*

Hopfner, I. (1919): 'Ogam und das Christentum', *Zeitschrift für katholische Theologie* 43, 105-111.

Hull, V. (1967): 'Miscellanea Hibernica', *ZCP* 30, 7-11.

Hutton, M. (1970): *Tacitus, Agricola, Germania, Dialogus, LCS.*

Hyde, D. (1932): 'Aguisín ii', *Lia Fáil* 4, 170-173.

Illinois Greek Club (1923) *Aeneas Tacticus, LCS.*

Jackson, K.H. (1946): (Review of *Corpus*) *Speculum* 21, 521-3.

(1949): 'Primitive Irish *w* and *b*', *EC* 5, 105-115.

(1950): 'Notes on the Ogam inscriptions of southern Britain', *The early cultures of north-west Europe* (H.M. Chadwick Memorial Studies, ed. Sir C. Fox and B. Dickins), 197-213.

(1953): *Language and history in Early Britain.*

(1971): 'Ogam stone', *Argyll, an inventory of the ancient monuments, 1, Kintyre* (The Royal commission on the ancient and historical monuments of Scotland), no. 244.

(1973): 'An Ogam inscription near Blackwaterfoot', *Antiquity* 47, 53-4.

(1980): 'The Pictish language', *The problem of the Picts* (ed. F.T. Wainwright), 129-160.

(1983): 'Ogam stones and early christian inscriptions', *The companion to Gaelic Scotland* (ed. D.S. Thomson), 220-221.

Jensen, H. (1970): *Sign, symbol and script* (trans. by G. Unwin).

Jones, C.W. (1943): *Bedae opera de temporibus* (The Medieval Academy of America, no. 41).

Joseph, L.S. (1982): 'Old Irish *tuir*, "house-post"', *Ériu* 33, 176-7.

Keller, W. (1936): 'H. Arntz, Das Ogom', *Beiblatt zur Anglia* 47, nr.2, 33-37.

(1938): 'Die Entstehung des Ogom', *BGdSL* 62, 121-132.

Kelly, F. (1976): 'The Old Irish tree-list', *Celtica* 11, 107-124.

(1979): 'Notes on Irish words', in Bieler, L. (1979), 242-248.

(1988) *A guide to Early Irish law.*

Kenney, J. F. (1929) *The sources for the early history of Ireland, Ecclesiastical.*

Kermode, P.M.C. (1907): *Manx Crosses.*

Killeen, J.J. (1965): 'The word *ogam*', *Lochlann* 3, 415-19.

Koch, J.T. (1990): '*Cothairche, Esposito's theory, and Neo-Celtic lenition', *Britain 400-600 Language and History* (see above under Gippert (1990) ), 179-202.

Korolev, A.A. (1984): *Drevnejšie pamjatniki irlandskogo jazyka.*

Krause, W. (1970): *Runen* (Sammlung Göschen Band 1244/1244a).

Krusch, B. (1905): *Ionae vitae sanctorum Columbani, Vedastis, Iohannis* (*Scriptores rerum Germanicum*).

Kuryłowicz, J. (1961): 'Note sur l'ogam', *Bulletin de la Société de Linguistique de Paris* 56, 1-5.

Lambert, P-Y. (1979): 'Gaulois IEVRV: irlandais (*ro*)-*ír* "dicavit" ', *ZCP* 37, 207-13.

Lejeune, M. (1970/71): 'Documents gaulois et para-gaulois de Cisalpine' (= *Lepontica*), *EC* 12, 357-500.

   (1988): *Recueil des Inscriptions Gauloises*, vol. ii, fasc. i, *Textes Gallo-Étrusques, Textes Gallo-Latins sur pierre.*

Lindsay, W.M. (1911): *Isidori Hispalensis Episcopi etymologiarum sive originum*, 2 vols.

Lionard, P. (1960/1): 'Early Irish grave-slabs', *PRIA* 61, 95-170.

Mac Airt, S. (1951): *The annals of Innisfallen.*

Macalister, R.A.S. (1897, 1902, 1907): *Studies in Irish epigraphy*, 3 vols.

   (1914): 'The DRUUIDES inscription at Killeen Cormac, Co. Kildare', *PRIA* 32, 227-238.

   (1928): *The archaeology of Ireland.*

   (1935): *Ancient Ireland.*

   (1937): *The secret languages of Ireland.*

   (1940): 'The inscriptions and language of the Picts', *Féilsgríbhinn Eoin Mhic Néill* (ed. an t-athair Eoin Ua Riain), 184-226.

   (1945, 1949): *Corpus inscriptionum insularum Celticarum*, 2 vols.

Mac Aogáin, P. (1968): *Graiméir Ghaeilge na mBráthar Mionúr.*

Mac Cana, P. (1961): 'VOTEPORI', *BBCS* 19, 116-7.

   (1980): *The learned tales of Medieval Ireland.*

McCone, K. (1979): 'Pretonic preverbs and the absolute verbal endings in Old Irish', *Ériu* 30, 1-34.

   (1982): 'Further to absolute and conjunct', *Ériu* 33, 1-30.

   (1985): 'Varia II', *Ériu* 36, 169-176 (on Old Irish *broimm* 'fart' and *olc/luch* 'wolf').

   (1987) *The Early Irish verb*, Maynooth Monographs 1.

   (1989): 'A tale of two ditties: poet and satirist in *Cath Maige Tuired*', *Sages, saints and storytellers* (Celtic studies in honour of Professor James Carney, ed. D. Ó Corrráin, L. Breatnach, K. McCone), Maynooth Monographs 2, 122-143.

   (1990): *Pagan past and christian present*, Maynooth Monographs 3.

McManus, D. (1983): 'A chronology of the Latin loan-words in Early Irish', *Ériu* 34, 21-71.

   (1984): '*Linguarum Diversitas*: Latin and the vernaculars in early medieval Britain', *Peritia* 3, 151-188.

   (1986): 'Ogam: archaizing, orthography and the authenticity of the manuscript key to the alphabet', *Ériu* 37, 1-31.

   (1988): 'Irish letter-names and their kennings', *Ériu* 39, 127-168.

   (1989): 'Runic and Ogam letter-names: a parallelism', *Sages, Saints and Storytellers* (see under McCone, (1989) ), 144-48.

Mac Mathúna, S. (1985): *Immram Brain, Bran's journey to the Land of the Women*.

MacNeill, E./J. (1907): 'Mocu, Maccu', *Ériu* 3, 42-49.

   (1909): 'Notes on the distribution, history, grammar, and import of the Irish Ogham inscriptions', *PRIA* 27, 329-370.

   (1910): 'The Dési genealogies', *Journal of the Waterford and S.E. Ireland Archaeological Society* 13, 44-51, 81-87, 151-157.

   (1911): 'Early Irish population groups: their nomenclature, classsification and chronology', *PRIA* 29, 59-114.

   (1919): *Phases of Irish History*.

   (1922): 'A pioneer of nations', *Studies* 11, 13-28; 435-46.

   (1931): 'Archaisms in the Ogham inscriptions', *PRIA* 39, 33-53.

   (1932): 'Varia', *Ériu* 11, 130-35.

   (1932a): 'De origine Scoticae linguae', *Ériu* 11, 112-129.

Mac White, E. (1960/61): 'Contributions to a study of Ogam memorial stones', *ZCP* 28, 294-308.

Marshall, P.K. (1968): *A. Gelli Noctes Atticae*, 2 vols.

Marstrander, C. (1910): 'Hibernica', *ZCP* 7, 357-418.

   (1911): 'Ogham XOI', *Ériu* 5, 144.

   (1928): 'Om runene og runenavnenes oprindelse', *NTS* 1, 85-188.

   (1930): 'Killaloekorset og de Norske Kolonier i Irland', *NTS* 4, 378-400.

   (1945): 'The *Druuides* inscription at Killeen Cormac', *NTS* 13, 353-356.

Meid, W. (1968): 'Zum Dvandva-Kompositum im Irischen', *Studien zur Sprachwissenschaft und Kulturkunde* (Gedenkschrift für Wilhelm Brandenstein, ed. M. Mayrhofer), 107-8.

Menninger, K. (1969): *Number words and number symbols: a cultural history of numbers*, (trans. by P. Broneer of the original German, *Zahlwort und Ziffer*, 1958).

Meroney, H. (1947): 'A druidic liturgy in *Ogam Bricrenn*?', *Modern Language Notes* 62, 187-9.

Meroney, H. (1949): 'Early Irish letter-names', *Speculum* 24, 19-43.

Meyer, K. (1905): *Cáin Adamnáin. An Old Irish treatise on the law of Adamnan* (Anecdota Oxoniensia).

   (1908/10): 'Brian Borumha', *Ériu* 4, 68-73.

   (1910): 'Conall Corc and the Corco Luigde', *Anecdota from Irish manuscripts III* (ed. O.J. Bergin, R.I. Best etc.), 57-63.

   (1912): 'Zur Bezeichnung des Patronyms im Irischen', *ZCP* 8, 178-9.

   (1912a): 'Zur keltischen Wortkunde I/II' *Sitz.* 38, 790-803, 1144-1157.

   (1912b): 'Cormac's Glossary', *Anecdota from Irish manuscripts* (ed. O.J. Bergin, R.I. Best etc.), vol. 4, 1-128.

   (1912c): 'The Laud genealogies and tribal histories', *ZCP* 8, 291-338.

   (1914): 'Zur keltischen Wortkunde V', *Sitz.* 1914, 630-642.

   (1915): 'Das Wörterbuch der kgl. Irischen Akademie', *ZCP* 10, 361-383.

   (1917): 'Über die Anordnung des Ogamalphabets', *Sitz.* 376-378.

Miller, M. (1977/78): 'Date-guessing and Dyfed', *Studia Celtica* 12/13, 33-61.

Moltke, E.(1985): *Runes and their origin: Denmark and elsewhere*.

Motta, F.(1978): 'Contributi allo studio della lingua delle iscrizioni ogamiche (A-B)', *Studi e saggi linguistici* 18, 257-333.

(1982): 'Ogamica', *Studi classici e orientali* 32, 299-304.

Nash-Williams, V.E. (1950): *The early Christian monuments of Wales*.

Ní Dhonnchadha, M. (1982): 'The guarantor list of *Cáin Adomnáin*, 697', *Peritia* 1, 178-215.

Ní Shéaghdha, N. (1977): *Catalogue of Irish manuscripts in the National Library of Ireland*, fasc.iv.

O'Boyle, S. (1980): *Ogam; the poets' secret*.

O'Brien, M.A. (1956): '*Der-, Dar-, Derb-* in female names', *Celtica* 3, 178-9.
(1962): *Corpus Genealogiarum Hiberniae*, vol. 1.
(1971): 'Notes on Irish proper names', *Celtica* 9, 212.
(1973): 'Old Irish personal names', *Celtica* 10, 211-236.

Ó Cathasaigh, T. (1977): *The heroic biography of Cormac mac Airt*.
(1984): 'The Déisi and Dyfed', *Éigse* 20, 1-33.
(1986): 'The sister's son in early Irish literature', *Peritia* 5, 128-160.

Ó Corráin, D. (1969): 'Studies in West Munster history II *Alltraighe*', *JKAHS* 2, 27-37.
(1971): 'Topographical notes-II', *Ériu* 22, 97-99.
(1972): *Ireland before the Normans*, ( The Gill History of Ireland 2).
(1979): 'Onomata', *Ériu* 30, 165-180.
(1985): 'Irish origin legends and genealogy: recurrent aetiologies', *History and heroic tale: a symposium* (ed. T. Nyberg et al.), 51-96.

Ó Corráin, D./Breatnach, L./Breen, A. (1984) 'The laws of the Irish', *Peritia* 3, 382-438.

Ó Corráin, D./Maguire, F. (1981): *Gaelic personal names*.

Ó Cróinín, D. (1983): 'The Irish provenance of Bede's computus', *Peritia* 2, 229-47.

Ó Cuív, B. (1965): 'Linguistic terminology in the medieval Irish Bardic tracts', *TPS* 141-164.
(1966): 'Miscellanea: A fragment of Bardic linguistic tradition', *Éigse* 11, 287-88.
(1973): Review of Binchy (1972), *Éigse* 15, 160-163.
(1973a): 'The linguistic training of the mediaeval Irish poet', *Celtica* 10, 114-140.
(1980): 'Irish words for "Alphabet"', *Ériu* 31, 100-110.
(1986): 'Aspects of Irish personal names', *Celtica* 18, 151-184.

O'Curry, E. (1861): *Lectures on the manuscript materials of ancient Irish history*.

O'Grady, Standish, H. (1892): *Silva Gadelica* 2 vols (Texts and Translations).

Okasha, E. (1985): 'The non-Ogam inscriptions of Pictland', *CMCS* 9, 43-69.

O'Kelly, M.J. (1945): (Review of *Corpus*), *JCHAS* 50, 152-3.
(1945a): 'Some prehistoric monuments of Imokilly', *JCHAS* 50, 10-23.
(1952): 'St Gobnet's House, Ballyvourney, Co. Cork', *JCHAS* 57, 18-40.
(1957/9): 'Church Island near Valencia, Co. Kerry', *PRIA* 59, 57-136 (with contributions by S. Kavanagh and R.A. Breatnach).

O'Kelly, M.J./Kavanagh, S.(1954): 'An Ogam inscribed cross-slab from County Kerry', *JCHAS* 59, 101-110.
(1954a): 'A new Ogham stone from County Kerry', *JCHAS* 59, 50-53.

O'Kelly, M.J./Shee, E.(1968): 'Three souterrains in Co. Cork', *JCHAS* 73, 40-47.

Olsen, M. (1954): 'Runic inscriptions in Great Britain, Ireland and the Isle of Man', *Viking antiquities in Great Britain and Ireland* 6 (ed. H. Shetelig), 151-233.

O'Neill Hencken, H. (1942): 'Ballinderry Crannóg No 2', *PRIA* 47, 1-76.

O'Rahilly, C. (1967): *Táin Bó Cúalnge* from the Book of Leinster.

(1976): *Táin Bó Cúailnge* Recension I.

O'Rahilly, T.F. (1931): 'Etymological Notes III', *Scottish Gaelic Studies* 3, 52-72.

(1942): '*Iarann, Lárag* etc.', *Ériu* 13, 119-127.

(1942a): *The Two Patricks.*

(1946): *Early Irish history and mythology.*

(1950): 'Notes on *Early Irish history and mythology*', *Celtica* 1, 387-402.

Ó Riain, P. (1985): *Corpus Genealogiarum Sanctorum Hiberniae.*

Page, R.I. (1962): 'The use of double runes in Old English inscriptions', *Journal of English and Germanic philology*, 61, 897-907.

(1983): 'The Manx Rune-stones' (*The Viking age in the Isle of Man*, ed. Christine Fell et al.), 133-146.

(1987): *Runes*, (British Museum, *Reading the past*).

Paton, W.R. (1925): *Polybius: The Histories* vol. iv, *LCS.*

Pedersen, H. (1909, 1913): *Vergleichende Grammatik der keltischen Sprachen* 2 vols.

Pellegrin, E. (1978): *Les manuscrits classiques latins de la Bibliothèque Vaticane* (vol II, pt. I).

Petrie, G. (1872, 1878): *Christian inscriptions in the Irish language* (ed. by M. Stokes), 2 vols.

Pilsworth, W.J. (1972): *History of Thomastown and district*, Kilkenny Archaeological Society, sec. ed.)

Plummer, C. (1910): *Vitae Sanctorum Hiberniae*, 2 vols.

(1923): 'On the meaning of Ogam stones', *RC* 40, 387-90.

Pokorny, J. (1915): 'Ogom CI "hier"', *ZCP* 10, 403.

(1915a): 'Ogom NET(T)A(S) NIOT(T)A(S)', *ZCP* 10, 405-7.

(1918): 'Zur Chronologie der Umfärbung der Vokale im Altirischen', *ZCP* 12, 415-426.

(1919): 'Einiges zur irischen Synkope', *ZCP* 13, 31-42.

(1921): 'Nachlass Kuno Meyer', *ZCP* 13, 166-194; 370-382.

(1922): 'Hibernica', *Zeitschrift fur vergleichende Sprachforschung* 50, 41-53.

(1927): 'Das nicht-indogermanische Substrat im Irischen', *ZCP* 16, 231-266.

(1955): 'Zur irischen Namenbildung und Urgeschichte', *Münchener Studien zur Sprachwissenschaft* 7, 56-67.

(1959/69): *Indogermanisches Etymologisches Wörterbuch*, 2 vols.

Pulgram, E. (1947): 'Indo-European personal names', *Language* 23, 189-206.

(1976): 'The typologies of writing systems' (in *Writing without letters*, see under Brice above), 1-28.

Raftery, B. (1969): 'A late Ogham inscription from Co. Tipperary', *JRSAI* 99, 161-164.

Raftery, J. (1959/60): 'A travelling-man's gear of christian times', *PRIA* 60, 1-8.

(1960): 'National Museum of Ireland, Arch. acquisitions 1958', *JRSAI*, 90, 1-40.

(1966): 'The Cuillard and other unpublished hanging bowls', *JRSAI* 96, 29-38.

(1969): 'Nat. Mus. Irl. arch. acquisitions 1966', *JRSAI* 99, 93-111.

(1970): 'Nat. Mus. Irl. arch. acquisitions 1967', *JRSAI* 100, 145-65 (no. 218).

Rhys, J. (1879): *Lectures on Welsh philology*.

Richards, M. (1960): 'The Irish settlement in South-West Wales', *JRSAI* 90, 133-162.

Richardson, J.D. (1941): 'Agma, a forgotten Greek letter', *Hermathena* 58, 57-69.

(1943): 'The word *ogham*', *Hermathena* 62, 96-105.

Robins, R.H. (1979): *A short history of linguistics*.

Rolfe, J.C. (1979): *Suetonius: De Vita Caesarum*, 2 vols. *LCS*.

Rynne, E. (1962): 'Nat. Mus. Irl. arch. acquisitions 1960', *JRSAI* 92, 139-173.

Schmidt, K.H. (1957): 'Die Komposition in gallischen Personennamen', *ZCP* 26, 33-301.

Schaffs, G. (1923): 'Die lateinischen Bemerkungen auf den Ogamsteinen Camp I und Calday Island', *ZCP* 14, 164-172.

Stevenson, J. (1989): 'The beginnings of literacy in Ireland', *PRIA* 89, 127-165.

Stokes, W. (1891): 'Adamnan's second vision', *RC* 12, 420-443.

(1897): 'Cóir Anmann (Fitness of names)' in Windisch (1897), 285-444.

(1900): *Acallamh na Senórach* = Windisch (1900).

(1903): 'The death of Crimthann son of Fidach', *RC* 24, 172-207

Stokes, W./Strachan, J.(1901, 1903): *Thesaurus Palaeohibernicus*, 2 vols.

Süss, W. (1923): 'Über antike Geheimschreibemethoden und ihr Nachleben', *Philologus* 78, 142-175.

Thurneysen, R. (1886): 'Du langage secret dit ogham', *RC* 7,369-374.

(1891): 'Mittelirische Verslehren' in Windisch (1891), 1-182.

(1909): *Handbuch des Alt-Irischen*.

(1912): (Review of MacNeill, 1909), *ZCP* 8, 184-5.

(1926): 'Cóic Conara Fugill' *Abhandlungen der preussischen Akademie der Wissenschaften* (1-87).

(1928): 'Auraicept na nÉces' (a review of Calder (1917) ), *ZCP* 17, 277-303.

(1928a): 'Die Bürgschaft im irischen Recht', *Abhandlungen der preussischen Akademie der Wissenschaften* (1928) 1-87.

(1933): 'Colmān mac Lēnēni und Senchān Torpēist', *ZCP* 19, 193-209.

(1937): 'Zum Ogom', *BGdSL* 61, 188-208.

(1946): *A grammar of Old Irish*.

Uhlich, J. (1989): '*DOV(A)*- and lenited *-B-* in Ogam', *Ériu* 40, 129-133.

Van Hamel, A.G. (1933): *Compert Con Culainn and other stories*.

(1946): 'Primitieve Ierse taalstudie', *Mededelingen van de Koninklijke Nederlandse Akademie van Wetenschappen, afdeling Letterkunde* 9, 295-339.

Vendryes, J. (1941): 'L'écriture ogamique et ses origines', *EC* 4, 83-116.

(1955): 'Sur un emploi du mot *AINM* "nom"', *EC* 7, 139-146.

Verworn, M.(1917): 'Die angeblichen "Runensteine" von Biere. Gefälschte Ogham-Inschriften', *ZCP* 11, 305-7.

Wagner, H. (1969): 'The origin of the Celts in the light of linguistic geography', *TPS* 203-250.

Warner, G.F. (1906, 1915): *The Stowe Missal*, 2 vols, (Henry Bradshaw Society, 31, 32).

Watkins, C. (1962): *Indo-European origins of the Celtic verb.*

  (1970): 'Language of Gods and Language of Men: Remarks on some Indo-European metalinguistic traditions', *Myth and Law among the Indo-Europeans* (ed. Jaan Puhvel), 1-17.

Williams, H. (1899): *Gildae de Excidio Britanniae* (Cymmrodorion Record Series no. 3).

Williams, I. (1943/4): (Review of *Corpus*), *The Transactions of the Honourable Society of Cymmrodorion*, 152-6.

Windisch, E. (1880): *Irische Texte mit Wörterbuch.*

  (1884): *Irische Texte* 2nd series, vol. I.

  (1891): *Irische Texte* 3rd series, vol. 1.

  (1897): *Irische Texte* 3rd series, vol. 2.

  (1900): *Irische Texte* 4th series, vol. I.

Wright, R.P./Jackson K.H. (1968): 'A late inscription from Wroxeter', *The Antiquaries Journal* 48, 296-300.

Zimmer, H. (1909): 'Über direkte Handelsverbindungen Westgalliens mit Irland im Altertum und frühen Mittelalter', *Sitz.* 21, 363-400, 430-476, 543-613 (continued in 1910, 1031-1119).

# Indices

Index 1: Irish and foreign technical terms, source texts and/or authors and persons.
Index 2: Forms quoted from inscriptions.
Index 3: General references to incriptions.
Index 4: Personal, tribal and place names discussed with reference to form.
References are to paragraphs except when they follow an asterisk, in which case they are to the notes. Ap2 denotes Appendix 2 and when not followed by a Roman numeral it refers to the introductory section on inscriptions in the *Corpus*.

## INDEX 1

*Acallamh na Senórach*: * 8.13.
Adamnán (*Life of Columba*): 4.9, 6.27, 6.30 * 5.33, 5.46, 6.61.
*ad-cumaing*: 8.11.
*Æmancholl*: 7.14.
*ætt, ættir*: 2.4, 3.6, 3.8.
Aeneas Tacticus: * 2.17.
*Agma*: 3.9-13, 7.17, 8.6.
*aicme*: 1.4, 3.6, 3.8-9, 3.11, 7.9.
*Aided Con Culainn*: * 8.13.
*Aided Crimthainn*: * 8.13.
*Aided Etarcomail*: 8.8.
*Aided Ferghusa*: 8.8.
*aidhm*: 8.6.
*aig taig*: 8.5.
*ail anscuichthe*: 8.13.
*Ailm*: 1.3, 3.15 * 7.41.
*ainm n-oguim*: 5.4, 8.6, 8.8, 8.10-11 * 7.9, 8.15.
Amairgein Glúngeal: * 8.4.
*Amharcholl*: 7.17.
*Amra Choluim Chille*: 5.33.
*ám [t]hám*: 8.5 * 8.10.
*Annals of Inisfallen*: 4.7, 7.7

*Auraicept Muman*: 7.14-15.
*Auraicept na nÉces*: 1.4-5, 3.13, 4.9, 7.8-9, 7.13-17, 8.1-4 * 4.39, 7.14, 7.36, 8.2, 8.4.
Babel (Tower of): 3.2, 8.3 * 8.6.
*Baile in Scáil*: 8.10 * 8.18.
*Baile mac Búain*: * 2.2.
*Balovuseni*: 3.8.
*Bardic Grammatical Tracts*: 7.17, 8.2, 8.6 * 7.48.
Bede (*De Computo Digitarum*): 2.9 * 2.18-19.
*Beithe*: 1.3, 3.15, 8.4.
*Beithe bog*: * 7.49.
*Beithe-luis-nin*: 1.4, 7.2, 7.9, 8.2-3, 8.6 * 1.2.
Bellerophontês: * 8.19.
*benaid*: 8.11.
*Bérla n-etarscartha*: 8.3-4 * 8.7.
*Bérla Féne*: 8.3 * 8.7.
*Bérla na filed*: 8.3 * 8.7.
*Bérla tóbaide/teipide*: 8.3 * 8.7.
*Berrad Airechta*: 8.13.
Bible: 3.2, 4.9, 8.1, 8.3, 8.10 * 8.1.

197

# INDEX 2

(Bracketed references are to the *Corpus*)

FECT CUNURI (176): 4.10.
FECT QENILOC (170): 4.10.
FILI(I): 4.13, 6.14, 6.22.
FILIA: 6.25, 6.27.
GAMICUNAS (191): 5.14, 6.3, 6.9, 6.24, 6.26.
GATTAGN[I] (307): 5.27, 6.8, 6.12, 6.28.
GATTEGLAN (239): 6.8-10, 6.12, 6.26, 6.28.
GENITTAC. . . (30): 6.13, 6.17, 6.26.
GIRAGNI (69): 6.12.
GLANNANI (i): 5.27, 6.12.
GLASICONAS (159): 6.3-4, 6.9, 6.26.
GLASICONAS (252): 6.3-4, 6.9, 6.15, 6.24, 6.26.
GLUNLEGGET (118): 6.18.
GOSOCTAS (283): 6.13, 6.24.
GOSOCTEAS (216): 6.13, 6.24.
GOSSUCTTIAS (190): 5.11, 6.13, 6.24, 6.28.
GRILAGNI (85): 5.14, 6.12.
HIC IACIT: 4.6, 4.11-2. 4.14, 6.27 * 4.49, 4.53.
IARNI (44): 5.11, 6.11.
ICORIGAS/ICORI (380): 5.23, 5.32, 6.7, 6.22, 6.24.
IGENAVI/INGENVI (466): 4.14, 6.20.
ILVVETO (342): 5.32.
-INBIR (187): 5.4.
INEQAGLAS (40): 2.2, 4.7, 6.4, 6.9-10, 6.17, 6.26, 6.29.
INIGENA/FILIA (362): 5.32, 6.25, 6.27 * 6.18.
INISSIONAS (161): 6.24.
IRCCITOS (168): 6.13.
[I?]USTI/IUSTI (484): 4.14, 6.20.
IVACATTOS (19): 6.3, 6.6, 6.9, 6.18 * 6.8.
IVAGENI (259): 5.14, 6.6-7, 6.9, 6.29.
IVODACCA (269): 5.23, 6.6, 6.18.
IVVEN/RE DRVVIDES (19): 4.10.
KOI: 4.6, 4.13, 5.3-4, 6.27 * 4.13, 4.18.
KOISIS TRUTIKNOS: 4.6.
LADDIGNI (138): 6.12, 6.28.
LADIMANI (64): Ap2.
?LAIDANN (139): 6.12, 6.28.
LA[TI]NI/LATINI (470): 4.14, 6.20.
LIE (1): 4.6., 7.1.
LITUBIRI (131): 6.8, 6.26, 6.28, Ap2.
?LLATIGNI (220): 6.12, 6.30.
LLOMINACCA (121): 6.30.
LLONNOCC (194a): 6.30.
LOBACCONA (266): 6.3.
LOGIDDEAS (xiv): 6.13, 6.17, 6.24, 6.26, 6.28.
LOGITTI (231): 6.13.
LOSAGNI (236): 6.12.

LUBBAIS (152): 6.24.
LUGA (266): 6.18.
LUGA (267): 6.18.
LUGADDON (4): 6.5, 6.19, 6.24, 6.26, 6.28-9 * 6.72.
LUGUAEDON (1) 6.5, 6.7, 6.26, 6.28-9 * 6.72.
LUGUDEC (4): 5.12, 5.17, 6.5, 6.7, 6.19 * 6.72.
LUGUDECA (286): 5.17, 6.7, 6.24.
LUGUDECCAS (263): 5.12, 5.17, 6.7, 6.24, 6.26, 6.30.
LUGUDUC (108): 2.2, 6.7, 6.28.
LUGUNI (41): 6.13.
?LUGUNI (112): 6.13.
LUGUNI (113): 6.13.
LUGUNI (307): 6.17.
LUGUQRIT. . . (68): 6.5.
LUGUQRIT (146): 6.19.
LUGUTTI (251): 6.13.
LUGUVVEC (221): 5.15, 6.5, 6.7, 6.28, 6.30 * 5.41.
LUGUVVECCA (140): 5.15, 6.5, 6.7, 6.29, 6.30.
MAC: 5.6-7, 5.19, 5.28, 5.33, 6.24, 6.27, 6.29-30.
MACCI (1): 4.10, 5.6, 5.18, 5.33, 6.27, 6.30.
MAC(C)V-: 5.18, 5.32, 6.14 6.27. * 5.45.
MACCV-DECCETI (326): 5.32.
MACCV-DICCL.. (442): 5.32.
MACI: 5.4, 5.6, 5.18, 5.27, 5.33, 6.27, 6.29-30.
?MACORBO (28): 6.17 * 6.59.
MACV (433): 5.32.
MACV-DECETI (440): 6.14, 6.22.
MACVS (xxi): 4.14, 5.18, 6.22, 6.27.
MAEL-MAIRE: 7.6 * 7.7.
MAEL-UADAIG: 7.6 * 3.27, 7.7.
MAGANN (204): 6.12.
?MAGLAGN[I] (353): 5.27.
MAGLANI (317): 5.27.
MAGLICUNAS/MAGLOCVNI (446): 5.32, 6.3-4, 6.15, 6.21-2, 6.26.
?MAGL[I]DUBAR (427): 6.4, 6.26.
?MAIC (83): 5.6, 5.19, 6.27, 6.30, Ap2.
MAILAGN[I] (60): 5.27, 6.12.
MAILAGNI (160): 6.12, 6.28.
MAILAGNI (258): 6.12.
MAILAGURO (82): 5.14, 6.16, 6.24 * 6.53, 6.63.
MAILE-INBIR (187): 6.16, 6.24, 6.28 * 6.52.
MAKINI (216): 6.13.
MAQ: 5.6-7, 5.15, 5.18-19, 5.28, 5.33, 6.24, 6.27, 6.30.
MAQA (160): 5.11, 6.25 * 5.38.

**QVENATAVCI** (462): 6.31.
**QVENVENDANI** (364): 4.14, 5.18, 5.27, 5.32, 6.6, 6.9, 6.22, 6.31.
RETAGIN (viii): 5.14, 6.5, 6.7, 6.28 * 5.39.
**RINACI** (448): 6.13.
?RINI (34): 6.18.
RITTAVVECC (211): 5.34, 6.5, 6.7, 6.24, 6.26, 6.30 * 5.39, Ap2, Ap2 (viii).
RITTAVVECAS (250): 5.15, 5.34, 6.5, 6.7, 6.24, 6.26, 6.30 * 5.39, Ap2, Ap2 (viii).
RITTECC (iv): 2.2, 5.34, 6.5, 6.7, 6.24, 6.26, 6.28-30, Ap2 (viii).
ROC[A]T[O]S/**ROCATI** (500): 6.3, 6.9, 6.19.
?RODAGNI (75): 6.12, 6.28.
?RODDOS (171): 6.11, Ap2.
RON[A]NN (145): 4.6, 5.16, 5.18-19, 6.12, 6.25.
ROTTAIS (277): 6.17, 6.24 * 6.60.
SAGARETTOS (172): 2.2, 6.13.
SAGITTARI (56): 3.2, 6.20.
SAGRAGNI/**SAGRANI** (449): 2.2, 5.16, 5.27, 5.32, 6.12.
SALICIDUNI (341): 6.26.
SAMMNN (ii): 6.18.
?SANGTI (189): 4.9.
**SCI FINTEN** (186): 4.10.
SCILAGNI (85): 6.12.
?SECIDARI (130): 6.26.
SEDAN[I] (46): 5.12, 6.13, 6.24.
**SENEMAGLI** (400): 6.26.
**SENOMAGLI** (370): 5.23.
S[I]B/M[I]L[I]N[I]/**SIMILINI** (399): 6.20.
SILLANN (vi): 4.7, 6.12.
SOGINI (126): 6.7-9, 6.17, 6.28.
?SOVALINI (281): 6.9 * 6.22.
SUVALLOS (158): 6.9 * 6.22.
TALAGNI (181): 6.12.
?TASEGAGNI (28): 6.12.
TEGANN (256): 6.12 * 6.36, 6.38, 7.46.
TEMOCA (55): 6.18.
TENAC[I] (148): 6.13.
**TIGERNACI** (432): 6.13.
TIGIRN (206): 6.11, 6.24, 6.28.
TOGITTACC (172): 5.7, 5.11-12, 5.17, 6.13, 6.26, 6.30.
TOICAC (200): 5.3, 5.7, 6.18.
TOICACI (198): 5.3, 6.13, 6.18.
TOICAKI (197): 5.3, 5.7, 6.18.
**TOICTHEG** (774): 6.13.
TOROQR. . . (54): 7.6.
**TOTAVALI** (375): 6.7, 6.28.
[TO]VISACI/**TOVISACI** (399): 6.13.
TRENACCATLO/**TRENACATVS** (353): 2.2, 5.32, 6.3, 6.6, 6.9.

TRENAGUSU/**TRENEGVSSI** (428): 4.14, 5.32, 6.6-7, 6.9, 6.22, 6.26.
?TRENALUGGO (26): 6.18.
-TTRENALUGOS (120): 6.6, 6.24 * 6.12.
TRENU (57): 6.11.
TRIA (160): 5.11, 6.25.
?TUCACAC (218): 6.18.
TULENA (79): Ap2.
TULOTANAGIA (37): 6.18.
TURANIAS (66): 5.14, 6.13, 6.17.
TURP[I]L[LI]/**TVRPILLI** (327): 4.4, 5.3, 6.20.
UDDAMI (217): 6.18.
ULCAGNI/**VLCAGNI** (467): 2.2, 5.16, 5.32, 6.12, 6.30.
ULCCAGNI (100): 6.30 * 6.5.
**VLCAGNVS** (370): 4.14 * 6.5.
**VALAMNI** (125) * 6.22.
VALUVI (302): 6.8, 6.18, 6.29 * 6.22.
VATTILLOGG (vi): 4.7, 6.26 * 4.26, 6.12.
VEC[REG/C] (227): 6.7.
VEDABAR (298): 6.4, 6.8.
VEDACU[NA] (126): 6.3, 6.8.
VEDDELLEMETTO (xiv): 6.13, 6.24.
VEDELMET[TO] (206): 6.13, Ap2 (xiv).
**VEDOMALI** (408): 6.8.
VEDUCERI (94): 6.8.
VELITAS (251): 4.6, 6.24, * 4.21.
VENDOGNI (422): 5.23, 6.12.
**VENDVBARI** (368): 6.4, 6.9-10, 6.26.
**VENDVMAGLI** (1028): 6.4.
VEQIKAMI (113): 4.7, 6.26.
VEQOANAI (129): 6.13, 6.24, 6.26.
VEQREQ (118): 5.34, 6.7, 6.24, 6.28-9 * 6.70.
VERGOSO (121): 5.11, 5.14, 5.17, 6.7, 6.10, 6.24.
[VIC]TOR/**VICTOR** (430): 4.14, 6.20.
?VIRAGNI (70): 6.12, 6.18.
VIRI-CORB (303): 6.16, 6.18.
VITALIANI/**VITALIANI** (445): 4.14, 6.20.
VITALIN (166): 6.20.
?VLATIAMI (185): 6.13, 6.18.
?VOBARACI (310): 6.13.
?VOCAGNI (304): 6.12.
VOENACUNAS (164): 2.2, 6.3, 6.28.
VORGOS (200): 5.7, 6.11, 6.24, 6.29.
VORRTIGURN (97): 2.2, 6.9, 6.28.
VORTIGURN (297): 2.2, 6.9, 6.28.
VORUDRAN (225): 6.9.
VOTECORIGAS/**VOTEPORIGIS** (358): 4.7, 5.18, 5.32-3, 6.7, 6.22, 6.29 * 4.22.
VRAICCI (12): 6.11, 6.28-9.
**VROCHANI** (460): 6.28.
VURUDDRANN (255): 5.27, 6.9.

## INDEX 3

155: 4.5, 5.3, Ap2.
156: 4.5-6, 4.8, 5.3, 5.6, 5.24 * 4.13,
     4.28, Ap2.
157-8: 4.5, 5.24, Ap2.
159: 4.5, 5.26, Ap2.
160: 4.5, 4.8, 5.24 * 4.12, 4.28, Ap2.
161: 4.5, 5.24 * 4.28, Ap2.
162: 4.5, 5.24, Ap2.
163: 4.5, 4.8, 5.3 * 4.28, Ap2.
164: 4.5, 5.24 * 4.28, Ap2.
165: Ap2.
166: 5.26, Ap2.
167: * 4.32.
169: 4.5-6, 5.27.
170: 4.8-10, 5.26 * 4.32, Ap2.
171: 4.8 * 4.28, Ap2.
172: 4.5, 5.7, 5.26, Ap2.
173-4: 4.5.
175: 5.26.
176: Ap2.
177: * 4.32.
178: 5.26 * 4.36, Ap2.
179: 4.5, 5.24.
180: 4.5, 4.8, 5.24 * 4.28, 4.30, 4.32,
     Ap2.
181: 5.24 * 4.36, Ap2.
182: Ap2.
183: 4.8, 7.5.
184: 4.8, 5.26 * 4.28.
185: 4.8-9 * 4.17.
186: 4.8, 4.10, Ap2.
187: 4.6, 5.3-4, 5.6, 5.29, Ap2.
188: 5.24 * 4.28, Ap2.
189: 4.9, Ap2.
190: 4.6, 5.24, Ap2.
191: 4.6, 5.24 * 4.32, Ap2.
192: * 4.32, 4.36, Ap2.
193: 4.7, 4.9, 5.3, Ap2.
194: 4.5 * 4.28.
195: * 4.32, 4.36, Ap2.
196: 5.24, Ap2.
197: 4.6-7, 5.3-4, 5.7, 5.25 * 4.28, Ap2.
198: 4.7, 5.3-4, 5.25, Ap2.
199: Ap2.
200: 4.7, 5.3-4, 5.6, 5.26, Ap2.
201: 5.3.
202: Ap2.
203: Ap2.
204: 4.8, 5.3-5, 5.6-7, 5.27 * 4.28, 5.48,
     Ap2.
205: * 5.11, Ap2.
211: 5.26, Ap2.
214: 4.5 * 4.16.
215: 4.6, 5.2, 5.26 * 4.19.
216: 5.3, Ap2.
217: 4.8 * 4.28, Ap2.
218: Ap2.
218a: 4.5.

219: 5.4, 5.28.
220: 4.5 * 4.16, 4.32, 4.36.
221: 5.6, 5.29.
223: 5.2-4, Ap2.
225: 4.5.
227: 4.4, 5.29.
228: 5.24.
229: 5.4.
230: 5.3.
231: 4.8, 5.3 * 4.28.
233: 4.8, 5.5, 5.29 * 4.28, 4.30.
235: 4.8, 5.3-4, 5.6, 5.27, 5.29 * 4.28,
     4.30.
239: 5.3-4, 5.28.
240: 5.3.
241: 4.4, 4.7 * 4.25, Ap2.
243: 4.7, 5.4, 5.27, 6.18 * 6.71.
244: 4.6, 4.7, 5.2, 5.4, 5.25, 5.27, 6.18 *
     6.71, Ap2.
245: 4.5.
246: 5.25.
246b: 7.5.
247: 4.5, 7.5.
250: 4.6, 5.26, 6.18, Ap2.
251: 4.6, 5.24.
252-4: Ap2.
255: 5.4, 5.27.
256: 5.3-4, 5.22, 5.28, Ap2.
258: 5.24.
262: 4.6, 5.24, 6.19 * 4.12, Ap2.
263: 4.9.
265: 4.8 * 4.28, Ap2.
266: 5.26 * 4.15.
268: Ap2.
269: 4.5 * 4.28.
270: * 4.17.
272: * 6.59.
273: * 4.32.
275: * 4.17, 4.19.
281: * 4.32.
283: * 6.59.
285: 5.27, Ap2.
286-7: Ap2.
288: 4.6, * 4.17.
290: Ap2.
291: 4.8.
298: * 4.28.
300: 5.24 * 4.36.
301: 4.8, 5.3.
303: 5.28.
307: 5.24, 6.18.
308: 4.5.
311: * 4.28.
316: * 4.36.
318: * 4.53.
319: 4.12 * 4.53.
320: * 4.53.
326: 4.12 * 4.53.

## INDEX 4

*Iustus*: 6.20.
*Kynyr*: 6.3, 6.7 * 6.11.
*Kynri*: 6.3, 6.7 * 6.11.
*Labraid*: * 6.8.
*Lachtnae*: * 6.44.
*Latinus*: 6.20.
*Lily*: * 6.32.
*Litugenus*: 6.8, 6.10.
*Litumarus*: 6.8, 6.20.
*Loígde*: 6.13, 6.24, 6.26, 6.28, Ap2, n6.
*Luccreth*: 6.5.
*Lug*: 6.5.
*Lugáed*, gen. *-adon* etc.: 5.29, 6.5, 6.7,
    6.26, 6.28 * 6.14.
*Lugaei*, gen. *Lugech*, *Lugach*: 6.5, 6.7, *
    6.26.
*Lugbe*: 6.8, 6.29.
*Lugbeus (gente) mocu Min*: 6.27.
*Lugna*: * 6.44.
*Luguid*: 5.17, 6.5, 6.7 * 6.17.
*Luigne*: 6.13, 6.18, 6.24.
*Luigtheg*: 6.13.
*Mac-Áine*: 6.24.
*Mac-Caírthinn*: 4.7, 6.14.
*Mac-Cárthinn*: 4.7.
*Mac-Coirpri*: Ap2 (xvii).
*Mac-Cuill*: 6.14, Ap2 (v).
*Mac-Cuilinn*: 6.14, Ap2 (xxi).
*Mac-Deichet*: 6.14, 6.30.
*Mac-Erce*: 6.14, 6.24 * 6.47.
*Mac-Iair*: 6.14.
*Mac-Liac*: 6.14.
*Mac-Rithe*: 6.14, 6.24.
*Mac-Rúadáin*: 6.14.
*Mac-Táil*: 6.14.
*Mactaleus*: 6.14.
*Mac-Tréin*: 6.14.
*Mac-Tréoin*: 6.14.
*Máelán*: 6.12.
*Máel-Augrai*: * 6.53.
*Máel-Gaimrid*: 6.16 * 6.52.
*Maelgwn*: 6.3-4, 6.15, 6.21 * 6.16.
voc. *Maglocune*: * 6.11.
*Maicnio*: * 6.48.
*Mailcun*: * 6.11.
*Marianus*: 6.20.
*Marinus*: 6.20.
*Martius*: 6.20.
*Medb*: 6.11, 6.29.
*Meilic*: 6.3-4, 6.15, 6.21 * 6.16.
*Menraige*: * 6.25.
*Midgen*: 6.7.
*Mílchú*: * 6.6.
*Miliucc*: * 6.6.
*mocu Alta(i)*: 6.17.
*Mocu Min*: * 6.25.
*Múadán*: 6.12, 6.28 * 7.7.
*Muirchú*: 6.3, Ap2 (xiv).

gen. *Nadcaeir*: 6.11, 6.15.
*Nad-Froích*: 6.15, 6.28.
*Nad-Sáir*: 6.15.
*Nad-Segamon*: 6.13, 6.15, 6.18.
*Nad-Slúaig*: 6.15, 6.28.
gen. *Nemaidon*: * 6.14.
*Nemnall*: * 5.47.
*Níadchú*: 6.15.
gen. *Núadat*: 6.28.
*Odrán*: Ap2 (xi).
*Odrige*: 6.17.
*Olcán*: 6.12.
*Olchú*: 6.3 * 6.7.
*Ollo-dagus*: 6.10.
*Penno-vindos*: 6.10.
*Pompeius*: 6.20.
*Reo*: Ap2, n2.
gen. *-Rithe*: 6.5.
gen. *Rethech*, *Rethach*, *Ráthach*: 6.5,
    6.7, 6.30, * 6.26, Ap2 (iv).
*Rian*: 3.2.
gen. *Ríata*: 6.11.
*Rocatus*: * 6.29.
*Rochad*: 6.3, 6.9.
*Ródán/Rúadán*: 6.12, 6.28.
*Roddanus*: 6.30.
*Rónán*: 5.16, 6.12.
*Rothrige*: 6.17.
*Rúad*: 6.11.
*Sagittarius*: 6.20.
*Saidliu*: 4.7.
*Samán*: Ap2 (ii).
*Sáraid*: 6.13.
*Sárán*: 5.16, 6.12.
*Segomo*: * 6.46.
*Sétnae*: 6.13, 6.24.
*Sílán*: 4.7, 6.12.
*Sillán*: Ap2 (vi).
*Similinus*: 6.20.
gen. *Sogain*: 6.7.
*Sonid*: * 7.8.
*Suibne*: 6.9.
*Tálán*: 6.12.
*Tecán*: 6.12 * 6.36.
*Tigern*: 6.11.
*Toicthech*: 5.7, 5.17, 6.13, 6.26, 6.30.
*Tornae*: 5.14, 6.13.
*Tóthal/Túathal*: 5.20, 6.7, 6.28.
*Trén*: 6.11.
gen. *Tréno*: * 6.35.
*Trian*: 6.11.
*Trianlug*: 6.6, 6.24 * 6.12-13.
*Túatán*: * 6.36.
*Tudwal*: 6.7.
*Turpillius*: 6.20.
*\*Úadach*: * 7.7.
*Uí Aicher*: 6.17-18.
*Uí Chuirbb*: 6.17.